Wives and Work

WIVES AND WORK

Islamic Law and Ethics Before Modernity

MARION HOLMES KATZ

COLUMBIA UNIVERSITY PRESS *NEW YORK*

Columbia University Press
Publishers Since 1893
New York Chichester, West Sussex
cup.columbia.edu

Library of Congress Cataloging-in-Publication Data
Names: Katz, Marion Holmes, 1967– author.
Title: Wives and work : Islamic law and ethics before modernity / Marion Holmes Katz.
Description: New York : Columbia University Press, 2022. | Includes bibliographical references and index.
Identifiers: LCCN 2021058006 (print) | LCCN 2021058007 (ebook) | ISBN 9780231206884 (hardback) | ISBN 9780231206891 (trade paperback) | ISBN 9780231556705 (ebook)
Subjects: LCSH: Marriage—Religious aspects—Islam. | Domestic relations—Religious aspects—Islam. | Women in Islam. | Muslim women. | Women (Islamic law) | Housekeeping—Islamic countries.
Classification: LCC HQ525.I8 K38 2022 (print) | LCC HQ525.I8 (ebook) | DDC 297.5/63—dc23/eng/20211230
LC record available at https://lccn.loc.gov/2021058006
LC ebook record available at https://lccn.loc.gov/2021058007{to come}

Cover design: Milenda Nan Ok Lee
Cover image: *The Makamat of Hariri.* Copy decorated with paintings by Yahya ibn Mahmoud ibn Yahya ibn Aboul-Hasan ibn Kouvarriha al-Wasiti. Bibliothèque nationale de France.

Contents

Acknowledgments

THE BULK OF the initial research for this book was carried out while I was the 2014–2015 Gladys Krieble Delmas Foundation Member of the Institute for Advanced Study, Princeton. That year's research was also supported by a Fellowship from the American Council of Learned Societies.

I will be forever indebted to the late Patricia Crone for giving me the opportunity to be a member of the Institute for Advanced Study. My time there coincided with the final year of her life; her resolution and humor in the face of catastrophic illness were unforgettable. I am also deeply grateful to her successor, Sabine Schmidtke, to the other members of the Islamic Studies seminar—particularly Anver Emon—for their thoughts and conversation, and to Joan Wallach Scott for her generous feedback.

This project also benefited from the input of hosts and participants at a number of venues where I was honored to speak, including the Boston University Institute on Culture, Religion and World Affairs; the Abdallah S. Kamel Lecture at Yale Law School; the VIII International Conference of the International Society for Islamic Legal Studies at Leiden University; the Gender and Sexuality in Middle Eastern History lecture series at the University of Chicago; the Vanderbilt Legal History Colloquium; the Columbia Arabic Seminar; the Willis D. Wood Lecture at Amherst College; and the University of Texas at Austin and Harvard Law School. Particular thanks go to Kecia Ali at Boston University; to Samy Ayoub, Dale Correa, and Hina Azam at the

University of Texas; to Leor Halevi and Thomas McGinn at Vanderbilt; and to Mariam Sheibani and Intisar Rabb at Harvard.

I am also grateful to everyone who read and commented on part or all of the evolving manuscript, including Mariam Sheibani, Sohaira Siddiqui, Najah Nadi, Saadia Yacoob, Ahmed El Shamsy, and the anonymous readers from Columbia University Press. Thanks also to Karen Bauer for her thoughtful comments at more than one conference. I owe a debt of gratitude to Maggie Sager for her meticulous and intelligent work assembling the bibliography and checking the footnotes of the manuscript. My father, Stanley Katz, and my brother, Derek Katz, offered needed moral support as I finished this project in a pandemic. Last but not least, I thank my mother, Adria Holmes Katz, whose endless unpaid labor made everything in my life possible and whose judicious copyediting helped to polish this manuscript. This book is dedicated to my husband, Bradley Marshall McCormick, whom I can never thank enough.

Wives and Work

Introduction

THIS BOOK EXAMINES a series of iterations of the Islamic legal discussion of wives' domestic labor. While it is generally assumed that classical Islamic law monolithically denies that wives have any obligation to do housework for their husbands, the material examined here shows this was subject to serious reflection and debate. The topic elicited such attention both because ownership of the wife's work raised fundamental questions about the claims and obligations exchanged between the spouses under the marriage contract and because denial of a wifely duty to do housework stood in conflict with what most premodern scholars understood to be right and good. Scholars' efforts to resolve this tension resulted in a range of solutions, from delineating a clear distinction between legal claims and ethical ideals to forging a complete synthesis of the two. As a result, the issue of wives' domestic labor offers a unique lens for questions about the relationship between Islamic law and ethics that have long been debated by scholars in the Western academy. By offering a systematic and sustained exploration of this issue, this book offers new insights both into the content of premodern Muslim scholars' views of family and work and into the evolving logic and dynamics of *fiqh*—the Islamic scholarly discipline of law. In addition, while much of the literature on Islam and gender has focused on issues of sex and sexuality, this study is premised on the idea that labor is equally central both to the ways in which people live gender, family, and status and to the ways in which Muslim scholars sought to think them.

Wives' domestic labor: The state of the discussion

Sometime in the 1890s an elite Ottoman woman imagined a cordial yet polemical exchange with a pair of European Christian visitors to Istanbul. In response to the accusation that "among you [Muslims], men treat the women like servants," her protagonist retorts that

> Among us, it is the duty of the wife to manage the household, and of the husband to pay its expenses. . . . If men have the means, they employ a servant and a cook. If [the husband's] means suffice only to feed [the couple], his wife takes care of the housework as a matter of good character[1]; otherwise, the man cannot compel her to do that as a matter of law. It came to pass in the caliphate of ʿUmar [ibn al-Khaṭṭāb, ruled 634–644 CE] that a man from among the noble Companions [of the Prophet Muḥammad] came to the caliphal palace as a petitioner, with a complaint against his wife. He saw ʿUmar coming out of the women's quarters while speaking sharply. [The man] said, "What happened, O Commander of the Faithful?" ʿUmar replied, "The ways of women are well-known and require no explanation; it is my wife who has caused me to be sharp in this way. As for you, what has brought you here?" The man replied, "I came to you to complain to you of my wife, but having found you in a state like this, I see no room for complaint!" ʿUmar said to him, "Be still! We should not raise our voices, because our wives manage our households, despite the fact that it goes beyond their duty; they suckle our children, and they are not obligated to do so. Thus, if we were to raise these matters, it would cause us harm." From this story it is manifest that women are neither obligated nor required to engage in [household] service as a matter of divine law.[2]

The author of this passage, Fatma Aliye (1862–1936), was the daughter of the Ottoman statesman Ahmed Cevdet Pasha and a pioneering author of Turkish fiction "who at the same time cherished feminist ideals and struggled with Western feminism."[3] Fatma Aliye's brief discussion of housework frames it within a nexus of ethical and legal duties: wives have no enforceable obligation to provide domestic labor but if necessary do so voluntarily as a matter of magnanimity. In the anecdote about the exemplary early caliph ʿUmar, the significance of a wife's lack of obligation to do housework is not that she actually refrains from doing so (apparently, even if her husband rules an empire) but that she places her husband morally in her debt.

In raising the issue of wives' domestic labor, Fatma Aliye anticipated a lasting motif both in the defense of Islamic gender norms vis-à-vis orientalist critics and in the internal argumentation of Muslim circles sympathetic to women's rights. In the United States in the late twentieth century, wives' exemption from domestic labor was routinely cited among the elements of the classical Islamic law of marriage that were recuperable for a gender-egalitarian project. As the leading Muslim American lawyer Azizah al-Hibri wrote in 2000, "the wife is under no duty to do any housework although she may engage in such work on a volunteer basis."[4] The importance of this point, in the eyes of Muslim gender activists, is twofold. On the one hand, it offers a genuine precolonial precedent to challenge modern, Western-derived ideals of feminine domesticity, thus "counter[ing] the arguments of those who insist on a gendered division of household labor."[5] On the other hand, it has useful implications on a material level. In particular, "some traditional jurists suggested that the wife was entitled to monetary compensation for her volunteer housework activity"[6]—a rule that "could be crucial in the distribution of assets upon the divorce of a stay-at-home wife and breadwinning husband."[7] Discussions of this issue among American Muslim scholars has been informed in part by legislative initiatives in Iran and Morocco in the 1990s and 2000s, which themselves inspired lively discussions of historical Islamic doctrine on this point.[8]

The issue of wives' domestic labor has retained its currency; as Asifa Quraishi observes in a 2013 essay, "Muslim women's rights advocates today regularly point to [the] old Islamic legal principle" that "a wife has no Islamic obligation to do housework."[9] However, the discussion of this point has been both enriched and complicated by the increasingly detailed analyses of Islamic legal history produced in the last two decades. Such work has not only added substance to academic and public knowledge of premodern legal argumentation but also raised foundational issues about its systematic assumptions and contemporary relevance. In an essay published in 2003, Kecia Ali raised the concern that "by focusing on isolated rights without paying attention to how they are embedded in a system of interdependent spousal obligations," progressive Muslim interpreters have failed to recognize the problematic nature of the classical Islamic legal argumentation from which they selectively cite.[10] In that essay and in her 2010 monograph

Marriage and Slavery in Early Islam, Ali argues that in Islamic legal texts of the formative period (i.e., the third century AH/ninth century CE), argumentation about issues of marriage and divorce reflects a model in which the marriage contract is conceptualized as the husband's "purchase" of sexual rights over the wife, metonymically represented as the "vulva" (*buḍʿ*). This understanding of the transaction is explicitly grounded in an analogy between marriage and the purchase of an enslaved concubine who becomes sexually licit to her male enslaver by virtue of his ownership (*milk*) over her.[11]

Although formative-period jurists recognized that marriage was not literally a sale and that its legal effects diverged in significant ways from those of slave ownership (not least in that a man could under no circumstances sell his wife), Ali demonstrates that both the concept of "ownership of the vulva" and the parallel with slave concubinage were pervasive elements of legal reasoning on issues of marriage and divorce. Most importantly, this model posited an asymmetrical and gendered exchange of entitlements and obligations between the spouses in which the wife's sexual availability was compensated by the husband's material maintenance. Within this framework, "the wife's performance of household duties is not expected, and is certainly not a condition of her support."[12] In short, Ali argues, formative-period jurists exempted wives from housework because in their view "wives were bound to provide service, but sexual rather than domestic."[13] Based on this analysis of the legal argumentation supporting early jurists' denial of a wifely duty to provide housework, Ali argues that progressive Muslims should exercise caution in appropriating the fruits of a legal discourse on marriage whose fundamental (if often tacit) premises they would find deeply distasteful.

Other scholars have placed the issue of domestic labor within a broader context of Muslim ethical debates, in which legal discourses are only a single component. In her 1999 PhD dissertation Ingrid Mattson addresses this theme within a complex field of early Islamic attitudes toward work, slavery, and social hierarchy. Rather than celebrating the ways in which early doctrine and practice fulfilled an Islamic ethic of equal human dignity, she examines how the constraints of political rule and of legal reasoning often compelled Muslim authorities to compromise this ideal.[14] Refusing to equate the prerogatives of wives with the status of "women" writ large, she asks, "If most women [i.e., wives] did not have to perform housework, who did the work? Male servants could draw water and perform many other tasks, but it was female servants who helped women with most of their chores."[15] Thus, "for every woman freed from the burden of such work, there is another woman or man made to bear that same burden."[16] Her analysis of the legal doctrine on wives' domestic labor foregrounds the status distinctions jurists draw between wives who are and are not entitled to exemption from housework.

Another scholar who has placed the *fiqh* doctrine on wives' domestic labor in a broader discursive context is Karen Bauer, who addresses this topic in a study on gender hierarchy in works of Qur'anic exegesis. Her major finding is that beginning in the sixth century AH/twelfth century CE, some of the most prominent interpreters explicitly assert a wifely obligation to provide housework. Hypothesizing that this shift may reflect the historical transition of the Muslim community from a wealthy conquest elite to a vast community comprising believers of all social classes, she observes that "in this case, social custom prevails even over an interpreter's school of law." Although evolving social mores did not consistently trump scholarly precedent, Bauer argues that they did so in this instance because it was a case in which "social custom support[ed] the gender hierarchy."[17]

This book builds on the findings of all of these scholars. By focusing systematically on the question of wives' domestic labor, I extend and nuance their arguments. Like Ali, I am attentive to the systemic assumptions underlying juristic arguments about marriage. This study extends her analysis of the structure of the marriage contract beyond the formative period that was the subject of her study, showing how scholars of the classical and postclassical periods elaborated and modified the underlying logic she has identified. Like Mattson, I place the legal discussion of domestic labor within the context of broader Islamic approaches to the ethics of labor and status. However, by focusing explicitly on the multiplicity of Islamic normative discourses and the overlaps and ruptures between them, this study traces the contours of a more diverse discursive landscape. Like Bauer, I emphasize change over time and consider how Muslim thinkers responded to social developments. However, based on evidence from additional sources, this study argues that the shift in practice she posits by the twelfth century CE in fact was already under way by the middle of the tenth century, opening up a perceived gap between legal doctrine and social mores that would evoke scholarly reflections for centuries.

Context and motivation of the project

Although I hope that this book will be of interest to those pursuing constructive projects on Muslim marriage, my own investment in the subject is rooted in a different set of experiences and concerns. The initial idea for the project arose in the early days of my marriage, when the distribution of household tasks was a matter of daily negotiation. However, as a Jewish woman married to a Christian man, I did not approach medieval Islamic legal texts on this subject in search of personally applicable religious norms. Rather, I was drawn to the subject by the perception that work—and particularly work in its most mundane and quotidian forms—is fundamental to the constitution and performance of both gender and social status.

As an American child in the 1970s, I learned to be a girl while happily playing with a toy carpet sweeper, a toy ironing board, a toy oven, and a toy sink in which to wash my toy dishes. In addition to experiencing housework as an apprenticeship in proper female selfhood, I learned that household labor held deep messages about status, dignity, and moral personhood. I remember that my mother (the wife and daughter of academics) insisted on scrubbing our kitchen floor on her own hands and knees, despite having a "cleaning lady" who came once a week. Questioned about this, she explained that scrubbing the floor on hands and knees was simply not something one could ask another person to do. Meanwhile, one of my best friends reported that her own mother (an immigrant from the Global South) had expressed her hope that scrubbing a floor on her hands and knees was something her daughter would never have to do for herself. Scrubbing the floor, I concluded, had meanings that went far beyond the need for a clean floor. Housework had the potential to lower a person (in this case, quite literally); to lower oneself voluntarily might be praiseworthy, but to debase another person was improper. People of different backgrounds varied in the meanings that they brought to housework and in what they could lose or gain by subjecting themselves to its indignities.

Premodern Muslim scholars, like twentieth-century American parents, often believed that (in the words of one twelfth-century Ḥanafī jurist), a girl "needs to know the manners of women, and teaching her the manners of women involves having her do housework."[18] They also placed domestic labor within the context of much broader issues of familial and social hierarchy. As we shall see, Muslim jurists often designated housework under the rubric of "service" (*khidma*), a word that (like its English counterpart) carried overtones both of virtuous humility and of social subordination. This concept has resonance (and provokes conflict) across different domains of my own life, from the home where I share chores with my husband, to the academic career where "service" is both a professional ideal and a differentially gendered burden, to a congregational life where "service" is seen both as a religious obligation and as the socially conservative counterweight to progressive advocacy.[19]

As Reva Siegel has demonstrated in her work on nineteenth-century U.S. labor statutes, contemporary American assumptions about wives' domestic labor have been shaped by a legislative and judicial history of which most Americans are unaware. As a result of this history, she observes, "we live in a world in which [wives'] unwaged labor in the home stands as an anomaly: lacking explanation but not requiring one either."[20] In the early nineteenth century, U.S. law perpetuated the model inherited from British common law, which "charged a husband with responsibility to represent and support his wife, giving him in return the use of her real property and absolute rights in her personality and 'services'—all products of her labor."[21] Beginning in the 1850s, this "doctrine of marital service" was modified by state statutes giving wives the right to their own wages. These statutes explicitly applied only to wages earned from "separate" or "personal" labor.[22] However, they also gave rise to material claims by wives on the basis of domestic work performed in the marital home. In their unanimous rejection of such claims, courts articulated a new domain of familial labor that was conceived of as untainted by market exchange.

Siegel argues that in denying claims to compensation for work done for the family within the home, judges did not simply retain an archaic element of the older common law but constructed a new doctrine of "separate spheres" appropriate to an industrialized society where men's work was increasingly associated with a monetized economy from which the family was to be insulated.[23] Over time, the result was that, in the words of Katharine Silbaugh, "the U.S. legal system conceptualizes housework as solely an expression of affection, the currency of familial emotions."[24] From the nineteenth century through the end of the twentieth, contracts between spouses granting a wife a monetary consideration for housework or care labor (whether a monthly wage or a bequest in the husband's will) were thus consistently invalidated by U.S. courts on the grounds that they were contrary to public policy.[25] The issue of housework, and of compensation for housework, is thus key to comprehending the emergence of current American attitudes toward marriage and the family. Despite profound differences in social, intellectual, and religious context, this study suggests that a deeper history of Islamic debates on this subject offers instructive resonances with those of our own time and place.

Source base and approach

This book is most centrally a study of the issue of domestic labor in selected works of pre-Ottoman *fiqh*.[26] Its source base consists primarily of comprehensive manuals of Islamic substantive law (*furūʿ al-fiqh*) that set forth the legal doctrines of a given school of Islamic law (*madhhab*) across the entire range of subject matter covered by the Sharia, from ritual to penal law. Despite the voluminous size of such compilations and their recognized importance to the Islamic legal tradition, until recently they have received surprisingly little sustained attention in Western academia. Their unmanageable length and sometimes mind-numbing level of detail has discouraged secular scholars from approaching them as anything but reference books from which to retrieve the relevant lines on a given point of doctrine. Unlike the more vivid examples of the fatwa genre, which (at least in their longer and unedited form) may offer engaging indications of their social and political context and of the jurists' intervention in concrete conflicts, the *furūʿ* works' endless and impersonal recitation of rules often seems to offer little purchase for analysis of their authors' legal projects.

However, in recent years a number of scholars have begun to delve into this genre in new and promising ways. In studies examining a range of concrete topics, scholars including Khaled Abou El Fadl, Kecia Ali, Hina Azam, Behnam Sadeghi, Mairaj Syed, and Nurit Tsafrir have offered deep thematic readings of material from works of Islamic substantive law.[27] Rather than approaching works of *furūʿ* as mere repositories of rules whose only significance lies in their implementation (or lack thereof) on the ground, these authors have recognized them as works of Islamic thought whose articulation of individual rules reflects broader concepts, values, and assumptions that can be retrieved through systematic analysis. As Syed notes,

> scholars examining premodern Islamic law have tended to pay only instrumental attention to texts of positive law (*fiqh*). . . . The result was a dearth of knowledge on the structure of reasoning present in the positive law texts, especially on concrete issues of legal and moral thought beyond the narrow question of legal change. Yet, the positive law texts are especially rich sources documenting not only the laws of each tradition but also how the tradition's laws were justified.[28]

This study examines just such "concrete issues of legal and moral thought" through analysis of the modes of justification used in its sources' discussions of domestic labor. Accordingly, my objective will not be primarily to assess whether classical legal texts really "require wives to do housework" (and therefore are disadvantageous to women "on the ground"), or the converse, but to understand *why* jurists affirmed or denied a person's obligation to do housework and what role this obligation played in their overall models of marriage and the family. Like Michael Chamberlain's 1995 work *Knowledge and Practice in Medieval Damascus, 1190–1350* (with whose subject matter it peripherally intersects), this study treats the terminology and logic of its source texts as objects of inquiry in their own right rather than as imperfectly transparent media for the reconstruction of realities beyond the text.[29] Like Kecia Ali, I seek primarily to "offer an analysis of the jurists' conceptual system."[30]

The issue of wives' domestic labor has no single, uniform location in the *fiqh* literature. *Fiqh* manuals are organized in a loose but fairly consistent conventional order, placing issues related to marriage and divorce in the middle sections falling between ritual law (which opens such compilations) and criminal law (which often closes them). It is notable that the standard divisions of *furūʿ* works include sections on the conclusion and dissolution of marriage contracts and on a small number of potentially litigable issues (such as the allocation of time and resources among co-wives) relating to ongoing marriages. Significantly for the argument of this book (which will argue that *fiqh* was historically a discipline largely distinct from Islamic ethics in its various forms), there are traditionally no sections devoted directly to the ideal behavior of spouses within a functioning marriage.[31] Within this organization, the issue of domestic labor is most often raised in the section on the maintenance (*nafaqa*) that husbands are obligated to provide for wives. Since jurists held that at least some husbands were required to pay the expenses of domestic help for their wives, the topic of *nafaqa* generally occasions some discussion of the conditions under which a wife could demand this or (conversely) the conditions under which she might be obliged to do the housework herself. Scholars also sometimes addressed the scenario that an elite wife could propose to do housework herself and pocket the wages of the servant to whose services she was legally entitled. The topic of *nafaqa* is generally allotted its own section, nested within neither the section on marriage nor the section on divorce. Spatially as well as thematically, it is at least as closely linked to divorce as to marriage, as spousal support was often quantified and imposed only when a couple separated.

The other section of a typical *furūʿ* work where the existence of a spousal obligation to provide domestic labor may often be encountered is (perhaps more surprisingly) the chapter on contracts of hire (*ijāra*). When exploring the theme of valid and invalid contracts of hire, jurists sometimes take the opportunity to ask whether husbands and wives (and sometimes other family members) can freely contract with each other to receive wages for services such as housework, or whether their relationship implies mutual duties that would preempt the possibility of contracting to receive pay. In the case of the wife, the issue of working for pay is most often raised by the possibility that a wife could contract to receive wages from her husband to nurse their child. Nursing is acknowledged as a remunerative form of labor in the Qur'an (verse 65:6), and sometimes provided a model for other forms of work that might be performed within marriage. References to domestic labor can also occur in the sections on legal claims (*daʿwā*, pl. *daʿāwā*), where jurists may discuss claims made by wives for items produced with their labor, and on dower (*mahr/ṣadāq*), where they may discuss whether a man can fill this requirement by contracting to serve his wife.

The discussion of wives' domestic labor in *fiqh* texts is thus both dispersed and complex. A representative sample of this discussion can be drawn from the following selection of opinions attributed to the tenth-century Ḥanafī jurist Abū'l-Layth al-Samarqandī (d. AH 375/985 CE):[32]

> [According to the Ḥanafī authority al-Khaṣṣāf (d. 261/874), if a husband brings his wife unprocessed food and she refuses to cook or bake it, she is not compelled to do so and he must bring her prepared food.] Abū'l-Layth al-Samarqandī said, "That is if she has an illness and is incapable of baking bread and cooking, or if she is from a noble family; in that case, the husband must bring her someone to

> bake bread and cook. [As for] if she is capable of that and is the kind of person who [customarily] serves herself, she is being obstinate [if she refuses to bake and cook] and she is not entitled to do so. That is because the Prophet assigned the work inside of the house to the wife and the work that is outside of the house to the husband; that is the verdict he reached between [his son-in-law] ʿAlī and [his daughter] Fāṭima."[33]

> If [a jurist] is asked for a legal opinion about [a man] who carries flour to his home and hires his wife to make bread from it, is the wage due [to the wife]?, he is in error if he replies either "yes" or "no." He ought to say, "If he wants her to make bread for sale, she is entitled to the wage, because she is under no obligation to do that. If [on the other hand] he wants her to make bread for them to eat, the wage is not due [to her] because she is under an obligation to do that as a matter of custom (*dhālika mustaḥaqq ʿalayhā ʿādatan*)."[34]

> If a man buys cotton and [his] wife spins [it], to whom does the [resulting] thread belong? It is transmitted from Abū Ḥanīfa that he said: If he gives her cotton and says to her, 'Spin!' the thread belongs to the husband. . . . The jurist [Abū'l-Layth] said: . . . As for if he gives it to her and does not say anything, then the thread belongs to the husband, because it is customary that if [a husband] gives cotton to his wife he is doing so only so that she will spin it, so her spinning becomes tantamount to housework (*bi-manzilat khidmat al-bayt*). This is like the case of [a husband who] bought flour and [his wife] made bread; the bread belongs to the husband.[35]

In these examples, the issue of the obligatoriness and the ownership of a wife's labor in the home is elicited by several different questions. One is the question of the husband's obligation to materially provide for his wife, which may or may not include financing the labor required to process her food. Another is the scenario of her contracting to receive wages for her labor in the home. A third is the issue of the spouses' competing claims to a product produced with the wife's labor and the husband's raw materials. It is notable that Abū'l-Layth, writing only a century after al-Khaṣṣāf, modifies his doctrine to the point of reversing it; the privilege of declining to cook and bake becomes an exception limited to the aristocratic or disabled wife. The default is that a wife is indeed obligated to provide housework, a position that he grounds both in social custom and in an alleged ruling of the Prophet

Muḥammad. However, custom dictates that the wife must work without compensation only for household consumption; the husband cannot force her to work without wages for the market.

Due to the dispersal of questions about wives' domestic labor across different sections of classical *fiqh* manuals, this study brings together material scattered across widely separated sections of these works, including those that are not primarily devoted to issues of marriage and divorce. To the extent that this material is not located in the sections of *fiqh* manuals explicitly related to the mutual duties of the spouses, it has not generally been drawn into the discussion of marriage in Islamic law. However, this study's contention is that despite the scattered nature of such passages, they cumulatively reflect systematic efforts to think through the structure of the marital relationship. In particular, the nature and limits of the spouses' ability to contract with each other for benefits (such as labor) that went beyond the core rights and duties of the marriage contract raised fundamental questions about the scope and nature of marriage as a legal institution.

The multiple frameworks of Islamic normativity

It is a central argument of this book that *fiqh* can best be understood as a single normative Islamic discourse (albeit a very authoritative one) that was always, implicitly or explicitly, in dialogue with other frameworks for the religious guidance of believers. To return to the example of Abū'l-Layth al-Samarqandī, he addresses the norms of marital life not only in his legal works but in his moral-didactic work *Tanbīh al-ghāfilīn* ("Rousing the Heedless"). In that context, he recounts the story of ʿUmar ibn al-Khaṭṭāb cited above. In Abū'l-Layth's version, ʿUmar declares that he tolerates his wife's insolence "because of all of the things I owe to her. The first is that she is a curtain between me and Hellfire; by her my heart is quieted from [longing for] what is forbidden. The second is that she is a treasurer for me; when I leave my home, she guards it for me. The third is that she is a laundress for me; she washes my clothes. The fourth is that she is a wet-nurse for my child. The fifth is that she is a baker and a cook for me."[36]

In this version of the anecdote, it is the fact that the wife's domestic tasks could be performed for the market (by a laundress, a wet-nurse, or a baker) that underlines her husband's moral indebtedness to her. Unlike in the legal opinions attributed to Abū'l-Layth, however, what is at stake here is not the wife's ability to refrain from working or to demand wages for doing so but the spouses' mutual kindness. According to Abū'l-Layth's legal doctrine, ʿUmar's wife presumably could decline to wash, bake, or cook for her husband and be awarded domestic help by a judge; by any reasonable standard she is noble (*sharīfa*). However, what is at stake in the context of this ethical work is not the spouses' enforceable legal claims but the ideal conduct that ensures their marital harmony.

Abū'l-Layth al-Samarqandī is not unusual in offering such a multifaceted (or fragmented) view of wives' domestic service. Rather, this issue is embedded in a series of broader complexes of ideas about social and religious status. Consider, for instance, the following anecdote about the North African Sufi holy man Abū Yiʿzzā (d. 572/1177):

> One of the companions of Abū Yiʿzzā got married. His wife asked him for a female slave, but he did not have one. So Abū Yiʿzzā said to him, "I will substitute myself for the female slave," for he was black and had no hair on his face. He dressed himself in the clothes of a female slave and served the man and his wife for an entire year. He ground wheat, kneaded dough, made bread, and poured the water—all at night—while in the day he performed his devotions in the mosque. After a year had gone by, the wife said to her husband, "I have never seen anything like this slave! She does all that is [normally] done during the day at night, and never appears in the daytime." Her husband turned away from her and neglected to answer, but she continued to ask him until he said, "No one works for you but Abū Wanalgūṭ, and he is no female slave!" Then she knew it was Abū Yiʿzzā and said, "By God, this one will never work for me again, and I swear that I will do my work myself!" From that time on, she did her work herself.[37]

In this story a new wife demands to be relieved of domestic labor by a servant, perhaps on the basis of her social status or of her understanding of *fiqh*. Abū Yiʿzzā's engagement in the menial tasks of food preparation is simultaneously a manifestation of his sanctity and an inversion of proper social roles so flagrant that it shames the wife into doing the work herself—implicitly chastening her into behavior superior to her initial insistence on exercising her entitlement to a servant. The saint's performance of service (*khidma*) is a powerful signifier conditioned by its association with gender, status, race, and spiritual prowess. In contrast, the wife's performance of the same tasks immediately becomes invisible when the story is resolved with the unmasking of the saint; had she taken on the cooking without demur, this tale would never have been told.

This hagiographic story is not unique in suggesting the contrasting and sometimes conflicting ways that humble household tasks could figure in the pious projects of premodern Muslims. In his *Iḥyāʾ ʿulūm al-dīn* ("Revival of the Religious Sciences"), Abū Ḥāmid al-Ghazālī (d. 505/1111) presents an anecdote in which a Sufi aspirant (*murīd*) takes a wife and insists on serving her. The mortified wife finally goes to her father to complain that he will not allow her to use the bathroom without his carrying the water for her to cleanse herself.[38] Here a sustained performance of pious humility collides with a spouse's sense of propriety, which may reflect considerations of both gender and status.

Such entertaining anecdotes do not merely reflect the idiosyncrasies of unusually (and, in the second anecdote, perhaps misguidedly) pious individuals. Rather, they reflect structural tensions between multiple normative frames that were available to Muslim thinkers as they pondered issues of work and marriage. Al-Ghazālī also entertained the scenario that a husband might choose to do the housework himself in his more strictly legal work. (In this context, the implied motive is to save money on domestic help rather than to cultivate personal humility.) He concluded that the husband was entitled to take on the cooking or the sweeping, but that his wife could draw the line at his carrying water for her bath or for her ablutions after using the bathroom, both because she would be embarrassed (*tastaḥī*, the same word used in the anecdote about the Sufi) and as a matter of personal dignity (*murūʾa*, further discussed below).[39] Again, household labor stands at the intersection of considerations of economic entitlement, personal honor, and social rank.

While it focuses primarily on the *fiqh* discussion of wives' domestic labor, this study places that discussion within the context of the various ideas about social convention and moral rightness that animated the jurists' analysis of the marital relationship. It thus deals with multiple, largely autonomous and yet often complementary forms of Islamic normativity. Accordingly, each chapter begins with an account of one of the normative discourses that paralleled and supplemented *fiqh*. Rather than seeing the diversity of these frameworks as evidence of incoherence, we will see how individual authors could skillfully wield multiple discourses to navigate various concerns about work, gender, and the Islamically good life. The result was not necessarily a seamless whole or an unproblematic synthesis but a complex negotiation that could strategically highlight different discourses in different contexts.

Recent work has emphasized the extent to which the moral worlds inhabited by modern Muslims are multiple and fractured rather than monolithic or homogeneous. This is only an instantiation of what Robert Hefner has termed "the larger *ethical* plurality that characterizes all human societies";[40] the need to make this case about Islam in particular reflects the unusually totalistic way in which this tradition has often been approached in the western academy. In a study of the everyday practices of young Muslim men in an Egyptian village, the anthropologist Samuli Schielke emphasizes that for his informants "morality is not a coherent system, but an incoherent and unsystematic conglomerate of different moral registers that exist in parallel and often contradict each other."[41] His analysis identifies six distinct "moral registers" that may guide their behavioral choices and value judgments: religion; social justice; community and family obligations; good character; romance and love; and self-realization.[42] These registers may stand in tension with each other; for instance, the "ascetic" pious values of chastity and gender segregation may conflict with the ideal of "male virtues based on virility and sexuality."[43] In a similar vein, Lara Deeb and Mona Harb argue in an ethnographic study of leisure spaces in Beirut that their informants operate under "multiple moral rubrics" that "reflect different sets of ideals and values."[44] They identify three such rubrics (social, political-sectarian, and religious) while acknowledging that "these categories are constructed and overlap."[45]

Schielke, Deeb and Harb approach "religion" as a single category sharing a larger moral field with competing values that are implicitly outside of religion. In each case, the "religion" category is implicitly identified primarily with the Sharia. This study, in contrast, approaches *fiqh* as only one of multiple frameworks within a larger religious field.[46] Because it focuses on normative texts produced by long-deceased authors, this study does not address the issue of "moral subjectivity" foregrounded by Schielke.[47] Rather, it examines how Muslim scholars placed the issue of domestic labor at the intersection of multiple schemas of value comparable to Schielke's "moral registers" or Deeb and Harb's "moral rubrics." Thus, it posits that improvisational maneuvering among concurrent and potentially conflicting normative frameworks is characteristic not only of the everyday practice of ordinary individuals but of the scholarly projects of some of the great authorities of the Islamic tradition.

In taking this approach, I follow the lead of the late Shahab Ahmed in rejecting the tendency to define Sharia in the sense of "Islamic law" as the single standard of Islamic normativity.[48] In bringing the *fiqh* discussion of domestic labor into dialogue with other Islamic discourses, I follow his insight that "to privilege the law and legal discourse as somehow being the arbiter and determiner of the theoretical object 'Islam' is to endorse just one authority claim among many within the human and historical phenomenon of Islam."[49] However, rather than focusing on what Ahmed labels "the *Sufi-philosophical* (or *philosophical-Sufi*) amalgam," in which an epistemological hierarchy privileging non-discursive forms of knowing synthesizes the various forms of Islamic authority, this study foregrounds the continuing multiplicity and autonomy of the discourses that could be brought to bear on a given issue of importance to Muslims.[50]

Our exploration of ethical pluralism focuses specifically on the ways in which different ethical frameworks complement or inform legal analyses of the marital relationship. Its specific emphasis on law and on marriage creates resonances with other contexts, including that of the modern United States. Writing about the legal interactions of a group of largely female working-class Americans, Sally Engle Merry argues that "the lower courts contain three analytically distinguishable discourses, only one of which is that of law. One is based primarily on categories and remedies of law, one on the categories and remedies of morality, and one on the categories and remedies of the helping professions. The same discourses exist outside the courts as well."[51] Perhaps unsurprisingly, because it lies at the intersection of so many moral, social, and material concerns, marriage seems to be particularly subject to this kind of multiple framing. In her influential study *Talk of Love*, sociologist Ann Swidler examines how her middle-class white informants draw eclectically on multiple distinct and partially contradictory frameworks in their analysis of marital love, including invocations of "utilitarian individualism and its theory of contract, fundamentalist Christianity and its theory of obedience of divine authority, and the therapeutic ethic with its theory of the authentic, expressive self."[52] For modern Americans as well as premodern Muslim jurists, there are diverse concurrent models of the marital relationship that may be elicited by different contexts in which they are situationally useful.

As Zahra Ayubi has recently discussed, "Islamic ethics" is a broad concept that can evoke a number of different forms of "Muslim morals and values"; in the context of premodern intellectual history, scholars have located it in multiple scholarly disciplines including "*kalam* (theology), *fiqh* (jurisprudence), *tasawwuf* (mysticism or Sufism), and *akhlaq* (philosophical ethics)."[53] As Ayubi also notes, Muslim scholars themselves saw these discourses as independent, if complementary; her sources "viewed *akhlaq* as disciplinarily distinct from the legal rules found in the *fiqh* genre and the spiritual relationship with the Divine found in Sufism."[54] For our purposes, the discussion of wives' domestic labor is embedded in at least four distinguishable (if often overlapping) discourses, which can be somewhat schematically labeled as *fiqh*, *zuhd* (with later incorporation of the relevant motifs into Sufism[55]), *akhlāq*, and *murūʾa* ("manliness" or honor).

It is, again, *fiqh* that will be the primary focus of this study. As is well known, *fiqh* is a discipline that was pursued by an increasingly distinct and self-conscious body of scholars beginning in the second century AH/eighth century CE. It has a characteristic framework and repertoire of terminology, most importantly the five legal statuses (*aḥkām*) of mandatory (*wājib/farḍ*), recommended (*mustaḥabb/mandūb*), neutral (*mubāḥ*), disapproved (*makrūh*), and forbidden (*ḥarām*).[56] It is the central role of these categories—the *aḥkām taklīfīya*, which Bernard Weiss has rendered as "normative categories" and Kevin Reinhart calls "determination[s] of moral status"[57]—that has perhaps played the greatest role in convincing modern Western scholars that *fiqh* is fundamentally an ethical discourse rather than a legal one in the modern Western sense of the term. As Reinhart notes, "statutes that 'recommend' but do not 'require,' rules that are not enforceable, are not ordinarily considered by philosophers of law to be part of the law but belong rather to the domain of morality."[58] Given the fact that (in Reinhart's formulation) works of *fiqh* "include 'oughts' and 'ought-nots' " in addition to enforceable rules, one might expect jurists to resolve the tension between a wife's lack of contractual obligation to do housework and the socioethical expectation that she do so by invoking the category of *mustaḥabb/mandūb* ("recommended").[59] In fact, however, this approach is rarely encountered in our sources. As we shall see, juristic discussions of a wife's domestic labor more often address whether she can be compelled (*tukrah*) to provide it or invoke distinctions between different kinds of obligation (among which legal obligation is only one). This may be because the focus of the *fiqh* discussion is on the marriage contract, which involves potentially enforceable duties vis-à-vis another human being (rather than ideal behavior vis-à-vis God).[60]

In addition to the "normative categories," *fiqh* discourse involves a separate set of legal statuses that pertain to the effectiveness of a legal action rather than to its ethico-legal evaluation. These are the *aḥkām waḍʿīya*, which Weiss renders as "nonnormative categories" and Reinhart as "determination[s] of validity"; the most important of these are the dichotomy *ṣaḥīḥ/bāṭil* (valid/invalid), which designate whether a given action fulfills its required components and conditions.[61] Much of the *fiqh* discussion examined here is framed in terms of the validity of various possible terms in the marriage contract or of various other contracts (particularly contracts of hire) between the two spouses. Rather than using the terms *ṣaḥīḥ* and *bāṭil*, however, we will most often encounter jurists asking whether a given thing is *jāʾiz* (usually "permissible," but here in the sense that it would be enforceable as a contractual provision or acceptable as a way of discharging one's contractual obligations).[62]

Zuhd ("renunciation") may have emerged as a counter discourse to the prosperity and power of the early Islamic empire.[63] The ideals of *zuhd* did not, of course, produce a set of explicit norms for the structuring of marital life; indeed, they sometimes led aspiring renunciants to shun marriage altogether (although this decision was controversial, given the Prophet Muḥammad's clear disapproval of celibacy). However, whether in the context of marriage or of relationships of brotherhood or discipleship, renunciants modeled an approach to the mundane labor of everyday life that was sharply distinct from that of the *fuqahāʾ*. Whereas jurists asked if and when a wife could demand to be relieved of household tasks, the *zuhhād* used such chores to inculcate humility and to forge relationships with spiritual models. Later, as the structures and conventions of Sufism began to crystallize, service (*khidma*) similarly played a role in moral self-cultivation and in spiritual apprenticeship, sometimes involving the same tasks (food preparation, sweeping, laundry) referenced by jurists in the context of the marital home.

The genre of *akhlāq* is a heterogeneous one; this rubric is primarily used to designate literature focusing on the cultivation of virtuous moral characteristics. As we shall see, such works could be based on hadith, on pre-Islamic Iranian sources, or on material drawn from the Greek philosophical tradition, or they could incorporate more than one of these elements.[64] The subgenre of *akhlāq* most relevant to this discussion is philosophical ethics, which, as Ayubi notes, is "located within the disciplinary boundaries of *falsafa* (after the Greek discipline of *philosophia*), in a branch of knowledge called practical philosophy/wisdom (*hikmat-i 'amali*)."[65] Islamic philosophical ethics was a tradition with its own distinctive authorities, terminology, and genre conventions. It contributed to the scholarly discussion of domestic labor in two ways. One was through the framework of Aristotelian virtue ethics, which envisioned the cultivation of desirable moral traits through the habituation of appropriate actions, with the ultimate goal of taming the passions and refining the soul (*nafs*). Ayubi writes that "this focus on the *nafs* is predominantly what sets *akhlaq* apart from *fiqh*."[66] Unlike Sufism, which also focuses on the *nafs* (although understood in different terms), "*akhlaq* is centered on managing the worldly" rather than on "withdrawing from the worldly as a means of self-transformation and annihilation in God."[67] In this context, as Ayubi demonstrates, wives are envisioned as running the household not to pursue their own moral perfection but to facilitate their husbands' pursuit of that goal by freeing them from mundane concerns.[68]

The second, and more direct, way in which the *falsafa* tradition contributed to Muslim scholars' discussion of domestic labor was through a Greek work that has survived only in Arabic translation, titled "Household Management" (*Tadbīr al-manzil*) and attributed to an otherwise obscure philosopher known as Bryson.[69] This work reflects one of the three branches of practical philosophy, which addressed the governance of the self, the family, and society. Bryson's analysis of a wife's role in the household is placed within a philosophical account of the social and personal prerequisites for the fulfillment of human beings' material needs. Thus, rather than emphasizing the role of engagement in household tasks (or of exemption from them) in the moral refinement of the husband or wife, this work promoted a view of marriage as an enterprise devoted to the shared prosperity of the family. The terminology and assumptions associated with this model were just as distinctive to the *falsafa* tradition as the language of ethical self-refinement. Most obviously, as we shall see, this set of ideas was routinely associated with the Arabic phrase *tadbīr al-manzil* ("household management") rather than with the concept of *khidma*.

The third ethical frame for domestic labor that we will explore was far less overtly and systematically developed than *zuhd* and *falsafa*. As Hefner notes, "not all ethical registers that operate in society achieve such an explicit and authoritative standing. Other moral currents might be less formal or articulate or may not be officially recognized or publicly discursivized at all."[70] While this study focuses solely on textual sources (and thus on motifs that received some form of literary expression), another set of moral resonances that accrued to domestic labor took a more diffuse form that was not associated with a specific genre of writing or form of scholarly expertise. These were the terms and assumptions relating to the preservation of social rank and personal dignity, which could be impaired by engaging in work considered inappropriate or demeaning. Like the ideal of *khidma*, this framework did not represent a separate discipline with its own terminology or body of experts. However, the scholars' pervasive concern with this set of issues can be roughly encapsulated in the term *murūʾa*. The word *murūʾa* (sometimes also *muruwwa*; literally, "manliness") can be used very broadly as a term for high moral character;[71] however, its more distinctive usage places it at the intersection of moral and social nobility. It is not the only term associated with the preservation of rightful rank that features in the discussion of domestic labor; other relevant keywords include *sharaf* or *nāmūs* (honor), *manṣab* (social position), and *martaba* (rank). I use it here to exemplify the terminology associated with personal dignity as a value worthy of religious consideration not only because of the frequency of its use but because it has been the object of the most overt analysis by premodern Muslim scholars, who thematized it as a modest topic of its own.[72] *Murūʾa* is strongly associated with the possession and proper disposal of wealth; it is frequently defined as involving "the improvement of livelihood" (*iṣlāḥ al-maʿīsha/al-māl*[73]) and the exercise of a respectable occupation (*al-ḥirfa*[74]). *Murūʾa* in this sense is gendered but can be cultivated by or through women; a woman's *murūʾa* involves remaining within her home, and a man's *murūʾa* deters him from marring his daughter to a social inferior.[75]

The ideal of *murūʾa* impinges on the discussion of domestic labor in that the elevated dignity associated with this ideal was understood to be conditioned on the work that one engaged in and the service that one received. A well-kept home and an impeccably provisioned table were particularly vital to the magnanimous and refined public presentation required by *murūʾa*. The management of such a household involved staff; one epigram equated *murūʾa* with (among other things) "the spaciousness of one's home and the numerousness of one's servants."[76] The woman of the house also had a role to play; the Umayyad prince Maslama ibn ʿAbd al-Malik is said to have declared, "There is no aid to a man's *murūʾa* like a good wife!"[77] An anonymous poet opined,

> If there is in a man's home no noble woman
> Managing, the *murūʾa* of his house is lost.[78]

Here, as in the philosophical discourse of *tadbīr al-manzil*, a woman is involved in running the household; she does so not as a domestic drudge but as a manager (*mudabbira*), a role commensurate with her explicit status as a noblewoman (*ḥurra*). In considering whether deprivation of a servant would conflict with a bankrupt man's *murūʾa*, or whether an elite wife's *murūʾa* would be impaired by engaging in housework, scholars invoked a distinct set of values and assumptions in which the maintenance of social status was understood not simply as a widespread human desire but as a moral value.[79] Labor, and particularly domestic labor, was central to the articulation of that ideal. Nevertheless, as we shall see, Muslim scholars also sometimes noted that the desire for rank or leisure could be an expression of vanity or arrogance. Regardless of an individual author's specific doctrinal conclusions, labor and its relationship to social status was a topic of independent and lively concern.

These various discourses intersected with and impinged on each other in many ways. Thus, a *fiqh* text need not exclusively reflect the distinctive framework associated with *fiqh*. As we shall see, jurists sometimes introduced the terminology or assumptions of the other discourses into their legal writing, whether overtly or more obliquely. Different frameworks presumably also intertwined as individuals sought to apply their religious values in everyday life. Nevertheless, each of these discourses had its own terminology, conventions, and logic; in the sources examined here, their autonomy never completely gives way to an overarching synthesis.

As may already be suggested by the examples cited thus far, the case of domestic labor was one in which *fiqh* rules (which generally denied that wives as a category had any affirmative obligation to do housework) did not directly correspond either to practical social mores or to the ideals of marriage and femininity articulated in other normative frames or other genres of Islamic literature. It is a central argument of this study that the resulting discrepancy gave rise to an unusual amount of overt reflection about the relationship between *fiqh* and Islamic ethics. In its most pronounced form, this mismatch juxtaposed a legal doctrine that denied that a wife had any duty to do housework with a moral conviction that she would be a bad wife (and perhaps a bad person) if she failed to do so.

This work seeks, in part, to examine whether and how individual scholars chose to incorporate other ethical discourses into the discipline of *fiqh* and to trace the trends in such choices over time. It is my contention that whether or not they directly invoked other normative frameworks, Islamic jurists always operated in the context of a rich set of discourses offering alternative ideals for human conduct in general and the marital relationship in particular. This was particularly true in an area, like domestic labor, that lay close to the heart of concerns about status, gender, and morality. Thus, I juxtapose *fiqh* discussions of domestic labor with parallel materials from the other disciplines even in cases where the legal texts do not directly invoke them. Opting to exclude relevant normative discourses was as much an authorial choice as opting to incorporate them.

Islamic law and ethics in Western scholarship

On one level, then, this book is a study on the relationship between Islamic law and ethics (in its various forms). This relationship has been one of the most durable and contested themes in the Western academic study of Islam. Over time, Western scholars have variously argued that the Sharia is too legal (in the sense of coercive) and thus lacks the moral character of "true" religion; that it is too moral (in the sense of offering nuanced personal guidance rather than enforceable "bright line" rules) and thus cannot be categorized with Western systems of law; and that it offered a harmonious synthesis of the legal and the moral until this was disrupted by the advent of colonialism. This study builds on the insights of Baber Johansen, who has pointed to the multiple ways in which Ḥanafīs of the classical period terminologically acknowledged divergences between enforceable *fiqh* and Muslim ethical ideals. However, rather than focusing on one school's classical solution to the problem of law and ethics, this study argues that the relationship between premodern *fiqh* and ethics was a negotiable one that was subject to scrutiny and revision as scholars addressed concrete problems.

One strand of Western academic engagement with Islam has been located in the evolving tradition of religious studies, which engages with "religion" as its object of investigation. As has been widely observed, the secular European study of religion is rooted in the Enlightenment, one of whose foundational documents was Immanuel Kant's 1793 work "Religion Within the Limits of Bare Reason."[80] In this work he dismisses religious law (in the sense of concrete and potentially enforceable rules of conduct) as incompatible with his fundamental premise that a good action is one that is freely chosen on the basis of moral principles. "Coercive laws" fail Kant's criteria for religious guidance not only because they impede the free exercise of conscience but because "they deal only with external actions."[81] While Islam is addressed only in passing, Kant asserts that its laws (like those of Judaism) coincide with those of morality only incidentally and are disqualified as expressions of true religion by the resort to force.[82]

As G. A. Lipton has demonstrated, Kant's ideas contributed to the "popular religio-philosophical ideals" of Western observers of Islam in the nineteenth century.[83] In particular, Europeans often "found in Sufism"—erroneously understood as uniformly antinomian—"a Kantian universal religion that has evolved from the immature Semitic theocracy of Islam (like Christianity from Judaism) and has thus disassociated itself from the coercive commandments of historical faith."[84] As discussed by Tomoko Masuzawa, similar themes and assumptions informed the construction of "world religions" by academic scholars of religion in the late nineteenth century.[85] Kantian assumptions were reproduced by Dutch scholar Cornelis Tiele (1830–1902), who influentially distinguished between "nomistic . . . religions or religious communities, founded on a law or sacred writing," and "universal or world religions, which start from principles and maxims."[86] While at one point acknowledging Islam as a representative of this final and highest category, Tiele elsewhere describes it as being grounded in "the absolute sovereignty of the one God, towards whom man . . . has only one duty, that of tacit obedience," and claims that it "therefore neglects the development of ethics."[87]

If Western scholars in the nascent field of religious studies had reservations about the prominent role of Sharia in the Islamic tradition, Western scholars of law did not find it legal enough. Johansen notes that European jurists' initial encounter with Sunni *fiqh* took place in "the practical context of colonialism."[88] Among the most lastingly influential contributors to this tradition was the Dutch scholar and colonial administrator Snouck Hurgronje (1857–1936), who argued (as Johansen writes) that "*fiqh* is not a legal system but a deontology because it mingles religion, ethics and politics in an unsystematic way in order to construe the image of an ideal society. Therefore, [Western] jurists are mistaken when they try to analyze it in legal terms."[89]

The Western academic study of *fiqh* was further developed by Joseph Schacht (1902–1969), who nuanced the assumptions of scholars like Hurgronje; while he held that "the sacred Law of Islam is an all-embracing body of religious duties," he nevertheless affirmed that it comprised a body of "properly . . . legal subject-matter" that he felt able to isolate in his popular *Introduction to Islamic Law* (1964).[90] A similar approach was adopted around the same time by the Egyptian jurist Chafik Chehata, who pointed to the historical evidence for the application of *fiqh* as a body of legal norms by the courts of Muslim-ruled societies and emphasized the distinction drawn by *fuqahāʾ* between the law of interpersonal transactions (*muʿāmalāt*) and that of acts of worship (*ʿibādāt*).[91] Although they proceeded from different premises and pursued different aims, scholars as different as Schacht and Chehata sought to distinguish between the ethical and the legal elements of classical *fiqh* in order to yield a body of rules legible as "law" within the context of the modern project of codification.

While these scholars attempted to address the imperfect fit between the content of premodern *fiqh* and modern Western categories of law, religion, and ethics, since the late 1980s Johansen has produced a deeper analysis of the historical discourse of *fiqh* on its own terms. Based on his readings of classical Ḥanafī law (particularly the works of Shams al-Aʾimma al-Sarakhsī [d. 483/1090] and ʿAlāʾ al-Dīn al-Kāsānī [d. 587/1189]), he argues that "the rational generalization of juristic principles in Islamic law" gave rise to "systematic constraints," with the result that

> in many cases . . . religious and moral considerations could not be taken into account, or could be taken into account only insufficiently. The Muslim jurists saw that as a problem. In their discussions they describe the relationship between the legal regulations to be applied by judges and the demands of morality and religion in terms that make it clear that there is a relationship between the two semantic fields, which together constitute the meaning of Islamic law, but which nevertheless are not identical to each other.[92]

Surveying various instances of discrepancies between legal doctrine and ethico-religious ideals, Johansen enumerates several ways in which his sources accommodate such ruptures. One is to distinguish between the "rulings of this world" (*aḥkām al-dunyā*) and the "rulings of the afterlife" (*aḥkām al-ākhira*). It is to this distinction that, for instance, the Ḥanafī jurists resort to justify their doctrine that the blood money of a non-Muslim murder victim is equal to that of a Muslim; the two are not equal in the eyes of God, but they are equally entitled to the authorities' protection of their lives on the earthly plane.[93] Another distinction jurists used to navigate divergences between systematized *fiqh* and Muslim ethics was that between the *ẓāhir* (that which is manifest) and the *bāṭin* (that which is hidden). This dichotomy grounds the acknowledgment that judges are obligated to rule on the basis of objective, external phenomena rather than of the internal intentions (and thus the ethico-religious guilt or innocence) of criminal defendants.[94] The *ẓāhir*/*bāṭin* dichotomy may also have implications for the individual who, for instance, knows himself to be guilty when the law acquits him, or knows his divorce to be valid when the external evidence does not allow a judge to enforce it. In such a case, the individual may have an obligation "between himself and God" (*fī mā baynahu wa-bayna Allāh*) that is extralegal in its force.[95]

The jurists similarly invoke the concept of sin (*ithm*), which may or may not coincide with legal liability.[96] The positive counterpart of sin is religious merit (*thawāb*). The distinction between religious merit and legal validity underlies, for instance, the famous Ḥanafī doctrine that a formally adequate prayer performed for purely hypocritical motives (and thus lacking any religious merit) nevertheless discharges the legal obligation to pray.[97] Finally, Johansen finds that jurists occasionally assert a moral obligation where no legal obligation exists (for instance, to recompense a worker who lacks a legal claim to a wage, or to donate gains that are legally licit but morally tainted).[98] Johansen argues that the jurists' employment of these concepts gives rise to two complementary semantic fields, one (signaled by terms such as *dunyā*, *ẓāhir*, and *qaḍāʾ*) associated with political sovereignty and judicial practice and the other (signaled by terms such as *ākhira*, *bāṭin*, and *ithm*/*thawāb*) associated with "the personal relationship to God." The two fields are also, particularly in the work of al-Sarakhsī, linked respectively with the genres of *ḥukm* (or legal verdict) and fatwa (or legal opinion).[99]

Although he focuses his analysis on the internal terminology and argumentation of classical texts, Johansen also examines the ways in which the discourse of *fiqh* maps onto (or fails to map onto) the categories of modern Western academic study. He does so explicitly in order to create a rigorous basis for comparative work that could integrate the study of Islamic law with that of other legal systems.[100] Since the early 2000s, a very different approach has been initiated by Talal Asad. Rather than accepting modern Western categories as the basis of analysis, Asad produces an archaeology of these concepts that reveals their problematic historical entanglements and the ways in which they are embedded in distinctively modern and Western assumptions.

Basing himself on the work of Egyptian reformer Muḥammad ʿAbduh (d. 1905), Asad characterizes " 'Sharīʿa' as a traditional discipline" as having constituted "not as a set of rules to be obeyed but as the condition that enables the development of virtues."[101] In contrast, "the modern idea of a secular society included a distinctive relation between state law and personal morality," one grounded in a "distinction between law (which the state embodied, produced, and administered) and morality (which is the concern ideally of the responsible person generated and sustained by the family)."[102] The heart of Asad's analysis focuses on the modern period, which lies outside of our concentration here; as Khaled Fahmy has recently observed (and as Asad largely concedes[103]), his argument about the conceptual shifts from traditional to modern models is based exclusively on modern sources.[104]

A scholar who has advanced arguments closely paralleling Asad's on the basis of profound familiarity with the literature of premodern *fiqh* is Wael Hallaq. In his magisterial work *Sharīʿa: Theory, Practice, Transformations*, Hallaq emphasizes the harmonious integration of social, ethical, and legal values in premodern Muslim societies, where "legal norms and social morality, if they could be at all separated, were symbiotic beings, one feeding on and, at the same time, sustaining the other."[105] While Hallaq's comments focus primarily on the practical implementation of the law, he similarly sees "jurist's law" as having "guided and promoted" but not "superimpose[d] itself upon, social morality. . . . Thus, the shared communal values of honor, integrity, shame and religio-social virtue entered the arena of the court as part of a dialectic with the assumptions of *fiqh* law."[106] Critiquing the modern tendency to sever the "ritualistic" and "private" elements of *fiqh* from those now regarded as properly legal, he argues that the ritual subject matter addressed in the opening sections of classical *fiqh* manuals played an integral role in the law, "laying as it did the foundations for achieving willing obedience to the law that was to follow, that is, the law regulating human affairs."[107] Like Asad, Hallaq thus emphasizes the role of the *fiqh* in the cultivation of virtuous ethical dispositions. Also like Asad, he emphasizes "the distinction between—and the segregation of—the legal and the moral" in the nineteenth-century colonial context and argues that it led to the erasure of "theistic teleology, eschatology, socially grounded moral gain, status, honor, shame . . ."—in short, of "the unimpeded integration of the moral force within the Islamic legal world."[108]

The examples cited by Asad and Hallaq show that the premodern *fiqh* tradition can be understood as a component of an overall ethical system that could be both normatively understood and concretely experienced as a harmonious whole. The present study does not seek to refute this possibility, which was realized in many different ways. Instead, it focuses on cases in which premodern legal scholars themselves articulated ways in which the potentially enforceable claims of *fiqh* could variously coincide with, complement, or (occasionally) diverge from the ideals emerging from other normative Islamic discourses such as the "theistic teleology, eschatology, socially grounded moral gain, status, honor, shame" enumerated by Hallaq. The claim is not that these discourses necessarily contradicted each other but that participants in the tradition sometimes found them to answer different questions and respond to different needs. Rather than representing an achieved synthesis, the relationship between *fiqh* and various ethical discourses was an open and negotiable work in progress.

By focusing on an issue central to the conduct of one of life's most important relationships, this project seeks to cast light on the broad and structural ways in which *fiqh* could diverge from ethics (rather than merely on minor or isolated discrepancies between the two). Rather than seeing such divergence as a flaw, I argue that it helps us to understand the distinctive work that *fiqh* is doing within a set of religious discourses addressing different contexts and needs. In particular, it can help us to move beyond the popular formulation that "in Islam, marriage is a contract" to the more accurate observation that "in Islam, a contract regulates certain aspects of the marital relationship." The logics and assumptions of *fiqh* thus do not have to be identified with the values attached to marriage as such.

Scope and limitations of the study

This study explores the meanings that are attached to domestic labor in premodern Islamic legal texts and (to a lesser extent) in the parallel Islamic normative discourses that sometimes informed their analyses. It is not a work of social history and does not attempt to reconstruct the actual nature of the work performed by wives or others in the times and places examined. In part this is because the materials for such a reconstruction are largely lacking. As Craig Perry notes of what is perhaps the richest trove of documents from the pre-Ottoman Middle East, the Cairo Geniza, "when we try to describe the precise nature of female work before 1250, we encounter the limits of the medieval sources. Although the Genizah is enormously rich in information for the period between the tenth and thirteenth centuries, it sheds surprisingly little light on the topic of domestic labor."[109] Similarly, Torsten Wollina remarks of the diary of the late fifteenth-century Damascene Ibn Ṭawq (otherwise a remarkable source of granular information about daily life in the pre-Ottoman period) that "the internal division of labor in the household is usually not addressed at all."[110]

Our information about domestic labor is thus, like that about many other aspects of daily life that contemporaries took for granted, fragmentary and anecdotal. The rare glimpses of housewives in action offered by our sources suggest that the legal model of marriage cannot be understood as a direct reflection of social mores. Thus, for instance, al-Samarqandī's doctrinal statements cited above can be contrasted with a famous passage from the work of his contemporary Badīʿ al-Zamān al-Hamadānī (d. 398/1008). Hamadānī's "Maqāma al-Maḍīrīya" features the comic tale of a hapless guest whose nouveau riche host boasts of the luxuries of his household until the narrator flees in despair of ever being fed. The host's long-winded disquisition on the desirable features of his possessions is preceded by an equally proud description of the good qualities of his wife:

> He was saying, "Good sir, if only you could see her with a dishcloth around her waist, going round from room to room, from the oven to the pots and from the pots to the oven, blowing on the fire with her mouth, and pounding spices with her hands! If only you could see how the smoke [of the cooking fire] has smudged that beautiful face and marked that radiant cheek, you would see a sight that

> dazzles the eyes. I love her passionately because she loves me passionately. Happy is the man who is granted help from his spouse and who is fortunate in his wife."[111]

This brief comic vignette contrasts in several ways with the guidelines and assumptions of contemporary legal literature. The merchant, whose boasts imply great wealth if little breeding, represents his wife's hands-on involvement in kitchen work as a credit to both him and her, rather than an as impairment of their status. The household explicitly includes servants, but the merchant (like many a modern elite man) prefers to boast of the labors of his wife.[112] The only obvious intersection with the *fiqh* model of marital conduct is the implication that the guest cannot, in fact, literally see the wife; indeed, the host's eager verbal breaching of her privacy may be one of his many faux pas.

As this example illustrates, we cannot assume that it is possible to read social behavior (or even social mores) directly out of *fiqh* texts. We cannot even be sure that the vague terminology of the legal sources' discussion of domestic labor reflects a consistent set of concrete tasks; indeed, we can be fairly confident that it does not. Cooking is an instructive case in point. Ingrid Mattson points out that in the early Islamic period, grinding grains and making bread were unremitting daily tasks for ordinary women.[113] In contrast, it has been widely noted that in pre-Ottoman Cairo very little cooking may have been done in most private households; not only bread but most other foodstuffs were routinely bought prepared from the marketplace.[114] (While the shortage of wood for cooking was unusually acute in Egypt, a similar situation may have pertained in other localities as well.[115]) Neither the site, nor the status associations, nor the gendering of cooking were consistent over time or place. Thus, for instance, Nawal Nasrallah finds that in ʿAbbasid Baghdad "proficiency in the art of cooking. . . . was one of the desirable accomplishments of the 'Abbasid man, especially the aspiring boon companion, who wished to win the favors of his superiors."[116] In contrast, Paulina Lewicka finds that in medieval Cairo cooking was an overwhelmingly female pursuit, whether in domestic or professional contexts.[117]

The other forms of daily labor involved in the running of the household are, if anything, more elusive in our sources.[118] It is thus next to impossible to reconstruct the daily routines of premodern Muslim wives or of their servants. Based on the comments of various jurists that will be cited over the course of this study, it seems reasonable to conclude very broadly that household labor was gendered, with a general pattern of indoor consumption-related labor being performed by wives and other female members of the household (although the concrete content of this work varied, and wives also engaged in various forms of outdoor or commercial labor depending on social context). However, this study does not use legal texts as proxies for the primary sources that we lack. Rather, it is a study of the legal texts themselves, using them as sources for the history of Islamic thought rather than of Muslim people's daily lives. As Hina Azam eloquently writes of her own project, this book attempts to "step into these edifices and study their structure from the inside."[119] One implication of this approach is that this study does not define its own rigorous category of "domestic labor" and then apply it to the texts but identifies and analyzes the terminology used within the sources and pursues its changing lineaments and connotations through time.

By far the most frequent term most used to refer to "housework" in the sources examined here is *khidma*, a term whose dense and shifting connotations reflect the range of social, political, ethical, and theological contexts in which it is used. This word occupies a semantic range closely paralleling that of the English "service"; it can be used for household service or for the service of God or of a king. Its active participle, *khādim*, is the most common word for "servant" (in the sense of a person, free or unfree, employed in a household to perform routine indoor work).

In the earliest legal texts addressing wives' domestic labor, the term *khidma* appears quite neutral and would probably be best translated as "work" or "labor." To the extent that the recipient of the service is specified, it is the house (*bayt*).[120] In many contexts, the word *khidma* continues to be used in later *fiqh* texts in this generic sense. As we shall see, however, by the tenth and eleventh century in the Islamic East the term *khidma* had also accrued a dense set of ethical and political resonances. In this context, the emphasis was on the relational and hierarchical dimensions of "service." *Khidma* was a basic building block of bilateral hierarchical relationships between worshipers and God, between parents and children, between vassals and rulers, between masters and apprentices, and between Sufi adepts and their disciples. The concept of *khidma* was important to premodern Muslim scholars' ethical vision not only because it was within such hierarchical relationships that they envisioned the project of moral self-formation as being pursued but also because of its intimate relationship to the concurrent and sometimes competing ethico-religious ideals of personal dignity and of pious humility. In this context, to discuss a wife's *khidma* was to place her domestic labor within a set of ethically charged relationships including those between parent and child and ruler and subject.

In part because the term *khidma* directs attention to the relational aspects of work, it is quite vague and elastic with regard to its concrete content. Classical sources sometimes enumerate specific tasks such as cooking or sweeping but often remain strikingly (and perhaps strategically) unspecific about the nature of tasks that surely varied according to time, place, and social class. In the book's analysis, I have focused on tracing and analyzing what my sources have chosen to say rather than attempting to fill in the gaps with a more rigorous or consistent terminology from outside of their own historical and socioreligious context. However, rather than ventriloquize the religiously specific language of my medieval sources, in my own discussion I have used the English expressions "housework" and "domestic labor" interchangeably as general designations for routine household chores. To the extent that more specific parameters are in play in given cases, this will be made clear in the analysis of individual texts.

As several authors have acknowledged, English terms such as *housework* and *domestic labor* are themselves ill-defined, whether on the level of sociological theory or of empirical studies of the division of labor within households.[121] Margrit Eichler and Patrizia Albanese note that they "searched for a definition of housework, and found none in most studies. . . . Instead, housework is operationalized through a list of pre-established activities."[122] Not only do such "lists of household tasks remain theoretically unfocused," but "the activities listed (e.g., cleaning, shopping) are taken as self-evident. This means that there is usually no examination of *how* the work is done. Does cleaning always equal cleaning?"[123] One of the major, insufficiently examined assumptions of the academic literature on housework / domestic labor is that it is routinely defined in terms of the unpaid nature of the work involved.[124] On a theoretical level, this is because the domestic labor literature of the 1970s and 1980s explicitly sought to address the economic and conceptual invisibility of women's unpaid contributions. On the level of empirical research, it reflects the fact that studies of the allocation of unpaid housework within the family and of professional domestic workers belong to separate literatures that rarely address each other.[125]

The unspoken assumptions of this book's source materials both parallel and diverge from those associated with the English terms *housework* and *domestic labor*. They are similar in that to the extent that there is any specificity about the work involved, it tends to come in the form of lists of tasks (cooking, baking bread, cleaning) that, while sharing certain core items, are both open-ended and vague; they gesture toward shared contextual expectations more than they inform us about the specifics involved. The focus is on the routine, repetitive tasks of daily life. As suggested by the discussion of the term *khidma*, in some cases Muslim jurists seem also to envision a component of "waiting on" another person—activities, such as carrying water for a person's bath, that are more gestures of deference than "housework" in the modern English sense.[126]

One notable contrast with modern Western assumptions is that, as we have already seen in the examples above, premodern Muslim jurists explicitly acknowledged that housework had monetary value and that it was at least hypothetically thinkable that a wife might demand compensation for it. The scenario of a wife's demanding wages for housework from her husband is a minor but recurring motif in the medieval *fiqh* literature; pending further evidence, I have not been able to determine if it was one based on concrete legal cases or social demands, but at the very least it was a provocative test case for legal reasoning. As in the case of antebellum America, the fact that this issue was even raised by Muslim jurists as early as the third/ninth century may appear as "a startling anticipation of contemporary feminist critiques of housework."[127] In both cases, it is necessary to understand the issue in its historical context. Rather than dramatically rescuing wives' quotidian labors from their structural invisibility, these conversations took place in the era before the Industrial Revolution decisively separated the male-gendered commercial workplace from a feminized domestic sphere and before the nineteenth-century cult of family and domesticity established the assumption that family relations were antithetically opposed to those of the market.[128]

In the middling-to-elite circles from which most early jurists emerged, much of this labor was performed by enslaved persons whose monetary value was known to reside in their work capacity. Many of its component tasks (such as grinding grain, baking bread, and laundering clothing) were also commonly pursued on a commercial basis outside of the home. Thus, the idea that routine household labor had a quantifiable monetary value would have been familiar and intuitive. However, it is unclear how often housework performed within the home was directly monetized in practice. Yossef Rapoport notes of the Mamluk period that while women frequently worked for pay (primarily but not exclusively in the textile industry), "salaried domestic servants were completely absent."[129] Both the ubiquity of enslaved labor and the stigma of women's exposure to unrelated men may have contributed to the rarity of domestic service as an occupation for free Muslim women; there seems to have been no equivalent of (for instance) the life-cycle service of medieval and early modern Europe.[130]

In contexts where cooking and cleaning were routinely performed either by unsalaried wives or by unsalaried slaves, it thus seems to have made intuitive sense to many jurists that such work was inherently unpaid labor. Even as they recognized that routine cooking and cleaning had a monetary value (and, accordingly, that it was possible to posit a "standard wage" for such services), jurists thus often drew clear distinctions between routine consumption-oriented labor and the labor associated with production for the market. Wives' demanding pay for housework was thus both eminently thinkable and (at least from the point of view of male religious scholars) obviously and viscerally wrong. Thus, as we shall see in chapter 2, some scholars engaged in logical acrobatics to deny wives even the theoretical possibility of demanding wages for housework. In distinguishing between consumption-oriented and market-oriented labor, many scholars defined a category roughly corresponding to the modern idea of "housework," placing the former within a complex field of legal, customary, and moral obligations that distinguished it from the kinds of work conventionally done for wages. However, the boundaries between these categories seem to have been variable both in principle and in practice.

* * *

Finally, I would like to address some notable limitations of this study. This book does not seek to offer a comprehensive overview of premodern jurists' views on domestic labor. Rather than surveying the maximum possible number of sources, I have preferred to focus deeply on a small set of individual authors and works. This approach makes it possible to tease out the linkages among apparently disparate sections of the same work of *fiqh*, showing how statements about wives' domestic labor are implicated in broader patterns of argumentation. The source texts are chosen in part for the length and richness of their treatment of the book's themes, which make it possible to access a single author's views on the broadest possible range of relevant issues. Despite its advantages, this approach limits the number of texts that can be addressed.

This study is also limited in its doctrinal scope. Each chapter focuses on one of what came to be regarded as the four canonical schools (*madhāhib*, singular *madhhab*) of Sunni legal thought. There are many other schools, both extinct and surviving, that would have been eminently worthy of examination; I have limited myself to these four both because of their retrospective importance for Sunni Muslims and for simple reasons of time and space. These four schools were also in more intimate and explicit dialogue with each other than, for instance, with Shi'i thinkers, so the authors discussed here are all contributing to the same broad shared conversation. The chronological order in which the schools are discussed is a factor of the specific authors whose work I found to illuminate the themes of the book. Each of the scholars featured is an eminent thinker whose work enjoyed lasting prestige within his school; however, they are presented as illustrative examples of the different potentialities and pathways that could be explored rather than as definitive exemplars of school doctrine. At the end of each chapter I offer a brief account of how the individual authors discussed fit into the larger trends within their schools.

As a study of scholarly thought, this book does not attempt to reconstruct the views or experiences of the mass of Muslims who were not versed in the technical discourses of the ulama. However, neither does it envision the ulama as an elite hermetically sealed from the beliefs and values of "popular" Islam. Rather, it shows how Muslim jurists strove to harmonize their legal doctrines with social expectations and religious values that they shared with the wider society, including deeply held assumptions about the proper conduct and religious value of gender roles within the household. Furthermore, the texts examined have gained broader significance through the authority they have been accorded over the centuries. They remain in circulation—in most cases in multiple modern printed editions, and more recently in digital forms available on the internet—due not primarily to the efforts of secular academics but to the texts' ongoing life as references for believing Muslims. Nevertheless, today as in the past many elements of their analyses would be unfamiliar (and perhaps jarring) to many believers; there is no one-to-one correspondence between their categories and values and those of average Muslims.

Relatedly, given the fact that all the scholars whose work is analyzed here were male, this book lacks any direct account of how domestic labor might have been incorporated into women's own moral and religious projects. For the periods and places studied here, we have only occasional glimpses of views attributed to women in male-authored texts. Women's household tasks could certainly be a source of religious imagery and metaphor.[131] As Rkia Cornell has observed (and as is discussed in chapter 3 of this study), there is some reason to think that early female renunciants and mystics had a particular affinity for *khidma* (in the overlapping sense of service to God and of personal service, including food preparation, to a spiritual mentor) as a form of religious devotion.[132] Looking at a much later historical period, Richard Eaton has described how in one region of southern India, "the bulk of the folk poetry written by Sufis was sung by village women as they did various household chores," the two most common subgenres being associated with grinding grain and with spinning.[133] I have not identified such materials for the centuries and regions addressed here (which of course does not mean that they do not—or did not once—exist). While there are certainly didactic works exhorting women to do housework, one can only speculate on the moral and religious meanings women themselves may have brought to these activities.[134]

Structure and chapter summaries

In order to access the diversity and development of the *fiqh* discussion of domestic labor, each chapter this study offers a snapshot of a different period and school of law. To place the *fiqh* discussion within the broader landscape of normative Islamic discourses that were available in those contexts, each of the first three chapters begins by introducing a relevant non-*fiqh* discourse and examining its approach to the issue of domestic labor. As we shall see, in some cases these parallel discourses are explicitly drawn into the *fiqh* discussion and in others they remain tacit alternatives to the legal framework. This project seeks to position the *fiqh* discussion among the available normative discourses regardless of the extent to which they are overtly referenced in the legal texts.

Chapter 1 focuses on the formative period of Islamic law, the second to third centuries AH / eighth to ninth centuries CE. It opens with a discussion of the early Islamic literature of *zuhd* (renunciation), which reflects the situation of an early Islamic community grappling with the moral implications of the wealth and power of the Umma in the wake of the conquests. In this context, personal performance of menial daily tasks appears as a virtuous alternative to the ubiquitous use of enslaved labor, and wives' desire for servants is seen as morally suspect. The remainder of the chapter focuses on the discussion of wives' domestic labor in early works of the Mālikī legal school. The *Mudawwana* of Saḥnūn (d. 240/854) uses exemption from domestic labor as the key legal distinction between the status of free wives and of enslaved women. In contrast, several other early Mālikī texts reflect deep commitment to the idea that wives are morally and socially (if not legally) obligated to do housework. The three authors produce different resolutions to the resulting tension between their ethical ideals and the school's dominant early legal doctrine.

Chapters 2 and 3 move to the classical period of Islamic law; each focuses on an individual scholar of the fifth/eleventh century. Chapter 2, which focuses on the Shāfiʿī Abū'l-Ḥasan al-Māwardī (d. 450/1058), opens with an examination of the issue of domestic labor in Islamic philosophical ethics. As a representative of elite Baghdadi culture, al-Māwardī incorporates into his scholarship a wide variety of discursive traditions including philosophical ethics. His legal manual, *Al-Ḥāwī al-kabīr*, adheres to a strictly legal analysis of the marital relationship, focusing rigorously on the contractual exchange of the husband's financial maintenance for the wife's sexual availability. This model explicitly excludes any obligation for the wife to provide labor and emphasizes her right to abstain from any task that would impair her social standing according to the mores prevailing in her milieu (although he resolutely evades the implication that she could claim wages from her husband). In contrast, al-Māwardī's ethical manual, *Adab al-dunyā wa'l-dīn*, deprecates sexual enjoyment as a motivation for marriage and affirms the legitimacy of marrying for the sake of a wife's labor. Despite the apparent tension between the two, careful reading suggests that they are not incompatible; rather, for al-Māwardī the genres of *fiqh* and *akhlāq* ask different questions and address different concerns.

Chapter 3 focuses on the Central Asian Ḥanafī al-Sarakhsī and his legal manual, *Al-Mabsūṭ*. It opens with a discussion of the moral resonance that had accrued to the concept of service (*khidma*) in this time and place. Rather than simply alluding to unavoidable mundane tasks, *khidma* (in both concrete and metaphorical senses) had come to be a central motif in the articulation of a wide range of bilateral hierarchical relationships on the social, political, and theological levels. This pattern is reflected, among other places, in the ideals and practices of Sufi discipleship that were crystallizing in greater Khurasan in al-Sarakhsī's lifetime. Al-Sarakhsī's legal analysis of *khidma* within the family gives it a new moral weight by positing a specifically ethical obligation for wives to serve husbands and for children to serve parents. His analysis of housework thus makes an explicit distinction between the legal and the moral while incorporating both into his work of *fiqh*. While he never overtly invokes the discipline of *akhlāq*, his analysis is also informed by Islamic philosophical ethics. Like the Islamic philosophers, he assumes that wives have a managerial role that contributes to the prosperity of the household. For al-Sarakhsī, the legal requirements of the marriage contract ultimately represent only a fraction of the mutual duties of the spouses, which must be complemented by the demands of love and ethics.

Chapter 4 moves to the postclassical period and focuses on a radical reimagining of the law of marriage in the fourth Sunni school of law, the Ḥanbalīs, in eighth-/fourteenth-century Damascus. It begins by examining the doctrines of the leading Damascene Ḥanbalī authority of the early thirteenth century, Muwaffaq al-Dīn Ibn Qudāma (d. 620/1223). In keeping with the distinctive doctrinal approach of his school, Ibn Qudāma treats the marriage contract as a limited legal agreement that does not preclude the two spouses' freedom of contract on other matters. Thus, not only does he deny any wifely obligation to provide housework but he explicitly affirms that a wife could validly contract to receive wages for housework from her husband. In the early fourteenth century, the Ḥanbalī status quo was sharply challenged by Taqī al-Dīn Ibn Taymīya (728/1328), who promoted a radically new vision of the marital relationship. Rather than understanding the marriage contract as a strictly legal transaction of limited scope, Ibn Taymīya melds his legal analysis with a vision of the ethics of marriage directly grounded in the Qur'an and hadith. In this new synthesis, a wife is obligated to provide housework to her husband not as part of an exchange of concrete benefits under the marriage contract but in the context of an overall moral relationship in which the husband's benevolent domination and nurture is reciprocated with the wife's obedience and service. Ibn Taymīya accordingly denies that a wife could, even hypothetically, contract to receive wages for housework from her husband.

The conclusion briefly examines the modern trajectories of the doctrines examined in the body of the book. In the twentieth century Ibn Taymīya's doctrine that wives are obligated to provide domestic labor rose to new prominence, due both to the introduction of modern Western ideals of domesticity and to the modern rediscovery and dissemination of Ibn Taymīya's works. Meanwhile, the doctrine that wives are exempt from domestic labor has been used as an Islamic precedent for modern legislation giving divorced wives and widows new claims to marital assets (on the grounds that they have contributed labor that they were not legally obligated to provide). Most strikingly, however, since the early twentieth century the legal issue of wives' domestic labor has been incorporated into a gendered ethical vision in which housework and family care are seen as the actualization of a divinely implanted feminine essential nature (*fiṭra*). This unprecedented synthesis of Islamic law and ethics inverts the most widely accepted model, in which the modern period is understood to have seen an unprecedented rupture between Islamic law and ethics.

ONE

Domestic Labor in the Literature of *Zuhd* (Renunciation) and in Early Mālikī Texts

THE *JĀMIʿ* OF Maʿmar ibn Rāshid (d. AH 153/770 CE) transmits a letter in which the Prophet's Companion Abū'l-Dardāʾ (d. 32/652) offers a series of moral exhortations to Abū Dharr al-Ghifārī (also d. 32/652–653).[1] It includes, for instance, the Prophetic counsel that a man who finds himself hard of heart should soften it by feeding and comforting an orphan. It finishes by declaring, "O brother! I am told that you have bought a servant; I heard the Messenger of God say, 'The human being (*ʿabd*) belongs to God and God to him as long as he is not served; when he is served, the judgment becomes incumbent upon him.'[2] [My wife] Umm al-Dardāʾ asked me for a servant, and I was well-to-do at the time; but I disliked that for her and was fearful of the Judgment."[3]

In this piece of counsel attributed to a respected early Muslim, being the recipient of the service of a fellow human being is incompatible with the purest form of a person's servanthood to God. Reading between the lines, however, it is not Abū'l-Dardāʾ himself who is implied to be performing the chores in his household; rather, it is his wife who seeks (and is denied) the relief of being provided with domestic help.

While we cannot be certain of the historicity of this anecdote, it conveys a clear sentiment—one that is somewhat surprising in light of early Islamic legal norms of marriage. According to the majority doctrines of the *fiqh* of the formative period, a Muslim husband is required to provide domestic labor for his wife if he is financially able; Maʿmar ibn Rāshid's contemporary

Abū Ḥanīfa, for instance, held that a husband was obligated to financially support his wife's enslaved servant.[4] Thus, it may be unexpected to find an exemplary early figure represented as denying his wife such help (despite his prosperity) on pious moral grounds. Rather than being an isolated anomaly, however, this anecdote reflects the complex meanings of mundane labor in an early Islamic society where pious individuals were coming to terms with the moral and religious implications of prosperity and power.

This chapter will place the wife's domestic labor within the larger landscape of ethical discourses in the Islamic community of the formative period (specifically, the second to third centuries AH/eighth to ninth centuries CE). After a brief introduction to the issue of domestic labor in this period, the chapter examines the role of domestic service—and of the menial tasks that comprise it—in early texts about pious renunciation, or *zuhd*. This material is juxtaposed with early juristic doctrines on the same subject, focusing specifically on the *Mudawwana* of Saḥnūn, the earliest comprehensive collection of legal teachings within the school of Mālik ibn Anas (d. 179/796). As suggested by the example above, these two genres take profoundly divergent approaches to the question of who should perform mundane daily chores and why. This mismatch, I argue, reflects both the evolving social composition of the early Muslim community and the diversity of the frameworks that were brought to bear on questions of everyday personal conduct. By the third/ninth century, Muslim thinkers drew on a repertoire of ideas about the moral valence of humble labor and the mutual obligations of spouses that could have sharply divergent implications for the behavior of husbands and wives. The remainder of the chapter examines how three influential early Mālikī scholars navigated this complex ethico-legal landscape, ranging from the substantive separation of the moral and legal dimensions of the question of wives' labor to different forms of synthesis.

Domestic labor in the literature of *zuhd* (renunciation)

The *Jāmiʿ* of Maʿmar ibn Rāshid is arguably the earliest thematic compilation of reports about the sayings and doings of the Prophet and the earliest Muslims preserved to us today.[5] The traditions collected in it reflect the assumption that availability of servants was the norm even in the latter part of the life of the Prophet Muḥammad, who is reported to have advised,

"When the servant brings one of you his food, having borne the heat, the hardship, the smoke, and the trouble of [its preparation]," the believer should allow him to sit or offer him a bite of food.[6] Relegation of mundane tasks such as food preparation to servants is depicted as a norm whose violation is cause for surprise; in one anecdote, a man who comes to the Prophet's Companion Salmān al-Fārisī and finds him kneading dough exclaims, "Where is the servant?" (Salmān explains that he has sent him on an errand.)[7]

Nevertheless, domestic tasks such as cooking and serving food are also pervasively associated with wives. In one report, the Prophet hosts some of his followers for a meal, crying out to his young wife, "Bring us food, ʿĀʾisha! . . . Bring us something to drink, ʿĀʾisha!"[8] Indeed, the admonition of Abū'l-Dardāʾ is not the only expression of ambivalence about acquiring servants to relieve wives of household work. Maʿmar presents an anecdote transmitted from the Prophet's great-grandson ʿAlī ibn al-Ḥusayn recounting,

> The Messenger of God's daughter Fāṭima came to him to ask him for a servant from among the prisoners of war he had received; her hands were worn from the handle of the millstone because she had been grinding so much [grain]. He said to her, "I will inform you of something better than that; when you go to bed, say 'Glory be to God!' thirty-three times, 'Praise be to God!' thirty-three times, 'God is most great!' thirty-three times, and say 'There is no god but God' to make a complete hundred [invocations]." She went home with that; he did not provide her with a servant.[9]

As we shall see, this tradition was to play a complex role in the legal debate over wives' domestic duties.

Other early sources reinforce the impression drawn from the *Jāmiʿ* of Maʿmar that slave servants were ubiquitous in the early Islamic period. In one widely cited report, the Prophet's widow ʿĀʾisha (who lived into the Umayyad period) declares that a full bath before Friday prayers is not obligatory; it had merely been advisable for believers in the early days of the faith, when Muslims had no servants and themselves became sweaty from their labors.[10] In the postconquest period, it could be felt as a hardship for the female relatives of a well-connected Muslim to be obliged to engage in domestic toil. An anecdote in an early source depicts Maʿmar's scholarly mentor at the Umayyad court, Ibn Shihāb al-Zuhrī, successfully appealing to the caliph ʿAbd al-Malik to grant him a slave "because when I left my family, they had no one to serve them except for one of my sisters—she has to make the dough and bake the bread for them."[11]

As Ingrid Mattson has observed, even early figures known for their asceticism are often depicted as having servants.[12] This is reflected in reports (such as the opening anecdote) about Abū Dharr, who is otherwise best known for his pious renunciation of worldly goods.[13] In one report, the Umayyad governor Ḥabīb ibn Maslama sends Abū Dharr three hundred dinars. He refuses them, declaring that God is his sufficiency; he has nothing but some shade to shelter him, a few sheep to sustain him, and "a freed slavewoman of ours who serves us as an act of piety."[14] In the absence of slaves—or in addition to their services—wives are implied to be the main sources of routine household labor such as the processing of food. Indeed, it seems to have been regarded as an unusual show of renunciation for even the most pious men to eschew the services of their wives. Al-Ḥasan al-Baṣrī (d. 110/728) is quoted as declaring, "I have met—by the One Who holds my soul in His hand—a number of people, none of whom ever ordered his wife to prepare food; if something was served to him he ate it, and otherwise he stayed silent."[15] Even here, one suspects that the men in question humbly waited for their wives or servants to prepare their food.

Despite the pervasiveness of references to enslaved servants, early Islamic normative sources also valorize the believer's personal engagement in humble labor. *Khidma*, or service—the word most widely used to designate the humble tasks of daily living—is a minor but pervasive theme in the genre of religious works devoted to *zuhd*, renunciation or self-denial.[16] In this context, personal performance of such labor is seen as both an expression of humility and a means to its cultivation. The *Kitāb al-Zuhd* of the Kufan traditionist Wakīʿ ibn al-Jarrāḥ (d. 197/812) has a chapter titled "Service and Humility" (*Bāb al-khidma wa'l-tawāḍuʿ*) that describes the Prophet and exemplary early Muslims engaging in lowly household chores such as sweeping floors and feeding and milking livestock. For an elite man, even minor tasks such as pouring the water for one's own ablutions and attending to one's own lamp may be seen as exemplifying humility (*tawāḍuʿ*).[17]

Engaging in such tasks is implied to be an act of virtue rather than a matter of necessity; in one anecdote, the early Kufan authority al-Rabīʿ ibn Khuthaym is told of his sweeping, "You have someone to do that for you!"; he replies, "I like to take my share of chores."[18] In another report, the Prophet is said to have spent his time at home "doing chores for his wives" (*fī mihnat ahlihi*), suggesting that such work might ordinarily be performed by the women of the household.[19] Ibn Saʿd (d. 230/845) includes in his chapter on the Prophet's exemplary character (*akhlāq*) a series of reports in which ʿĀʾisha describes him as engaging in homely tasks such as sewing and fixing sandals.[20] Nevertheless, he also includes a chapter enumerating the Prophet's servants, including both enslaved persons and two women who served him voluntarily.[21]

In some cases, personal performance of menial tasks (and eschewal of the services of a slave) may have been a broad life commitment. The Baṣran devotee Kahmas ibn al-Ḥasan (d. 149/766–767) is known for his extreme devotion to his mother, for whom he performed humble tasks such as sweeping despite an admirer's offer of funds to buy a servant.[22] However, pious men's engagement with mundane tasks appears more often to be a gesture of humility than a genuine renunciation of the labor of others, whether servants or wives. The *Kitāb al-Zuhd* of ʿAbd Allāh ibn al-Mubārak (d. 181/797) presents a report admiringly describing how the elderly Companion of the Prophet Abū Barza "used to go and get water in the middle of the night and perform his ablutions [for prayer] without waking any of his servants."[23] Of the pious Umayyad ʿUmar ibn ʿAbd al-ʿAzīz (d. 101/720) it is said, "When he became caliph he renounced the world (*zahida fī al-dunyā*) and refrained from being served (*taraka an yukhdam*)." Nevertheless, his renunciation of service seems to have been largely symbolic: "When his food was prepared for him, it was set out and covered; when he came in, he took it and ate."[24]

There is little in such reports to suggest that even the most austere pious figures of the early Islamic period genuinely relinquished the labor of servants or of wives. The primary contexts in which men are depicted as fully assuming the burden of daily chores are in homosocial groups outside of the home. A story from the eleventh-century source *Ḥilyat al-awliyāʾ* depicts Ibrāhīm ibn Adham al-Balkhī (d. 161/777–778) renting a house with three companions while on pilgrimage in Medina; he suggests that they undertake the housework (*khidmat al-bayt*) in rotation.[25] The *Kitāb al-Jihād* of ʿAbd Allāh ibn al-Mubārak presents a number of reports emphasizing the religious merit of service to one's fellows, whether on a journey, in a military campaign, or as a personal disciple.[26] The Prophet is said to have invoked blessings on any man he saw serving his companions.[27] The merit of performing humble labor for one's fellows was sufficiently rich that pious men sometimes vied for the privilege.[28]

Such anecdotes do not allow any systematic conclusions about the quantitative prevalence of servants in early Muslim households or the allocation of domestic chores. Nevertheless, the ubiquity of references to domestic servants is telling; both textual allusions and historical context suggest that the availability of slave captives was a significant factor. Maʿmar himself is said to have been a slave of Persian origin who rose to frequent the caliphal court during the final decades of Umayyad rule. He was thus both a member of the vast wave of prisoners of war and an upwardly mobile Muslim whose views were informed by "the wealth, power, and prestige of the new Islamic-conquest elite."[29]

Although the broad context of Muslim ascendancy and abundant servile labor is historically well-grounded, the texts cited above were not created or primarily intended as historical records; rather, they are normative sources offering guidance for a virtuous Muslim life. Regardless of the authenticity of individual anecdotes, they communicate the resonances and concerns associated with domestic labor by early religious thinkers and teachers. The *zuhd* works of the second and third centuries AH suggest that exemption from the menial toil of everyday life was simultaneously a defining privilege of the Muslim conquest elite and a potential moral hazard to the pious individual. However, paradoxically, it was also an opportunity: it was precisely the ready availability of servants that rendered personal engagement in such activities salient as a moral gesture.

Nevertheless, this gesture was not equally available to everyone. Normative texts of the second-third century AH suggest that the ubiquity of servants posed a challenge not only to religious ideals of humility and egalitarianism but to the gendered structure of the pious household envisioned by male scholars. In the *Kitāb Mujābū al-daʿwa* ("People Whose Prayers Were Answered") of Ibn Abī'l-Dunyā (d. 281/894), the wife of the early Syrian ascetic Abū Muslim al-Khawlānī greets him on his return home each day by taking his cloak and shoes and serving him his meal. One day he instead finds her moping in the dark. Asked what is wrong, she complains that if he would only approach Muʿāwiya (presumably then either governor or caliph), he would provide them with a servant. Abū Muslim exclaims, "O God, may whoever has spoiled my wife be struck blind!" The interfering woman promptly loses her vision, and Abū Muslim's wife resumes her virtuous ways.[30] Here the nameless wife's engagement in humble service is not in itself noteworthy, despite the easy availability of servile labor; it is her refusal to serve that is visible and (negatively) legible as a moral gesture.

Only in rare cases is it a wife whose insistence on personal performance of humble chores appears as notable and exemplary. One anecdote set in the early second century AH (albeit preserved in a later source) recounts that after the Baṣran ascetic Riyāḥ al-Qaysī got married, he arose to find his new wife at work making bread.[31] He asked, "Why don't you find a woman to take care of that for you?" and she retorted, "I married Riyāḥ al-Qaysī; I did not think that I had married an obstinate tyrant!"[32] Here it is the wife who assumes the role of pious admonisher—and also, as in the case of Umm al-Dardā', the wife who engages in household toil to spare her husband the moral odium of acquiring a servant. Despite individual differences, the early sources' many anecdotes about men and women performing or avoiding humble household labor, seeking or eschewing servants suggest that the distribution of routine chores within the household was an area of moral concern.

Wives' domestic labor in early *fiqh*

As we have seen, to the extent that materials of the second and third centuries AH drawn from the edifying literature associated with *zuhd* thematize domestic labor, they praise personal performance of the mundane tasks of daily life as an aid to the cultivation of humility. At the same time, they pervasively imply the ubiquity of enslaved servants; exemplary early male figures' involvement with menial chores appears both voluntary and intermittent. It is primarily with respect to wives that acquisition of servants is itself seen as a moral problem, and personally undertaking the heaviest and most time-consuming household tasks is depicted as a virtuous alternative even when a servant might be available.

A very different picture emerges from the *fiqh* literature of the formative period. Unlike the works of ethical guidance discussed above, in the early legal texts no misgivings are expressed about the moral effects of keeping servants, whose financial maintenance is discussed as a matter of enforceable entitlement. This section surveys the role of wives' domestic labor in early works of *fiqh*, whose distinctively legal project gave them a very different perspective on the allocation of household chores.

Surveying the doctrinal positions accumulated up to his own time, Abū Jaʿfar al-Ṭaḥāwī (d. 321/933) observes that legal scholars "were in agreement (*lam yakhtalifū*) that a wife is not obligated to serve herself, that it is her husband's obligation to provide that [labor] for her, and that if she has a servant, the husband . . . is obligated to pay the maintenance of the servant according to her need for it."[33] Ibn al-Mundhir (d. 318/930) describes early legal disputation in this area as revolving around the number of servants a husband may be compelled to support for his wife, with some jurists holding that the obligation is limited to one and others arguing that some wives may legitimately require more.[34]

As Ibn al-Mundhir notes, the doctrine of "the husband's being obligated to maintain the wife's servants is not based upon an authoritative text such as a hadith that must be accepted; rather, it is an opinion of the scholars."[35] The husband's duty to support his wife's servant emerged from the internal logic of the jurists' analysis of the marital contract; the obligation of spousal support (*nafaqa*), which included the provision of food and clothing, was understood to imply responsibility for the labor required to render them usable.[36] Some scholars (notably al-Shāfiʿī [d. 204/820][37]) made the wife's prerogatives in this area dependent on her social status; Ibn al-Mundhir notes that "all of the scholars whose opinions are taken into account/recorded (*kull man yuḥfaẓ ʿanhu min ahl al-ʿilm*) make incumbent [on the husband] the maintenance of a single servant for a wife *who does not serve herself*" (*la takhdim nafsahā*).[38]

A wife's entitlement to the costs of keeping a servant may be taken to imply that she herself owes her husband no domestic labor, but no direct statements on this subject are attributed to the school founders in the earliest available sources. What is clear is that none of the scholars retrospectively regarded as school founders are remembered to have articulated an affirmative duty for wives to provide housework for their husbands.

The early *fiqh* discussion of responsibility for domestic labor seems strikingly focused on the scenario that the wife possesses an enslaved servant. This may be because the focus is on the strictly legal issue of the quantity and nature of the material support that a man may be judicially compelled to disburse to his wife rather than with the broader question of how to allocate labor in an ideal Muslim household. It may also reflect the socio-economic realities of the early Islamic period; Karen Bauer has argued that "the wife's right to service was an early legal norm, possibly put in place as a consequence of the number of readily available slaves in the earliest period, plus the fact that in the period before mass conversion, Muslims were the political and military elite and could afford slaves."[39]

The concrete implications of the doctrine that a husband's duty of *nafaqa* included tasks such as food preparation were vividly imagined by the early Hanafi jurist Abū Bakr al-Khaṣṣāf (d. 261/874). In his manual for judges, he writes, "If the judge orders that [a wife] be provided with the maintenance that she requires, including flour and other foodstuffs, and she says, 'I will not work, or bake, or cook, or process any of that,' she is not compelled to do so, and the husband is obligated to provide her with someone who will take care of baking, cooking, and the like."[40] Al-Khaṣṣāf's scenario of a wife stubbornly refusing to engage in food preparation offers a stark contrast to the anecdotes in works of moral guidance, where exemplary wives eschew the help of servants and toil over their own millstones and cooking pots. However, the contrast is largely a function of the distinct objectives of the genres in which these passages appear. While the edifying narratives discussed above provide guidance for a pious project of self-fashioning as a good believer and a good spouse, al-Khaṣṣāf's scenario addresses the proper disposition of a conflict that could be brought before a judge. Neither the husband nor the wife is assumed to be acting ideally. The issue is not what people ought to do but what they can be made to do in the context of litigation. In this case, the husband can be compelled to provide the labor that will render his wife's rations edible, while the wife cannot be compelled to do the work herself.

The Mudawwana *of Saḥnūn*

Perhaps the earliest explicit statement about the legal status of wives' domestic labor is found in the *Mudawwana* of ʿAbd al-Salām ibn Saʿīd al-Tanūkhī (d. 240/854), known as Saḥnūn. This work is a compilation of legal opinions attributed to the Medinian authority Mālik ibn Anas by the first generation of his students, whom Saḥnūn encountered in Egypt, particularly Mālik's long-term disciple ʿAbd al-Raḥmān ibn al-Qāsim (d. 191/806).[41] In this work the authorial voice (implicitly, Saḥnūn) asks, "Is it your opinion that a wife is obligated to perform any service (*khidma*) for herself or her house, according to the doctrine of Mālik?" His interlocutor (implicitly, Ibn al-Qāsim[42]) replies decisively, "She is obligated to perform no service, either for herself or her house!"[43] The context implies that this statement may be Ibn al-Qāsim's own extrapolation from Mālik's transmitted teachings rather than a direct quotation from Mālik. The *Mudawwana* also reports Mālik's teaching that "the husband is responsible for the maintenance (*nafaqa*) of his wife and of one maidservant belonging to his wife."[44] There were divergent views on the implication of this doctrine if the wife lacked a servant or if the husband lacked funds to support one. An opinion attributed to al-Rabīᶜ (probably al-Rabīᶜ ibn Sulaymān al-Azdī, d. 256/870) specifies that if the husband "does not have the means to provide her with a servant, the two of them both contribute to service.[45] The wife is entitled only to sufficient clothing and food; as for [domestic] service, she is relieved of responsibility for it if he is prosperous and she contributes with her means if he is needy."[46]

Here the wife's entitlement to domestic help financed by her husband is contingent on his financial resources; if they are lacking, the spouses are to join forces, perhaps in paying for a servant rather than in doing the work themselves (although this is ambiguous). Saḥnūn himself seems to have placed the burden of financing domestic service on all husbands without distinction: "His inability [to provide domestic] service is like his inability to provide maintenance [i.e., food, clothing and shelter]; it is obligatory [for the judge] to separate the couple if he is unable to provide it."[47] This statement rather shockingly implies that any husband too poor to provide a servant is subject to judicial dissolution of his marriage. Despite their differences, these opinions associate household labor with servants rather than with wives, and the position that a wife of any status could demand household help on pain of divorce was at least thinkable.

Indeed, Saḥnūn's statement about the impecunious husband is not the only instance in the *Mudawwana* that domestic service is regarded as a legitimate basic need even of able-bodied adults. For instance, it is stated that an indigent father may be required to sell his house if this will provide for his subsistence after the purchase of a more modest residence, but not so his slave.[48] In the *Mudawwana*'s discussion of rightful recipients of funds collected from obligatory alms (*zakāt*) or of food distributed in expiation of an oath, a person is considered "poor" if he possesses only a house and a servant sufficient for his own needs.[49] The "needs" involved may involve the maintenance of social status as well as the provision of physical care; describing the legitimate recipients of food distributed in expiation, Mālik specifies that such persons may own only a house adequate to their needs and have "a maidservant who saves the family's face."[50]

It is notable that, at least in principle, the *Mudawwana* appears to envision all wives as being entitled to expect domestic service; it deploys no special labels of status or prestige to characterize the individuals who are entitled to it. The text as a whole certainly displays awareness of distinctions of status and wealth within the Muslim community, for instance, when it specifies that a woman who is "poor" (*miskīna*), "lowly" (*danīʾa*), and "of no account" (*lā khaṭba lahā*) may designate any respectable man to contract her marriage, while a woman of "property, wealth and rank" must be married off by a male guardian.[51] As we have seen, it also designates destitute Muslims as recipients of charity and rules on scenarios where an economically struggling husband may be unable to support his wife. All of this may suggest that the social world envisioned in the *Mudawwana* is not one of uniform Muslim wealth and privilege. Nevertheless, it implicitly regards exemption from unpaid domestic service (even to oneself) as a prerogative of the free Muslim of either sex. It is also consistently assumed that the servants in question are enslaved; thus, the text speaks of maintenance (*nafaqa*) rather than of wages, and it treats servants as economic assets when gauging a person's wealth.

The fact that the normative model envisioned in the *Mudawwana* associates domestic labor with servants rather than with wives does not mean that such labor is not gendered. Rather, different kinds of tasks are associated with enslaved men and women.[52] One passage enumerates building, goldsmithing, dyeing, and carpentry as skills that enhance the value of an enslaved man; for an enslaved woman, they are cooking, spinning, weaving, and cleaning.[53] In another source Ibn al-Qāsim is cited as describing the gainful occupations (*ṣunʿa*) of enslaved women as including cooking, baking, and embroidery; the comparable qualifications of male slaves are trade (*tijāra*), eloquence (*faṣāḥa*), and intelligence (*nafādh*).[54]

The *Mudawwana* thus reflects a general assumption that Muslim households routinely enjoyed the labor of enslaved servants and that this labor freed wives of any obligation to provide housework. As we have seen, this assumption may have been sociologically accurate for many if not all Muslim households as long as Muslims represented a small conquest elite. In this study, however, the focus is not on the concrete practices of Muslims "on the ground" but on the significance of domestic labor within the discursive projects of different Islamic genres. In this context, the key question is what role this assumption plays within the larger conceptual structure of the *Mudawwana*. One answer may be found in the distribution of the work's references to the exemption from domestic labor. Tellingly, the person whose obligation to perform domestic labor the *Mudawwana* most insistently and emphatically denies is not the wife but the *umm walad*, the enslaved woman who has borne her master a child.

The *umm walad* occupies a status somewhere between that of an ordinary slave and that of a wife. She cannot be sold and automatically becomes free at the death of the owner who impregnated her.[55] Ingrid Mattson notes that as a result of the *umm walad*'s "liminal position," "in any legal case in which the outcome was affected by the free or slave status of a woman, jurists had to decide whether to treat the *umm walad* as a slave or as a free woman."[56] In the most direct statement regarding the labor of a woman of this status, Mālik is quoted as declaring, "The master of an *umm walad* is not entitled to use her for service (*an yastakhdimahā*) or to fatigue her with tasks such as drawing water, grinding [flour], or the like."[57] Mālik's specific examples of drawing water and grinding flour might be taken as emblematic of particularly onerous or heavy household tasks, and indeed later Mālikīs sometimes allowed the use of *umm walads* for "light" household service.[58] However, in the *Mudawwana* it is consistently asserted that the *umm walad* is not subject to domestic service at all; as Mālik declares in another passage, "All her master is entitled to from her is sexual enjoyment, just as he is entitled to sexual enjoyment from a free [wife]."[59]

The *Mudawwana* reiterates, with striking frequency, that the owner of an *umm walad* is not entitled to her labor. This point arises in a number of scenarios where the owner of an *umm walad* for some reason forfeits the right of sexual access to her; in each case, it is asserted that she then becomes free altogether. In the absence of any right to her labor, a master who loses the right to sexual enjoyment of his *umm walad* has no remaining right to her at all.[60] Altogether, the *Mudawwana* manages to inform us that an owner is not entitled to his *umm walad*'s labor (or that he is entitled only to sexual enjoyment of her) at least nine times. Even bearing in mind that the work is a compilation of legal reports rather than a tightly synthesized authored composition, this point is asserted rather insistently. On the one hand, the strong affirmation that an *umm walad*'s owner is entitled to sexual access rather than domestic work reflects the *Mudawwana*'s understanding of marriage; the primary feature of the *umm walad*'s status as compared with that of other enslaved women is precisely that it is more wife-like. On the other hand, if it is necessary to assert the ways in which an *umm walad* is similar to a wife, it is also necessary to assert the ways in which she is different from an ordinary slave. In this respect, ownership of one's own labor functions as the key differentiator between slave and (partially) free statuses.

The view that a man was not entitled to the labor of his *umm walad* was not shared by all early jurists. Al-Shāfiʿī affirmed that an *umm walad* could be used for service and derisively dismissed the view that she would be rendered free if her owner forfeited the right to sexual access.[61] Similarly, the followers of Abū Ḥanīfa held that an *umm walad* could be used for service.[62] However, what is at stake in this juristic dispute is whether an *umm walad* is more like a slave or more like a free wife. All parties implicitly agree that being subject to the involuntary exploitation of one's labor without pay is definitive of servile status.

Indeed (and perhaps unsurprisingly), ownership of one's own labor is explicitly the key component of free status regardless of gender. To become free is to become entitled to wages for one's own labor; if the owner acknowledges having used a slave for service after manumission, then the freed person is entitled to the market value of any service performed since manumission.[63] In one passage Ibn al-Qāsim replies tersely that manumitting a slave woman is equivalent to "gifting her service to her."[64] To own one's own labor (and thus to be entitled to wages for it) is to be free, and vice versa. This fact sheds light on Mālik's categorical denial that a wife does not owe her husband her service.

The equation between free or enslaved status and ownership of labor is complicated by the fact that, according to the legal model reflected in the *Mudawwana*, to own a male slave is to possess two analytically distinct things: the slave's person (*raqaba*) and his service or labor (*khidma*). Ordinarily the two go together, with the right to the enslaved individual's service accruing to the person who possesses his *raqaba*, who may then exploit it personally for domestic or other work (*istikhdām/istiʿmāl*) or use it to earn wages or profit (*istighlāl*), which accrue to the owner.[65] However, ownership of the slave's person and of his labor are also potentially separable. The *Mudawwana* examines multiple scenarios in which a person bequeaths an enslaved person's *raqaba* to one person and his *khidma* to another.[66] The two are distinct in the sense that a person who has received the bequest of an enslaved person's service for a certain duration cannot sell the slave. Nevertheless, at any given point in time an owner's right over an enslaved man is reducible to the right to his labor.[67]

In the case of a woman, the picture is complicated by the fact that labor is not the only benefit at stake; the right to sexual access is also involved. Just as the right to a person's labor ordinarily accrues to the owner of the *raqaba*, the right of sexual access to a woman is conceptualized as accruing to the owner of her *buḍ*ᶜ. The exact meaning of the word *buḍ*ᶜ is debated; according to the lexicographer al-Azharī (d. 371/981), "some people say that it is the genitals, others that it is sexual intercourse; it has also been said that it is the marriage contract."[68] As Kecia Ali has demonstrated, according to the model developed by the jurists of the formative period, the ownership of a woman's *buḍ*ᶜ can be transferred from the woman either to a husband or to her owner, if she is enslaved.[69] This situation gives rise to several possible permutations. A single, free adult woman owns both her own *buḍ*ᶜ and her own labor. If she is enslaved, both her *buḍ*ᶜ and her labor belong to her owner, who is entitled to both sexual enjoyment and service. If she marries, she transfers ownership of the *buḍ*ᶜ to a husband in exchange for the dower (*ṣadāq*); however, she retains ownership of her own labor. An obvious complication ensues if an enslaved woman is married; in this case, her husband is entitled to sex on demand, but her owner remains entitled to her labor.[70] On a purely conceptual level, assigning a husband the right to a free wife's domestic labor would fundamentally disrupt this schema.

In the *Mudawwana*, the one prominent exception to the wife's exemption from domestic labor is the breastfeeding of infants. This is an activity that might not intuitively be categorized as labor, let alone as economically valuable labor, but in fact wet-nursing is recognized as a wage-bearing activity in the Qur'an (2:233, 65:6), and commercial wet-nursing was widespread in early Islamic societies.[71] The *Mudawwana* explores this issue in detail. Ibn al-Qāsim recounts, "I asked Mālik whether a married woman is required to nurse her child. He said, 'Yes, whether she wants to or not, unless she is someone who is not made to do that.' I said to Mālik, 'And who is not made to do that?' He said, 'A woman who is noble and very wealthy, the likes of whom does not nurse or care for children; [in such a case] I consider [paying for nursing] the obligation of [the child's] father, even if she has milk.' "[72] This passage introduces a status distinction between wives whose social prestige renders it inappropriate for them to nurse or tend children and those (apparently the majority) who are liable to provide nursing.

A wife who is obligated to nurse her child is entitled to no compensation for doing so because nursing is treated as one of the entitlements accruing from the husband's payment of *nafaqa*.[73] However, the obligation to nurse is specific to the couple's own child; it is not a form of labor to which the husband is categorically entitled. Saḥnūn asks, "What is your opinion of my hiring my wife for wages to nurse a child of mine from another woman?" Ibn al-Qāsim replies, "That is valid, although I did not hear it from Mālik, because that was not her obligation, and since it was not her obligation, it is valid to hire her for that."[74] The specific rule that a wife who is not noble must nurse her own child thus does not affect the broader principle that a free wife is entitled to her own labor and to its proceeds.

In general, the *Mudawwana* is consistent in treating family members as individuals who are proprietors of their own labor; thus, Ibn al-Qāsim affirms that a man may validly hire his mother, sister, or other female relative to nurse his child for wages.[75] However, just as the husband is understood to have certain entitlements from his wife while he provides her maintenance, a similar principle applies to other dependents. Saḥnūn asks, "What is your opinion if a father hires his son to serve him, and [the son] did so; is the son entitled to the wages, according to the doctrine of Mālik?" Ibn al-Qāsim replies, "If this son of his has reached puberty, then the son receives the wage if he contracted for it, because Mālik said: The father is not responsible for the son's maintenance after he reaches puberty."[76] In this case, Ibn al-Qāsim implicitly reasons that the child is obligated to provide service to his father for free as long as he remains his dependent. The fact that Ibn al-Qāsim does not apply the same logic to the domestic labor of wives suggests that, in his view, the maintenance of a wife primarily entitles the husband to something else—presumably, sexual access. A wife is thus in principle free to dispose of her own time and energies as she pleases, within the limits of her husband's specific prerogatives regarding sexual availability and public mobility. In response to the query, "Is it your opinion that if a man's wife wants to engage in trade, her husband is entitled to prevent her from doing that?" Ibn al-Qāsim cites Mālik as declaring, "He is not entitled to prevent her from engaging in trade, but he is entitled to prevent her from going out [of the house]."[77]

Throughout the *Mudawwana*, it is generally assumed that domestic service (*khidma*) consists of routine daily chores with no direct commercial product. Although it is not envisioned that a wife may be compensated for doing housework, the same is not true of work such as spinning or weaving. In these cases, the wife is potentially entitled to the value of her labor. A report transmitted in the *Mustakhraja* of Muḥammad ibn Aḥmad al-ʿUtbī (d. 255/869) recounts Ibn al-Qāsim's response to a legal fact pattern involving a man who dies leaving spun flax in his home: "If it is known that the flax belonged to the husband and the wife spun it, the wife is made to swear by God that she did not spin it for him; if she swears, the value of her spinning is assessed and the value of the flax is assessed, and the thread is divided between them [i.e., between the wife and the deceased husband's estate] according to that proportion."[78] In this scenario, the wife's productive work performed during the marriage is treated as her own property, and it is regarded as having monetary value even if she performed it in the home without demanding payment. Her word (supported by an oath) suffices to establish that she did not labor with the intent of donating the product to her husband.

Textile production was a major industry in the early Islamic world, and women were integral parts of it.[79] Ibn al-Qāsim is said to have opined that spinning did not qualify as an occupation (*ṣunʿa*) that would enhance the value of a slave woman because "all women spin."[80] Although many wives must have spun and woven primarily to supply the needs of their own families, spun thread or yarn was also a commercial product that could contribute significantly to the household economy. In another passage of the *Mustakhraja*, Mālik's student Ashhab (d. 204/820) is asked about "a man whose wife reproached him, saying, 'We eat from my spinning, the work of my hands and my earnings'[81]—so he swore not to eat anything [paid for] from her work."[82] In this scenario, the couple's actual financial situation diverges from the male-provider model underlying the *fiqh* analysis of the marriage contract. However, this model appears to be more than a theoretical construct; the wife's de facto role of provider seems to be a source of moral leverage for her and of chagrin for her husband, who vows to eschew the proceeds of her work.

Overall, the *Mudawwana* presents a clearly defined legal model in which marriage entitles a husband to his wife's sexual availability but not to her labor. For her part, the wife is entitled to material support including the labor required to maintain the household (implied to be provided primarily by enslaved servants). Within the larger discursive structure of the *Mudawwana*, the wife's exemption from providing unpaid labor to her husband is the key distinction conceptually distinguishing the status of the wife from that of the enslaved concubine. This model addresses only the concrete entitlements of the spouses and the circumstances under which a judge might redress infractions (for instance, if a husband defaults on his obligation to fund service for his wife). In this sense, it represents a legal discourse that appears sharply divergent from the ethical motifs associated with daily chores in the literature of *zuhd*.

Works attributed to Ibn Ḥabīb

Saḥnūn's was not the only effort to articulate the implications of Mālik's teachings for the issue of domestic labor in the first half of the third/ninth century. The other most lastingly influential contribution was associated with ʿAbd al-Malik Ibn Ḥabīb (d. 238/852), a Cordoban who journeyed to the East and studied with several prominent disciples of Mālik. The works attributed to Ibn Ḥabīb suggest that even in the early third/ninth century, some Mālikīs resisted the idea that wives were exempt from domestic labor. Even in the absence of a clear legal mandate for wives to do housework, some early Mālikīs fulsomely celebrated the religious merit of their engagement in humble chores.

Ibn Ḥabīb's major legal work, *al-Wāḍiḥa*, survives only in fragments, but his relevant comments are cited in a number of later works.[83] Ibn Abī Zayd al-Qayrawānī (d. 386/996) quotes the relevant passage as follows:

> If the wife is of high standing (*dhāt qadr*) in terms of her person and her dower (*ṣadāq*) and the husband is well-to-do, she is obligated to do none of the work of her house—neither spinning, weaving, kneading bread, cooking, sweeping, nor anything else—and he is obligated to provide her with a servant. If she is of rather low status in her person and her dower, and her dower does not suffice to buy a

> servant, the husband is not obligated to provide her with a servant and she is obligated to do the indoor work, including kneading bread, cooking, sweeping, spreading [bedding], drawing water if she has it [within the household], and all of the housework (*ʿamal al-bayt*). [The same is true] if her husband is well-to-do but is of the same [low] status as she or slightly superior, as long as he is not one of the noblemen who do not degrade their wives with work even if they are of lower status. He said: As for spinning and weaving, he is not entitled to that from her under any circumstances, unless she does it voluntarily. If he is poor (*muʿsir*) he is not obligated to provide her with a servant even if she is high-status and noble, and she is obligated to do the indoor work just as a base woman is. This is what was explained to me by Ibn al-Mājishūn and Aṣbagh.[84]

The doctrine transmitted by Ibn Ḥabīb is distinctive in asserting that some wives have a positive obligation to perform housework, rather than merely (as in the doctrine attributed to al-Rabīʿ in the *Mudawwana*) that some wives lack the entitlement to be provided with service. By itemizing basic domestic tasks and distinguishing them from work ordinarily done for financial profit, this passage lays the foundations of a concept analogous to the modern category of "housework." The term *muʿsir*, which is widely used in legal discussions of individuals lacking the means to fulfill basic needs and obligations, suggests that this duty devolves on a high-status wife only if her husband is genuinely needy. However, overall the passage seems to stack the deck in favor of the wife's obligation to do housework; she may be obliged to do so if she is low status even if her husband is well-to-do, and if he is needy even if she is of high status.

Ibn Ḥabīb attributes this doctrine to two distinguished authorities of his school. ʿAbd al-Malik ibn ʿAbd al-ʿAzīz Ibn al-Mājishūn (d. 212–214/827–829) was a leading student of Mālik.[85] Aṣbagh ibn al-Faraj (d. 225/839), a student of several of Mālik's star students including Ibn al-Qāsim, was a leading exponent of Mālik's teachings in Egypt.[86] Ibn Ḥabīb is said to have studied with both of them. It is impossible to know who originated the specific wording reported by Ibn Ḥabīb, to what extent it reflects the opinions of these two figures, or (if so) whether they attributed it to Mālik. Another report suggests that Aṣbagh may have been distinctively concerned with class differentiation among wives; he is said to have argued that a very noble or wealthy woman might be entitled to maintenance for more than one servant, up to as many as four or five a wife for the daughter of a king or a member of the

Prophet's Hāshimite clan.[87] Ibn al-Mājishūn and Aṣbagh may not have been alone among Mālik's early followers in placing an affirmative duty to do housework on at least some wives; Al-Qāḍī ʿIyāḍ (d. 544/1149) states that Mālik's disciples Ibn Nāfiʿ (d. 186/802) and Ibn Maslama (d. 216/831) decisively asserted a wife's duty to provide housework, with the latter itemizing "cleaning, spreading [bedding], sweeping and serving" as wifely obligations.[88] However, these reports are difficult to evaluate and seem to have had little impact.

Following this exposition of legal doctrine, Ibn Ḥabīb goes on to introduce an additional element into the Mālikī discussion of this issue: a Prophetic precedent for wives' providing domestic labor. He writes, "Similarly, the Prophet (peace be upon him!) ruled that Fāṭima was responsible for the indoor work of the house, and that ʿAlī was responsible for the outdoor work."[89] In addition to providing authoritative support for the doctrines advanced, this observation casts them into a rather different light; eschewing all mention of social status and financial means, it suggests a divinely sanctioned model for wives' doing housework as a general gendered norm. The parallelism between the work assignments of Fāṭima and ʿAlī suggests complementary between the spouses, and the distinction between indoor and outdoor work potentially evokes ideas of female modesty.[90] Furthermore, the report specifically describes the Prophet's allocation of the indoor work to Fāṭima as a legal ruling. (It is notable that while the wording of this report varies, it consistently involves verbs—*ḥakama* and *qaḍā*—specifically referring to judicial verdicts.[91]) No narrative setting explains when or why the Prophet might have resolved a legal case between his daughter and son-in-law, and the report itself did not fulfill the standards of authentication that were then in the process of crystallization.[92] Its wording may thus suggest efforts to clarify the issue of domestic labor as a matter of enforceable law on the basis of the Prophetic Sunna and its citation by Ibn Ḥabīb reflects a new development in the Mālikī discussion of this issue.

In *al-Wāḍiḥa*, then, Ibn Ḥabīb appears to have promoted a strand of the Mālikī legal tradition that (in contrast to that of Ibn al-Qāsim as transmitted by Saḥnūn) limited the scope of wives' prerogative to be provided with domestic help and asserted a positive duty for poorer and humbler wives to do household chores. However, the approach remains soberly legal; the central focus is on the nature of the husband's financial burdens under the marriage contract. A very different view of the issue of marriage and domestic labor emerges from another text attributed to Ibn Ḥabīb, a didactic work on the conduct of women and the ideals of marriage, published under the title *Adab al-nisāʾ* ("Etiquette for Women"). ʿAbd al-Majīd Turkī has argued convincingly for Ibn Ḥabīb's authorship of this text;[93] at the very least, it would appear to be a very early expression of views within the Mālikī school.

In that work the author declares,

> It is meritorious and virtuous[94] for [a wife] to spin, weave, grind [flour], sweep, and do other work of that sort, but she is not obligated to do so unless she wishes. She is responsible to do only light tasks[95] unless her marriage contract stipulated that condition.[96] This [kind of work] is obligatory only for a poor person[97] who, if she did not grind [flour] for her husband, would do so for others in order to earn her keep; [in that case], that is obligatory for her.[98]

This formulation seems both broadly compatible with that in the *Wāḍiḥa* (in that poorer wives are affirmatively obligated to do housework) and meaningfully distinct from it (in that exemption from housework seems to be the default rule rather than the prerogative of the wealthiest and most elite wives).

There are many possible explanations for the apparent discrepancy between this statement and the corresponding passage of the *Wāḍiḥa*, ranging from a doctrinal shift on Ibn Ḥabīb's part to misattribution of this text. It is also possible that one of the works is intended to express Ibn Ḥabīb's own preferred doctrine, and the other what he takes to be the dominant doctrine of the school. Even if we infer that *Adab al-nisāʾ* was not produced by Ibn Ḥabīb, however, its treatment of the theme of wives' domestic labor suggests the complexity of this issue in the worldview of Mālikīs of the early third/ninth century. What is most striking is that, following its brief and sober affirmation of the legal doctrine that most wives are exempt from housework, it goes on to elaborate on the religious merit of women's domestic efforts at great length and in the most fulsome terms.[99] It does so largely through lengthy proof texts attributed to early Islamic authorities, albeit without the full chains of transmission that would soon become indispensable. The book culminates with a long passage enumerating the rewards (*thawāb*) for wives who serve their husbands and perform acts of kindness for them. It cites various forms of personal service (such as bringing water and serving food), and housework such as washing clothes, cooking, and baking bread. In each case, the wife is promised lavish otherworldly recompense. It includes such statements as

> ʿAbd al-Malik [ibn Ḥabīb] said: Jaʿfar ibn Muḥammad[100] told me: "Any woman who engages in the service of her husband (*qāmat bi-khidmat zawjihā*) for a single day, God will grant heaven to her and will give her the reward for twelve saints (*walī*). Any woman who serves her husband for a day and a night, God will forgive her all sins, and on the Day of Resurrection she will be clothed in a green garment and God will record for her the reward of a martyr for every hair on her body and will build her a city of musk for every hair on her body, and she will not leave this world before seeing her place in heaven. Any woman who serves her husband for a single day will emerge from her sins as [pure as] on the day when her mother gave birth to her; God will give her the reward of a thousand obligatory pilgrimages to Mecca and a thousand supererogatory pilgrimages, and a thousand angels will ask forgiveness for her. Any woman who sweeps her husband's house and spreads a robe for her husband to sit on out of love of God, God will open the gates of mercy upon her and will cleanse her grave of worms and scorpions; God will bring seventy houris into her house to keep her company, and every day a thousand angels will visit her grave bringing her the felicity (*naʿīm*) of heaven, and God will make her grave spacious."[101]

The passage's authority statements on the virtues of wifely labor prominently include a version of the story, already cited above, in which the Prophet's daughter Fāṭima asks her father for a servant. It is notable that in this case the narrative is carefully crafted to avoid the suggestion that Fāṭima objects to housework per se:

> ʿAbd al-Malik [ibn Ḥabīb] said: It was reported to me that prisoners of war were brought to the Messenger of God; ʿAlī ibn Abī Ṭālib said, "Fāṭima, go to the Messenger of God and ask him for a servant!" She came [to the Prophet] but was ashamed to speak to him [about this]. The Messenger of God said, "Did you come because you needed something, Fāṭima, or simply to visit?" She burst into tears and said, "O Messenger of God! As for water, I draw it from the well within the courtyard and no one sees me. As for kneading dough, I make bread in my house and no one sees me; and I wash clothes in my house and no one sees me." She showed him her hands, which were worn with work. "But, O Prophet, the thing that is difficult for me is the firewood, which I gather from far away; O Prophet,

> a woman is a thing to be concealed (*ʿawra*), so that is what is difficult for me." The Messenger of God said to her, "For things to be like that is better for you than any number of servants (lit., "a servant and a servant and a servant"). When you go back to your house, make your husband's bed. When he comes home, receive him at the door and take his cloak from him; then when he sits down on his bed, take off his sandals."[102]

As in other versions of this report, the story culminates with the Prophet instructing Fāṭima in an invocation to perform at bedtime.

As we have seen, this anecdote was in circulation as early as the first half of the second century AH, when it appeared in the *Jāmiʿ* of Maʿmar ibn Rāshid. Maʿmar places it in a chapter on invocations to perform before going to sleep and after waking in the morning, focusing attention on the efficacy of prayer rather than on the division of labor in the household.[103] By the middle of the third century AH/ninth century CE, the story was circulating in multiple versions with details suggesting different views on wives' involvement in domestic labor. At this point, the story had clearly been drawn into the debate over wives' domestic duties; thus, Bukhārī (d. 256/870) includes versions of this report both in the section of his *Ṣaḥīh* devoted to pious invocations and in a chapter titled "A Woman's Work in Her Husband's House" (*ʿAmal al-marʾa fī bayt zawjihā*), which frames it as a proof text for a wife's obligation to do housework.[104]

The version presented in *Adab al-nisāʾ* goes to great lengths to affirm wives' domestic duties. Rather than simply emphasizing that a prayer bestowed by the Prophet is more precious than a prisoner of war, this version elaborates in some detail on the services Fāṭima ought to supply to her husband. Unlike the more common versions of this anecdote in which Fāṭima "complains" (*shakat*) of the rigors of her household labors, which are seen as a tribulation and an indignity, Ibn Ḥabīb's text has Fāṭima affirming her willingness to cook and clean; her sole concern is with exposure to the public gaze.[105] The different renditions of the story suggest very different messages about the status of housework.

Even more striking than the extravagant praise of wives' engagement in routine housework in *Adab al-nisāʾ* is the work's emphasis on their performance of productive labor, particularly textile production. As we have seen, in the *Wāḍiḥa*, even while affirming a non-elite wife's obligation to provide housework, Ibn Ḥabīb denied that wives had any obligation to spin or weave for their husbands' benefit. In this he followed the Mālikī mainstream, which (as we have seen) allowed a wife to claim the value of her labor in a dispute over ownership of the resulting textile. In contrast, the emphasis in *Adab al-nisāʾ* is on the abundant otherworldly rewards to be reaped by wives who spin and weave:

> [It is reported] from ʿĀʾisha that she looked at a woman who had a spindle in her hand and was spinning and said to her: Rejoice in the good news of the reward that God has in store for you; if you knew that, you would not cease to spin and weave day and night! Then she said to her: For every garment you weave for yourself or for someone else to wear, there is a palace in heaven bigger than the distance between the East and the West, and for every thread you spin there are 120,000 cities! For the hum of the spindle seven heavens are opened up until it reaches the [divine] Throne; it buzzes like a bee, and in God's eyes it equals the confession that there is no god but God. It does not stop or become still until it reaches God and He looks at it and says, "Welcome! I have forgiven the woman who made you! O angels, I ask you to bear witness that I have forgiven her sins for her, even if they are [as numerous] as the foam of the sea or the sands of a river or of the oceans."
>
> The Messenger of God said: Any woman who spins enough to clothe herself and her children, the angels of seven heavens and seven earths and all that is within them ask forgiveness for her. She comes forth from her grave [on the Day of Judgment] wearing a garment like the light of the sun, with a veil on her head like the light of the full moon, with light before her and to her left.[106]

Juxtaposition of the relevant passages from the *Wāḍiḥa* and *Adab al-nisāʾ* suggests the profound difference between legal and homiletic approaches to wives' domestic labor. Regardless of whether the latter is accurately attributed to Ibn Ḥabīb, together they suggest the potential tension between legal doctrines and socioreligious ideals in this area for early Andalusian Mālikīs. The most prestigious jurists of the school denied that a wife had an obligation to do daily domestic tasks, and none required her to provide commercially productive labor such as spinning and weaving. In contrast, this didactic text both broadly acknowledges these doctrines and juxtaposes them with powerful affirmations that a pious and virtuous wife will humbly accept her domestic chores and be devoted to her spindle. Carefully bracketing the issue of contractual obligation, the text vividly elaborates an alternative framework of divine favor and otherworldly rewards.

Fatwas attributed to Muḥammad ibn Saḥnūn

One of the most sustained discussions of the issue of wives' labor occurs in a work purporting to record the responses of Saḥnūn's son, Muḥammad ibn Saḥnūn (d. 256/870), to a wide range of legal questions.[107] It is notable that this particular issue proves particularly knotty, leading to an extended series of follow-up questions and clarifications. Although the work's attribution to Ibn Saḥnūn is subject to debate, the passage suggests that some early Mālikīs perceived tensions not only between different forms of textual authority but between received legal rules and widespread social practices.

The exchange begins:

I SAID: Is a woman obligated to provide her husband with any service or not?
HE SAID: With respect to that [question] there are distinctions and differences of opinion. It is reliably transmitted from the Prophet (peace be upon him!) that he ruled[108] that [his daughter] Fāṭima was obligated to do the indoor work (*al-khidma al-bāṭina*), such as grinding [flour], cooking food, making flour into bread, and tending[109] the house—which is sweeping it and spreading out the bedding, no more—and reached a verdict[110] that ʿAlī ibn Abī Ṭālib was responsible for the remaining work outside of the house.[111]

It is notable that this response refrains from mentioning the doctrine attributed to Mālik, instead alluding to juristic disagreement and then adducing a prophetic precedent in circulation among hadith scholars. This is striking because in this work as a whole, the authority identified as Muḥammad ibn Saḥnūn is represented as strongly committed to the doctrines of Mālik.[112] It does, however, fit Ibn Saḥnūn's historical reputation for having based his legal rulings heavily on hadith reports.[113] The questioner immediately notes this divergence from the school of Mālik, although he again frames it in terms of hadith criticism rather than of Mālik's legal teachings:

I SAID: The followers of Mālik say that the Prophet did not rule that Fāṭima was obligated to do any [housework].
MUḤAMMAD SAID: May God forgive their error! Do they not know that the Prophet (peace be upon him!) sent Bilāl to bring the switch on the day of

ʿUkkāsha; Bilāl went to [get] the switch and met Fāṭima (may God be pleased with her), who had come out with her face dripping sweat. She said, "I was grinding barley for al-Ḥasan and al-Ḥusayn, because their stomachs are empty."[114] Know that all of the kinds of indoor work I have mentioned to you are incumbent on the wife, including grinding [grain], making dough, kneading, spreading the [coverings of] the house and tending it, and drawing water from a nearby place.[115]

The rueful exclamation "May God forgive their error!" suggests that in this particular case, Ibn Saḥnūn simply cannot identify with the doctrine of the school. He again resorts to hadith in support of his position, this time citing a narrative report in which Fāṭima is incidentally encountered in the midst of her domestic labors.[116]

The questioner then opens another line of inquiry, probing the limits of a wife's duty to provide household labor.

I SAID: Is it the husband's obligation to transport firewood?

HE SAID: Yes, and the wife is not obliged to do anything other than what we have mentioned. As for working with wool, cotton, linen, and hair, gathering firewood and hay, taking care of domestic animals by tying, loosing, and milking them, carrying and harvesting fruits, and carrying crops, she is not obliged to do any of that unless she volunteers to do so by her own free will.[117]

There are two criteria implicitly at work in this exchange. One is a distinction between indoor and outdoor labor, and the other is between the labor directly involved in economic production (such as the raising of livestock and the gathering of crops) and that involved in consumption and maintenance (such as cooking and cleaning). Wives need do no labor outside the home, and no commercial labor within it.

The remainder of the passage reflects the questioner's concern that these guidelines may not, in fact, inform actual practice. He begins by inquiring about the legal consequences of a husband's failure to abide by them.

I SAID: If [the husband] compels her to do the things that you have mentioned that she is not obliged to do, or some of them, does that impair his standing as a witness?

HE SAID: Yes, it impairs his standing as a witness [and his eligibility to serve as a prayer leader]; have you not heard God's statement, "Do not seek to harm[118] [your wives] (*lā tabghū ʿalayhinna sabīlā*)" (Q 4:34). "*Baghy*" [the verb used in the Qur'anic verse], which is injustice and aggression, is forbidden against the wife or anyone else; there is no disagreement that engaging in that which is forbidden impairs one's standing as a witness or a prayer leader.[119]

The issues of witnessing and prayer leadership are significant because they are the primary areas of *fiqh* in which actions that are not in themselves legally punishable nevertheless have legal consequences. A person may be barred from witnessing or prayer leadership if he is persistently sinful, even if he has not committed a crime with any concrete sanction.[120] In this case, both the leading question and Ibn Saḥnūn's response suggest that a husband's legally unwarranted exploitation of his wife's labor is an ethical infraction severe enough to forfeit his reputation for moral probity. However, the questioner is not content to suggest that usurpation of the wife's labor impairs the husband's moral standing; he goes on to pursue the question of material compensation.

I SAID: If [the husband] uses her to work at something that you have mentioned that she is not obliged to do and wishes to return to the right way, what should he do for her?

I SAID: . . . If she waives his debt for what she has done for him of her own free will there is no problem [with this]. If she refuses, the two of them [share the proceeds] according to the value of each one's contribution; the husband['s share] is the value of the unworked wool, linen, or hair, and the wife's is the value of her work, whatever it comes to. For taking care of domestic animals or harvesting and carrying fruit she gets a fair wage (*ujrat mithlihā*).

I SAID: Is all of this the doctrine of Mālik?

HE SAID: Yes, it is the doctrine of Mālik and his followers.[121]

As we have seen, the doctrine assigning a wife the value of her labor on a textile is attributed to Mālik; here it is extended to other forms of productive or outdoor work.[122] Following the doctrine of Mālik, he thus understands the husband to have a claim on his wife's time, but not on her productive labor.

Thus far, the questioner has treated the husband's possible exploitation of his wife's labor as an individual infraction. At this point, however, he acknowledges that wives' involvement in economically productive or outdoor work may be a social norm. In this case, he suggests that there may be an enforceable expectation that the wife perform such kinds of work—but also suggests that as an explicit provision, such a condition could invalidate the marriage contract.

I SAID: If it is the custom in a locality for women to be made to do all the kinds of work you have mentioned, including both indoor and outdoor work, is a woman instructed by a judge to do [these things] if she refuses to work, and does that [i.e., the requirement that the wife do these kinds of work] cause the invalidity of a marriage as does a sale [added to the marriage contract], or not?[123]

Ibn Saḥnūn responds that "the scholars have different opinions about that." His answer does not directly address the initial question whether a husband could receive a judicial verdict directing his wife to do kinds of work that are customary in the couple's region but begins with the premise that "if custom and usage continues over time it is like an explicit condition [of a contract]."[124] This argument might seem to support the husband's right to his wife's labor, but in fact such a contractual stipulation would be legally problematic. This is because by adding the wife's labor to the benefits ordinarily purchased by the husband's payment of dower, such a contract conflates two separate transactions and makes it unclear how much of the dower is paid in consideration for each benefit. Such indeterminacy is problematic in the Islamic law of sales.[125] Having surveyed the range of opinion on this subject, Ibn Saḥnūn selects the most restrictive: "My opinion is that Mālik's doctrine—that a marriage is invalidated by the husband's stipulating the wife's work or its being customary—is correct; but God Most High knows best." His rationale is that "the wife's work is unknown and indeterminate, and its duration is also unknown, because it lasts until death or separation."[126] The husband cannot purchase sexual access to his wife and labor of unspecified nature and quantity in a single transaction.

Ibn Saḥnūn goes on to address the possible objection that wives' performance of various kinds of customary labor is merely one of the many subsidiary effects of the marriage contract. In his view, this is not the case because for many people, acquiring the right to the wife's labor is not a subsidiary aspect of marriage but one of the primary motivations for taking a wife. He notes bitterly that "the wife's work is the greatest objective [of marriage] among the people whose custom it is" for wives to do these kinds of work, since women's labor "is the greatest occupation among the sources of their livelihood, because it is renewed among them every day and night. It is the confirmed basis [of marriage] among them, more certain than children and sex; know this and consider it." After this stinging critique, the conclusion of the answer is surprisingly mild: "If the wife offers voluntarily [to work] after the marriage is contracted, this is better and stays further from [areas of juristic] disagreement."[127]

The *Fatāwā* attributed to Ibn Saḥnūn take a strictly legal approach to the issue of wives' labor, focusing on the validity and enforceability of different contractual provisions or informal agreements. Even the moral transgression of a husband who misappropriates his wife's productive labor is treated through the lens of eligibility for legal witnessing. Nevertheless, the work's approach to the issue of wives' labor is not without tensions. Despite the author's general commitment to the doctrines of Mālik, on the question of wives' domestic labor he both promotes a dissenting opinion and overtly expresses his disapproval of the received Mālikī ruling that wives are responsible for no work within the house. Formally this choice reflects his commitment to the authority of hadith, but substantively it may also reflect a deeply felt preference for a sharply gendered division of duties within the household. Nevertheless, he is emphatic in his assertion that a wife cannot be compelled to provide any labor beyond food preparation and the daily maintenance of the home. It is good for a wife to volunteer her commercial or agricultural labor but legitimate for her to demand pay and sinful (to the point of forfeiting legal probity) for a husband to demand such work against her will. In cases where the local economy is based on women's outdoor and productive labor, however, he seems to concede that there is no solution but a wife's voluntary assent to this arrangement after the marriage is contracted. In the end, the force of Ibn Saḥnūn's pointed critique of the exploitation of women's labor is less to offer a practical alternative to wives' involvement with crops, livestock, or textile production than to place communities that are heavily dependent on women's work—such as peasants and pastoralists—outside of the normative model of the Muslim household.[128]

For both urban and rural wives, Ibn Saḥnūn's legal model presents both opportunities (notably the entitlement in principle to demand pay for economically productive labor) and pitfalls (notably the tension between the ideal model of the marriage contract and deeply engrained social expectations for wives' labor). His emphasis on the scenario of a wife's voluntarily relinquishing the material claims arising from her labor suggest the possibility of coercion. The *Fatāwā* attributed to Ibn Saḥnūn do not probe these tensions, but they are explored deeply in a fatwa attributed to the tenth-century Mālikī authority Ibn Abī Zayd al-Qayrawānī (d. 386/996).

A fatwa attributed to Ibn Abī Zayd al-Qayrawānī

Despite the efforts of Mālikī scholars like Ibn Ḥabīb and Ibn Saḥnūn to dispute the doctrine denying any wifely duty to provide household labor, it was the doctrine of Ibn al-Qāsim that prevailed in the school. As already suggested by the discussion above, as the Muslim community became larger and more socially and economically diverse, there was thus a potential mismatch between social expectations that wives provide housework and legal doctrines suggesting they had no such obligation. A lengthy examination of the moral conundrums arising from this situation is attributed to the most prominent Mālikī authority of the fourth/tenth century, the North African Ibn Abī Zayd al-Qayrawānī.[129] The attribution of the fatwa is not secure; like the other legal responsa attributed to Ibn Abī Zayd, it is found only in sources dating centuries after his own lifetime.[130] Whether or not it actually issued from his pen, however, it offers a fascinating glimpse of the legal and ethical considerations that would have presented themselves to a pious Mālikī surveying the doctrines inherited from the great authorities of the third century AH.

The text of the original question has not been preserved; in its existing form the fatwa is prefaced with the terse statement, "Ibn Abī Zayd and others were asked what service a woman is obligated to perform for her husband." However, based on allusions within the response, it must have been a longer and more circumstantial inquiry than this summary would imply. The mufti repeatedly addresses himself to the questioner in the second person singular and in one place refers to his own production as "this letter of mine" (*kitābī hādhā*).[131] The fact that the inquiry is said to have been addressed to Ibn Abī Zayd "and others" suggests that its author considered it to be of some moment. Because it addresses personal moral scruples rather than actionable legal claims, consultation of multiple authorities is unlikely to have been an effort to sway the opinion of a judge; it might reflect the questioner's perception either of the question's wide social relevance or of its subtle and problematic character.

Based on the text of the fatwa, it is possible to reconstruct three components of the initiating question. First, the mufti observes that "you say that [the wife] imagines (*taẓunnu*) that she is obligated to do [housework] because of what she sees [other] women doing."[132] He also quotes the questioner as having posed the scenario of a woman's promising to do housework in order to induce a man to marry her. Finally, he alludes to the questioner's concerns about the propriety of ordering a wife to do housework or perform personal service to her husband, when she may be assumed to believe (arguably wrongly) that she is obligated to comply.

In answer, the fatwa begins by presenting the opinions of the most prominent disciples of Mālik, beginning with Ibn al-Qāsim's categorical denial that a wife is obligated to do any housework at all.[133] The mufti notes that if one follows the opinion of Ibn al-Mājishūn and Aṣbagh (discussed above), there is simply no problem; the questioner's concerns all revolve around the possibility of misappropriation of his wife's labor, and according to this doctrine he is entitled to it (assuming, apparently, that he is not both noble and rich).[134] He then proceeds to examine the issues raised on the assumption that his questioner either subscribes to the opinion of Ibn al-Qāsim or wishes to act within the limits of the stricter doctrine as a pious precaution.

To the first concern "that she imagines (*taẓunnu*) that she is obligated to do that because of what she sees [other] women doing," he responds briskly, "This is an unlikely thing (*amr baʿīd*); I do not think that she is ignorant of that."[135] His response to the scenario that the woman might have promised to provide domestic service in order to secure her husband's hand in marriage is similarly dismissive: "As long as he did not make this a condition in the [marriage] contract itself, there is not harm in it."[136] Having dispatched this concern on a purely contractual level, however, he proceeds to address the inquirer's ethical scruples:

> At the very most, if she were to be told that housework is not mandatory for a wife it would be an excess [of caution] for someone who follows the doctrine of Ibn al-Qāsim. After doing that, he[137] need not worry about what she imagines, or what might be imagined about her, that she fears that if she ceases to do that that antipathy or hatred for her might grow in his heart or he might leave her. He need not concern himself with that; rather, he must not punish her for this or ostracize her (*yahjuruhā*) for it. As for if she loses esteem in his eyes because of this or he neglects her because of an antipathy he feels for her because of that, he has done no wrong (*lā shayʾ ʿalayhi*) unless he uses his neglect of her [to pressure her] while still wanting her, wanting to return her to work by means of that neglect, while he still loves her and wants her. This is something he ought not to do.[138]

Later in the letter the mufti returns to this theme:

> He is entitled to say nothing to her if she continues to work, as long as she knows that if she falls short in the work or refrains from doing it she is safe from his manners toward her changing. The principle (*al-maʿnā*) in this is an excess [of caution] in matters and an element of compassion (*nāḥiya min al-ishfāq*). As for if he neglects her because of that but without omitting any of [his] obligations toward her, he is entitled to do that; similarly, if he neglects her without harming or wronging her but simply out of dislike for her and her behavior, as I have clarified to you at the beginning of this letter of mine, it is as I have mentioned to you.[139]

In response to the questioner's concern about ordering his wife to do housework that she is arguably not obligated to provide (but that she may do out of fear of her husband's reaction), and about ordering her to do personal service beyond housework, the mufti writes:

> As for his ordering her to do housework, he is entitled to do that according to the doctrine of Ibn al-Mājishūn and Aṣbagh, as we have stated before. As for his personal service (*mā yakhuṣṣuhu*), he may ask her to do that, and she is not obligated to think that that is mandatory for her; if she knows that, he may ask her as he asks his personal friends and not concern himself with anything beyond that in terms of imagining that if she does that she does so to protect herself

> from what has been mentioned above. If he followed his [request] with "if you like," that would be better and more fitting in making the matter clear.[140]

In addition to his analysis of the concrete scenarios raised by his questioner, the mufti offers a more general discussion of the Islamic ethic regarding wives' domestic labor. "In the early days of this [Muslim] community the women used to serve their husbands in difficult tasks. It is reported that Fāṭima (may God be pleased with her!) used to grind [grain], and that Asmāʾ used to guide[141] al-Zubayr's horse, saddle it (?), and serve him in similar ways.[142] The women of the Anṣār used to carry water in waterskins and do other kinds of work."[143]

There follows an anecdote in which Abū'l-Dardāʾ admonishes his new wife for adorning their home with draperies; she responds in part, "It is for the sake of God (*huwa fī sabīl Allāh*); satisfy me with kindness, and I will satisfy you with heat—the heat of the bread and the oven."[144] This story seems to address issues of luxury and consumption (raised by the disputed draperies) more directly than those of domestic labor. Reframed in the context of the fatwa, it suggests that Abū'l-Dardāʾ has reservations about his entitlement to his wife's work in decorating their home rather than merely about the moral licitness of the decorations. His concerns are dispelled when she suggests that their relationship involves a reciprocal exchange of kindness and warmth, one that goes beyond the formal framework of the marital contract.

The mufti continues:

> The early Muslims (*salaf*) that we have mentioned did not concern themselves with whether [working] was obligatory for [a wife] or not, or inform her that it was not obligatory for her; rather, if she did serve he accepted it and approved of it, and he did not provide her [with service] except for what God willed, or with respect to a tiring task that was not appropriate for her. There is nothing to fear for women of this time from what they are required to do of that; and God knows best![145]

Despite his apparent personal preference for the behavior modeled by the earliest Muslims, however, the mufti does not regard it as dispositive in terms of legal doctrine. Rather, he frames the problem in terms of a choice between the doctrines of early Mālikī authorities: "As for according to the doctrine of Ibn al-Mājishūn, all of that is permissible for him, and you are relieved of concerning yourself with it; my [own] opinion on that subject is the other opinion, as I have told you."[146]

In this text, the questioner's concerns revolve around a perceived tension between the doctrine of Ibn al-Qāsim, which denies that women have any legal obligation to do housework, and a social environment that leads women to believe they do. His underlying anxiety appears, however, to be less about the exploitation of wives than about the moral standing of husbands. If a wife does housework out of the mistaken belief that she is obligated to do so, or out of the possibly accurate belief that there will be dire marital consequences if she does not, has her husband misappropriated her labor? Under these circumstances, he could be understood to have obtained her services either through false pretenses or through coercion. Given the questioner's assumption that the wife is innocently oblivious of any discrepancy between the social expectations placed upon her and the legal rights she enjoys, the inquiry seems to be driven by the moral scrupulosity of the husband; while this-worldly consequences seem unlikely, he wants to know whether he is behaving wrongfully.

Although the mufti, by his own account, personally subscribes to the doctrine of Ibn al-Qāsim, he consistently minimizes the ethical and interpersonal implications of the ruling that wives are exempt from domestic labor. He encourages the gratuitous assumption that the wife is already aware of the law and characterizes the simple precaution of informing her of her rights as a "*mubālagha*," or exaggeration (here presumably referring to excessive moral scrupulosity). Similarly, his analysis of the questioner's implicit scruples about coercion does little to address sincere concerns about wrongful exploitation of the wife's labor. In this area his argumentation evokes the terminology and concerns of Mālikī discussions of the issues surrounding *khul*ᶜ (a divorce initiated by the wife, who pays a consideration to the husband in return for her release from the marriage). Mālikī scholars were distinctively concerned with the possibility that a husband might inflict harm (*ḍarar*) on his wife in order to induce her to pay for her release. Whereas the Mālikī rules of *khul*ᶜ seek to prevent wrongful appropriation of the woman's property, this fatwa addresses concerns about the wrongful appropriation of her work. In both cases the husband's genuine antipathy toward his wife is accepted, but manipulative mistreatment is not.[147]

The question and answer also evoke the distinctive Mālikī concern with intention (*nīya*), although the term is not explicitly used. The mufti argues that if the husband neglects his wife simply because she has lost his affection or provoked his resentment by failing to do housework, he is both legally and morally in the clear; in contrast, if he still loves her, he should not use neglect instrumentally as a means of prevailing on her to work. This emphasis on motivation is reminiscent of the approach attributed to Mālik regarding a man who takes an oath to refrain from sexual intercourse with his wife (*īlāʾ*) or who engages in sexual intercourse with one wife rather than another; in each case, it is the husband's intent that determines the ethico-legal status of his action.[148] As Kecia Ali has observed, these arguments suggest that early Mālikī jurists' "real concern was not with the woman's experience of harm so much as with the husband's willful infliction of it."[149]

The mufti also instructs that the husband must not "punish (*yuʿāqib*) or ostracize (*yahjur*)" his wife in retaliation for her failure to do housework. The allusion to ostracism (*hajr*) evokes the wording of Q 4:34, the scriptural basis of the husband's disciplinary authority over his wife; widely understood as his refusal to have sex with her, ostracism is the intermediate step in the verse's ascending series of punishments (between admonition and physical chastisement). Although it is a commonplace of the legal and exegetical literature that the wife is obligated to obey her husband, this statement alludes to the fact that, in more concrete terms, jurists limited the husband's disciplinary authority to the enforcement of his legitimate rights vis-à-vis the wife. Denial of the husband's right to her labor would thus imply denial of his right to discipline her for failing to work.[150] This principle limited not only his ability to enforce his orders but the legitimate scope of the orders themselves; as the mufti observes later in the fatwa, he may ask her nicely to perform non-obligatory tasks, but he cannot command her to do so.

The mufti's final argument, which circumvents all of the subtleties of his analysis to that point, is that the early Muslims—whose example was authoritative for later generations of the faithful—received their wives' exertions with approval and did not feel obligated to inform them of the absence of any wifely obligation to work.

Ultimately, this elaborate fatwa is less about the domestic lives of wives than about the ethical lives of husbands. The perceived gap between a law that (arguably) relieves women of housework and the social conventions and marital dynamics that compel them to do it raises concerns about the moral standing of a man who takes advantage of the situation. (His legal situation does not seem to be at issue, in the sense that not even the hypothetical possibility of judicial recourse or monetary compensation for the wife is raised.) It is notable that the discussion never contemplates the notion that a husband who prefers the doctrine of Ibn al-Qāsim should simply relieve his wife of her domestic duties. This fatwa addresses the ethical tensions arising from an anomalous gap between Mālikī legal doctrine and social sensibilities of right and wrong strictly through the tools of the discipline of *fiqh*.

Wives' domestic labor in a changing social and discursive landscape

At the close of the formative period, then, Mālikī doctrine reflected diversity of both doctrine and practice on the issue of wives' domestic labor. The Iraqi Mālikī Ibn Khuwayz Mandād, writing in the tenth century, describes the diversity of opinion within the school as follows:

> The members of our school have differed on the question of whether a wife is obligated to provide domestic service (*khidma*) or not. Some of the members of our school say: A wife is not obligated to provide any domestic service. Do you not see that [the marriage contract] is not a contract of hire or of acquisition of her person [i.e., as a slave]; it is merely a contract for sexual enjoyment (*istimtāʿ*). What [the husband] is entitled to by virtue of the contract is sexual enjoyment to the exclusion of anything else, so he may not demand more than that; consider [God's] statement [in the Qur'an], "If they obey you, then do not seek to harm them" [verse 4:34].[151]
>
> Some [other] members of our school say: She is obligated to provide the domestic service appropriate to someone like her (*ʿalayhā khidmat mithlihā*). If she is of noble status because of her father's wealth or [her own] affluence, then she is obligated to manage the household (*al-tadbīr li'l-manzil*) and give instructions to the servant; if she is of middling rank she is obligated to spread the bedding and the like, and if she is of lower status than that she is obligated to sweep the house and cook. If the women of the Kurds, the Daylamites, and the mountainous region of Iraq[152] are in their own territory, they are made to do what their women are made to do; this is because God said, "[Wives'] entitlements are equivalent to their

> obligations, according to what is customary (*bi'l-maʿrūf*)" [Q 2:228]. The custom (*ʿurf*) of the Muslims in their [various] countries in all historical periods (*fī qadīm al-amr wa-ḥadīthihi*) has gone as I have described; do you not see that the wives of the Prophet (peace be upon him!) and his Companions were made responsible for the grinding [of flour], the baking and cooking, the spreading of bedding, the serving of food, and the like. We know of no woman who refused to do that, nor would it have been permissible for her to refuse; rather, they used to beat their wives if they were remiss in that and compel them to do service.[153] If [service] were not something they were entitled to, they would not have required it of [their wives]."[154]

Given the clear and categorical nature of the doctrine attributed to Mālik, why would such tensions have arisen around this issue beginning in the century following his death? One approach would place the evolving Mālikī discussion of wives' domestic duties within the context of the changing social practices and economic fortunes of the Muslim communities within which the jurists worked. As we have seen, Karen Bauer convincingly relates the early scholarly consensus around a husband's obligation to support his wife's servant to the prosperity of the early Islamic conquest elite and to the ubiquity of enslaved servants. In this view, the increasing appearance of scholarly opinions asserting wives' obligation to do housework would reflect the Muslim community's transition from a small conquest elite to an economically diverse society embracing peasants and artisans as well as warriors and administrators.

Indeed, the social dispensation assumed in the *Mudawwana* was already beginning to unravel by the time of its compilation. For instance, in 218/833 the Arab aristocracy of Egypt ceased to receive a lifelong government pension; its elimination "depriv[ed] the elite of both an important source of income and a major signifier of social status."[155] Thus, while Ibn al-Qāsim lived in a world where membership in the Muslim elite implied a level of socioeconomic privilege that could have ensured access to domestic servants, this would not necessarily have been the case a generation later. Overall, it is possible that social conditions diverged very swiftly from the situation implied by early authoritative texts such as the *Mudawwana*, thus creating a discrepancy between theory and practice.

Without minimizing the role of changing social practices on the ground, this study argues that the evolving discussion of wives' domestic labor equally reflects a shifting discursive terrain. Another factor in the disruption of Mālikī doctrine on a wife's exemption from domestic labor is the rising role of hadith in legal discussions of the third century AH. Reports potentially relevant to the issue of wives' domestic duties, like the anecdote about Fāṭima's request for a servant, were presumably in circulation long before this; there is no reason to exclude the possibility that they accurately report events of the Prophet's lifetime. However, hadith texts seem to be only secondarily drawn into the legal analysis of this issue. To the extent that we can speculate about the evidentiary grounds of Ibn al-Qāsim's doctrine that wives are not responsible for domestic labor, it appears to be an inference from the juristic model of the marital bargain. Even later Mālikīs did not attempt to ground it textually in hadith but derived it from the structural logic of the marriage contract, in which the dower and maintenance provided by the husband were understood to purchase the wife's sexual availability rather than her work.[156] In contrast, arguments in favor of a wife's obligation to do housework—which seem to arise in the generation of Mālik's students—were almost invariably supported by reference to the practice of the Prophet and the early Muslim community.

The late second and early third century AH saw the growing dominance of a legal theory that gave primacy to hadith texts in the derivation of legal rules, a development that was centered on (but not limited to) the doctrines of al-Shāfiʿī. Indeed, Ahmed El Shamsy has argued that it was precisely the eroding dominance and homogeneity of the Arab conquest elite that led to the transition from Mālik's dependence on the living tradition of the community to later jurists' emphasis on textual hermeneutics.[157] It was also in this period that scholars began to gather legally relevant reports from the Prophet and early Muslim authorities and compile them into thematically organized works; the voluminous *Muṣannaf*s of the Yemeni ʿAbd al-Razzāq al-Ṣanʿānī (d. 211/826) and the Kufan Ibn Abī Shayba (d. 235/849) are the most notable examples.[158] As we have seen, both of these collections contain reports—particularly those revolving around the division of labor between Fāṭima and her husband, ʿAlī—that became central to the discussion of wives' domestic duties. Ibn Abī Shayba himself is said to have adduced the report that the Prophet assigned the indoor work to Fāṭima in support of the claim that all wives were obligated to do housework; the same argument is attributed to his contemporaries Abū Isḥāq al-Jūzajānī (d. ca. 259/873) and Abū Thawr (Baghdadi, d. 240/854–855).[159]

Overall, one gets the impression that in the early to middle third century AH this argument became prevalent in hadith circles in the Islamic east. This was not, by this time, the core territory of the Mālikī school; however, the third century AH was also a period that saw a vastly increased interregional circulation of hadith texts. Jonathan A. C. Brown notes that "during that time of Mālik . . . hadith transmission was localized" such that the Medinian Mālik was not exposed to hadith texts current in other regions of the Islamic empire; "it was only among the generation of Mālik's students, and even more so among their students, that hadith scholars traveled widely in order the unify the corpus of hadith."[160] As we have seen, Ibn Ḥabīb knew the report that the Prophet had assigned the housework to Fāṭima (a report that Mālik either did not know or did not cite in his *Muwaṭṭaʾ*) and brought it to bear in the legal discussion of this issue in his *Wāḍiḥa*. He was himself an exemplar of the trend toward long-distance travel in pursuit of knowledge (*al-riḥla fī ṭalab al-ʿilm*) in the third century, having traveled east to perform the pilgrimage and studied in Medina and Egypt before returning to Andalusia.[161] In this period hadith was also being made more widely available within the Islamic West by figures such as Baqī ibn Makhlad (d. 276/998), who is said to have brought Ibn Abī Shayba's *Muṣannaf* to Andalusia. The introduction of this material is said to have evoked some consternation from Andalusian jurists who objected to its deviations from the doctrines of Mālik.[162]

On one level, then, the complexity of Mālikī sentiment on wives' domestic labor in the third century reflects the cross-fertilization of early legal reasoning with the increasingly systematic and transregional deployment of reports about the Prophet and his Companions. In conjunction with the growing discrepancy between a legal model premised on the privileges of a small conquest elite and a Muslim community that was growing in size and diversity, this methodological shift could lead to serious reevaluation of received ideas about marital duties.

However, the resulting diversity of opinion did not merely reflect different views on the comparative weight of received legal doctrine and the texts of hadith. Rather, divergent approaches to the issue of wives' domestic labor also arose from different visions of the relationship between *fiqh* and Islamic ethics. While this is not the only factor that was at play, the negotiable and changing relationship between *fiqh* and ethics is the factor least examined in the secondary literature thus far and the one of most interest to this study.

As suggested by the examples from the *zuhd* genre at the beginning of this chapter, works with an ethical focus approached the issue of domestic labor with a quite different set of premises and concerns than works of *fiqh*. This contrast can be further illustrated by contrasting the already-cited *Kitāb al-Nafaqāt* ("Book of Maintenance") of al-Khaṣṣāf (an Iraqi contemporary of Saḥnūn who died in d. 261/874) with the *Kitāb al-ʿIyāl* ("Book of Dependents") of Ibn Abī'l-Dunyā (a younger Iraqi who died in 281/894). These two texts both originated in third/ninth century Iraq and reflect a similar social context (the milieu of the Abbasid court) but are very different in theme. Khaṣṣāf's is a legal work focusing on the claims that each party could make (or be subject to) in a court of law and the remedies that would be available if they defaulted on their obligations. He thus asks, for instance, "is the husband compelled (*yujbar*) to pay maintenance for [his wife] and for one servant?"[163] He similarly discusses whether a wife is compelled (*tujbar*) to breastfeed, whether she would be awarded wages (*yuqḍā lahā*) for breastfeeding by a judge, and whether the husband could be compelled (*yujbar*) to pay or imprisoned for failing to do so.[164] In contrast, Ibn Abī'l-Dunyā focuses on the ethical challenges and rewards of providing for one's dependents. He is unconcerned with the legal parameters of maintenance for the wife or any other member of the family, approaching the subject primarily through hadith that emphasize the moral and affective dimensions of familial care. Although this material is compatible with the legal tradition, it is framed in very different terms; here the focus is on the male provider's earning of merit and on his cultivation of proper moral dispositions including love and mercy for the more vulnerable members of the family. Familial relationships are ultimately placed within the context of theocentric ethics; God will have compassion on those who have compassion on others, and he who honors his wife honors God. A legal entitlement to maintenance of a servant has no place in this ethical vision.

The one place where Ibn Abī'l-Dunyā focuses on domestic labor is in the separate chapter devoted to the moral and religious value of women's spinning, whose meritorious nature is reiterated with great emphasis.[165] In addition to being an appropriate activity for a pious and well-behaved woman, spinning is emphasized to be a source of licit earnings. ʿAlī is cited as declaring that "the spindle is one of the pure sources of livelihood," and the early Kufan ascetic ʿAmr ibn Shuraḥbīl is quoted as glossing the Qur'anic verse "O prophets, eat from the things that are pure" with the observation that "Jesus used to eat from [the proceeds of] his mother's spinning."[166] Again, there is a clear contrast with a strictly legal approach to the issue of right livelihood; as we have seen, Ibn al-Qāsim gave the husband no legal right to the products of his wife's work and raised the possibility that a woman might in some situations demand compensation for her spinning. In *Kitāb al-ʿIyāl*—as in Ibn Ḥabīb's *Adab al-nisāʾ*—a woman's spinning is placed within a framework of meritorious action and personal humility.

Indeed, the valorization of women's spinning—and its treatment as a source of morally irreproachable livelihood for the pious male—is a hallmark of an ethics focused less on legal technicalities than on hadith. There are hadith texts (although poorly authenticated ones) that praise women's spinning and advocate that they be trained in it, and the reported personal practice of a number of early figures reflects the view that a woman's spinning is a pure and virtuous source of livelihood for her husband, son, or brother.[167] Aḥmad ibn Ḥanbal himself is said to have subsisted in part on the spinning of his womenfolk, a practice in which he in turn may have been inspired by Sufyān al-Thawrī.[168] Bishr ibn al-Ḥārith is also said to have lived off his sister's spinning.[169] The dying Abū Dharr, afraid that he would be buried in a shroud of tainted origin, gratefully accepted one from a passing stranger who assured him that it was the product of his mother's spinning.[170] Of course, from a strictly legal perspective the handiwork of a wife, mother, or sister was not obviously exempt from moral concern; a husband or son had no inherent right to it, and a gift from a female kinswoman was no less subject to suspicions of subtle coercion or moral debt than a gift from anyone else. However, the implicit model of the household in works like that of Ibn Abī'l-Dunyā treats its members as components of a larger unit whose moral solidarity transcends individual property rights.

All of the considerations described above—the evolving socioeconomic composition of the Muslim community, the wider dissemination of hadith, and the desire to bring legal doctrines into dialog with ethical ideals—seem to have contributed to diversity of opinion on wives' domestic labor among Mālikīs starting in the third century. Certainly, by the early fourth century the doctrine that provision of domestic service was the obligation of the husband was capable of inspiring indignation and incredulity. It is reported of the pious Cordoban scholar and moderate renunciant Aḥmad ibn Khālid (d. 322/934) that he declared, "I am astonished by the members of our [Mālikī] school; on what grounds have they made it obligatory for a husband to provide a servant for his wife, to the point that they made it equivalent to maintenance? I consider that despicable." He then cited the hadith stating that the Prophet required Fāṭima to do household service.[171] His objections may have related to gender roles in marriage or to the general frivolity of retaining servants; his own rather austere personal piety involved "serving with his own hands" (*yakhdim bi-yadihi*), although the work in question was agricultural rather than domestic.[172] The legal status of women's work may also have mattered to him because it played a role in his own religious ethic; he is quoted as declaring, "My mother used to spin; I would sell what she spun and buy parchment and books."[173] A legal doctrine that wives were under no obligation to contribute work to the household might have conflicted with his belief in the virtue of a modest life supported by the earnings of the women in the family. Wives' domestic labor, in the third Islamic century no less than in the first, stood at the intersection of a complex of concerns about legal entitlement, ethical virtue, and gendered hierarchy within the family.

* * *

The earliest layer of legal doctrine, among Mālikīs and followers of the other Sunni schools, appears to assume that wives are entitled to household labor (implicitly from enslaved servants) financed by their husbands. As Kecia Ali has demonstrated, this rule is the logical outcome of a legal model of marriage in which the husband's payments entitle him to sexual access rather than to labor; it also reflects the discursive means by which the doctrine of Mālik distinguishes between free wives and enslaved concubines. However, debate appears to have arisen as soon as the generation following Mālik. Works attributed to figures such as Ibn Ḥabīb and Ibn Saḥnūn suggest not only that contemporary social customs in fact dictated that wives engage in housework but also that some scholars were articulating such expectations in normative religious terms. By the time of Ibn Abī Zayd, the mixed legacy of Mālikī teaching in this area seems to have raised perplexing issues of law and ethics for a thoughtful husband. Early Mālikī thinkers approached these issues in a variety of ways that reflected the legal or ethical nature of their immediate projects and their approaches to the relationship between these two discursive fields.

In terms of the contrast between legal and ethical frameworks, the material collected in the *Mudawwana* falls firmly on the legal side. It approaches the issue of domestic labor rigorously within the context of the enforceable obligations arising from the marriage contract. Its language in the sections on marriage and divorce is saturated with the language of contract—the entitlements (*li-*) and obligations (*ʿalā*) of the two parties, and what is valid (*jāʾiz*) with respect to the contract itself—rather than deploying a more nuanced language embracing the recommended (but not obligatory) and the reprehensible (but not forbidden). One would look in vain for material relevant to the ideal conduct that spouses should pursue voluntarily within the household.

In contrast, ʿAbd al-Majīd Turkī notes that the didactic and ethical focus of *Adab al-nisāʾ* is reflected in its terminology, with terms like "ought" (*yanbaghī*) and "it is desirable" (*yustaḥabb*) appearing frequently and legal terminology only rarely.[174] The complex treatment of wives' domestic labor in *Adab al-nisāʾ* juxtaposes the legal doctrine familiar from the *Mudawwana* with a vision of the virtuous Muslim household familiar from the ethical literature, one that that combines idealized family solidarity with gendered hierarchy. Giving little attention to the legally enforceable provisions of the marriage contract, it lingers on issues of kindness (*iḥsān*) between spouses and on themes of merit and divine reward. Like the work of Ibn Abī'l-Dunyā, it lavishly praises wives' engagement in textile production despite the lack of any legal obligation for them to do so.

Issues of law, custom, and morality are more thoroughly synthesized in the fatwa attributed to Ibn Abī Zayd, where they all contribute to the complexity of the decisions facing a morally committed Mālikī husband. Here the mismatch between legal doctrine and social practices gives rise to ethical scruples regarding what the husband must tell his wife about her rights and what he may instruct her to do in the house. The ethical evaluation of his behavior is in turn incorporated into the mufti's legal analysis, which parses the husband's motivations to distinguish between his legitimate prerogatives of discipline and divorce and the possibility of illegitimately manipulating his wife.

Despite the diversity of Mālikī legal opinion on the issue of domestic labor, and despite the social expectations and moral scruples that potentially made it problematic, the opinion of Ibn al-Qāsim seems to have been established quite early as the most authoritative doctrine of the school. *Adab al-nisā'* describes it as the legal status quo; Ibn Saḥnūn acknowledges it as the Mālikī position while indignantly rejecting its authority; and the fatwa of Ibn Abī

Zayd nods to its authority while clearly favoring another substantive outcome. Over time, the doctrine of Ibn al-Qāsim in the *Mudawwana* was formally canonized as the majority doctrine (*mashhūr*) of the mature Mālikī school.[175] The Mālikī school thus emerged from the formative period of its development with a legal doctrine that in some ways contrasted with what many Muslims perceived to be both customary and right. As we shall see, this was also true of the other schools that ultimately became the classical *madhāhib* of Sunni Islam.

TWO

Falsafa and *Fiqh* in the Writings of al-Māwardī

THIS CHAPTER MOVES our inquiry from the fourth/tenth century, where our examination of Mālikī doctrine concluded in chapter 1, to the first half of the fifth/eleventh century. It also shifts in geographic focus from the Islamic West (North Africa and Andalusia) to the capital of the Abbasid caliphate in Baghdad. This was an intellectual milieu deeply shaped by ethical discourses adopted from the Greek, Persian, and other traditions that were mediated through translation and incorporated into vigorous new syntheses with Islamic thought. I focus specifically on the Greek tradition, elements of which played an especially prominent role in later Islamic constructions of marriage and the family.

The chapter first introduces the Greek-derived practical philosophy of marriage and the household and its incorporation into the works of Islamic thinkers up to the eleventh century. It then explores the relevant ideas of Abū'l-Ḥasan al-Māwardī (d. AH 450/1058 CE), a Shāfiʿī jurist who also produced an ethical work incorporating elements of Greek philosophical thought on marriage.[1] Beginning with an examination of al-Māwardī's analysis of the marriage contract and the status of wives' domestic labor in his legal manual *Al-Ḥāwī al-kabīr*, this chapter shows that his strictly legal model of marriage strongly emphasizes the contractual exchange of the husband's material support for the wife's sexual availability (a model that we have already encountered in the Mālikī legal work *Mudawwana*). Al-Māwardī thus firmly denies that a wife has any obligation to provide housework while at the same time resisting the implication that she controls her own time and labor and (at least hypothetically) might thus demand wages from her husband.

Turning to al-Māwardī's ethical work *Adab al-dunyā wa'l-dīn*, we find that he deprecates sexual enjoyment as an objective of marriage and accepts that a man might marry for the sake of his wife's domestic services. Despite the apparent conflict between these two stances, some passages of *Al-Ḥāwī* suggest that even when writing in a legal mode, al-Māwardī was mindful of broader ethical values that sometimes diverged from the enforceable provisions of the law. In the end, rather than contradicting each other, al-Māwardī's works of law and of moral guidance complement each other by answering different questions and responding to different needs. Finally, the chapter briefly places al-Māwardī's discussion of wives' domestic labor (and his approach to the relationship between law and ethics) in the broader context of Shāfiʿī doctrines in this area.

Marriage and domestic labor in Islamic *falsafa*

The translation movement that flourished approximately from the mid-eighth to the late-tenth century CE made available to readers of Arabic a vast corpus of Greek thought, including ethical works by Aristotle and other philosophic authorities. As Dimitri Gutas has emphasized, the translation movement was "supported by the entire elite of ʿAbbāsid society: caliphs and princes, civil servants and military leaders, merchants and bankers, and scholars and scientists; it was not the pet project of a particular group in the furtherance of their restricted agenda."[2] Like the vocabulary and assumptions of *zuhd*, terminology and assumptions drawn from Greek philosophical works would come to lastingly pervade Islamic ethical literature, including analyses of the roles and duties of the spouses.

Undoubtedly the most influential Greek ethical work to be translated into Arabic in this period was Aristotle's *Nicomachean Ethics*.[3] This book was reportedly translated by Isḥāq ibn Ḥunayn (d. 289/910–911) and is referenced by the Muslim philosophers al-Kindī (d. 252/866) and al-Fārābī (d. 339/950).[4] In this work, Aristotle places marriage within the context of his discussion of *philia* ("friendship" or "love"). *Philia* is seen as both an aid to and an occasion for the exercise of personal virtue, and the ideal relationship is based on the mutual recognition of the two parties' virtue.[5] Aristotle argues that while friendship may also result from considerations of either pleasure or utility, such relationships are quick to dissolve.[6] The highest caliber of friendship is between equals in virtue; Aristotle categorizes marriage among the relationships (like those between parents and children) that are inherently characterized by asymmetry.[7] Both human and animals are inherently inclined to form couples for the sake of reproduction.

> With the other animals the union extends only to this point, but human beings live together not only for the sake of reproduction but also for the various purposes of life; for from the start the functions are divided, and those of man and woman are different; so they help each other by throwing their peculiar gifts into the common stock. It is for these reasons that both utility and pleasure seem to be found in this kind of friendship. But this friendship may be based also on virtue, if the parties are good; for each has its own virtue and they will delight in the fact.[8]

Brief as these remarks are, they suggest a very different framing of marriage than either the ideals of *zuhd* or the legal model of male maintenance in exchange for female sexual availability. In terms of the goals of marriage, Aristotle's framework relegates both pleasure and material benefit to a subordinate and depreciated status. In terms of its dynamics, rather than being premised on a dichotomy between a male provider and a female consumer, it suggests that both spouses contribute by their activities to the shared welfare of the marital household.

While the *Nicomachean Ethics* established some of the themes and assumptions that informed Muslim philosophers' approach to marriage, it offered little detail on the management of the household. The work that contributed most to the development of a Muslim philosophical understanding of marriage was one that achieved little fame in its Greek original, now long lost, but achieved wide circulation in Arabic translation. This is the treatise "Household management" (*Tadbīr al-manzil*) of Bryson, the nom de plume of a figure whose historical identity and dating remain uncertain. Simon Swain places the origin of the Greek text in the first century AD and its translation into Arabic around the beginning of the tenth century CE.[9]

This work offers advice to the male owner of a landed estate, including sections devoted to counsel on the proper management of slaves, wife, and children. It is framed in economic terms, focusing on the material needs of the individual and the household. The treatise's opening premise is that the human body, in a constant state of flux, requires continuous replenishment. Its need for nourishment leads to the development of numerous crafts and thus to the interdependence of human beings, none of whom can individually master them all. From this interdependence results also the need for money to serve as a medium of exchange.

From these premises, the text then turns to the earning and management of wealth. It is in this context that Bryson frames his discussion of the aristocratic household. While he grounds the need for slaves in the multifarious demands of the household, he regards the wife in first place as a proxy for her husband. Arguing first from "common sense," he reasons that since "most of the man's business is outside his estate," he must often be away from home. "Given this, there is no alternative for him but to have someone to keep it safe and manage the contents of it for him. It is impossible for someone to give another's affairs the attention he gives his own. Since this is so, the best thing for the man is to have a partner in his estate to possess it as he possesses it, to care for it as he cares, and to manage it as he manages."[10]

This is, of course, the wife. Bryson argues that the Creator "gave the woman a nature which makes her prefer to stay still and keep out of sight," thus suiting her to remain at home and guard the household while the husband ventures forth. What is more, He placed the spouses in a relationship uniquely suited to this cooperation:

> Next, He established between them a feeling of love and intimacy, which leads to the removal from each one of them of jealousy, rivalry, and meanness towards his companion with regard to the property which the one permits the other (to use) and over which the one gives the other unrestricted control in respect to its management. Even if this were not so, each one of them would be preoccupied with his companion more than he would be with another owing to their association and partnership and readiness to take (from each other). But He made both of them as if they were one person.[11]

Bryson's analysis of marriage is distinctive in its emphasis on the wife's role in preserving the material well-being of the household, which is depicted as a joint economic unit. He strongly emphasizes the affective bond between the spouses, but in keeping with the economic theme of the treatise as a whole, this relationship is first and foremost "expressed in terms of financial trust."[12] The wife is a partner (*sharīk*) to the husband, and her role is an executive one; as Bryson states with great emphasis, "she is without any doubt the caretaker and manager of the estate, who calculates what is good for it, and who is charged with ruling the servants and the other persons within it."[13]

The Muslim author whose work ultimately played the largest role in disseminating the ideas of Greek philosophers on love and marriage was Abū ʿAlī Miskawayh. Said to have died in 421/1030 at the advanced age of one hundred, he pursued a successful career as a secretary to some of the leading luminaries of the Buyid aristocracy in the second half of the fourth/tenth century.[14] His work—"The refinement of moral characteristics and the purification of dispositions" (*Tahdhīb al-akhlāq wa-taṭhīr al-aʿrāq*)—is closely modeled on Aristotle's *Nicomachean Ethics*, drawing from it not only much of its terminology and argumentation but also its structure and organization; it also quotes directly from Bryson's *Tadbīr al-manzil*.[15] Miskawayh frames his brief comments on marriage within Aristotle's model of the three bases for love, distinguishing between bonds based on pleasure (which form swiftly and dissolve swiftly), those based on material benefit (which form slowly and dissolve quickly), and those based on virtue (which form slowly and dissolve slowly).[16] Like Bryson, he places a heavy emphasis on human beings' need for bonds of cooperation and affection based on the individual's inability to subsist without help.[17]

In his brief comments on the marital relationship, Miskawayh writes:

> The pleasure shared by a man and a woman is the cause of love between them. The two loves [i.e., his and hers] may exist together, since the cause is the same, namely, pleasure; or the one may cease and the other endure, since pleasure, as we have already explained, changes and is almost never stable, and thus the cause affecting one of the two lovers may change while that affecting the other may persist. Moreover, there exists between a man and his wife common goods and mixed benefits, which they seek in cooperation. By this I mean the goods external to us, which are the causes of the prosperity of home life. The wife expects these goods from her husband because it is he who earns and procures them; while the husband expects his wife to administer these goods because she is the one who keeps and manages them in order that they may become fruitful and not wasted. When either of them fails, their love changes and complaints

begin to arise, and things continue in this way until love either ceases, or remains along with complaints and reproach.[18]

Swain convincingly notes the "Brysonian terminology" of this passage, which stresses the wife's role in the management (*tadbīr/tudabbir*) of the household and her partnership role (*sharīk/mushtarak*) in preserving its material prosperity.[19] It is also Aristotelian in its analysis of the objectives underlying the marital relationship and their consequences for its longevity, with the stability of shared material interests mitigating the volatility of mutual sexual desire.

The second author whose assimilation and transformation of Greek ideas about marriage and household management may have contributed most to the developing Islamic ethical literature is Abū ʿAlī Ibn Sīnā (known in English as Avicenna). A Persian speaker born near Bukhara as the son of a bureaucrat in the Samanid administration, he served as a physician and an administrator and died in 428/1037.[20] In his "Treatise on the Division of the Intellectual Sciences," he divides "practical wisdom" into the management (*tadbīr*) of individuals, households, and cities, citing Bryson as the authority on household management.[21] The most extensive discussion of marriage attributed (albeit less firmly) to Ibn Sīnā is a separate treatise on governance (*siyāsa*, a term he uses interchangeably with *tadbīr*).[22] The author's premise in this work is that every person (implicitly, every free adult male) is necessarily engaged in governance, whether of a kingdom, a province, or a household.[23] Following Bryson, he begins with the observation that the human being needs nourishment. The accumulation of a surplus (which distinguishes man from beasts who seek their sustenance day by day) requires the acquisition of dwellings to store and protect it, and of a wife to guard and manage it.[24] (Like Bryson, he appears to assume that the actual labor of producing and preparing food will be relegated to servants.[25]) In the remainder of the work, much like Bryson, he proceeds to discuss the individual's self-governance, followed by the governance of wives, children, and servants.

The author opens his comments on the wife by observing that "a virtuous wife is the man's partner (*sharīka*) in his possessions, the administrator (*qayyima*) of his wealth, and his deputy when he travels."[26] She is "devoted to the service of her husband" (*mubtadhila fī khidmat zawjihā*), managing well (*tuḥsin tadbīrahā*) and increasing his limited assets by her frugality (*tukaththir qalīlahu bi-taqdīrihā*).[27] Here the wife's role in managing the household and ensuring its prosperity is reframed as a dimension of her service (*khidma*) to her husband. This emphasis on proper gender hierarchy within marriage is amplified when he proceeds to stress the importance of maintaining the awe (*hayba*) with which the wife regards her husband, without which she may become his manager (*mudabbira*) rather than the subject of his management.[28] Nevertheless, he should also honor her; a free and noble wife will strive to maintain her honorable status in her husband's eyes.[29] Finally, it is stressed that a wife should be kept busy with domestic tasks, for an idle wife will only incline to mischief. This means that "she occupies herself with governing her children, managing her servants, and attending to the chores of her chamber; for when she has no duties or concerns, she will be interested only in attracting men with her charms and preening herself, and will think only about demanding more [from her husband]."[30]

While Muslim philosophers differed in the details of their analyses of the marital relationship, overall they (and the Greek sources by which they were partially inspired) concurred with the aphorism attributed to an anonymous female philosopher (*ḥakīma*) in an Arabic work of the tenth-eleventh century CE: "a wife is desired for only two things: for children, and for aid in [securing] a prosperous life (*al-maʿūna ʿalā ṣalāḥ al-ʿaysh*)."[31] As Simon Swain has noted, the philosophical emphasis on the managerial and economic roles of the wife diverged sharply from the Muslim jurists' analysis of the marriage contract, which highlighted the husband's right to sexual enjoyment and the wife's right to sustenance.[32] In the broad model adopted and adapted by the Muslim *falāsifa*, the wife is an active contributor to the welfare and prosperity of the household rather than a passive consumer of her husband's support. This shared investment in the couple's economic well-being sustains (and is sustained by) a relationship of mutual affection. Rather than comprising the mundane and subservient toil evoked by the term *khidma*, her activity within the household is understood in terms of supervision and authority. The idea of a wife as a household manager and contributor to the household's wealth was not necessarily foreign to the broader Islamic tradition or to the social practices of Muslims;[33] nevertheless, it was the Greek ethical tradition that most thoroughly developed this motif on a discursive level.

Marriage and domestic labor in the work of Abū'l-Ḥasan al-Māwardī

The remainder of this chapter looks at the analysis of marriage and domestic labor by a scholar of the fifth century AH/eleventh century CE, Abū'l-Ḥasan al-Māwardī. As a legal scholar who was immersed in the lively intellectual milieu of caliphal Baghdad, al-Māwardī offers a multifaceted view of the different frameworks that a cultivated person of the classical period could bring to bear on the question of the Islamic good life. Chief among these were *fiqh* and *falsafa*, both of which contributed to his views on wives' domestic labor. Al-Māwardī both produced one of the leading works of Shāfiʿī *fiqh* and contributed to the philosophically influenced ethical literature of his time; thus, his work offers an unusual opportunity to see the same mind at work in these two genres of writing. This chapter first examines the legal framework through which he analyzed the issue of wives' obligation to do housework in his legal manual *Al-Ḥāwī*, then explores how this framework relates to his philosophical ethics in his work *Adab al-dunyā wa'l-dīn*.

Al-Māwardī was born in Basra (364/974) and settled in Baghdad, where he died in 450/1058. He had a distinguished public career, serving both as a judge and as a diplomat in the service of the Abbasid caliphs al-Qādir and al-Qāʾim. In the latter capacity he engaged in negotiations with the Buyid rulers of Iraq, who had exercised effective suzerainty over the caliphs since they seized control of Baghdad and claimed the title of "supreme commander" (*amīr al-umarāʾ*) in 334/945. Al-Māwardī positioned himself as a staunch defender of the authority of the Abbasid caliphate in a period when it was struggling to meet military and ideological challenges both from the Buyids (themselves probably Zaydī Shi'ites but patrons of the Imāmī Shi'ites of Baghdad) and from the Ismāʿīlī Shi'ite Fatimid caliphate of Egypt and Syria. Although over time al-Māwardī was closely aligned with the Abbasid rulers, his relationship with the Buyids was at least initially good. Nor was he rigidly committed to the Sunni normativity articulated by al-Qādir; his work shows clear Muʿtazilī influences.[34]

The legal work of interest here is his monumental survey of Shāfiʿī legal doctrine *Al-Ḥāwī al-kabīr* ("The Great Comprehensive [Treatise]"). This work is a commentary on the *Mukhtaṣar* of al-Muzanī (d. ca. 264/877), which itself is an abridgment of the doctrine of the school founder al-Shāfiʿī. Al-Māwardī subsequently produced a shorter epitome of this work, *Al-Iqnāʿ*, reportedly at the initiative of al-Qādir, who commissioned a legal manual to serve as a reference for judges from each of the four Sunni schools of law.[35]

Al-Ḥāwī was perhaps al-Māwardī's greatest claim to fame before modern scholars identified *Al-Aḥkām al-sulṭānīya* as a crucial work of premodern Muslim constitutional law.[36] However, al-Māwardī also produced work in a number of other fields, including Qur'anic studies, Arabic grammar, and ethics. Cumulatively, these works reflected the rich intellectual culture of an elite Iraqi of the eleventh century. However, the various sources of al-Māwardī's erudition are not evenly represented in all of his works; some "draw heavily on the Persian and Hellenistic traditions," while others "hew strictly to the Arabo-Islamic tradition."[37] The degree to which his works of different genres reflect a well-integrated overall outlook has been disputed.[38] Christopher Melchert posits a chronological progression, proposing that "Māwardī put away the Persian and Hellenistic traditions as the Sunni revival progressed and he transferred his principal loyalties from the Būyids to the caliph."[39] Both because the precise dates of his works are uncertain and because we do not know if he genuinely disavowed any element of his scholarship over time, this chapter juxtaposes his views expressed in different genres without positing any specific chronological development.

Domestic labor and the logic of the marriage contract in Al-Ḥāwī al-kabīr

By the fifth/eleventh century, basic school doctrines had largely crystallized and had been honed through generations of interschool polemic. Rather than striving to determine the content of the law, scholars of this period worked to refine their concepts and to articulate lines of legal argumentation that discursively justified existing doctrine. Like other classical jurists, al-Māwardī treats the marriage contract as a sale-like exchange in which the dower functions as the countervalue (*ʿiwaḍ*) for the woman's sexual capacities, represented by the *buḍʿ* (a term variously interpreted either as a metonymic reference to the wife's genitalia or to the right to sexual intercourse). As Kecia Ali has demonstrated, this fundamental model underlies the legal reasoning about the marriage contract established in the formative period.[40] However, as a scholar writing long after the crystallization of basic school doctrine, al-Māwardī articulates a more nuanced conceptual framework. Most importantly for our purposes, he distinguishes the initial sale-like transaction in which the husband acquires the right of sexual access to the wife from the ongoing rent-like transaction in which he provides maintenance (*nafaqa*) in exchange for her continuing sexual availability.

Like other transactions of rent or hire, this second exchange involves the acquisition of a usufruct (*manfaʿa*), which al-Māwardī consistently identifies with the right of sexual enjoyment (*istimtāʿ*). He explicitly juxtaposes and contrasts the usufruct of sexual enjoyment with the usufruct of labor (*istikhdām*). Al-Māwardī rigorously maintains that a married woman has alienated her usufruct of sexual enjoyment and not of labor; her husband thus has no direct claim on her work (or, by implication, on the daytime hours usually devoted to work rather than to sex). Nevertheless, he systematically evades the implication that a free wife's labor capacity remains at her own disposal. Instead, he carefully constructs an argument in which a wife's right to her own labor, while not transferred to her husband, is nevertheless preempted by his claim to her sexual usufruct.

A wife's lack of obligation to provide domestic labor does not necessarily imply a corresponding right to have household help provided by her husband. Following the received doctrine of the Shāfiʿī school, al-Māwardī limits this prerogative to wives whose social status would render personal engagement in housework inappropriate. In his discussion of this issue, his focus moves from the mutual exchange of entitlements under the marriage contract to questions of social custom and propriety. Household labor emerges as a major signifier of social rank, and the privilege of exemption from it is a corollary of al-Māwardī's general view that social capital is an asset rightly protected by the law.

We now examine al-Māwardī's arguments in greater detail, beginning with his overall analysis of the balanced exchanges involved in the marriage contract. Al-Māwardī's analysis of domestic labor in *Al-Ḥāwī* reflects the complexity of the contract, which involves both a one-time and enduring transfer with irreversible implications (for instance, the woman's loss of marriageability or virginity through consummation) and a continuing exchange of material maintenance on the part of the husband for sexual availability on the part of the wife. Al-Māwardī addresses and conceptualizes both aspects of the exchange. On the one hand, he understands the *buḍ*ᶜ as being consumed or destroyed (*mustahlak, mutlaf*) by the consummation of the marriage, such that it cannot be returned to the woman if the contract is invalidated but must be indemnified with a fair dower.[41] On the other hand, he states in a number of places that what is being purchased by the husband is actually the usufruct (literally "benefit," *manfa*ᶜ*a*) of the wife's sexual parts.[42] Specifically, "maintenance is in exchange for making herself available to the husband for sexual enjoyment."[43] Although al-Māwardī does not seem to articulate this explicitly, it can be inferred from his argumentation that he views dower (*mahr/ṣadāq*) as the countervalue of acquiring the woman's *buḍ*ᶜ (analogous to the price in a sale) and maintenance (*nafaqa*) as the countervalue of her ongoing sexual availability (analogous to wages in a contract of hire).

Thus, al-Māwardī's analysis of the marriage contract involves not only an analogy with sale but an analogy with rent in which the wife is likened to the proprietor of a rental house and the husband "leases" her usufruct. In his analysis of the wife's sexual recalcitrance (*nushūz*), he notes that

> maintenance becomes due [to the wife] by virtue of her making herself available for sexual enjoyment (*al-tamkīn bi'l-istimtā*ᶜ), just as the rent for a house becomes due by virtue of [the proprietor's] making it available for residence. It has been established that if the landlord prevents the renter from taking up residence [in the house], he is no longer liable for rent. Similarly, if the wife prevents [her husband] from sexual access to her, he is no longer liable for maintenance.[44]

The same model informs al-Māwardī's justification of the doctrine that a wife must bear the cost of her own medical treatment, where he writes, "The wife is equivalent to a landlord (*mukrī*) who is obligated to rebuild what has collapsed of the rented house, rather than the renter."[45] Here the wife is seen as the proprietor of her own body, which she is obligated to maintain; the husband is merely hiring out one function of her body, that of sexual enjoyment.

The conceptualization of the ongoing marital exchange as analogous to a contract of rent or hire has a number of concrete implications. Based on this parallelism, al-Māwardī consistently understands maintenance as a countervalue (ᶜ*iwaḍ* or *badal*) in a contract of exchange (ᶜ*aqd mu*ᶜ*āwaḍa*).[46] One implication of interpreting *nafaqa* as a countervalue is that it is approached as an economic asset rather than as a need-based form of support. Accordingly, al-Māwardī holds that the food component of marital maintenance should be provided in the form of unprocessed grain because (unlike bread) grain has durable value; it can be stored or planted (or, as we shall see, resold).[47] In short, in the Shāfiʿī view, it is the husband's duty to pay the wife, not to feed her (even if much of her pay comes in the form of foodstuffs). As a countervalue, maintenance is set at a determinate quantity (*muqaddar*) rather than calibrated to the wife's needs. The precise amount due depends on the husband's level of wealth, not on the wife's appetite; if it exceeds her needs, she may save or resell the surplus.[48] As a payment due in return for specific benefits, unpaid-back *nafaqa* also accumulates as a debt against the husband.[49]

Key to this analysis is the concept of *manfaʿa* (pl. *manāfiʿ*), meaning "benefit" or "usufruct." It is *manāfiʿ* (whether of houses, fields, human beings, or beasts of burden) that are transferred in contracts of lease or hire.[50] A free adult disposes over his or her own *manāfiʿ*; the *manāfiʿ* of an enslaved person ordinarily belong to the owner and are restored to the individual by manumission.[51] Based on a teaching attributed to al-Shāfiʿī, the *manāfiʿ* of a free person (like those of a house or a field) have inherent economic value. Thus, for instance, if a free person's labor is misappropriated (*ghaṣb*), he or she is entitled to a standard wage (*ujrat al-mithl*) for the work.[52] Similarly, a free man may use his labor (including *khidma*, household service) as dower in a marriage contract.[53] This doctrine contrasts with that of Abū Ḥanīfa, according to which the labor of a free person becomes a commodity only if it is assigned value under a contract of hire; Ḥanafīs thus hold that a free man's labor is not indemnified if it is misappropriated, and it cannot be used as dower in a marriage contract.[54]

Al-Māwardī implicitly assumes a male (whether enslaved or free) to possess one kind of *manfaʿa*, his labor capacity.[55] In contrast, he states repeatedly that a enslaved woman (or, indeed, any woman) has two usufructs (*manfaʿatān*), her capacity for labor (*istikhdām*, literally the capacity of "being used for service") and her capacity to be used for sexual enjoyment (*istimtāʿ*).[56] The implicit reason for this distinction is that the sexual capacities of a man are never the object of a legitimate economic transaction.[57] As we have seen, al-Māwardī envisions the marriage contract as involving the husband's compensation of the wife only for her sexual usufruct; as he states in one place, the dower "is a countervalue for one of her two usufructs" (*iḥdā manfaʿatayhā*[58]), that of *istimtāʿ*.

Al-Māwardī often treats a woman's two usufructs of sex and labor as parallel for the purpose of analogical reasoning. For instance, in support of the Shāfiʿī doctrine that a woman's male guardians (*awliyāʾ*) have no right to object if she accepts a substandard dower (*mahr*), al-Māwardī argues:

> She has two usufructs, the usufruct of labor (*manfaʿat al-istikhdām*) and the usufruct of sex (*manfaʿat al-istimtāʿ*). Since the male guardians do not have the right to intervene against her with respect to her labor if she hires herself out for less than the standard wage for someone like her, they do not have the right to intervene against her with respect to her sexual usufruct if she marries herself off for less than the standard dower for someone like her.[59]

However, al-Māwardī does not always posit that *istimtāʿ* and *istikhdām* should be treated alike. Rather than using core concepts such as *manfaʿa* to generate a rigorously consistent set of legal rulings, he uses them primarily to provide ex post facto rationales for preexisting Shāfiʿī doctrines.[60] Thus, he is quite willing to abandon the parallelism between a woman's sexual and labor capacities when this is required by his school's ongoing rivalry with the Ḥanafīs.[61]

Nevertheless, the parallelism between the two usufructs of labor and sexual availability is a structural feature of his legal reasoning about marriage and slavery, and is central to the way in which al-Māwardī treats the two as both similar and different from each other. Of course, they differ fundamentally in the sense that the husband does not own his wife's person (*raqaba*) and thus cannot sell her. In terms of the rights and duties associated with enslavement and marriage as ongoing relationships, however, it is the fact that a husband does not possess the usufruct of his wife's labor that most fundamentally distinguishes her legal status from that of a slave. (As we have seen in chapter 1, the same was true of the Mālikī model elaborated in the *Mudawwana*.)

Indeed, despite the fact that a male owner is legally entitled to sexual access to his female slave, al-Māwardī pervasively associates slaves with labor and wives with sex. Discussing the defects that render a slave ineligible for manumission as an act of expiation (*kaffāra*), he observes that only defects that affect the slave's ability to work are relevant since "the objective of slaves is work, because they are held for service or earning. . . . Similarly, since the objective of marriage is sexual enjoyment, the defects that affect [sexual enjoyment] give rise to a choice [that is, to an option of annulment on the part of the new spouse], and whatever does not affect it does not give rise to [a choice]."[62]

Al-Māwardī is aware that it is legitimate for a man to have sexual intercourse with his slave woman, and that some do.[63] As we shall see, he is also aware that wives often do housework and that men may marry for this purpose. Nevertheless, his legal model treats labor as the defining function of enslavement and sexual enjoyment as the defining objective of marriage.[64] This model is the basis for his reasoning on subsidiary points of doctrine; thus, in the passage quoted above, it is used to support the doctrine that a man may annul his marriage if his wife proves to have an obstacle to sexual enjoyment, but not if she proves incapable of working in his home. Formally speaking, marriage is contracted for sexual access, and maintenance is the wage that the husband pays to his wife for her sexual availability.

The direct linkage al-Māwardī establishes between *nafaqa* and *istimtāʿ* plays a consistent and salient role in his legal reasoning. Thus, he argues that the husband must pay for any grooming products and cosmetics used to enhance the wife's attractiveness (and she in her turn must use them if provided) because "his entitlements with respect to her include the use of adornments that encourage him to enjoy her sexually."[65] Al-Māwardī's rigorous focus on the husband's claim to sexual enjoyment extends even to his analysis of her entitlement to food and clothing. He writes that the wife is not at liberty to sell the clothing provided by her husband and buy cheaper garments (in order to pocket the difference or buy additional food) because her personal adornment contributes to his sexual enjoyment. In contrast, she is entitled to sell excess food; her husband may prevent her from doing so only if her meager consumption leaves her too weak to have sex or too gaunt to be alluring.[66] Whether she remains vigorous enough to perform any other household duty is irrelevant to this logic.

Indeed, in the model elaborated by al-Māwardī, it is the defining feature of the marriage contract that it relates specifically—and exclusively—to sexual rights. It is this limitation to the sexual usufruct (*manfaʿa*) of the woman that distinguishes the legal status of marriage from slavery. As we have seen, al-Māwardī (like other jurists) recognizes a sale-like component to the marriage contract, which is understood as involving the husband's acquisition of the wife's *buḍʿ*. This is a limited form of ownership right over the wife; as al-Māwardī states, "the only [aspect] of the woman married that becomes the property [of the husband] is the right of [sexual] enjoyment."[67] He observes, "Ownership of a slave (*milk al-yamīn*) is more powerful (*aqwā*) than the marriage contract because the marriage contract is limited to the ownership of the *buḍʿ*, and the ownership of a slave compromises ownership of the [the enslaved woman's] entire person (*raqaba*)."[68]

The contrast between marriage and enslavement is particularly direct in the case of an enslaved woman who is also married. In this case, the enslaved woman's labor belongs to her owner while sexual rights are transferred to the husband. Al-Māwardī writes,

> As for the slave woman, if her master marries her off, she differs from the free woman in terms of the obligation to make herself available ([for sex]: *al-tamkīn*), because the free woman is obliged to make herself available to her husband [both] in the nighttime and in the daytime. [As for] the slave woman, the master (*al-sayyid*) is obliged to make her available to her husband at night, but he is not obliged to make her available to him during the day. The difference between the two [cases] is that the right to the slave woman's labor is possessed by the master, and the right to her sexual enjoyment is possessed by her husband. Neither right is voided by the other because of their difference from each other and the distinction between their times: service is associated more with daytime than with nighttime, so it is assigned to the master and he is not obliged to deliver her [to her husband] during it; the nighttime is associated more with sexual enjoyment than the daytime, so it is assigned to the husband and the master is obliged to deliver [the wife to the husband] during it.[69]

If a married slave woman's time is to be divided between the master who owns her labor and the husband who is entitled to her sexual company, this raises the question of the time and labor of the free woman. Al-Māwardī continues, "The free woman is different from [the slave] woman, because there is no one entitled to her labor who shares [her time] with her husband; for that reason, she must deliver herself [to her husband both] during the nighttime and during the daytime."[70]

The obvious objection to this argument is, of course, that the wife may retain the right to her own time and effort during the daytime hours that are associated with work rather than with sexual enjoyment. This idea is duly raised by al-Māwardī's hypothetical interlocutor:

> If it were asked, "She is the possessor of her own labor, so why isn't she entitled to withhold herself from her husband during the time of work, which is the daytime, like the slave woman?" it would be replied: "Because no one else possesses her labor (*al-khidma ghayr mamlūka ʿalayhā),* so her being married nullifies her right to [her own] labor (*ṣāra fī tazwījihā tafwīt li-ḥaqqihā min al-khidma*); she thus differs from the slave woman, whose labor is owned by someone else."[71]

Al-Māwardī is astute in pinpointing the question of the free wife's labor, which is raised by his single-minded focus on sexual access as the raison d'être of marriage. Although it is clear that he does not, in fact, regard the time and work capacity accruing to the owner of an enslaved wife as remaining at the disposal of the free wife, the line of reasoning by which he reaches this conclusion is less obvious. It appears that the free woman loses her right to dispose of her own labor (and of the daylight hours in which it would ordinarily occur) not because that right has been acquired by another person but because it simply falls into abeyance as a result of her marriage.[72]

The idea that a free wife in principle owns her own labor yet is not free to dispose of it because of the conflicting rights of the husband also emerges from al-Māwardī's comments about breastfeeding. His starting point is that (as stated explicitly by al-Shāfiʿī in the base text on which he is commenting), a wife cannot be compelled by her husband to breastfeed regardless of her social status.[73] Al-Māwardī observes that if the husband were entitled to breastfeeding from his wife, "he would [similarly] be entitled to compel her to serve him, and he is not entitled to that."[74] Here he treats breastfeeding and domestic service (*khidma*) as parallel forms of labor; the husband does not have an enforceable right to either of them. Conversely, if the wife wants to breastfeed, al-Māwardī writes that the husband is not entitled to prevent her unless he does so "for the sake of enjoying [her] sexually (*li-ajl al-istimtāʿ*) and in the times appropriate to it (*fī awqātihi*)."[75]

Thus far it appears that the husband's rights over his wife are rigorously limited to sexual access and perhaps to the nighttime hours. However, the fact that her husband has no personal claim on her work does not imply that she is free to dispose of it as she wishes. Al-Māwardī observes that while a husband is entitled to forbid his wife from breastfeeding under some circumstances, "his [right to] prevent her from nursing does not indicate that he is entitled to nursing from her; [rather], it is like his [right to] prevent her from serving someone else, despite the fact that he is not entitled to have her serve himself. Don't you see (*a-lā tarā*) that someone who hires a tailor is entitled to prevent him from [engaging in] building, despite the fact that he is not entitled to building from him?"[76]

Here the husband's rights with respect to his wife's labor are purely negative; his sexual rights prevent her from freely exercising her ownership of her own labor capacity, without giving him any direct right to her work. He is like someone who has a tailor on retainer; the employee is prohibited from hiring himself out as a builder not because his employer is entitled to his labor as a builder but because the employer has acquired the right to have him on call for tailoring.

Al-Māwardī's second argument against the wife's entitlement to dispose of her own time and labor is based on the idea that the marriage contract is analogous to an exclusive contract of hire for a stated period of time rather than to a contract for piecework:

> It is not permissible for the wife to hire herself out to breastfeed a child other than her own or to serve someone other than her husband, because her usufructs are [already] claimed by virtue of the husband's [right to] sexual enjoyment of her (*li-istiḥqāq manāfiʿihā fī istimtāʿ al-zawj bihā*), so she became like someone who hired himself out for a month to serve Zayd and then hired himself out for that [same] month to serve ʿUmar; this would not be permissible, because his usufructs are already claimed by virtue of the prior contract. . . . [Similarly], if she hired herself out to breastfeed her [own] child and serve her husband [for pay], this would not be permissible, but if she [breastfed or served] voluntarily it would be permissible. [This is] because by hiring herself out she would be compensated (*muʿāwaḍa*) by the wage, and she has already received compensation for her usufructs in the form of maintenance (*nafaqa*), and there cannot be two countervalues for the same thing. [In contrast], if she does so voluntarily she is not receiving compensation [twice for the same thing]; rather, she has gratuitously given (*badhalat*) an additional usufruct. According to this [principle], if she sews a garment for him she is not entitled to a wage, because he could not validly hire her to sew it, [so] she [is considered to have] done it voluntarily.[77]

In this complex passage, al-Māwardī begins by stipulating (in a syntactically and logically difficult formulation) that by virtue of the husband's right to sexually enjoy his wife, all of her usufructs (*manāfiʿ*) have been placed outside of her disposal. The key word here is the technical term *istiḥqāq*, which refers legally to the establishment of a prior claim of ownership in favor of another party.[78] It is significant that he does not state that it is the husband himself who owns any nonsexual usufructs but simply that, as a result of his sexual rights, there is a prior claim on those usufructs, such that the wife no longer disposes over them. He clarifies this claim with the example of a person who hires himself out for a month's service to two different employers. A contract of *khidma* is understood to place the employee generally at the service of his or her employer for the duration of the contract. Thus, while it would be possible to contract to perform specific tasks for two different people concurrently (for instance, to sew a cloak for Zayd and a shirt for ʿAmr), it is not possible to provide "service" to them both simultaneously. The parallel to the case of the wife is at first not obvious; it is clear from al-Māwardī's discussion of spousal maintenance that he does not define *nafaqa* as compensation for the wife's domestic labor. The common denominator here is that she is already being paid for an exclusive full-time job (i.e., being sexually available to her husband).[79]

Another passage that may shed light on al-Māwardī's understanding of the wife's right (or lack thereof) to control her nonsexual usufructs occurs in his discussion of the reasons for the husband's responsibility to provide maintenance. He writes that the rational (*maʿqūl*) reasoning supporting this obligation is that

> the wife's usufructs are reserved for him (*al-zawja maḥbūsat al-manāfiʿ ʿalayhi*) and she is prevented from disposing [of them] because of his entitlement to sexual enjoyment of her; thus, she is entitled to her support and maintenance, as [an owner] is obliged to provide for the slave who is retained (*mawqūf*) to his service and as the ruler is obligated to pay the maintenance for soldiers because they are retained (*li-iḥtibās anfusihim*) for the purpose of jihad.[80]

Here the wife's obligation to be available for sex corresponds to the slave's obligation to be available for service and the soldier's duty to be ready for war. The key words (*maḥbūsa*, *mawqūf*, *iḥtibās*) point to the individual's retention or detention for the service in question, which constrains him or her from other pursuits. This approach, which defines spousal maintenance essentially as compensation for the opportunity cost of being a wife, plays only a minor role in al-Māwardī's broader argumentation. It is of limited utility to him because (as he explicitly notes elsewhere) the Ḥanafīs use the same logic to support their argument that the quantity of a wife's maintenance is based on need rather than being stipulated by law.[81] Just as a soldier receives support sufficient to his needs from the treasury in return for fighting as much as is required by the Muslim community, the Ḥanafīs argue, a wife receives as much support as she needs from her husband in return for making herself available for as much sexual intercourse as he requires. (I explore this argument in greater detail in chapter 3.) As we have seen, as a Shāfiʿī, al-Māwardī argues that the maintenance of a wife (unlike that of a slave) is a countervalue (*ʿiwaḍ*) rather than a need-based form of support. Although al-Māwardī is thus not willing to carry this logic very far, the analogy between a wife and a soldier is instructive. Like a soldier, she is retained for a specific duty, but the obligation to be available for that duty precludes other possible uses of her time or labor. She cannot work for pay (unless it is for a third party with her husband's permission) not because her husband owns her labor but because she is a full-time wife.

The wife's labor is thus not specifically alienated by the marriage contract; al-Māwardī concedes to his hypothetical opponent that she is technically its owner (*mālika*), and if her husband gave her permission to hire herself out for wages, nothing suggests that the wages would belong to anyone but her.[82] Nevertheless, because of her husband's claim on her sexual availability, she cannot actually exercise these ownership rights by disposing of her own work. Al-Māwardī's reasoning leads to the conclusion that (as he puts it in a parallel passage), "the free [wife] does not have an ownership claim to her own labor (*laysat al-ḥurra mustaḥiqqa li-khidmat nafsihā*), and for that reason, it is not permissible for the wife to hire herself out for pay."[83]

Al-Māwardī's legal reasoning revolves consistently around the principle that the marriage contract gives the husband a comprehensive right to sexual access to his wife, a claim that he deems to govern everything from the nature of her economic maintenance to the disposal of her time. This principle is rigorously applied and yet transparently artificial; it is difficult to imagine, for instance, that in the real world husbands' primary concern with respect to their wives' employment outside of the home was the possibility that they might temporarily be unavailable for sex. The logic of sexual access is also purely negative in its implications; it explains why a wife may be precluded from activities that make her unavailable to her husband but offers no rationale for her to offer her husband or the household anything but sex.

Nevertheless, al-Māwardī's consistent assumption is that wives—or at least most wives—do, in fact, supply domestic labor. For instance, he writes that an insane man may "be in need of the service of women, and a wife will be kinder to him."[84] This formulation suggests the gendering of labor: a man may stand in need of women's work (presumably, housework and personal care), and this may best be provided by a wife. The function that al-Māwardī envisions for wives may include not only mundane chores but the oversight of the household. Describing the skills that a young woman must display to demonstrate her competence to control her own assets, he suggests that she should be given some of her money "to spend on herself and on the management (*tadbīr*) of her servants and her home"; if she is found to be capable of overseeing "household affairs" (*umūr al-manāzil*) and of having garments spun, she has demonstrated mental maturity (*rushd*).[85]

The fact that al-Māwardī does not hold wives as a category legally responsible to provide domestic labor also does not mean that he considers them categorically entitled to have this labor provided for them. Following al-Shāfiʿī, al-Māwardī limits this prerogative to wives whose status makes it inappropriate for them to engage in household chores. Of course, in combination, these doctrines suggest that humbler wives are neither obligated to do housework themselves nor entitled to have service provided for them. Who would then perform the routine tasks required to run the household is not specified. The lack of attention to this presumably common scenario suggests that the relevant *fiqh* doctrines address a limited set of potentially litigable material claims, rather than seeking to guide the day-to-day conduct of Muslim spouses.

For al-Māwardī, the parameters of a wife's entitlement to maintenance for a domestic servant are firmly based in social custom. The recurring key word in his analysis is *al-maʿrūf*, a term that literally means "what is known" but also has connotations of "what is right or just."[86] In this context, al-Māwardī consistently interprets it as a reference to prevailing social mores. Citing the Qur'anic command to "consort with [wives] according to what is *maʿrūf*" (Q 4:19), he argues that for a woman of appropriate status, "the service [of a slave or servant] is something that is usual and customary (*min al-muʿawwad wa'l-maʿrūf*)." In contrast, "if [the wife] is not of a status to be served because she [ordinarily] serves herself,[87] he is not obliged to pay the maintenance of her servant because it goes beyond the 'customary' amount that is commanded with respect to her."[88]

A wife of the requisite status is also exempt from food preparation. As we have seen, Shāfiʿī doctrine dictated that a wife should in principle be provided with her rations in the form of grain rather than of prepared food. Al-Māwardī elaborates:

> If it is the custom of her peers (*ʿādat amthālihā*) to take care of the grinding and baking of their own rations, like the people of the countryside (*ahl al-sawād*), then she is obligated to undertake its grinding and baking rather than the husband. If it is not customary for her peers to undertake the grinding and baking of their rations themselves, the husband has the choice to pay her the fee for grinding [and baking] or to provide her with someone who undertakes its grinding and baking.[89]

Having established that a wife's entitlement to domestic help is contingent on its being customary for a woman of her social class, al-Māwardī goes on to analyze the criteria by which this can be determined. He writes,

> The relevant "custom" in that respect has two aspects. The first of them is the custom associated with rank and station (*ʿurf al-qadar wa'l-manzila*). It is the custom of people who possess [high] rank by virtue of nobility or wealth for others to serve them, so they do not serve themselves, and the custom of anyone whose rank is low and whose station is inferior to serve himself and not to be served. The second aspect is the custom of the locality (*ʿurf al-bilād*). It is the custom of the people of the cities (*al-amṣār*) to employ servants and not to serve [themselves], and the custom of the people of the hinterlands (*al-sawād*) to serve [themselves] and not to employ servants.[90]

A wife's entitlement to service apparently depends on both of these variables—that is, her husband must provide her with a servant only if she is both high-status and a town dweller.[91] She must have enjoyed the appropriate status in her birth family, and her personal sensibilities are irrelevant: "If she is the kind of person who is not [ordinarily] served and is too haughty to serve [herself], [her husband] is not obliged to pay the maintenance of her servant, and if she is the kind of person who is [ordinarily] served and debases herself by serving [herself: *tabadhdhalat fī'l-khidma*], he is [nevertheless] obliged to pay the maintenance of her servant."[92]

The high-status wife's entitlement to service is not contingent either on her possession of a slave or on the availability of funds to acquire one from her dower.[93] Rather, she must be supplied with the requisite services regardless whether her husband purchases an enslaved servant, maintains one she already possesses, or hires a free servant.[94]

Another possibility pondered by the jurists was that the husband might opt to do the work himself, thus saving the cost of a servant. This scenario raised the question of whether the wife's entitlement was simply to be relieved of the chores, or to be provided with service in a way that was honorable for her.

> As for if the husband wants to serve her himself, there are two views. One of them, which is the opinion of Abū Isḥāq al-Marwazī[95] and Abū ʿAlī ibn Abī Hurayra,[96] is that he is entitled to do that because her needs are filled by his service. The second view is that he is not entitled to do that, because she may feel bashful about using him for service (*taḥtashimuhu fī'l-istikhdām*) and experience a deficiency [in service].[97]

There was also the possibility that a wife might prefer to eschew the servant and claim the wages. Al-Māwardī continues, "If she were to say, "I want to serve myself and take the wages of my servant," she is not entitled to do that, like the working partner in a commenda partnership (*muḍāraba*); he is entitled to hire a carrier or porter (*ḥammāl wa-naqqāl*) for the goods, but if he were to take it upon himself to carry them he would not be entitled to take the wage for carrying them."[98]

In these comments al-Māwardī seems strikingly indifferent to the issue of gender hierarchy within marriage. The possibility that the husband might choose to do the work himself elicits no reflections on the inherent propriety of a man's waiting on his wife; it is rejected with reference not to the possible humiliation of the man but to the possible embarrassment of the woman. Al-Māwardī's rationale for denying the wife the option of serving herself and pocketing the corresponding wages is similarly ungendered. He compares her to a partner in a commenda contract, a role with no gendered valence (but often assumed to be held by a man). Such a partner is entitled to hire a worker for certain menial services but not to collect pay for performing them himself.[99] Al-Māwardī's concern is focused not on the ways in which the spouses' activities articulate a hierarchical and gendered relationship between the two of them but on the extent to which the wife's activities conform to her proper position in the broader social hierarchies prevailing beyond the marital home.

In al-Māwardī's analysis, exemption from performing one's own domestic labor is an expression of the status of families and of entire social strata. Being served by others is the custom and the prerogative of social elites; it distinguishes nobles from commoners, the wealthy form the poor, and urbanites from rustics. Possession of such status is not a matter of personal sensibilities and aspirations (or even primarily one of economic resources) but of shared social understandings of who is "the kind of person" who could customarily expect to be served.

In a parallel passage, al-Māwardī offers additional status terminology to describe the kinds of wives who are or are not entitled to be provided with domestic servants. He refers to the wife "the likes of whom are not usually served because of her *tabadhdhul*" and the wife "the likes of whom would usually be served because of her *ṣiyāna*."[100] *Tabadhdhul* (or *bidhla* or *ibtidhāl*) and *ṣiyāna* are widely distributed focal terms for al-Māwardī in *Al-Ḥāwī* and often appear in tandem as a contrasting pair.[101] The term *tabadhdhul* derives from a root meaning "to expend" (as money or effort); a *bidhla* is a worn-out work garment.[102] Derivations of the root take on the meaning of "common" or "vulgar." As used by al-Māwardī, *tabadhdhul* refers to being cheapened or degraded, in the sense of being exposed to hard usage or to the public gaze. *Ṣiyāna*, in contrast, means "preservation"; it evokes not merely physical protection or careful keeping (as of a valuable object) but being sheltered from unauthorized gazes and from unrestricted social contact. *Ṣiyāna* sometimes appears parallel with *ḥishma* (decency, decorum[103]) and is sometimes explicitly associated with the preservation of honor.[104]

In addition to signifying high status, *ṣiyāna* is also distinctively gendered.[105] When used in reference to a girl or woman, the contrasting pair *bidhla/ṣiyāna* references her degree of modesty or seclusion and, thus, of status. Attractive or high-class women should be discouraged from attending Friday prayers for the sake of *ṣiyāna* (as well as to avoid sexual temptation).[106] Enslaved women used for service are *mubtadhalāt*, while those kept as concubines are *maṣūnāt*.[107] A woman also becomes "shopworn" through an unsuccessful contract of marriage, for which she should thus be compensated.[108]

The *ṣiyāna/bidhla* pair is also used to rank and evaluate men. Whereas *ṣiyāna* can sometimes be associated with women as a class—who are, in al-Māwardī's view, distinctively subject to devaluation through exposure—when applied to males this dyad always signals a status distinction. Indeed, in a number of contexts *Al-Ḥāwī* posits two broad categories of people: *ahl al-ṣiyāna / dhawū al-ṣiyāna* (those who have reputations to preserve), and *ahl al-bidhla* (those who do not).[109] Like a woman (although to a lesser extent), a man is cheapened by exposure to the common view, particularly when engaged in mundane or intimate activities.[110] Avoiding overexposure to the common throng is particularly important for a man in a position of authority, such as a judge.[111]

Al-Māwardī's analysis of the elite wife's exemption from domestic labor is thus consistent with his pervasive assumptions relating to social status and the need to maintain it by refraining from activities regarded as common or degrading. His concern with evaluating and preserving social rank is also reflected in another section of *Al-Ḥāwī*'s Book of Marriage, that on *kafā'a* (social parity). The general principle of *kafā'a* is that a woman may marry a social equal or superior but may not degrade her own and her family's standing by contracting marriage with a social inferior. Fathers (who are understood to be uniquely concerned with the welfare of their children) have the prerogative of contracting their daughters' marriages with whomever they prefer (subject to the daughters' consent). However, a marriage contracted by any other guardian (*walī*) is subject to challenge and annulment by male affines on the grounds of lacking *kafā'a*, based on the logic that a mésalliance inflicts reputational damage not only on the bride but on her kin.[112]

Jurists considered multiple factors as possible criteria of *kafā'a*, notably including ethnicity and piety. As a Shāfiʿī, al-Māwardī also considers the source of the prospective groom's livelihood (*kasb*), thus raising issues of labor, rank, and personal dignity analogous to those raised by the question of a wife's domestic labor. Perhaps unsurprisingly, given the rough parallel between the two issues, here again al-Māwardī's focus is on the accepted mores of the specific social milieu. He writes:

> In well-known custom (*al-ʿurf al-maʾlūf*), means of livelihood come from four sources: through agricultural pursuits, trades, crafts, and military occupations (lit., "defenses," *ḥimāyāt*).[113] Each of these has ranks (*rutab*) that vary in comparative status; each one of them may be superior to any of the others based on the variation among places and times. In some lands trades are [regarded as] superior, and in others agricultural pursuits; in some times the soldiers providing defense (*ḥumāt al-ajnād*) are superior and in some more lowly. For this reason it is not possible to deem any of them superior in all places and times; rather, with respect to them one adheres to custom and convention.[114]

Al-Māwardī concludes that the four conditions of occupational *kafāʾa* are that one's craft not be a disreputable (*mutaradhdhil*) one like that of a weaver, one whose earnings are considered tainted (*mustakhbath*) like that of a cupper, lacking in honor (*murūʾa*) like that of a porter, or degraded by common use like that of a hired laborer (*mubtadhalan ka'l-ajīr*).[115]

Al-Māwardī's fifth condition of *kafāʾa* is wealth (*al-māl*). He justifies the consideration of this factor (whose relevance was denied by the Mālikīs) by invoking authoritative texts suggesting the importance of wealth.

> This is because of [the Prophet's] (peace be upon him!) statement, "A woman is married for the sake of four things: for her money[, her beauty, her status, and her piety]"[116] and because of what is transmitted from him that he said, "The claims to prestige (*aḥsāb*) of the people of this world (*ahl al-dunyā*) are this wealth."[117] It has also been said in interpretation of God's statement "Indeed, [the human being] is intense in his love of good things" [Q 100:8] that ["good things"] means wealth.[118]

It is notable that the texts al-Māwardī cites are subject to very different interpretations. The hadith in which the Prophet enumerates wealth as a motive for marrying a woman ends by advocating that one choose a bride for her piety;[119] and while verse 100:8 invokes the human love for lucre, it is almost universally understood to condemn it.[120] Here too, al-Māwardī ends up by referring the reader to the standards of the relevant social milieu:

> If [the family of the prospective spouse] are from among the people of the cities, who mutually boast and vie in terms of their wealth, then with respect to them wealth is taken into consideration as a condition of marriage equality. If they

> are from among the nomads and the tribes of the villages (*al-bawādī wa-ʿashāʾir al-qurā*) and mutually boast and vie on the basis of their genealogies rather than their wealth, there are two views on the consideration of wealth as a condition of marriage equality.[121]

For the purposes of al-Māwardī's legal analysis in this passage, neither the religious legitimacy of the grounds on which people boast and vie nor the inherent ethical valence of boasting and vying is subjected to serious scrutiny. In the framework of *Al-Ḥāwī*, social rank—evaluated according to whatever criteria are in fact prevalent in the relevant circles—is an asset subject to legal protection, and the moral praiseworthiness of the social values in question is a very muted concern.

Based on the excerpts above, it may seem that al-Māwardī's analysis of marriage is a cynical one. One might infer that, in his view, men marry for sex and women marry for money; and his discussion of domestic labor suggests pragmatic deference to social values that reinforce hierarchy and stigmatize labor. However, other comments in *Al-Ḥāwī* suggest that these features of his analysis reflect his understanding of the strictly legal entitlements at play rather than of marriage as a social reality (let alone as a religious ideal). This emerges from his scattered observations about the overall benefits of marriage. At one point he observes that "the objective of marriage to a free woman is affection and companionship (*al-ulfa wa'l-muwāṣala*[122]), rather than [simply] sexual intercourse . . ."[123] In another context he notes that in marriage (unlike the purchase of an enslaved woman) "the objective is intimate association and good companionship" (*al-ʿishra wa-ḥusn al-ṣuḥba*) in addition to "full sexual enjoyment" (*kamāl al-mutʿa*).[124] In his discussion of fair dower (*mahr al-mithl*), al-Māwardī similarly acknowledges that men prefer wives with personal qualities such as intelligence, beauty, and good conduct, who accordingly command higher dowers.[125]

Al-Māwardī is thus fully aware that, in the real world, people choose to marry (and select their spouses) for reasons having to do with love, companionship, and the desire for a capable helpmeet. It is the legal framework defining marriage as an exchange of dower for sexual rights, not his underlying view of the nature and benefits of marriage, that compels him to focus so systematically on the husband's right to sexual enjoyment. For instance, in discussing the defects that can entitle a spouse to annulment if discovered after contracting the marriage, he writes that "there is no option [of annulment] for simplemindedness (*al-balah*), because sexual enjoyment is unimpaired. Similarly, there is no option [of annulment] for stupidity or incompetence, because sexual enjoyment is unimpaired by either of them; they only affect other things, such as the management of the household (*tadbīr al-manzil*) and the upbringing of children (*tarbiyat al-walad*)."[126]

Such comments suggest that al-Māwardī was aware of the artificiality of the legal model of marriage he elaborated in such detail; the categories of *fiqh* did not capture the goals that people actually pursued when getting married. In addition to gesturing toward an important concern of actual life, his usage of the phrase *tadbīr al-manzil* in this passage suggests another dimension of his understanding of marriage: his knowledge of—and commitment to—the ethical heritage of *falsafa*.

Indeed, it is in such passing comments that *Al-Ḥāwī* also gestures to al-Māwardī's larger ethical commitments, which diverge in fundamental ways from the legal questions that are the work's central focus. Near the beginning of the Book of Marriage of *Al-Ḥāwī*, al-Māwardī comments on al-Shāfiʿī's statement that "whoever does not crave [sexual intercourse], I prefer him to devote himself to the worship of God [instead of marrying]."[127] This sentiment is in itself potentially controversial; marriage is a prominent and undisputed component of the Prophet Muḥammad's Sunna, and the virtues of celibacy were debated even among Muslim renunciants.[128] In his commentary al-Māwardī appears even less enthusiastic about the married state than al-Shāfiʿī; while al-Shāfiʿī states that he approves of (*uḥibb*) marriage for those who desire it, al-Māwardī merely declares it permissible or neutral (*mubāḥ*).[129] Among other textual and rational arguments, he observes, "Since the objective (*maqṣūd*) of marriage, which is sexual intercourse (*al-waṭʾ*), is not obligatory, a fortiori marriage must not be obligatory. [This is] also [true] because marriage involves nothing more than the fulfillment of desire and the achievement of pleasure, and that is not obligatory, like other desires."[130]

By identifying marriage with sexual intercourse and sexual intercourse with the satisfaction of lust, he gives it a subordinate place in a moral framework where virtue is associated with the disciplining of one's desires. This is not what one would expect based on the central role of *istimtāʿ* in his argumentation about the rights and duties of marriage. Ultimately, it is precisely the centrality of sexual access to his legal model of marriage that relegates marriage to such a low level in his moral schema. This passage suggests that al-Māwardī's legal analysis of marriage in *Al-Ḥāwī* coexists with a vision of ethics that relegates physical pleasure to a lowly level of human aspiration. However, it is in a work of another genre that we can most fully access his ethical vision of marriage and the place of labor within it.

Domestic labor in Adab al-dunyā wa'l-dīn

In most cases, we can only speculate about the extent to which a work of *fiqh* represents the ethical principles, as well as the legal doctrines, of its author (or try to elicit this from passing references in a legal work, as we have done above). In the case of al-Māwardī, however, we can juxtapose his treatment of marriage and labor in *Al-Ḥāwī* with that in a work of a different genre, his ethical manual *Adab al-dunyā wa'l-dīn* ("Good Conduct for This World and the Next"). As we have seen, the discussion of marriage in *Al-Ḥāwī* focuses overwhelmingly on issues that could potentially be adjudicated in a court of law (What maintenance payments can be imposed on a husband? Under what conditions can a marriage be annulled on grounds of social disparity?). While a concerned Muslim man could consult *Al-Ḥāwī* to avert the possibility of his marriage being invalidated for lack of *kafāʾa*, he would find little to guide him toward the selection of an ideal spouse or the forging of a happy marital life. In contrast, *Adab al-dunyā wa'l-dīn* raises sweeping questions about the objectives and virtues of marriage. Al-Māwardī's analysis of marriage in this work focuses not only on the moral and religious soundness of different motives for entering into wedlock (or for choosing a wife) but also—and perhaps most importantly—on the impact of such motives on the depth and durability of the emotional bond between the spouses. (Unsurprisingly, this bond is envisioned overwhelmingly in terms of the moral priorities and the feelings of the husband.) Within this framework, *Adab al-dunyā wa'l-dīn* explicitly marginalizes and devalues the element most central to al-Māwardī's legal analysis of the marriage contract, the factor of sexual enjoyment (*istimtāʿ*). It also asserts a universal criterion of preference among forms of labor and livelihood, based on the primacy of mind over body, that contrasts with *Al-Ḥāwī*'s deference to local social hierarchies of prestige.

As Mohammed Arkoun observed, *Adab al-dunyā wa'l-dīn* is composed in the style of belles lettres (*adab*), eclectically combining elements from the various intellectual currents that informed the ethos of "the aristocratic class of Buyid Iraq."[131] In it, "simple sayings of philosophers, ascetics, or poets are used in the same way as sacred texts," cumulatively contributing to "the justification and consolidation of a scale of values."[132] While the book eschews the explicit citation of sources, its content suggests familiarity with works of *falsafa*, including Miskawayh's *Tahdhīb al-akhlāq*.[133] Although the work is loosely constructed, some themes stand out by the voluminousness of their treatment—especially *ulfa*, affection or sociability.[134] Indeed, Arkoun argues that the importance of social solidarity is the one theme drawn from the *falsafa* tradition that al-Māwardī most centrally emphasizes.[135]

As suggested by its title, the work is divided into two major sections, devoted respectively to the concerns of religion and of earthly life. Al-Māwardī opens the book's second section, dealing with conduct in matters of this world (*adab al-dunyā*), with the premise that human beings are inherently dependent on cooperation with others of their kind.[136] He identifies the three factors necessary for a person's well-being in this world as an obedient soul (*nafs muṭīʿa*), comprehensive affection (*ulfa jāmiʿa*, in the sense of having abundant social and familial ties), and sufficient material means (*mādda kāfiya*).[137] His discussion of marriage falls within the extensive section on the varieties and causes of *ulfa*. While al-Māwardī's framework does not directly reproduce those of either Aristotle or Bryson, he incorporates elements rooted in each; Bryson's emphasis on human interdependence is combined with Aristotle's concern with the sources of *philia* (love or friendship). In *Adab al-dunyā wa'l-dīn*, al-Māwardī thus approaches marriage as one among a number of sources of human solidarity, which is one of the practical prerequisites for the pursuit of a good life.

Among the source of ties of affection, al-Māwardī lists kinship through marriage (*al-muṣāhara*).[138] Marriage involves the voluntary initiation of new kinship ties and the intermingling of lineages and may produce intense emotional bonds between the spouses.[139] He proceeds to analyze the possible motivations for contracting a marriage. His evaluation of the comparative virtues of these different motivations reflects Aristotle's analysis of the different bases for friendship, which Miskawayh had already applied to marriage. As we have seen, in the *Nicomachean Ethics* Aristotle represented *philia* (love or friendship) as resulting from three different kinds of motives, which have different implications for the stability of the relationship: pleasure, utility, and virtue. Miskawayh applied this model to his analysis of marriage, which he saw as combining the volatility of desire with the comparative durability of shared material interests. Al-Māwardī further develops this schema, enumerating five different motivations for contracting a marriage: money, beauty, religion, affection (*ulfa*, again meaning the multiplication of interpersonal ties), and the preservation of chastity (*al-taʿaffuf*, in this case meaning the prevention of illicit sexual activity).

If money is the primary motivation of a marriage, al-Māwardī says, it is possible that the union will endure if the financial incentive is combined with other factors; if money is the only basis for the marriage, however, the relationship is sure to deteriorate swiftly once the wife's assets are in hand.[140] (It is notable that in this context, al-Māwardī ignores the legal principle that a wife's wealth is not at her husband's disposal.) Desire for a woman's beauty is a more durable basis of affection than desire for her money since beauty (unlike wealth) is an intrinsic attribute. On the other hand, an outstandingly beautiful woman may be bold and coquettish, and her husband may be tormented by desire.[141] He then moves on to religion (*dīn*) as a foundation for marriage, affirming that it is the firmest and most lasting basis for the marriage bond, as suggested by the Prophetic hadith.[142] Although this observation would seem to establish the pursuit of piety as the proper and fundamental motivation of marriage, in fact al-Māwardī's discussion of this point is rather perfunctory; as we shall see, his discussion culminates elsewhere. A marriage contracted in pursuit of social ties (*ulfa*) may have two contrasting motives: either to cement one's bonds with a friendly group or to appease and win over a hostile one. A marriage alliance contracted on this basis will endure as long as the parties entertain their hopes or fears vis-à-vis the other group.[143] Al-Māwardī concludes, "If the contract [of marriage is concluded] out of the desire to preserve one's chastity, it is the true objective sought through the contracting of marriage (*al-wajh al-ḥaqīqī al-mubtaghā bi-ʿaqd al-zawāj*); all others are factors appended to it and associated with it."[144] Al-Māwardī's discussion suggests that "preservation of chastity" comprises the pursuit of a legitimate marital sexual life, including reproduction.

Having identified the legitimate channeling of sexuality as the proper motivation of marriage, al-Māwardī goes on to enumerate the wifely qualities that will enhance a marriage made on this basis. The list overlaps with that already discussed; this time, however, he is exploring not the objectives that may motivate one to contract a marriage, but the factors that will lead to the best possible marriage contracted for the sake of rightful sexuality and reproduction. A wife chosen with this objective in mind should be pious (once again, *al-dīn*) and intelligent. Her kin should also be social equals (*akfāʾ*) of her suitor; in this way, he will avoid shame (*ʿār*), acquire useful social allies, and ensure the respectable status of his children. However, al-Māwardī acknowledges that these criteria do not themselves ensure a successful and lasting union; rather, a good match involves factors that may vary with context and personal taste.[145]

At this point al-Māwardī moves on from his general and abstract analysis of different bases for marital love to consider the different concrete motivations that may sway a given individual man. Different personal desires or situations may dictate different choices of spouse. The first to be considered is the desire for offspring; a man who is primarily pursuing this objective should seek out a young virgin wife. Al-Māwardī endorses this motivation, stating that "marriage was established for it, and the [divine] law establishes it."[146] The second objective he considers is "the performance of what women undertake of the management of households" (*al-qiyām bi-mā yatawallāhu al-nisāʾ min tadbīr al-manāzil*). He remarks in this regard,

> Although this [work] is performed particularly by women, it is not the most characteristic function of wives,[147] because it can be performed by other women. For this reason it has been said, "A woman is a refreshing herb, not a household administrator" (*al-marʾa rayḥāna wa-laysat bi-qahramāna*). [However], this objective [i.e., contracting a marriage for the sake of acquiring a mistress for one's household] does not affect a person's religion or impair his honor (*murūʾa*).[148]

Al-Māwardī states that if one seeks a wife for this reason, it is best to choose one who is advanced in age and has skill and experience in household management and familiarity with the ways of men (implicitly, perhaps a widow).

Finally, one may marry for the sake of sexual enjoyment (*istimtāʿ*). Al-Māwardī declares, "This is the most blameworthy of the three cases and the one that most impairs [the man's] honor, because in [pursuing this motive] he obeys his bestial characteristics and follows his base desire." However, this does not apply "if he does that to break and subdue desire" so that he will not be tempted to engage in sexual misbehavior (*fujūr*) that would lead to stigmatization and shame; in that case there is no blame attached to his behavior, and he is in fact worthy of praise. Nevertheless, "If in this case he were to refrain from degrading (*istibdhāl*[149]) free women and resort to slave women, this would be more conducive to the protection (*ṣiyāna*) [of his status] and more perfect for his honor."[150] Al-Māwardī regards such a marriage as perilous for the woman involved because sexual desire does not endure; lust will ultimately turn to dislike. It was to spare their daughters this kind of degradation (*ibtidhāl*), he declares, that the pre-Islamic Arabs used to bury their infant daughters alive.[151]

Of course, this hierarchy of motivations diverges sharply from the legal analysis of *Al-Ḥāwī*. There *istimtāʿ* was not only identified as the prime objective of marriage but frequently used as the sole criterion for the analysis of a husband's prerogatives. In *Adab al-dunyā wa'l-dīn*, in contrast, the pursuit of *istimtāʿ* is not merely portrayed as less than optimal; it is stigmatized as uniquely degrading. It seems unlikely that al-Māwardī's dim view of sexual indulgence in this passage reflects an ascetic preference for renunciation; his discussion of marriage is couched in a larger framework that endorses the expansion of family ties, the pursuit of a respectable livelihood, and the preservation of social status.[152] Rather, in his denunciation of sexual indulgence as a form of obedience to one's "bestial characteristics," he evokes the Platonic tripartite soul posited by the philosophers.[153] Like Miskawayh, he advocates self-control but rejects asceticism.

Philosophical hierarchies also inform his evaluation of the impact on the wife of the different motivations for marriage. The legal analysis of *Al-Ḥāwī*, drawing overtly on social values and conventions, assumes that it is degrading for an elite woman to engage in mundane chores. Unlike household labor, sexual enjoyment is the defining obligation of wives of all status. Indeed, in his discussion of concubines al-Māwardī posits it is precisely the woman whom one has taken as a sexual partner who one will protect from the public eye and from cheapening activities.[154] In the ethical analysis of *Adab al-dunyā wa'l-dīn*, while someone who seeks a wife for household management may prefer to choose an experienced older woman, such activities are no threat to his honor (nor, apparently, to hers). It is taking a wife for pleasure, not using her for household tasks, that involves degradation (*istibdhāl*).

Another example of the sharp distinction between al-Māwardī's legal approach in *Al-Ḥāwī al-kabīr* and his ethical concerns in *Adab al-dunyā wa'l-dīn* involves his attitude toward social hierarchies. As we have seen, in *Al-Ḥāwī* both his discussion of a wife's entitlement to a servant and his treatment of the issue of social parity between spouses (*kafāʾa*) show a high degree of deference to time- and place-bound conventions of rank and status. In a legal context, al-Māwardī treats social prestige (defined by the prevailing conventions of the relevant circles) as an asset that enjoys enforceable protection. In *Adab al-dunyā wa'l-dīn*, in contrast, al-Māwardī evaluates the different sources of livelihood in terms of a normative distinction between occupations that reflect the primacy of the intellect (a central axiom of the work) and those that are limited to physical exertion.[155] Here he derives an absolute hierarchy of occupations directly from the hierarchy of moral capacities that underlies his ethical framework. A person intent on the cultivation of a virtuous self will not pursue work that develops only his physical and animalistic (*bahīmī*) capacities any more than he will pursue a marriage that indulges the animalistic quality of lust. As for wealth, it should be pursued only to the point of fulfilling one's basic needs. This approach perhaps complements, but is nonetheless completely distinct from, al-Māwardī's legal framework, which treats social and occupational status as a matter of convention and offers individuals enforceable means to protect the social capital accruing from it.

Overall, our comparison between these two works of al-Māwardī suggests that the legal project in *Al-Ḥāwī al-Kabīr* is substantially distinct from—and yet overall compatible with—the ethical project of *Adab al-dunyā wa'l-dīn*. While al-Māwardī does not perceive any provision of the Sharia to be immoral, his approach to *fiqh* suggests that it is not the project of *furūʿ al-fiqh* to offer a guide to the refinement of one's moral character. Rather, the genre of *furūʿ al-fiqh* aims to inform both judges and Muslim believers of the obligations to which they are liable and the rights that they may claim.

Al-Māwardī in the context of the Shāfiʿī school

As we have seen in chapter 1, although al-Shāfiʿī's own references to wives' domestic labor were ambiguous, by the tenth century members of his school adhered to the inter-*madhhab* consensus that elite wives were entitled to a domestic servant funded by their husbands. Al-Māwardī's contribution to the discussion of wives' domestic labor lay less in any major doctrinal innovations than in the refinement of the issue's conceptual framework and the exploration of subsidiary questions. His scholarship was influential; Christopher Melchert notes that although al-Māwardī directly trained few leading scholars, "he was a major figure in the elaboration of Shāfiʿī doctrine, especially at the level of positive law (*furūʿ*)."[156] Nevertheless, of course, he represents only one voice within a diverse Shāfiʿī school. In the generation before al-Māwardī, the Shāfiʿī *madhhab* had bifurcated into two sub-traditions (*ṭarīqas*) known as the Iraqi school (or school of Baghdad) and the Khurāsānī school (or school of Marw). In part due to the mobility of scholars, these labels primarily designate intellectual lineages rather than the geographical origins of their members.[157]

The two sub-schools generally agreed that, in the words of Abū Isḥāq al-Shīrāzī (d. 476/1083), the leading proponent of the Baghdadi Shāfiʿī school in al-Māwardī's time, a wife "is not obliged to serve [her husband] by making bread, grinding [grain], cooking, washing, or any other kind of work (*khidma*), because what she has contracted to provide is sexual access, so she is not obliged to provide anything else."[158] However, they disagreed about the implications of this analysis. The difference of opinion was expressed in their divergent approaches to a question that, whatever its social relevance, raised fundamental issues about the contractual relationship between the spouses: Can a wife validly hire herself out to her husband for pay? This question was primarily raised by the scenario of a wife's demanding wages from her husband to nurse their baby but was sometimes extended to include other tasks such as housework.[159]

Al-Māwardī's teacher Abū Ḥāmid al-Isfarāyinī (d. 406/1016), who is regarded as the focal figure of the Iraqi *ṭarīqa*, argued that it is not permissible for a wife to receive wages for nursing from her husband "because the husband is entitled to the time that she spends nursing in exchange for a countervalue (*badal*), which is maintenance (*nafaqa*), so it is not permissible for her to take another countervalue."[160] In this view, while the husband's payment of maintenance compensates the wife for her sexual availability and not her labor, it nevertheless secures for him the right to all of her time. As we have seen, al-Māwardī himself subscribed to this reasoning and extended it to domestic tasks such as sewing. ʿAbd al-Wāḥid al-Rūyānī (d. 502/1108), whose work is said to have drawn centrally on al-Māwardī's *Al-Ḥāwī*, similarly extended this logic to domestic tasks: "Similarly, if [the husband] were to hire her for housework (*khidma*) it would not be valid, because there is a prior claim on her capacities at all times (*li'annahā mustaḥaqqa al-manāfiʿ fī jamīʿ al-azmān*) except for [the time required] for duties that she must perform, such as acts of worship and relieving herself."[161] Another formulation of the Iraqi view focused not specifically on the wife's time but on the related idea that the husband's claim on his wife (while in itself limited) preempts all others. Imām al-Ḥaramayn al-Juwaynī (d. 478/1085) notes that the Iraqi authorities of the school held that such a contract would be invalid because "the husband's rights over her comprehend her capacities in general" (*innahā ʿalā al-jumla mustaghraqat al-manāfiʿ bi-ḥaqq al-zawj*).

In contrast, the Khurāsānīs held that because the right to a wife's labor was not alienated by the marriage contract, she could validly contract to receive wages from her spouse. Al-Juwaynī notes that the people of Marv "definitively held" (*qaṭaʿū*) that a contract for a wife to receive wages for nursing from her husband would be valid because nursing is not obligatory for her, and the husband is entitled to only one of her capacities, that of sexual enjoyment. Al-Juwaynī himself emphatically endorses this view.[162] His fellow Khurāsānī (and fellow student of Abū Bakr al-Qaffāl, the founder the of the Khurāsānī *ṭarīqa*) al-Qāḍī Ḥusayn al-Marwarūdhī (d. 462/1069) affirmed the validity of a wage contract between the spouses and extended it analogically to sewing and other tasks.[163] Al-Juwaynī's student Abū Ḥāmid al-Ghazālī endorsed this opinion and applied it to all contracts of hire between husband and wife. His commentator al-Rāfiʿī explicitly included domestic labor, stating that a contract to nurse the couple's child for pay would be valid "as if he had hired her to cook, sweep, or the like."[164]

Pending further evidence, it is unclear to what extent this discussion reflected issues that were socially relevant or actively disputed in courts. One factor in the controversy was certainly inter-*madhhab* and inter-*ṭarīqa* polemic. Al-Juwaynī dismisses the opinion of the Iraqi Shāfiʿīs not simply on its own merits but because it parallels that of the school's Ḥanafī rivals: "What [the Iraqis] have mentioned is the doctrine of Abū Ḥanīfa, and thus I give no weight to what they have transmitted, even if they state it decisively."[165] Indeed, al-Juwaynī's partisan motivation is more pronounced than his interest in affirming wives' ability to dispose over their own labor. He writes that, without her husband's permission, a wife cannot hire herself out to a third party "for any kind of work, including washing, baking bread, spinning, sewing, or the equivalent. This is not because the husband is entitled to these usufructs from her but because they are displaced (*mazḥūma*) by the entitlement of the husband; the husband's entitlement with respect to a free wife is comprehensive (*ʿalā al-istighrāq*)."[166]

Outside of the context of the immediate inter-*ṭarīqa* polemic, he thus adopts the argument of his Iraqi opponents. As Mariam Sheibani has demonstrated, while Khurāsānī Shāfiʿīs were most absorbed in polemics with their Ḥanafī interlocutors, Iraqis were chiefly preoccupied with the Ḥanbalīs.[167] Thus, al-Rūyānī (who, despite his geographic origin, sided with the Iraqi *ṭarīqa*) explicitly contrasted his rejection of contracts of hire between husbands and their wives with the Ḥanbalī insistence that they were valid.[168] The positions of the two Shāfiʿī *ṭarīqa*s may thus be largely artifacts of intergroup debate.

Based on the evidence at hand, it is impossible to know to what extent these doctrinal differences affected the behavior or the bargaining positions of spouses on the ground. What is clear is that debates over the control of the wife's labor could cut to the heart of scholars' differences over the implications of the marriage contract. Less explicitly but equally importantly, scholars differed in the ways in which they incorporated ethical considerations into their legal argumentation. As we have seen, al-Māwardī's legal argumentation followed a logic largely autonomous from his ethical framework on such issues as the objectives of marriage and the significance of social hierarchy. A fellow Shāfiʿī such as al-Juwaynī differed not only in terms of the concrete legal doctrines associated with the Khurāsānī rather than the Iraqi *ṭarīqa* but in the extent to which he sought to integrate legal argumentation with ethical judgments.

Al-Juwaynī's discussion of the elite wife's entitlement to domestic help is saturated with the terminology of social stratification, alluding repeatedly to the wife's rank (*martaba*), prestige (*qadar*), position (*manzila*), and honor (*murūʾa*).[169] He denies that such a wife can offer to do the work and pocket the wage on that grounds that by so doing she would have "diminished her own rank" (*asqaṭat martabat nafsihā*).[170] This emphasis on the preservation of social capital is also reflected on his discussion on the freeing of slaves as acts of expiation (*kaffārāt*), which he cross-references with his discussion of wives' entitlement to servants. There he argues that a person who owns only a home and a slave may resort to fasting if doing his own chores "is not befitting to his station (*manṣab*), and if he set forth [on his own errands] that would diminish his honor."[171]

These arguments might suggest that al-Juwaynī is highly deferential to—and, indeed, highly invested in—socially established standards of hierarchy and prestige.[172] However, the impression that he perceives an unproblematic harmony between the objectives of the divine law and human scales of social value is quickly dispelled by his editorial comments. Addressing the case of a man who can buy a slave to free in expiation only by impoverishing himself, he remarks that "most things that people reckon as points of honor are indulgences of the [lower] soul in the eyes of the wise!"[173] Al-Juwaynī's ambivalence toward social standards of prestige is particularly evident in his discussion of the social equality of marriage partners (*kafāʾa*), which revolves around the avoidance of the social stigma; the passage is peppered with words such as *shayn* (dishonor), *ʿār* (shame), and *shanār* (disgrace). Yet al-Juwaynī also subjects existing social values to a brisk and withering critique. "As for the doctrine on lineage," he remarks, "with respect to it no consideration is given to what the children of this world take into account/set store by" (*lā iʿtibār fīhi bi-mā yaʿtaddu bihi banū al-dunyā*).[174] (In this context, "the children of this world" clearly means "worldly people"—that is, people who lack an awareness of ultimate values.) He further remarks, "As for kinship to the grandees of this world (*ʿuẓamāʾ al-dunyā*), most of whom are oppressors who have seized power over people—they are revered out of hope [for their favors] and fear [of their wrath]; the divine law proclaims the lowliness[175] of their station. Thus there is no reliance on their lineages, even though they may boast of them (*qad yatafākharūna bihā*)."[176]

For al-Juwaynī, as for al-Māwardī, legal reasoning was thus an autonomous field that both intersected with his religious ethic and sometimes sharply diverged from it. The two were compatible parts of a larger whole; the protection of social capital, like the assertion of the spouses' separate rights under the law, could coexist with a wider moral framework where such considerations were petty or misguided. The ethical frameworks that they brought to bear were, however, not identical. While al-Māwardī was informed by an ethical heritage centrally featuring the Greek-derived *falsafa* tradition, al-Juwaynī invoked a broad critique of worldly values. In both cases, the enforceable claims that were the focus of contract law (including that of the contract of marriage) were always articulated against the background of other normative commitments.

* * *

Scholars have debated the degree to which al-Māwardī's diverse scholarly writings reflect a coherent overall worldview. Ovamir Anjum describes him as manifesting "a multiple-personality disorder," while Mona Hassan argues that he manifests "rich, human complexity" by "varying his style and approach when writing in different genres."[177] Anjum and Hassan are both addressing al-Māwardī's political writings, where the complement to his Islamic legal framework is a "Near Eastern, particularly Persian, model of kingship" rather than a philosophically informed ethical model of marriage.[178] A similar apparent polarity confronts us when we compare his views of marriage in his legal and ethical works. In this case, however, on further examination the different facets of al-Māwardī's intellectual culture reveal a deeper compatibility. Al-Māwardī the jurist who gives *istimtāʿ* a defining role in his legal reasoning about marriage in *Al-Ḥāwī* is still discernibly the same person who deprecates *istimtāʿ* as a motivation for marriage in *Adab al-dunyā wa'l-dīn*. Sexual gratification is, in al-Māwardī's consistent view, a subordinate and ignoble goal in the range of human objectives. It is nevertheless the benefit that a husband purchases with his material maintenance of his wife under the marriage contract and thus serves as the central criterion in analogical arguments about this maintenance. Similarly, the belief that the life of the mind is superior to other human pursuits is in the end perfectly compatible with the recognition that actually existing human societies rate the prestige of different occupations in various ways, many of which may conflict with this criterion. It is social status, not philosophical virtue, that is protected by the Sharia.

A notable feature of al-Māwardī's legal analysis is his reluctance to concede the rather obvious inference that a wife who has not alienated her labor under the marriage contract must logically retain the right to that labor herself. He insists that a husband, while not himself possessing a claim to his wife's labor, nevertheless preempts her right to dispose of it herself. This argument supports his doctrine that a wife cannot, even hypothetically, charge her husband wages for housework. The scenario of a wife's demanding wages for her labor in the home is "good to think with" because it isolates the issue of her legal claim to her usufruct of labor from the issue of her husband's right to control her mobility outside of the home and her interaction with strangers. Al-Māwardī's resolute yet weakly argued rejection of the wages-for-housework scenario may reflect his genuine feeling, reflected at various places in *Al-Ḥāwī* (as well as in *Adab al-dunyā wa'l-dīn*) that wives do in fact customarily provide housework, and that men may marry for this reason, without any claim to pay. However, our brief survey of the divergent opinions on this issue in the two sub-schools of the Shāfiʿī *madhhab* suggests that arguments on the subject may in part be motivated by inter-*madhhab* and inter-*ṭarīqa* polemic rather than by the various authors' substantive views on gender roles within marriage.

On the related issue of a wife's entitlement to domestic help funded by her husband, later Shāfiʿīs significantly amplified the school founder's differentiation among wives of different social statuses. Al-Māwardī's enhanced concern for this issue is in turn outdone by al-Juwaynī's lavish use of terms evoking social rank and prestige. However, in each case it appears that deference to prevalent social sensibilities as a criterion for a wife's legal entitlement to maintenance for a servant coexists with quite different criteria for genuine (moral or religious) nobility or worth. In al-Māwardī's case these alternative criteria are expressed in a separate ethical work and are rooted in Greek philosophical assumptions about the superiority of the intellect; in al-Juwaynī's case they are expressed in passing within his legal work and are rooted in Islamic values that deprecate or relativize worldly wealth and advancement. Al-Māwardī and al-Juwaynī draw the boundary between legal and ethical evaluation somewhat differently, but this boundary nevertheless exists for both of them.

THREE

Legal and Ethical Obligation in the *Mabsūṭ* of al-Sarakhsī

OUR STUDY NOW moves to the late fifth/eleventh century and to a new geographical focus, Greater Khurasan (the area comprising northeast Iran and Transoxania). In this period and region, the duty to provide mundane service to a superior—whether within the family or in family-like relationships of fealty or discipleship—was laden with ideas about the moral duties inherent in dyadic relationships of subordination. The first section of this chapter explores "service" (*khidma*) as a versatile concept that by this period played a central role in the articulation of a wide range of hierarchical bilateral relationships, from apprenticeship to Sufi discipleship.

The chapter then turns to the motif of domestic labor in the legal manual *al-Mabsūṭ* of the Ḥanafī jurist Shams al-Aʾimma al-Sarakhsī (d. AH 483/1090 CE).[1] Whereas al-Māwardī's legal analysis of labor obligations within marriage (examined in chapter 2) was almost completely distinct from his ethical analysis of the same issue, al-Sarakhsī wrote in a context where the provision of labor within the family was thoroughly saturated with ethical significance. It is thus unsurprising that his legal analysis of wives' obligation to do housework incorporated ethical considerations in new and central ways. However, rather than merging his legal and ethical analyses of the marital relationship, within this work of *fiqh* al-Sarakhsī articulates a domain of ethico-religious obligation that is distinct from the judicially enforceable provisions of the marriage contract. Al-Sarakhsī's ethical vision of marriage is based in part on hadith and on his broad understanding of Islamic ethics.

However, he also incorporates elements of the Greek practical ethics of the household examined in the first section of chapter 2, although without overtly identifying them as such. In particular, at certain points al-Sarakhsī's analysis of marriage clearly displays the terminology and concepts associated with Bryson. The final section of the chapter places al-Sarakhsī within the broader context of evolving Ḥanafī doctrine on the issue of wives' domestic labor.

The significance of service (*khidma*) in eleventh- to twelfth-century Khurasan

Over the course of the fifth century AH/eleventh century CE, layers of ethical meaning continued to accrue to the concepts and tasks associated with domestic labor. As we have seen, in the early Islamic period the personal performance of menial daily tasks such as cooking and cleaning could be a token of pious humility for a Muslim conquest elite with easy access to enslaved labor. When not performed for oneself as a sign of self-abnegation, service (*khidma*) was most often associated with wives and servants. By the eleventh century, the motif of *khidma* had vastly expanded in scope and significance. As demonstrated by such scholars as Antonio Jurado Aceituno, Jürgen Paul, Margaret Malamud, Marina Rustow, and Eve Krakowski, in this period *khidma* became one of the focal terms in a sociopolitical system fundamentally structured around bilateral hierarchical relationships of personal loyalty.[2] *Khidma* (in the sense of servitude or service) was understood as a central component in the individual's relationship to God, to rulers, to parents, and to mystical masters in the increasingly institutionalized spiritual discipline of Sufism. As we shall see, this view of *khidma* as a structural feature of hierarchical relationships within the family and beyond also came to inform the analysis of domestic labor in *fiqh* texts.

As Rustow has demonstrated based on documents from the Cairo Geniza, the terminology of *khidma* was not confined to the realm of political fealty but had entered the usage of ordinary Arabic speakers.[3] In the words of Eve Krakowski, *khidma* was one of a small set of core terms that "reflect a "common code" of social affiliation recognized by men [and women] at all levels of the social ladder."[4] Examining the family ties of Egyptian Jews, Krakowski argues that their "ideals of kinship centered neither on patrilinies nor on solidarity groups of any kind, but rather on dyadic relationships between individual relatives—relationships that were heavily gendered . . . in the obligations that they entailed."[5] Although no single body of documentary evidence for Muslim family relationships parallels the data on the Jewish community afforded by the Geniza, the Arabic vocabulary of affiliation and obligation was common to both communities. It is reasonable to infer, as Paul argues, that the model of *khidma* was originally derived from the vocabulary of family relations and served to extend symbolic kinship to individuals tied by bonds of political loyalty. However, as Krakowski argues, "by the Geniza period [in the tenth through twelfth centuries CE], the analogy seems more often to have worked the other way," with appeals for the help and loyalty of kin invoking the conventions of political patronage.[6]

A sense of the breadth and variety of relationships of *khidma* in Greater Khurasan in the eleventh to twelfth centuries CE can be drawn from the biographical notices assembled by ʿAbd al-Ghāfir ibn Ismāʿīl al-Fārisī (d. 529/1135). Receiving service was the prerogative of parents and elders; asked about his age, one man proudly declared that he was seventy years old and "served by (*yakhdimunī*) thirty-one children and grandchildren."[7] Students also served their teachers, most often teachers of hadith.[8] *Khidma* of a Sufi master was a central part of spiritual discipleship, and men involved in political life were described as "serving" a sultan or emir.[9] *Khidma* could be a form of apprenticeship; of one man it is noted that he served an emir in his childhood (*fī ṣibāhu*) and learned the scribal art from him.[10] The concrete details of such service, which must have varied widely from one context to another, are rarely specified. A child placed in the service of a teacher or mentor might well have performed daily chores or errands, while a courtier's service was surely more rarefied (or metaphorical).

Whereas the theological and political realms were linked to that of kinship through a broad ideology of service, they offer few concrete parallels to daily practices within the household.[11] The same is not true, however, of the Sufi practices of training and discipleship that were in the process of crystallizing in Greater Khurasan.[12] Sufism incorporated and developed many elements of the early ascetic movement discussed in chapter 1, including the motif of *khidma* as a form of self-abnegation.[13] The practices of spiritual apprenticeship are particularly germane to contemporary models of marriage because Sufis framed the master–disciple relationship in terms that mirrored, transformed, and sometimes inverted gender relations within the family.

The argument here is not that Sufi terminology and practices directly influenced contemporary *fiqh* discourses but that both Sufism and *fiqh* drew on common assumptions about the ways in which "service," embodied in the performance of mundane life tasks, could serve to articulate familial or family-like relationships of affiliation and hierarchy. It is impossible to construct a full empirical account of how and by whom such labor was performed, either within family homes or in the context of Sufi communities; our focus here is on the various normative models within which the chores of everyday living were charged with ethical significance.

As Malamud observes, Sufi "novices . . . were consistently enjoined to behave in a manner that closely matched the subordinate behavior women were urged to display toward fathers and husbands."[14] The deferential role of disciples was not only discursively but sometimes literally parallel to that of women within the household and often involved the kinds of mundane tasks traditionally associated with wifely *khidma*, including cooking, cleaning, and waiting on senior men. The Sufi model of *khidma* is accessible primarily through sayings and anecdotes associated with various Sufi figures. In many cases little is known about the individuals involved, and the historicity of specific events is open to debate; nevertheless, clear overall patterns emerge from this material.

A sense of the Sufi model of *khidma* current in Greater Khurasan in the eleventh century can be drawn from the biographical dictionary *Ṭabaqāt al-ṣūfiya* of Abū ʿAbd al-Raḥmān al-Sulamī (d. 412/1021). Bringing together anecdotes and teachings traced to figures ranging from the late second century AH/eighth century CE to his own time, al-Sulamī constructed a lineage that retroactively assimilated pious figures of the past to a contemporary vision of Sufism.[15] While the reports presumably contain a significant element of authentic information about thought and practice in the earlier historical periods they describe, in their selection and editing al-Sulamī communicated themes and concerns relevant to his own time and place.[16] Because the work includes entries on a significant number of female Sufis, it also allows some observations about the gendering of Sufi *khidma*.

In Sulamī's *Ṭabaqāt*, *khidma* is a minor yet pervasive theme. It is in the first place rendered to God, both in the form of explicit acts of worship and as a general stance of obedience and devotion.[17] In a number of sayings, service of human beings appears as an accessible form of behavioral conditioning for the service of God; as one holy man declares, "Spiritual discipline (*al-riyāḍa*) is breaking the ego (*kasr al-nafs*) with service."[18] In concrete terms, the main recipients of service are Sufi masters and one's fellow aspirants on the mystical path, although the ideal Sufi should humble himself by serving all people.[19]

If *khidma* is a distinct but minor theme in the material gathered by al-Sulamī in his thousand or so entries on male Sufis, it rises to prominence in his much smaller collection of sayings and anecdotes related to female mystics. I have located thirty-four explicit references to *khidma* in the 360 pages devoted to male mystics in a modern edition of the *Ṭabaqāt al-ṣūfīya*, and twenty-five in the 38 pages devoted to women.[20] Thus, on a per-page basis, the motif of *khidma* appears on average seven times more frequently in the entries on female Sufis. The result is that, while the content of the concept appears similar in both instances, its salience is vastly different. The parallel between physically serving one's fellow human beings (particularly mystics and saints) and the service of God, while familiar from the entries on men, plays a particularly prominent role in those on women.[21] In addition, as has been noted by Rkia Cornell, a number of the female figures are identified as the personal servants of male or female spiritual masters.[22] Cornell observes that "in as-Sulamī's book of Sufi women no theme is more prominent than that of servitude." This concept is conveyed above all through the term *taʿabbud* ("to make oneself a slave"); *khidma* is, in turn, "an essential aspect of . . . *taʿabbud*."[23]

Only rarely does al-Sulamī's material provide allusions to the concrete activities involved in *khidma*. For instance, a woman known as Zaytūna is described as having been a servant of al-Nūrī; an anecdote depicts her asking him, "Shall I bring you something to eat?" and asking what he would like her to prepare.[24] To the extent that service can be understood as involving domestic chores such as cooking, it is perhaps unsurprising that it is disproportionately—although far from exclusively—associated with women in the corpus collected by al-Sulamī. The *khidma* offered to spiritual mentors could directly parallel (or even replace) that normally performed by wives. Cornell notes a story (transmitted in a somewhat later text) in which a woman declares to her pious husband that "I do not love you in the way that married couples do. . . . I wanted to be with you only in order to serve you." The husband recounts that "every time she cooked a pot [of food], she would say, 'Eat it, sir! It has been cooked only by the glorification of God.' "[25] The pious practice of *khidma* could also involve the humble service of a man to his mother.[26]

If the materials collected by al-Sulamī construct an ideal of *khidma*, a composite picture of the concrete practice of *khidma* within a Sufi community can be extracted from the life narrative of al-Sulamī's younger contemporary (and possible student) Abū Saᶜīd ibn Abī'l-Khayr (d. 440/1049).[27] The fullest version of Abū Saᶜīd's life, *Asrār al-tawḥīd* ("Secrets of God's Mystical Oneness"), was produced more than a century after his death; thus, this material is filtered through later sensibilities and certainly contains a number of ahistorical components.[28] However, it seems reasonable to assume that the overall conventions of Sufi conduct reflected in the text are rooted in the period and place of interest to us here.

In *Asrār al-tawḥīd*, service is an important stage in the early training of the budding mystic. Significantly, service in the Sufi lodge (*khāneqāh*) appears as an extension of service within the family; after the young Abū Saᶜīd has been initiated into Sufism, his spiritual master sends him back to his village with the instruction, "Occupy yourself with serving your mother."[29] Abū Saᶜīd later devotes himself to the service (Persian: *khedmat*) of his brethren by cleaning the *khāneqāh*, including its latrine, and busies himself with sweeping the local mosques. These activities, like begging on behalf of the community, are explicitly described as a form of humiliation (*dhull*).[30] In another anecdote the young Abū Saᶜīd avidly serves a distinguished senior mystic; when the latter's robe is soiled with blood from a wound, Abū Saᶜīd launders, folds, and returns it.[31]

In these passages, *khidma* (Persian: *khedmat*) appears as a combination of menial household labor and personal service. The same pattern persists later in the work, when Abū Saᶜīd appears as a senior mystic disposing over the services of others.[32] His disciple and servant Ḥasan-e Moʾaddeb is depicted as being charge of provisioning and food preparation for the community.[33] In one anecdote Abū Saᶜīd offers Ḥasan's services in laundering a religious rival's clothes.[34] Significantly (and in contrast with al-Sulamī's depiction of the early Islamic predecessors of the Sufi movement) the then-new Sufi institution of the *khāneqāh* is depicted as a homosocial space where men undertake forms of quotidian labor and personal care that might otherwise be the domain of women. (Although Abū Saᶜīd does have female disciples, there is no indication that they participate in activities like cooking and cleaning for the *khāneqāh*.[35]) In this context it is ambiguous whether male Sufis' performance of domestic tasks that were ordinarily assigned to women was regarded as a beneficially humbling form of feminization, or whether the gendering of the tasks was simply not salient.

As discussed above, Sufi discipleship was only one of multiple instantiations of *khidma* in eleventh- to twelfth-century Khurasan and drew its complex valences from the many relationships of commitment and subordination with which such "service" was associated. A particularly rich cumulative account of the multifaceted significance of *khidma* (including, but not limited to, the performance of humble household tasks) is provided by the *Iḥyāʾ ʿulūm al-Dīn* ("Revival of the Religious Sciences") of Abū Ḥāmid al-Ghazālī. Throughout the book, al-Ghazālī invokes the language of *khidma* in his discussion of proper hierarchical relationships of political, religious, and familial varieties. Human beings engage in the *khidma* of God; worldly scholars devote themselves to the *khidma* of sultans; and children offer *khidma* to parents.[36] Similarly, a student of the religious sciences "should humble himself toward his teacher, and seek religious merit and honor by serving him."[37] Like al-Sulamī, al-Ghazālī also represents personal service as part of the spiritual training of the mystical aspirant, at least in its initial stages.[38] His discussion of the motif of "service" reflects all of the discourses encountered so far, including service as a mode of pious self-abnegation, "household management" as a motif rooted in Greek philosophical ethics, and service as a defining element in bilateral relationships of loyalty and subordination.

Although substantive or symbolic personal service played a central role in the articulation of hierarchical relationships among grandees, scholars, and Sufis, the primary context for the performance of daily life tasks was the household. Al-Ghazālī's attitude toward domestic service and the various menial tasks that it comprises is twofold. On the one hand, he regards some degree of self-abasement as an indispensable component of the spiritual path. Humility can be cultivated both through the performance lowly tasks (particularly when this occurs in public view) and through voluntary subordination to others; these components converge in the practice of *khidma*. He advises the reader to emulate the Prophet Muḥammad by engaging in such chores as tending domestic animals, mending clothes and sandals, and grinding flour;[39] he considers it a sign of self-conceit if a person "does not undertake with his own hands any work in his house."[40] He repeatedly describes high-status figures including the Prophet, caliphs, and prominent religious scholars performing humble tasks such as refilling the lamp or pouring water for a guest to wash his hands.[41] Nevertheless, cumulatively al-Ghazālī's many references to *khidma* or to the mundane tasks that it may comprise suggest that such acts of self-abasement are largely symbolic. On a practical level, household chores remain overwhelmingly associated with wives and servants.

As Zahra Ayubi has demonstrated in detail, when relegated to women or to lower-class men, *khidma* is divested of its ethical significance and instead defined as a mundane burden unworthy of elite males.[42] As is well known, in the *Iḥyāʾ* al-Ghazālī asserts that providing household service is one of the core functions of a wife.[43] The fourth benefit he enumerates in his discussion of marriage (after procreation, sexual satisfaction, and emotional refreshment) is

> freeing the heart from preoccupation with the management of the household (*tadbīr al-manzil*) and being responsible for the work of cooking, sweeping, spreading [bedding], washing dishes, and preparing the means of living. It would be impossible for a person to live in his home alone even if he did not desire sexual intercourse because if he were responsible for all of the household tasks most of his time would be wasted and he would have no leisure for knowledge or [pious] action. In this way a good woman who keeps the household in order is an aid to religion.[44]

It is notable that here and in other passages of the *Iḥyāʾ*, in discussing the duties of a wife al-Ghazālī uses the phrase *tadbīr al-manzil* (household management) or the close variant *tadbīr al-bayt* (management of the home).[45] As we have seen, this usage directly evokes the terminology of Arabic translations of works from the Greek philosophical tradition.[46] Simon Swain notes that although al-Ghazālī's depiction of the wife's role in the household is clearly derived, whether directly or indirectly, from that of the Greek philosopher Bryson, al-Ghazālī's is a far humbler vision of wifely duties; here the wife is directly engaged in household chores rather than acting as a manager and executive.[47]

As Ayubi has demonstrated, the model of philosophical ethics posits that the path of perfection is pursued not through bodily engagement in tasks that humble the spirit but through the leisure that enables rarefied contemplation. It is women and non-elite men who perform the labors that free up elite men for this pursuit.[48] Al-Ghazālī draws on the *falsafa* tradition to emphasize what Ayubi has termed "the construction of instrumental femininity in relation to rational masculinity, and the construction of elite masculinity in the context of homosocial relationships among men."[49] Indeed, in her function of freeing of a socially and spiritually elite man for more elevated pursuits, a wife is interchangeable with a male servant or volunteer.

In the *Iḥyā'*, al-Ghazālī enumerates "being served" (*al-istikhdām*) as one of the legitimate benefits of wealth, noting that "the tasks that are required for a person to prepare his means [of living] are many, and if he were to undertake them himself his time would be wasted and it would be impossible for him to follow the path of the next world."[50] To avail oneself of someone else's service in order to free one's time and attention for higher pursuits is thus not merely permissible, but godly. In al-Ghazālī's view, it is a virtue if one "loves the person who personally serves him (*yakhdimuhu bi-nafsihi*) by washing his clothes, sweeping his house, and cooking his food, and by that means affords him the leisure (*yufarrighuhu*) for [the acquisition of] knowledge or for [pious] action."[51] One should not personally take on a menial task such as washing one's clothes out of fear that it may not be done properly (a religious concern for reasons of ritual purity). To accept the voluntary help of a commoner (*ʿāmmī*) with such a task is licit for the recipient and meritorious for the commoner.[52] Indeed, the necessity for such hierarchical relationships mitigates the religious prohibition of the love of prestige (*jāh*). Nevertheless, al-Ghazālī warns that this is a slippery slope and that it may be preferable to hire a servant who will perform these tasks for wages rather than out of respect for one's perceived status.[53] Overall, humble service is both a path to moral self-improvement and a waste of time that the elite male audience of the *Iḥyā'* should relegate to those incapable of the heights of moral self-refinement. In al-Ghazālī's synthesis of law, Sufism, and philosophical ethics, *khidma* thus plays an ambiguous role that varies according to the gender and status of the individual.

The *Iḥyā'* is a work dating to the later years of al-Ghazālī's life, so we cannot directly juxtapose it with his earlier legal writings. However, it is worth noting that as a Shāfiʿī jurist al-Ghazālī acknowledges that, legally speaking, high-status wives are exempt from any obligation to provide domestic labor.[54] In the *Iḥyā'* (as in his other ethical works), in contrast, wives in general are pervasively associated with the performance of housework;[55] only in passing does he note the possibility that selection of a high-status wife will lead to the husband's being deprived of her service.[56] While it is possible that al-Ghazālī might have incorporated his mature ethical and mystical views into his later legal interpretations, it seems equally likely that for him these discourses simply addressed different concerns. The remainder of this chapter explores the views of a Ḥanafī jurist who, unlike al-Ghazālī, incorporated some of the ethical resonances of *khidma* into his legal analysis of labor obligations within the household.

Domestic labor in the *Mabsūṭ* of al-Sarakhsī

The remainder of this chapter examines the theme of domestic service in the magisterial legal work *Al-Mabsūṭ* ("The Extensive [Legal Manual]") of the influential Ḥanafī Shams al-Aʾimma al-Sarakhsī, who lived and worked in Transoxania.[57] Very little is known about al-Sarakhsī's life. He is known to have dictated his voluminous survey of Ḥanafī legal doctrine *Al-Mabsūṭ* from prison, having fallen afoul of the Qarakhanid ruler of Uzjand for reasons not clearly explained in the available sources. The composition of this work seems to have been spread over the fourteen years that he spent in prison between 466/1074 and 479/1087. Formally, it is a commentary on Muḥammad ibn Muḥammad al-Marwazī's (d. 334/946) abridgment (*Mukhtaṣar*) of the works of the early Ḥanafī authority Muḥammad ibn al-Ḥasan al-Shaybānī (d. 189/805).[58]

As we have seen in chapter 2, the Shāfiʿī interpretation of the marriage contract posited that the husband's provision of maintenance (*nafaqa*) directly compensated the wife for her continuing obligation to be available for sexual enjoyment (*istimtāʿ*). This model excluded the wife's labor, which was simply not involved in the contractual exchange. As a Ḥanafī, al-Sarakhsī worked on a quite different set of basic assumptions about the exchange of rights and duties under the marriage contract. Rather than conceptualizing the wife's sexual capacity (known as the *buḍʿ*) as a usufruct that was paid for on an ongoing basis by the husband's provision of maintenance, he approached it as a substance that was exchanged for the dower (*mahr*) in a one-time transaction. This raised the question of what it was that the husband was receiving in exchange for his continuing provision of maintenance. The answer, in the Ḥanafī view, was that *nafaqa* compensated the wife for devoting her time to her husband to the exclusion of other activities. While maintenance did not directly pay the wife for domestic labor, in this model it paid her for full-time preoccupation with the husband and his household—a preoccupation that was obliquely (and sometimes quite explicitly) understood to involve housework. Nevertheless, no payment directly compensated the wife for her labor; housework in this model was not a contractual obligation secured by a specific countervalue but a moral obligation embedded in wider assumptions about hierarchical duties within the family. In the following, we follow al-Sarakhsī's argumentation in detail.

Domestic labor and the logic of the marriage contract in *al-Mabsūṭ*

Like the Shāfiʿī al-Māwardī (and, indeed, like classical jurists in general), al-Sarakhsī interprets the marriage contract as a sale-like exchange in which the husband's payment of the dower purchases control over the wife's sexual capacity, metonymically represented by the "vulva" (*al-buḍʿ*).[59] However, whereas Shāfiʿīs understood the object of this transaction to be a usufruct (*manfaʿa*), as a Ḥanafī, al-Sarakhsī argues passionately that it is to be regarded as a substance (*ʿayn*).[60] What is at stake in this rather technical distinction between substance and usufruct? On one level, very little. Indeed, al-Sarakhsī openly acknowledges that the Ḥanafī doctrine is a legal fiction; the *buḍʿ* acquired in marriage simply has the formal status (*ḥukm*) of a substance rather than literally being one. As he frankly notes in passing, "what is claimed through sexual intercourse (*al-mustawfā bi'l-waṭʾ*) is actually a usufruct."[61] Nevertheless, the categorization of the *buḍʿ* as a substance carries significance. Al-Sarakhsī points to the fact that Islamic precepts treat illicit sexual use of one's own or another's body very differently than the misappropriation of other capacities, such as labor.[62] Conceptualizing the *buḍʿ* as a substance also emphasizes the sale-like quality of the marital transaction over its rent-like aspect, an emphasis that underlines the enduring nature of the contract. Due to the Shi'ite acceptance of time-limited marriage (*mutʿa*), the permanency (*taʾbīd*) of the marriage contract was a sensitive and symbolically important issue for Sunni jurists.[63]

For our purposes, the most important implication of the Ḥanafīs' decision to treat the *buḍʿ* as a substance is that it demanded a more explicit differentiation between the benefits accruing from the payment of dower (*ṣadāq* or *mahr*) and those accruing from the payment of ongoing spousal maintenance (*nafaqa*). In the Ḥanafī account, since the purchase of the *buḍ*ᶜ transfers ownership of an object-like asset, it should require no further payments for the continuing enjoyment of the item acquired through the sale. In al-Sarakhsī's account, the Shāfiᶜī approach is self-contradictory in that it treats both *ṣadāq* and *nafaqa* as compensation to the wife for sexual access, thus stipulating two kinds of payment for the same underlying asset. To al-Sarakhsī, this is an unsatisfactory approach that ultimately fails to explain why the husband must provide maintenance at all. If *nafaqa* is not compensation for ongoing sexual access (*istimtā*ᶜ), he reasons, then logically it is not a countervalue (*ᶜiwaḍ*) at all. This reasoning has wide-ranging implications for the Ḥanafī understanding of *nafaqa*.

Al-Sarakhsī writes,

> Maintenance is not a countervalue (*ᶜiwaḍ*) of the *buḍ*ᶜ (i.e., the right to sexual access); the dower (*mahr*) is the countervalue of the *buḍ*ᶜ, and one thing does not require two countervalues in the same contract. In addition, whatever is the countervalue of *buḍ*ᶜ must come due all at one time, because [possession of] the right to sexual access accrues to the husband all at one time. [Maintenance] also cannot be the countervalue of sexual enjoyment (*al-istimtā*ᶜ) and the exercise of authority over [the wife] (*al-qiyām ᶜalayhā*) because that is [the husband's] free disposition of his property (*taṣarruf minhu fī milkihi*), so it requires no countervalue from him. Thus, we know that it functions as an obligatory gift (*ṣila*).[64]

Al-Sarakhsī's reasoning here is, first, that *nafaqa* cannot be compensating the wife for the initial right of sexual access; this is paid for by the dower, and the husband cannot be required to pay for it in two different ways. Furthermore, if the husband has purchased sexual access to his wife once and for all, he cannot be understood to owe ongoing payments to avail himself of this access; that would be like requiring him to rent an item that he already owns. Al-Sarakhsī concludes from this process of elimination that a wife's maintenance is not a form of payment for a specific prerogative accruing to the husband in the marriage contract at all; rather, it is a *ṣila*—an obligatory transfer without any direct countervalue.[65]

Categorizing *nafaqa* as a *ṣila* has concrete implications for the law of maintenance, including the issue of expenses for domestic help. According to Ḥanafī doctrine, maintenance is not set at a determinate amount (as it would be if it were a countervalue) but gauged to the fulfillment of the wife's needs (*al-kifāya*).[66] As we have seen in chapter 2, as a Shāfiʿī, al-Māwardī approaches the husband's provision of the food component of *nafaqa* as the transfer of an asset owed to the wife pursuant to the marriage contract. Accordingly, he prefers that it be delivered in the form of unprocessed grain as a commodity that she can store and even sell. In contrast, as a Ḥanafī, al-Sarakhsī emphasizes that the husband is obligated to directly fill the wife's personal needs by providing her with food in edible form. This in turn implies that husband is responsible (at least financially) for one major form of household labor, the work of processing the wife's food—by a professional miller or baker or, when appropriate, by the wife's own servant. Following the precedent set by earlier Ḥanafī authorities, al-Sarakhsī writes, "If [the wife] has a servant, the judge imposes [on the husband the maintenance costs] for one servant because the husband needs to take care of her needs (*li'anna al-zawj muḥtāj ilā al-qiyām bi-ḥawāʾijihā*), and the minimum of that is for him to prepare her food; her servant does that in his place (*yanūb ʿanhu fī dhālika*), so he is required to pay the maintenance for her servant in the amount that is customary (*bi'l-maʿrūf*)."[67]

It is certainly open to question whether Shāfiʿī wives actually received measures of unprocessed grain while Ḥanafī wives received their meals ready to eat. What is definite is that there was a significant difference in the ways in which scholars of the two schools conceptualized *nafaqa*. Whereas al-Māwardī (like other Shāfiʿīs) treats *nafaqa* as a financial asset to which the wife is contractually entitled regardless of whether she requires or consumes it, al-Sarakhsī (like other Ḥanafīs) treats it as a form of personal care directly based on the wife's individual needs. This personal care includes the provision of food that is actually edible, which entails the husband's responsibility for the costs of food processing.

The Ḥanafī categorization of *nafaqa* as a *ṣila* rather than a countervalue affects not only their analysis of its quantity and nature but their fundamental rationale for spousal maintenance. As we have seen in chapter 2, al-Māwardī sees *nafaqa* as a countervalue (*ʿiwaḍ*) for the husband's ongoing sexual access to his wife (*istimtāʿ*); this direct reciprocal relationship between sexual access and material support pervasively informs his legal argumentation. As a Ḥanafī, al-Sarakhsī does not understand *nafaqa* as a countervalue for the wife's sexual availability. However, neither can he interpret it as strictly a response to the wife's need; like all other classical Islamic jurists, he recognizes that spousal maintenance (unlike the *ṣila* due to indigent kin) is incumbent on the husband regardless of the wife's poverty or wealth. This discrepancy is not lost on al-Sarakhsī, who explains, "A poor [relative's] entitlement to maintenance from the one who is wealthy and has means is based on need (*al-ḥāja*) because neither of two [relatives] with means is more entitled than the other to be assigned maintenance from the other. This differs from the maintenance of a wife; she is entitled to it on the basis of the contract because she devotes all of her time to him (*li-tafrīghihā nafsihā lahu*)."[68]

In this interpretation, a wife is entitled to support in consideration of the opportunity cost of making herself constantly available to her husband. (It is notable that al-Sarakhsī affirms this logic despite his repeated assertion that women are in any case incapable of supporting themselves; as he pungently declares at one point, "If a woman were told to earn [her living], she would earn it with her genitals."[69])

The view that *nafaqa* compensates a wife for devoting her time to her husband at the expense of other pursuits gives rise to a legal analogy with officials who offer services to the Muslim community. Al-Sarakhsī writes in another passage that maintenance is due to the wife

> because she is detained (*maḥbūsa*) for the interests of the husband and devotes herself exclusively to him. Thus, she is entitled to a sufficiency (*al-kifāya*) from his wealth. [She is] like the collector of alms-tax who, because he has devoted himself to work on behalf of the poor, is entitled to a sufficiency from their wealth [that is, from the alms taxes], and like the judge who, because he has devoted himself to the work of the Muslims, is entitled to a sufficiency from their wealth.[70]

Sarakhsī's observation that a wife is "like" (*ka-*) a tax collector or judge places marriage within a series of structurally similar relationships where someone is retained to perform a service on behalf of someone else outside of the parameters defining a legitimate contract of hire (*istiʾjār*). Such a person is entitled to a need-based stipend but should not draw a fixed wage.

In the Ḥanafī model elaborated by al-Sarakhsī, it is legally problematic for officials such as judges and prayer leaders to draw a salary for their services both because of direct textual prohibitions and because the duties violate the Ḥanafī guidelines for contracts of hire (*istiʾjār*).[71] On the one hand, the exact nature and extent of the tasks to be performed by the employee are indeterminate. On the other hand, they constitute acts of piety that should not be performed for financial benefit.[72] (The relevance of each consideration varies in each instance; the duties of a prayer leader are less indeterminate than those of a *qadi*—congregational prayers, unlike legal cases, occur in specific quantities at specific times—but they are more purely defined as acts of piety.)

However, in each case al-Sarakhsī (like other members of his school) argues that it is permissible for such an official to receive support payments from the treasury. Like the wife's *nafaqa* (as understood by the Ḥanafīs), this payment should ideally be calibrated to the needs of the individual and his family rather than set at a specified level, because it is not a wage; that is, it is not conceptualized as a direct countervalue (*ʿiwaḍ*) of services performed. The rationale for the legitimacy of paying a need-based stipend (*irtizāq*, as opposed to *istiʾjār*) to a public official is that he has devoted himself full time to performing a task on behalf of the public, to the exclusion of other activities.[73] Such a person is entitled to a stipend because his duties prevent him from earning a living by other means;[74] he is being paid not directly for his labor but for the opportunity cost of his availability. The key term in this context is *farragha/tafrīgh li-*, which literally means "to render oneself unoccupied for"; in context, it means to free oneself up for a given duty at the expense of other possible pursuits. It is this term that al-Sarakhsī consistently uses to refer to the wife's full-time devotion to her husband, which justifies her entitlement to maintenance.[75]

In other passages, al-Sarakhsī makes parallel arguments about *muʾadhdhins*, prayer leaders, muftis, and soldiers.[76] The case of the wife also appears (along with that of the judge or the tax collector) as a model for more specialized cases. Thus, al-Sarakhsī notes that a contract to perform the *ḥajj* on behalf of another person is illegitimate and void; however, if someone does perform the pilgrimage at another person's behest and for his benefit, he is entitled to maintenance from that person's wealth despite the invalidity of the contract:

> He is not entitled to this maintenance (*nafaqa*) by way of countervalue (*ʿiwaḍ*) but is entitled to a sufficiency (*kifāya*) because he devoted himself to a work from which the person who [invalidly] hired him benefits; so he is entitled to a sufficiency from his wealth, like the judge who is entitled to a sufficiency from the

> treasury, the tax collector who is entitled to a sufficiency from the alms funds, and the woman who is entitled to maintenance from the husband's wealth, not by way of countervalue.[77]

Here the stipend received by the agent is not conceived as a contractually required payment for his work but as deserved support that sustains him while he devotes himself to someone else's interests.

If a judge receives a stipend because he has made himself available for adjudication, and if a prayer leader receives a stipend because he has made himself available to lead regular congregational worship, for what purpose is a wife understood to have made herself available? As we have seen, al-Māwardī makes a similar argument that a wife is entitled to maintenance from her husband because "her usufructs are reserved for him (*al-zawja maḥbūsat al-manāfiʿ ʿalayhi*) and she is prevented from freely disposing [of them] because of his entitlement to sexual enjoyment of her (*li-ḥaqqihi fī'l-istimtāʿ bihā*)."[78] However, al-Sarakhsī posits that she has already been compensated for sexual access with the dower. Although he does not elaborate on the point in detail, he notes repeatedly in passing that a wife is entitled to maintenance because she devotes herself full time to the care of her husband and his home. In one place he states straightforwardly that the cause (*sabab*) of the wife's right to *nafaqa* is not the marriage contract (*al-ʿaqd*, i.e., the exchange of dower for the wife's *buḍʿ*) "but her devoting herself to the service (*khidma*) of the husband."[79] In another, he asserts that "the divine law (*al-sharʿ*) made [the husband] liable for [the wife's] maintenance so that she would take care of his housework (*khidmat baytihi*)."[80] In other passages, his language is less specific; in a number of different places he suggests that a wife is entitled to support because she "devotes herself to [her husband's] interests" (*tafrīghihā nafsahā li-maṣāliḥihi*).[81] The vagueness of al-Sarakhsī's comments regarding the wife's household duties reflects his legal argument that *nafaqa* is not a wage for specific services but a consideration for the wife's general occupation with her husband's needs.

Throughout the *Mabsūṭ*, al-Sarakhsī's operating assumption is that a wife's time is spent catering to her husband's welfare. For instance, he notes that women are exempted from the obligation of Friday congregational prayer in part because "a woman is busy serving her husband" (*al-marʾa . . . mashghūla bi-khidmat al-zawj*).[82] In justifying the rule that a divorced woman loses custody of her child if she remarries, he notes that "when she marries, she becomes occupied with the service of her [new] husband, so she does not have leisure to take care of the child."[83] If a woman hires a slave for service (*khidma*), she is entitled to have the servant work for her spouse as well as herself because "she is obligated to serve her husband," and she is assumed to have hired the help in part to relieve her of this burden.[84]

Domestic labor as an ethico-religious obligation

It is important to note that al-Sarakhsī does not consider the wife to be *contractually* obligated to provide household services. In his view, the marriage contract specifically comprises the exchange of dower for the husband's entitlement to sexual access to the wife. However, this does not mean that he believes wives to be exempt from housework. Rather, he understands the exchange of these considerations within the marriage contract (i.e., the dower for the *buḍʿ*) as a discrete transaction that does not exhaust the functions and objectives of marriage. In this context, he makes a distinction between two kinds of obligation incumbent on the wife, only one of which is contractual and binding but both of which are integral to his understanding of the marital relationship. The issue arises most prominently in his discussion of breastfeeding. In al-Sarakhsī's Ḥanafī view, a mother who remains married to the father of her child is not obligated to provide breastfeeding for their child, but neither can she claim payment for it. He writes:

> While [the husband and wife] remain married, she is not entitled to a wage for breastfeeding [their] child, according to our [Ḥanafī] doctrine, even if he were to hire her [to do so; that is, the contract would be void]. [This is] because while the marriage exists breastfeeding is one of the tasks that are religiously (*dīnan*) incumbent upon her; [in contrast,] after separation that is incumbent on her neither as a matter of religion (*dīnan*) nor as an enforceable obligation (*daynan*, literally "as a debt"). . . . If they are not separated she is entitled to no wage for breastfeeding, but if she refuses to breastfeed she is not compelled to do that, because what is incumbent upon her by virtue of the marriage [contract, *al-nikāḥ*] is for her to make herself available (*taslīm al-nafs*) to the husband for sexual enjoyment (*al-istimtāʿ*); she is ordered (*tuʾmar*) to do all other tasks—such as sweeping the house, washing clothes, cooking and baking, and similarly breastfeeding—as

> a matter of religion (*tadayyunan*) and is not forced to perform them as a matter of law (lit., "as a legal verdict," *ḥukman*).[85]

Taking up the subject of payment for breastfeeding in another section of the *Mabsūṭ*, al-Sarakhsī observes that "the decisive factor[86] in [this issue] is that this task is incumbent upon her as a matter of religion (*dīnan*) even if it is not incumbent upon her as an enforceable obligation (*daynan*); she is asked to do it as an advisory opinion (fatwa) but is not forced to do it as a matter of compulsion (*lā tujbar ʿalayhi kurhan*)."[87]

In these two passages, there is a systematic contrast between duties that are owed "as a matter of religion" (*dīnan*) and those that are owed "as a debt" (*daynan*); this play on two words derived from the same Arabic root separates moral obligations from ones that, like a monetary debt, can be extracted involuntarily through the intervention of a judge.[88] The degree to which the Arabic term *dīn* corresponds to the English term *religion* is, of course, limited; indeed, in its full contemporary sense "religion" is a distinctively modern and Western category.[89] However, recent scholarship that explores the historical usage of the Arabic term *dīn* (rather than excavating the genealogy of the English word "religion") suggests that there are nevertheless significant overlaps in the two terms' semantic fields. Rushain Abbasi observes that in medieval Islamic texts the adjectival form *dīnī* functions as a complement to *dunyawī* ("this-worldly"), concluding "that the medieval *dīn–dunyā* binary represented a conceptual separation of the world into distinct religious and non-religious spheres analogous to the modern religious–secular, with things like worship, prayer, and divine law on one side and all worldly matters on the other."[90] Focusing specifically on Ḥanafī legal terminology, Junaid Quadri has shown that the category of "*umūr dīnīya*" designates "those matters which are oriented toward the afterlife," contrasted with "worldly (*dunyawī*) matters that occur between people, and so raise the possibility of interpersonal conflict."[91] In contrast with Abbasi, Quadri argues that "this division between this-worldly and other-worldly ones is distinct from, and ought not to be confused with, the 'religious/secular' dichotomy," in part because the modern European category of the "secular" is predicated on a division of "this world" "into the religious world (the church) and the secular world proper (*saeculum*)."[92] In the context of al-Sarakhsī's arguments about wives' marital obligations, the qualifier *dīnan* can be understood to designate obligations the woman has toward God (a category

Ḥanafī terminology also designates as *baynahu wa-bayna Allāh* ["between (the individual) and God"][93]), as contrasted with interpersonal claims that could be adjudicated by a judge.[94]

The distinction al-Sarakhsī makes here between what I will call "ethico-religious" obligations and legal ones recurs elsewhere in *al-Mabsūṭ*, with the label *dīn* designating that which is morally right in contrast to that which is judicially enforceable.[95] For instance, he states that a property owner is entitled to the free use of his or her own property even in cases where this may harm a neighbor. Although the neighbor has no legal recourse against the free exercise of property rights, al-Sarakhsī notes that the angel Gabriel himself has enjoined consideration for one's neighbor; "refraining from bad treatment one's neighbor is obligatory as a matter of religion, but one is not compelled to do it as a matter of law (*fi'l-ḥukm*)."[96] Similarly, if a Muslim sojourns in hostile non-Muslim territory under the protection of a safe conduct (*amān*) and misappropriates the wealth of a nonbeliever there, the latter has no legal recourse against him if they then both enter Muslim jurisdiction. However, al-Sarakhsī states that such behavior is repugnant as a matter of *dīn* because the Prophet forbade treachery.[97] In these cases, a gap opens between conduct that is legally permissible and conduct that is morally admirable.

Al-Sarakhsī draws a closely related distinction between directing a wife to perform certain tasks as an advisory opinion (fatwa) and doing so as a legal verdict (*ḥukm*). This terminology also recurs in other contexts within the *Mabsūṭ*. Earlier in the passage discussed above, al-Sarakhsī states that if a Muslim borrows or misappropriates something from a non-Muslim in hostile non-Muslim territory, "he is legally advised to return it (*yuftā bi'l-radd*) but is not compelled to do so as a judicial verdict (*lā yujbar ʿalayhi fi'l-ḥukm*)."[98] The contrast between fatwa and *ḥukm* may be surprising in the light of al-Sarakhsī's clear declaration that "adjudication (*qaḍāʾ*) is in reality the issuing of legal advice (fatwa), except that it is binding (*mulzim*)."[99] The incongruity disappears if we understand the fatwa and the verdict as communicating the same overall doctrine in two different performative situations. The mufti, whose role is to provide nonbinding information about an inquirer's obligations, might truthfully tell a wife either "You should cook" or (more informatively) "You have a non-enforceable obligation to cook." The qadi, whose role is to reach binding legal verdicts, would either simply decline to enforce a demand that she cook or tell her that she cannot be compelled to do so. While substantively consistent with each other, the two could thus contrast sharply in their overt articulation. In effect, the fatwa would tell her that she ought to cook, while the *ḥukm* would tell her that she need not do so.

Although the contrast between religious and legal obligations is potentially applicable to a range of legal issues (and is thus distributed broadly, if sparsely, though the *Mabsūṭ*), it is most often elicited by concerns about the legitimacy of payment for specific kinds of activity. This concern arises from the general Ḥanafī doctrine regarding contracts of hire (*isti'jār*), which (as we have seen) holds that a person cannot validly contract to receive wages for a task that he or she is already religiously obligated to perform. It is for this reason that, Ḥanafīs hold, one cannot validly hire oneself out as a prayer leader or a Qur'an reader.[100] This principle was extrapolated to other tasks for which an individual could be understood to have a preexisting religious obligation. For instance, al-Sarakhsī observes that "if a Muslim rents from another Muslim a house in which to perform the obligatory prayers . . . it is not permissible and he is entitled to no rent," in part because "it is incumbent on every Muslim as a matter of religion to give another Muslim access to a place to pray when he needs it."[101] Similarly, one cannot contract to receive wages for teaching a fellow Muslim the Qur'an because "every Muslim is [already] commanded to do it as a matter of religion." In contrast, one can claim wages for other kinds of teaching because there is no religious imperative to do so for free; "it is a task whose performance is not [already] incumbent upon the teacher as a matter of religion or law (*dīnan wa-lā daynan*)."[102] The preexisting obligations in these cases are not legally actionable. One cannot legally demand access to another person's home in order to pray, nor can one obtain a court order compelling him or her to provide instruction in the Qur'an. The religious obligation to provide prayer space or to teach scripture is sanctionable only in an otherworldly forum. However, these religious obligations have a concrete legal consequence, which is the invalidity of a contract to receive wages for these actions.

Al-Sarakhsī treats wives' domestic labor in the same way: it cannot be the object of a valid contract of hire since there is a preexisting, if legally unenforceable, obligation. As he writes in connection with breastfeeding, "Hiring (*al-isti'jār*) [one's wife] for something of this kind is not permissible, like hiring [her] to sweep the house or to kiss or touch [her husband][103] or something of that kind."[104] While it may seem obvious (or at least uncontroversial) to assert that there is a religious obligation to teach a fellow believer the Qur'an, it is less obvious that wives have a preexisting duty to provide labor to their husbands. As we have seen above, regarding the prior obligations of teachers al-Sarakhsī distinguishes between a religious duty and one grounded in custom; a contract of hire is rendered invalid by either one. In the case of wives' duty to care for their husbands (including the provision of various kinds of domestic labor), he asserts that there is both a textually grounded religious obligation and one based on customary practice. He places this argument within a larger analysis of duties of service within the immediate family.

Al-Sarakhsī writes:

> If a husband hires his wife to serve him for a stated wage every month, it is not valid because the housework (*khidmat al-bayt*) is incumbent upon her religiously and required of her customarily by virtue of the marriage [contract] (*wa-maṭlūb minhā bi'l-nikāḥ ʿurfan*), according to the report that when the Prophet (peace be upon him!) married [his daughter] Fāṭima and ʿAlī (may God be satisfied with them!), he assigned the tasks inside the house to her and those outside of the house to him, and because the divine law (*al-sharʿ*) made [the husband] liable for [the wife's] maintenance so that she would take care of his housework (*khidmat baytihi*), so she is not entitled to an additional wage for that, even if it is stated [in a contract of hire]. [In contrast], if he hires her to breastfeed a child of his from another [woman], to tend his livestock, or to do [any] task other than housework it is valid, because this task is not incumbent upon her and not expected from her by virtue of the marriage [contract].[105]

In asserting a direct Prophetic mandate for a gendered division of labor within the marital household, al-Sarakhsī is perpetuating a report that by his time had already been thoroughly marginalized in the evolving field of hadith studies. The claim that the Prophet had assigned the housework to Fāṭima was a time-honored one but lacked a full or reputable chain of transmission.[106] Despite the lack of credence this report received from hadith specialists, however, it continued to be cited in Ḥanafī legal works for generations after al-Sarakhsī.[107] As Behnam Sadeghi has argued in the context of ritual law, it was only in the Mamluk period that Ḥanafī scholars undertook the systematic elimination of ill-authenticated hadith (or even reports that were never documented as hadith at all) from the school's legal argumentation.[108] In addition to adducing a binding precedent set by the Prophet Muḥammad, in this passage al-Sarakhsī directly asserts that a wife receives maintenance from her husband in exchange for her domestic labor. This is a claim that, as we have seen, he more often suggests obliquely than states overtly. Its casual incorporation into his larger argument here supports the idea that it may represent al-Sarakhsī's intuitive understanding of the marital bargain.

The wife's obligation to do housework is gendered and asymmetrical; al-Sarakhsī continues:

> If the woman hires her husband to serve her, it is valid because serving her is not incumbent upon the husband. [Muḥammad ibn al-Ḥasan al-Shaybānī] said in his *Kitāb al-Āthār*[109] that he is entitled to refuse to serve [her] because it is degrading for him to serve his wife, and that is a [valid] excuse to void the contract of hire. . . . If [the husband] does serve her [on the basis of the invalid contract], he receives the wage for it. The same is true if she hires him to tend her sheep or to do [any other] work for her; with respect to that he is like [any] other unrelated person (*ajnabī*).[110]

On the one hand, a husband can validly contract to receive wages for household labor he performs on behalf of his wife because he has no preexisting moral obligation to do so. On the other hand, such a contract would nevertheless be subject to annulment at the husband's discretion because such a contract would violate the proper gender hierarchy between the spouses. A similar point arises in another passage of the *Mabsūṭ*, where al-Sarakhsī discusses the scenario of a husband who contracts to serve his wife for a year by way of dower. He notes that some jurists distinguish a contract for the husband to serve his wife (which they reject) and a contract for him to tend her sheep, on the grounds that "she is commanded to honor [her husband] and show deference to his claims (*turāʿī ḥaqqahu*), and that is negated by her using him for service, and for that reason serving her cannot validly be a dower. The same is not true of tending [animals]; don't you see that a son cannot hire his father for service but can hire him for another kind of work?"[111]

Al-Sarakhsī continues his discussion of contracts for work within the family to consider other kinship relationships. The moral expectation of domestic service is not limited to wives but extends to other subordinate members of the household. Here again, the obligation arises both from ethico-religious principles and from social custom. Al-Sarakhsī continues:

> If a man hires his son to serve him in his house, it is not valid and [the son] is entitled to no wage because serving the father is incumbent on the son as a matter of religion and he is required to do so as a matter of custom, so he cannot take a wage for it; [demanding a wage] is considered unfilial conduct (*ʿuqūq*), and unfilial conduct is forbidden (*ḥarām*). The same is true if his mother hires him because he has an even greater obligation to serve her [than his father]; she needs it more and is more compassionate to him. If one of [the parents] hires him to have him tend sheep or to do something other than domestic service (*khidma*), it is valid; that is not [religiously] incumbent upon him, nor is it required according to custom.
>
> If a son hires his father, his mother, his grandfather, or his grandmother to serve him, it is not valid because he is forbidden to use these [people] for service (*istikhdām*) because of the degradation (*idhlāl*) it involves, so it is not permissible for him to become entitled to that from them by virtue of the contract of hire. . . . However, if [one of these people] does any of that work, [that person] receives the wage because after [the son or grandson] used [him or her] for service, the element of degradation would in it would be greater if he were not liable for the wage.[112]

Al-Sarakhsī goes on to examine various special cases in which the filial obligations of children to parents are modified by the enslaved or non-Muslim status of one or both of the parties. Although the filial duties of an enslaved son are superseded by his obligations to his master, a father's rights are not erased even by enslavement or unbelief.[113]

Al-Sarakhsī continues to specify that not all familial relationships entail obligations of service or preclude free contracting of the two parties' labor. Unlike the coerced labor extracted from an enslaved person, working for a wage is compatible with the dignity of free kin:

> Contracts of hire for service are valid between siblings and all other relatives, just as they are valid between unrelated persons, unlike requiring service by virtue of ownership [of a slave]; that [i.e., the service of a slave] is established by means of coercion (*bi-ṭarīq al-qahr*) without the agreement of the servant, and this is incompatible with close kinship (*al-qarāba al-qarība tuṣān ʿan mithlihi*). As

> for this [i.e., a contract of hire], it is a contract based on mutual agreement, and using someone for service on the basis of mutual agreement is not a cause of the severing of ties of kinship (*qaṭīʿat al-raḥm*) between them.[114]

This series of examples revolves around the principle that ties of kinship entail certain obligations and are incompatible with certain kinds of treatment. These obligations are not legally enforceable but nevertheless have concrete legal consequences; for instance, it is because a person is religiously (*dīnan*) obligated to serve his father and mother that he cannot legally contract to receive a wage for doing so. The frequent and consistent invocation of the concept of "religious" obligation in the specific context of labor relations among close kin suggests that the family is an arena where this category is distinctively salient. Based on the distribution of references to "religious" duties within the *Mabsūṭ*, it is within the immediate family (both natal and marital) that one most often has duties that are broadly moral in nature, located in a domain of virtuous personhood that is ordinarily outside of the ambit of courtroom enforcement. Labor (particularly "service," *khidma*) plays a central role in this morally governed familial domain.[115]

Al-Sarakhsī's vision of the obligations of kinship is rooted in moral principles including filial piety (*birr al-wālidayn*) and the duty of kindness toward kin (*ṣilat al-raḥm*). In the course of his discussion, he also repeatedly asserts the axiom (supported by a Prophetic hadith) that "a believer may not degrade himself (*laysa li'l-muʾmin an yudhilla nafsahu*)."[116] The prohibition on self-abasement may seem unexpected in the context of a religious tradition that generally emphasizes humility and condemns self-aggrandizement. Although al-Sarakhsī does not explicitly justify it (beyond citing it as a dictum of the Prophet), it may best be understood first in terms of a religious commitment to human dignity and second in terms of the special status of the Muslim community.[117] In his analysis of the household, it also functions to establish that individuals should not relinquish the personal dignity to which they are rightfully entitled in the context of hierarchical relationships. He invokes this principle to support the rules that a husband should not serve his wife, a father his son, or a Muslim a nonbeliever.[118] A concern with the avoidance of degradation of the self or others (*dhull/dhulla, idhlāl*) is thus pervasive in al-Sarakhsī's analysis of labor relations within the family and of marriage in general.

Taken together, the rules relating to obligations of service among family members imply certain assumptions about the ways in which work both creates and expresses hierarchy. However, not all labor is the same in this regard. The most socially degrading form of labor is that provided involuntarily by an enslaved person for a master; the least is that provided based on a mutually negotiated contract. However, service (*khidma*) appears to be degrading even when freely contracted. Put differently, *khidma* appears to be inherently an expression of social deference, whereas other forms of labor may be treated as symbolically neutral.[119] Although the hierarchical implications of *khidma* are mitigated by the free contracting of one's labor, they are never fully dispelled. For instance, al-Sarakhsī writes that while it is legally valid for a Muslim to hire himself out for service to a non-Muslim, "it is undesirable (*yukrah*) for a Muslim to serve a nonbeliever because of the element of degradation involved in it."[120]

What exactly is "service" in this context, and why is it assumed to be inherently humiliating in ways that do not apply to shepherding sheep or other unspecified tasks? One distinctive quality of *khidma* is that it is understood to involve placing oneself fully at the disposal of another person rather than simply performing one or more discrete tasks; thus, a contract of service requires that one "deliver oneself" (*taslīm al-nafs*) to the employer, as a wife is expected to deliver herself to her husband.[121] Elsewhere in *al-Mabsūṭ*, al-Sarakhsī provides a discussion (closely based on that of al-Shaybānī, whose works are condensed in the base text of *al-Mabsūṭ*[122]) of the parameters of the work falling under a contract of *khidma*. The services enumerated include lighting lamps, bringing water for ablutions, spreading bedding, washing clothes, baking bread, feeding and milking livestock, drawing water from the well, and sewing (albeit only for consumption, not for sale).[123] Although al-Sarakhsī acknowledges that the precise components of *khidma* are dependent on prevailing custom, it thus generally involves waiting on someone in ways often associated with modern Western maids and valets. It also encompasses a variety of household chores, including some aspects of the care of domestic animals (implicitly, those tasks that—unlike pasturing, *raʿy*, which is repeatedly contrasted with *khidma*—can be performed within or in the immediate vicinity of the house).

It is the first category of tasks involved in *khidma*, personal services such as carrying a superior's ablution water and laying out his or her clothes, that most clearly suggests why it is such a central motif in the construction of hierarchies within the family. One suspects that it is these small acts of deference, rather than heavy household labor, that may be the prime referent of the word "service" as it applies to a child's duties vis-à-vis his or her parents. However, al-Sarakhsī seems uninterested in drawing these distinctions explicitly; personal service and household labor together constitute a single discursive category applicable to servants, wives, and children alike.

Providing labor for near relations is not a reciprocal and egalitarian duty but a unidirectional and hierarchical one. Within the circle of close kin, service of superiors is incumbent upon subordinates, and the service of inferiors is forbidden for superiors.[124] There is no obligation of *khidma* between peers and, correspondingly, no prohibition on their contracting for it among themselves. The obligation to provide service to a parent or a husband parallels an enslaved person's obligation to his or her master closely enough that it is necessary to consider various scenarios where the two might conflict. The hierarchical relationship of serving and being served should also ideally parallel that between nonbelievers and believers within a Muslim polity.

Overall, both the obligation to serve and the entitlement to service seem to have more to do with hierarchy than with gender. A child is obligated to serve both a father and a mother and prohibited from employing either of them for service (although the mother is regarded as having somewhat greater claims in terms of both needs and desert). The spousal relationship, however, is at least a partial exception to this general pattern: while the provision of *khidma* between spouses may proceed in both directions, it is unambiguously gendered. The husband's financing of some kinds of *khidma* for his (elite) wife is an integral part of his role as a male provider (and contributes to the discursive constitution of the wife as an economic dependent), while the wife's service obligation to the husband parallels other familial relationships of subordination and deference.[125] Spouses' obligations for *khidma* within marriage thus link gender and hierarchy in ways that do not necessarily apply to other kinship relationships (such as that between a son and his mother).

The ethics of marriage in Al-Mabṣūṭ

In the *Mabsūṭ*, al-Sarakhsī does not elaborate on the point that a wife "is not compelled" to cook or clean. If her obligation to provide these services is purely moral, is her engagement in them purely voluntary? And if so, what happens if she exercises her option to refrain? Clearly a judge will not order her back to work, but this does not clarify what options remain open to her husband. The somewhat later Transoxanian Ḥanafī Burhān al-Dīn Ibn Māza (d. 616/1219) suggests that al-Sarakhsī did address this question, and in no uncertain terms. He writes,

> Shams al-Aʾimma al-Sarakhsī said: If the wife refuses to bake bread, cook, and do housework, the husband is entitled to refuse [to give her] condiments to eat with her bread. [He may] give her wheat bread that can be eaten [by itself] and say, 'It is food, and I am obligated only [to provide] food'; similarly, if she asks for fruit, the husband is entitled to refuse to [give her] any fruit. If he gives her barley bread he must [provide] a condiment because it cannot be consumed [alone], but he is not compelled to do this as a judicial ruling (*fī'l-ḥukm*). If she performs the housework, the husband should provide these things for her; he is counseled to do this as a matter of religion (*diyānatan*), not of compulsion or law.[126]

As the grandson of a leading student of al-Sarakhsī's, Burhān al-Dīn Ibn Māza fell within his direct scholarly lineage; his transmission of this report thus has some credibility. Whether or not this is an authentic verbatim quotation from al-Sarakhsī, its content passed in his name into some of the most authoritative works of the later Ḥanafī tradition.[127]

Assuming that this quotation indeed expresses al-Sarakhsī's sentiments, it suggests that the moral obligations he envisioned were not merely a matter of personal choice and individual conscience. By suggesting that a husband might literally put his recalcitrant wife on a diet of bread and water, he introduced an element of coercion—although not the kind of official compulsion associated with a judicial verdict. More importantly, however, he suggested that legally enforceable obligations of the marriage contract represented only one element of a proper relationship between husband and wife. Spouses who limit themselves to the bare minimum of mutual duties mandated by the marriage contract, he implies, are left with a bleak life indeed. The supererogatory but indispensable household duties of the wife are balanced by similar duties on the part of the husband, who provides his wife with the comforts of life not as a matter of law but of moral obligation (*diyānatan*).

Indeed, in the *Mabsūṭ* al-Sarakhsī explicitly regards the specific rights and duties exchanged between the spouses under the marriage contract as only a fraction of the overall benefits of wedlock. Thus, in justifying the relevance of social parity between spouses (*kafāʾa*), he observes that marriage "comprises goals and objectives including companionship, affection, intimacy, and the establishment of family ties (*taʾsīs al-qarābāt*)."[128] What distinguishes the binding provisions of the marriage contract is not that they are the only (or even the most important) components of the marital relationship as a whole but that they are gendered goods that are legally exchanged between the two individuals rather than mutual benefits that are shared by them. In al-Sarakhsī's words, "the objective of marriage [as a legal contract] is the 'ownership of enjoyment' rather than any other objective; don't you see (*a-lā tarā*) that it is the exclusive prerogative of the husband, so that he must remunerate [her] for it, while the rest of the objectives accrue to them both?"[129]

Al-Sarakhsī's conviction that spouses have marital obligations extending beyond the enforceable provisions of the marriage contract reflects a broader Ḥanafī model of marriage. This point emerges most clearly from his discussion of the punishment of amputation for theft. According to al-Sarakhsī, al-Shāfiʿī maintains that the amputation penalty applies to thefts committed by one spouse against the other, "based on his principle that beyond the rights and obligations (*ḥuqūq*) of the marriage contract (*al-nikāḥ*), the two of them are like strangers (*ka'l-ajānib*)."[130] In contrast, the Ḥanafīs hold that neither spouse can be subject to amputation for theft of the other's property. This is because "according to our [Ḥanafī] doctrine, as a result of being spouses an element of unification is established between them (*yathbut bi-sabab al-zawjīya maʿnā al-ittiḥād baynahumā*); for this reason the testimony of either of them on behalf of the other is not accepted, and either one's making free with (*tabāsuṭ fī*) the property of the other is like a child's making free with the property of his parent."[131]

In al-Sarakhsī's account of the Ḥanafī model of marriage, the spouses' complementary contributions of labor to their shared household are an integral component of the unifying function of marriage, which extends beyond the limited entitlements and obligations involved in the marriage contract itself. In his discussion of legal witnessing, he argues that one of the reasons for the inadmissibility of either spouse's testimony on behalf of the other is

> that the marriage contract was legislated [by God, *mashrūʿ*] for the sake of this, which is that each of them be intimate with (*yaʾlaf*) the other, favor him or her, and prefer him or her to [all] other people; God alluded to this in His statement, "He created for you mates from yourselves that you may take comfort in them, and He ordained affection and mercy between you" (Q 30:21). [Marriage] was legislated for the sake of unification in taking care of the needs of [their shared] livelihood (*al-qiyām bi-maṣāliḥ al-maʿīsha*). For this reason the Messenger of God (peace be upon him!) assigned the tasks inside of the house to Fāṭima (may God be satisfied with her!) and the tasks outside of the house to ʿAlī (may God be satisfied with him!). By means of both of [the spouses] the needs of their livelihood are taken care of, so with respect to that they are[132] like one person. It should not be said that this unification between them is [limited] specifically to the rights/obligations (*ḥuqūq*) of the marriage contract[133] because the element of unification in the obligations of the marriage contract is incumbent [upon the spouses] as a matter of law (*sharʿan*), and what is beyond that is established by custom. It is manifest that each [spouse's] partiality for the other and preference for him or her over other people is the same as that between parents and children, or rather, even more manifest; a person may come into conflict with his parents to satisfy his wife, and a woman may take her father's money and give it to her husband. The proof of this is that each of them considers the other's interests to be his own.[134]

The "unification" (*ittiḥād*) alluded to in this passage is one of the rationales that al-Sarakhsī cites for the impermissibility of a wife's demanding payment for services rendered to her husband. Such compensation would be improper not only because the woman has a preexisting moral obligation for service but because she would in some sense be working for herself. Al-Sarakhsī writes,

> Through the marriage contract, a unification is established between them with respect to the objectives of marriage (*maqṣūd al-nikāḥ*); having a child is an objective of marriage, so by breastfeeding she is in effect working for herself, and she is not entitled to wages from the husband [even if it is stipulated] as a condition, as is the case with kissing, touching, and sexual intercourse. We hold the same opinion with respect to all other kinds of housework (*aʿmāl al-bayt*), such as cooking, baking bread, washing, and anything [else] from which both of them benefit; he does not become liable for wages [even if it is stipulated] as a condition.[135]

Similarly, he argues that a woman is entitled to no reward for returning her husband's escaped slave not only because she is in any case morally obligated to serve him but because "each one of them makes free with the other's property and considers his benefit (*khayr*) to be his own."[136]

As we have seen in chapter 2, the Shāfiʿī jurist al-Māwardī approached the issue of marriage in two different modes, the legal and the ethical; these two approaches found expression in works of separate genres that applied distinct frameworks and conventions to the analysis of the marital bond. In contrast, in the *Mabsūṭ* the two strands appear as distinct and yet integral components of the same discourse. Entitlements that can be demanded in court are clearly distinguished from unenforceable ethical ideals, but both are attributed to the same fundamental sources, and both form integral parts of al-Sarakhsī's overall *fiqh* project in the *Mabsūṭ*.

For al-Sarakhsī, what kinds of work a person should do, and for what others he or she should do it, are questions that engage fundamental debates about Islamic values. His legal discussion of labor relations within the family is complexly intertwined with morally charged issues of status, dignity, and human worth. His discussion of *khidma* emphasizes the ethico-religious value invested in the upholding of proper forms of hierarchy, encapsulated in concepts such as *birr/ʿuqūq* (filial versus unfilial conduct) and the avoidance of *idhlāl* (abasement). In this sense, his analysis reflects similar assumptions about personal service and moral personhood as the Sufi sources discussed at the beginning of this chapter. Such concerns are on one level relegated to a sphere of voluntary moral conduct. However, they have concrete legal implications in that they limit the freedom of contract of the individuals involved; even if a husband reached an agreement with his wife to pay her wages for housework, the agreement would be legally void.

Whereas al-Māwardī's ethical work explicitly drew on Greek philosophical precedents and terminology, at first glance al-Sarakhsī's legal and ethical discourses would seem to be much more homogeneous. The two elements of his argumentation are smoothly integrated within the fabric of the *Mabsūṭ* and overtly draw on the same authorizing discourses of Qur'an and hadith. However, on deeper examination it appears that al-Sarakhsī also drew directly or indirectly on the Greek philosophical tradition on household management. Al-Sarakhsī does not use the phrase "*tadbīr al-manzil*" that so clearly signaled al-Māwardī's engagement with Bryson and his philosophical analysis of the household. Nevertheless, his approach is deeply informed by its broader arguments and assumptions and contains near-verbatim echoes of its wording. It has long been known that Sarakhsī was familiar with at least some of the contents of this work, whether directly or through an intermediary.[137]

As we have seen, the overall structure of Bryson's work on household management places the married couple within the context of the material needs of the human person, which cannot be fulfilled by any individual in isolation. These needs are met through the interdependence and exchange of peoples pursuing different crafts as well as through the cooperation of the members of the household. Bryson's wife is a partner who manages the couple's assets in the husband's absence. He reasons that since "most of a man's business is outside of his estate. . . . the best thing for the man is to have a partner in his estate to possess it as he possesses it, to care for it as he cares, and to manage it as he manages."[138] Accordingly, God "established between [the spouses] a feeling of love and intimacy, which leads to the removal from each one of them of jealousy, rivalry, and meanness towards his companion with regard to the property which the one permits the other (to use) and over which the one gives the other unrestricted control in respect to its management." In short, He "made the two of them as if they were one person."[139]

As Simon Swain observes in his analysis of Bryson's legacy in the Arabo-Islamic literature, this text's analysis departs in significant ways from basic *fiqh* doctrines on marriage. He notes that "the concept that couples are a kind of economic unit, which shares benefits and goods, is . . . not part of the Hadith or the law."[140] Bryson is most distinctive in "setting the wife in an economic and managerial framework" and in his emphasis on the "emotional and affective relationship between wife and husband," neither of which is typical of the Islamic legal tradition at large.[141] Al-Sarakhsī's allusions to the broader moral objectives of marriage closely parallel Bryson's overall framework, a resemblance that is all the more striking because these elements of al-Sarakhsī's discussion so clearly diverge from the traditional *fiqh* model of the marriage contract.

Thus, in more than one place al-Sarakhsī argues that the two spouses are "like one person" (*ka-shakhṣ wāḥid*) with respect to caring for the needs of their shared livelihood (*maṣāliḥ al-maʿīsha*), a claim that directly parallels Bryson's argument that God "made the two . . . [spouses] as if they were one person" in the management of the household.[142] It is notable that the distinctive phrase "*maṣāliḥ al-maʿīsha*" also occurs in the passage that Michael Bonner has already identified as suggesting al-Sarakhsī's direct or mediated usage of Bryson.[143] Also very much in the spirit of Bryson is al-Sarakhsī's observation that "each of [the spouses] considers the other's interests to be his own," a fact that he relates directly to the emotional bonds uniting the couple.[144] Al-Sarakhsī sees this affectively grounded cooperation in fulfilling the household's material needs as a (or perhaps the) fundamental objective of wedlock, writing that "marriage was instituted for the sake of survival (*al-baqāʾ*); it is by it that progeny is perpetuated, and similarly survival [is ensured] through taking care of the needs of [the household's] livelihood."[145] The wife's care for her husband and his needs appears in this context of human interdependence as an integral part of marriage. Overall, as we have seen, al-Sarakhsī envisions marriage as having a unitive function that is simultaneously affective and economic; by binding the couple together in their interests and sentiments, it ensures the family's material subsistence. This is, in essence, Bryson's view of marriage; and there is good reason to think that al-Sarakhsī was directly or indirectly aware of Bryson's discussion.

Al-Sarakhsī's incorporation of elements from Bryson, although it draws in terminology and assumptions from Greek philosophical ethics, does not place his discussion of marriage within the context of Aristotelian virtue ethics that has dominated the contemporary discussion of Islamic law and ethics.[146] As Swain has observed, Bryson is little concerned with the refinement of the self; his philosophical approach focuses on the function of marriage and the household in supplying and protecting a person's material needs.[147] Unlike al-Ghazālī or other Muslim exponents of virtue ethics, al-Sarakhsī directs no interest toward the spiritual or philosophical pursuits for which the elite man will be freed by the labor of his wife and servants. In general, neither does he reference the possible contribution of humble *khidma* to the moral improvement of wives or children;[148] service is owed to parents and husbands as an expression of deference, not as a means of self-refinement. However, al-Sarakhsī's apparent lack of interest in the cultivation of a virtuous self does not mean that his analysis of labor within the household is "ethical" only in the genealogical relation of some of its components to the Greek discipline of practical ethics. Instead, it forms part of his vision of a relationship that best fulfills the ultimate ends of marriage: a partnership in which the spouses cooperate for their shared prosperity and well-being is a *good* marriage in the deepest sense of the term.

Al-Sarakhsī in the context of the Ḥanafī tradition

It remains to place al-Sarakhsī's discussion of domestic labor within the broader development of Ḥanafī doctrine. At a fundamental level, al-Sarakhsī is elaborating on teachings attributed to the earliest authorities of the Ḥanafī school. As one might expect, his analysis is firmly grounded in the doctrines transmitted from Muḥammad ibn al-Ḥasan al-Shaybānī, whose works are summarized in the base text on which he is commenting in the *Mabsūṭ*. However, al-Sarakhsī himself does not clearly distinguish between his own comments and the elements incorporated from his base text. The recent publication of an edition presenting the fullest recoverable text of al-Shaybānī's magnum opus *Al-Aṣl* suggests both the continuities and the innovations reflected in al-Sarakhsī's analysis. As we have seen, al-Sarakhsī's discussion of domestic labor revolves centrally around the idea that a wife has a moral (although not a strictly legal) obligation to cook and clean for her husband. How innovative was this idea, and to what extent did al-Sarakhsī represent the evolving mainstream of the Ḥanafī school?

There is no apparent precedent for al-Sarakhsī's doctrine that a wife has an ethico-religious obligation to do housework in the teachings of Abū Ḥanīfa or his students. Abū Ḥanīfa himself is reported to have stated, "A wife is entitled to refrain from baking bread for her husband or cooking for him."[149] His disciple Muḥammad al-Shaybānī is cited as declaring that "a husband is not entitled to use his free wife for service."[150] Abū Ḥanīfa and his disciples are said to have agreed that a husband was responsible for the maintenance of his wife's servant if she had one, although they differed on the precise parameters of this obligation.[151] This overall approach seems to have retained its currency in the third/ninth century. As we have seen in chapter 1, the Ḥanafī authority al-Khaṣṣāf (d. 261/874) held that if a judge awarded a wife maintenance in the form of flour and other foodstuffs and she refused to cook or bake with it, the husband was obligated to hire someone to do so for her.[152]

However, the idea that many, if not most, wives were in fact expected to provide household labor was not a new notion in al-Sarakhsī's time. As we have seen in the introduction, the tenth-century Khurāsānī Ḥanafī Abū'l-Layth al-Samarqandī (d. 375/985) limited the prerogative of declining to cook or bake to the wife who was noble in status or who was prevented from doing so by a physical disability. In contrast, "if she is capable of [cooking and baking] and is the kind of person who [customarily] serves herself, she is [merely] being obstinate [if she refuses to cook or bake] and is not entitled to do so."[153] He justified this ruling with reference to popular custom. Thus, he held that a wife could contract to receive wages to bake bread for her husband if it was for sale in the market; however, "if he wants her to make bread for them to eat, the wage is not due [to her] because she is under an obligation to do that as a matter of custom (*dhālika mustaḥaqq ʿalayhā ʿādatan*)."[154]

Abū'l-Layth extended his principle that the ordinary, able-bodied wife was obligated to cook, bake, and do other kinds of labor devoted to household consumption. This approach appears to be in tension with the reported doctrine of Abū Ḥanīfa, who implicitly held that a husband had no inherent claim on his wife's spinning. Abū Ḥanīfa is said to have held that if husband brings his wife cotton and tells her to spin it, the resulting thread belongs to the husband; if she spins his cotton without his express permission, the thread belongs to her but she must reimburse him for the cotton.[155] (The implied logic is that if she spins the thread at his direction, she has implicitly volunteered her labor; if she does so without his permission, she has usurped (*ghaṣb*) the cotton and must pay him for the raw materials she has appropriated.[156]) In contrast, Abū'l-Layth argued that the thread belonged to the husband even if he had not instructed the wife to spin it, "because it is customary that if [a husband] gives cotton to his wife he is doing so only so that she will spin it; thus, her spinning becomes equivalent to housework (*khidmat al-bayt*). [This is] like the case of [a husband] who bought flour and [his wife] made bread; the bread belongs to the husband."[157]

Abū'l-Layth's conclusion that a wife customarily owed her husband basic household labor (and thus could not demand compensation for it) also informed his broader view of economic relations between the spouses. He held that if the couple used the proceeds of the wife's spinning to buy goods for their shared use or used fabric produced with her spinning to furnish their home, the goods belong to the husband "because a woman customarily works for her husband."[158] He also held that a wife could not charge her husband rent if they resided together in a house belonging to her because this would be "equivalent to his hiring her to cook or to bake bread."[159]

As we have already seen in chapter 1, it seems that by the fourth/tenth century, scholars were responding to the social realities of a growing Muslim community that included many households of modest means where wives customarily cooked and cleaned. The opinions advanced by Abū'l-Layth may also reflect the distinctive approach of the Ḥanafīs of the Khurāsānī or "Balkhī" school, whose contribution to the literature of the *madhhab* consisted primarily of collections of *fatāwā* (also known as *nawāzil* or *wāqiʿāt*) that often "contain details testifying to their origin in situations of daily life."[160] As Nurit Tsafrir has noted, Abū'l-Layth frames his own *Nawāzil* (the work in which he expressed the view that ordinary wives must provide housework) specifically as reflecting the responses of Khurāsānī muftis to "what they saw in their own time of the differing circumstances and the differing customs of the people."[161] As is evident from Abū'l-Layth's opinions, the practical significance of the legal question of a wife's duty to do housework related primarily to the material claims she might make on the basis of her labor.

Among Transoxanian Ḥanafīs of the tenth to twelfth centuries there was particularly sustained attention to the issue of ownership of thread or textiles produced by a wife's labor. Transoxania was a major center of cotton production, and many relevant fatwas deal specifically with cotton, sometimes designated by the Arabized Persian term *jūzaqa*.[162] (As Tsafrir observes, the use of Persian reinforces the probability of "the emergence of material from daily practice."[163]) Ṭāhir ibn Aḥmad al-Bukhārī (d. 542/1147–1148) presents an exhaustive analysis of various scenarios in which the spouses explicitly or implicitly make different agreements about the ownership of the products of the wife's spinning.[164] The wife may be entitled to a wage for her spinning if the spouses so agree, although if she spins at her husband's direction without mention of wages, she is understood to donate her labor. The working assumption is that if the wife's labor is for household consumption rather than for trade, it is an unpaid form of household service: "If he is not a cotton merchant, the thread belongs to the husband, as would be the case if she made bread from the husband's flour or cooked the husband's meat; the bread, the meat and the gravy would belong to the husband, and the same is true of this case."[165]

As in this example, the Khurāsānī legal analyses of the ownership of textiles generally accept and build upon the premise that wives are expected to perform routine household tasks such as cooking or baking without compensation.

Abū'l-Layth's doctrine limiting the prerogative of refusing to provide domestic labor to elite or disabled wives was widely reproduced in the Ḥanafī literature of the following several centuries and can be taken to represent the evolving doctrinal mainstream of the school.[166] It is impossible to know whether the intervention of Abū'l-Layth itself caused this change or whether it reflected a broader shift in practices and attitudes; it is probable that both were true, although Abū'l-Layth's statements were the precedent most often invoked. Tsafrir argues that as a general matter, the pragmatic doctrinal accommodations of the Khurāsānī Ḥanafīs historically came to predominate in the school as a whole;[167] the wide reception of this particular doctrine thus need not reflect a particular hostility to the prerogatives of wives. It seems reasonable to accept Abū'l-Layth's claim that these newer views were broadly based in contemporary custom and thus helped to conform the law to concrete social needs. It is nevertheless true that these shifts tended to erode the contractual prerogatives of non-elite wives.

Against the background of these developments, Al-Sarakhsī is neither innovative nor unique in arguing that wives in general have an obligation to provide housework. For instance, the leading Baghdad Ḥanafī, al-Qudūrī (d. 428/1037), is quoted as stating that it would be invalid for a husband to pay his wife a monthly wage for service "because a wife is obligated to do the housework" (*li'anna khidmat al-bayt talzam al-marʾa*).[168] Scholars of later generations also expressed this view in ways that appear to be independent of al-Sarakhsī's framework and wording. For instance, ʿUmar ibn ʿAbd al-ʿAzīz Ibn Māza (known as al-Ṣadr al-Shahīd, d. 537/1142–1143) writes that "the factor necessitating [the husband's] maintenance [of his wife] is [his] control of her, and control of her is achieved only by her being in the husband's house and her engaging in the husband's tasks (*iqāmatihā bi-aʿmāl al-zawj*) in the house."[169] What appears to be new and distinctive with al-Sarakhsī is the way in which he places the wife's domestic labor within a two-tiered vision of the marital relationship where the enforceable obligations of the marriage contract are contrasted with—and supplemented by—the couple's mutual moral duties.

The recognition of nonjusticiable moral claims was itself an old one within the Ḥanafī *madhhab*. As noted by the editor of al-Shaybānī's *Aṣl*, Mehmet Boynukalın, this work draws a distinction between moral duties and litigable claims in its analysis of many legal issues; in al-Shaybānī's terminology, the rule to be applied by a judge in court sometimes diverges from what morally binds the individual "between himself and God" (*baynahu wa-bayna Allāh*).[170] However, al-Shaybānī does not bring this two-tiered model to bear on the question of wives' domestic duties. Despite the closeness with which al-Sarakhsī parallels the concrete rules presented by al-Shaybānī (regarding not only the spouses but other familial relationships that preclude contracting wages for *khidma*), he is innovative in applying to these cases a concept of moral duty that is contrasted with legal obligation. For instance, al-Sarakhsī's statement that "if a man hires his wife to serve him for a specified monthly wage, it is not valid" is a verbatim quotation from al-Shaybānī; some scholars attributed it to Abū Ḥanīfa himself.[171] However, the terse rationale offered by al-Shaybānī is quite different from al-Sarakhsī's: He states that a man may not hire his wife to serve him for a monthly wage "because she is one of his dependents" (*li-annahā fī ʿiyālihi*).[172] This is the same criterion that he brings to bear on the question of monetary rewards (*juʿl*) for services rendered by a family member.[173] The implicit reasoning is that a dependent is expected to supply certain services gratis in exchange for economic support.

The idea that *khidma* was a distinctively subordinating form of labor was also not new; al-Shaybānī, like later Ḥanafīs, held that children owed *khidma* to parents and that it was improper for parents to serve children.[174] However, al-Sarakhsī gives domestic labor a newly central role both in the articulation of proper hierarchy between the spouses and in the elaboration of a sphere of moral obligation within the household. We can thus see al-Sarakhsī as reflecting the rich significance of *khidma* in eleventh-century Khurasan. Although he does not directly reference the forms of personal service that were then being developed in the context of Sufi discipleship, he invests domestic *khidma* with an ethical weight that is distinctive to this historical period.

Al-Sarakhsī's framing of housework as a wife's ethico-religious duty was widely adopted by later Ḥanafīs.[175] The idea that a wife had a conventional and moral (although not a contractual) obligation to provide cooking and cleaning informed ongoing legal discussions of the possibility of her claiming compensation for her work, whether in the form of wages or by claiming the material products of her labor. Based on both of these lines of reasoning, Qāḍī Khān (d. 592/1196) argued that a wife could not claim wages for cooking or cleaning; in contrast, if a husband hired his wife to wash his clothes, she was entitled to the wage in part "because she is not morally (*diyānatan*) obligated to do that."[176] Overall, Khurāsānī jurists of the eleventh to fourteenth century based their approach to domestic labor largely on social practice. Much of their argumentation seems straightforwardly aimed at ensuring that all parties can rely on the expectations raised by prevalent custom. Their deference to practice led them to acknowledge the labor that women customarily contributed to the household, significantly qualifying the doctrinal convention that a wife owed her husband nothing but sexual availability. This canonization of social expectations eroded the prerogatives that wives might have claimed based on earlier Ḥanafī doctrine. Nevertheless, the Khurāsānī jurists's painstaking efforts to define the parameters of unpaid domestic labor also reflect their default assumption that a married woman's labor belonged to her; if she did not work to meet the direct needs of the household, she worked for herself.[177]

* * *

In his pioneering examination on the terminology by which Ḥanafī scholars distinguish between moral and legal imperatives, Baber Johansen argues "that the jurists must largely disregard moral and religious considerations in order to systematically generalize the concept of the legally competent proprietor who is able to engage in transactions, such that it can be applied to all persons and used to legally protect the exchange of goods."[178] In his view, it is this valorization of the freely contracting proprietor that most fundamentally characterizes Ḥanafī legal discourse: "The formation of Hanafite law took place in a society in which private property played a decisive role. Almost everything could become property, even the human being. . . . As almost everything could become private property the proprietor became the prototype of the legal person in Hanafite law."[179]

In classical Ḥanafī analysis of domestic labor within marriage and the family, however, commercial contracts are ruled legally invalid due to supervening moral considerations.[180] Rather than treating a wife or adult child as free proprietors capable of contracting their own labor, al-Sarakhsī gives priority to the informal obligations entailed by relationships that are simultaneously intimate and hierarchical. Ethical principles thus play a generative role in his legal project.

Al-Sarakhsī's argument against the validity of a contract for a wife to receive wages for domestic labor is on one level the direct corollary of the Ḥanafī doctrine invalidating contracts of hire in the presence of a prior religious obligation. However, it also reflects a dimension of his overall analysis of marriage and the family, which pervasively asserts a sphere of filial and marital obligation paralleling and intersecting the demands of the law narrowly construed. His distinction between "religious" and "legal" obligations of the wife similarly do not reflect an isolated instance of divergence between ethical considerations and the internal logic of the legal argumentation but an overall vision in which the limited legal exchange of the marriage contract is supplemented by an ethics of the household. This ethical view reflects the deep significance that *khidma* had acquired in contemporary Khurasan, playing a central role in the articulation of bilateral relationships of loyalty and subordination. It is also rooted in the Greek philosophical tradition. While al-Sarakhsī's strictly legal analysis regards the spouses' assets as separate and denies a wifely obligation for housework, his ethical analysis posits the wife's labor as a key contributor to the shared flourishing of the marital household.

The doctrine that wives were morally obligated to provide housework destabilized the conceptualization of the marriage contract that had been constructed in the formative period of Islam. Rather than simply reconceptualizing the spousal relationship as involving an exchange of housework for maintenance, al-Sarakhsī and later members of the Ḥanafī school produced a complex vision of marriage as involving both a limited exchange of contractual prerogatives and a broad penumbra of moral obligations. The contract, in the end, did not exhaust their understanding of Muslim marriage.

FOUR

Marriage Reimagined

The Work of Ibn Qudāma and Ibn Taymīya

AS WE HAVE seen, by the end of the fifth century AH/eleventh century CE scholars working within the various schools of law produced fully developed conceptual frameworks for the law of marriage. While acknowledging in various ways that most wives were in practice expected to provide domestic labor, these mature doctrines nevertheless sustained the broad early consensus that they had no obligation to do so on a strictly legal level. In contrast, within the Ḥanbalī school in Damascus in the fourteenth century CE, existing legal doctrine on wives' domestic labor was dramatically challenged. As a baseline for the developments of the early fourteenth century, I begin with an analysis of the work of Ḥanbalī law regarded as most authoritative at the beginning of this period, the *Mughnī* of Muwaffaq al-Dīn Ibn Qudāma (d. AH 620/1223 CE).[1] Up to this time, the Ḥanbalī school had gone further than any other in affirming the limited scope of the marriage contract and the wide-ranging freedom of contract between the spouses. In the early fourteenth century, Taqī al-Dīn Ibn Taymīya (d. 728/1328) and his disciple Ibn Qayyim al-Jawzīya (d. 751/1350) proposed a new approach that fully integrated moral demands such as the wife's obligation to do housework into the law of marriage. This radical reimagining of the legal framework of marriage appears to reflect both the distinctive gender ideals of that time and place and the two scholars' effort to fundamentally revise the relationship between Islamic law and ethics.

The status quo: Muwaffaq al-Dīn Ibn Qudāma

While the birth and development of the Ḥanbalī school took place in Baghdad, Ibn Qudāma's lifetime saw the emergence of a substantial Ḥanbalī community in Damascus. The arrival of the Saljuqs in 468/1075 had initiated the city's transformation from a backwater on the periphery of the Fatimid Empire to a thriving center of Sunni scholarship graced with growing numbers of madrasas, the then newly introduced institutions of Islamic higher learning funded by waqf endowments.[2] Muwaffaq al-Dīn's family came to Damascus fleeing difficult conditions under Crusader rule in the Nablus region; there they settled the Ṣāliḥīya neighborhood on the slopes of Mt. Qāsyūn and became pillars of the growing Ḥanbalite establishment.[3] In this period Damascus gradually supplanted Baghdad (where Muwaffaq al-Dīn received some of his scholarly training) as the center of gravity of the Ḥanbalī school of law. Muwaffaq al-Dīn rose to leadership of the *madhhab* in a period when the Ḥanbalīs in Syria were flourishing and receiving increasing levels of state patronage.[4] When the Ayyubid sultan al-Muʿaẓẓam (ruled 615–624/1218–1227) added a prayer niche for the Ḥanbalīs to those of the other Sunni schools in the Umayyad mosque, it was Muwaffaq al-Dīn who was privileged to lead the first congregational prayers.[5] His voluminous and magisterial work *al-Mughnī* not only provides an exhaustive account of Ḥanbalī legal doctrine and its supporting legal argumentation but offers comparative data about the doctrines and argumentation of other schools of law. The book quickly achieved canonical status; Henri Laoust writes that "the *Mughnī* was often considered the repository of the school's doctrine, knowledge of which allowed a jurisconsult to rise to the status of *mujtahid*."[6]

Ibn Qudāma opens his main discussion of wives' domestic labor with a categorical statement attributed to the eponymous founder of his legal school: "A woman is not obligated to provide her husband with service by kneading [dough], baking [bread], cooking, or the like—Aḥmad [ibn Ḥanbal] stated this explicitly (*naṣṣa ʿalayhi Aḥmad*)."[7] He proceeds to acknowledge the dissenting opinions of the early hadith specialists Abū Bakr Ibn Abī Shayba (d. 235/849) and Abū Isḥāq al-Jūzajānī (d. ca. 259/873), which they supported with a report claiming that the Prophet assigned responsibility for housework to his daughter Fāṭima.[8] Ibn Qudāma proceeds:

> Our evidence is that what [the wife] has contracted to provide is sexual access (*al-istimtāʿ*), so she is not obligated to provide anything else, such as watering his livestock or harvesting his crops. As for the Prophet's dividing [the work of the household] between ʿAlī and Fāṭima, this was by way of what is appropriate to good morals (*al-akhlāq al-marḍīya*) and the course of custom, not by way of [legal] obligation (*al-ījāb*). Thus, it is transmitted about [the prominent female Companion of the Prophet] Asmāʾ bint Abī Bakr that she used to take care of [her husband] al-Zubayr's horse and gather date pits and carry them on her head, and that was not obligatory for her. For this [same] reason, it is not obligatory for the husband to take care of the [couple's] affairs outside of the home (*maṣāliḥ khārij al-bayt*) or to provide anything beyond what is obligatory to give her of maintenance and clothing. However, it is more appropriate for her to do the things that it is customary for her to take care of, because it is the custom and [because] the affairs [of the household] will prosper only by [her doing] it, and [the couple's] livelihood will not be well-ordered without it.[9]

In this passage, Ibn Qudāma's most straightforward and compelling appeal is to the transactional logic of the marriage contract. In the contract's balanced exchange of entitlements and obligations, the wife has traded a specific good (her sexual availability) for the financial benefits provided to her by her husband; this exchange excludes extraneous duties such as work in the house or the fields.[10]

Despite his sharply delineated view of the benefits exchanged between the spouses under the marriage contract, which in his view clearly do not include the wife's labor, Ibn Qudāma does not simply dismiss the idea that wives should keep house. Having argued quite compellingly that a wife is not obligated to provide labor to her husband, he spends the remainder of the passage arguing equally persuasively that she ought to do so. His reservations reflect the belief that, in his social world, wives are routinely expected to do housework and that, indeed, no good wife would refuse. He resolves this dilemma by drawing a distinction between the demands of law and those of social custom and ethics; the Prophet counseled Fāṭima to tend to the work within her home as a matter of good conduct, not as a statement of her contractual duties.

To illustrate the supererogatory nature of the labor of the exemplary women of the first Muslim generation, Ibn Qudāma then cites the case of

Asmāʾ (a prominent female Companion of the Prophet and the daughter of the first caliph, Abū Bakr). It clearly requires no explicit statement that wives are not legally compelled to serve their husbands as stable hands or field laborers; Asmāʾ is manifestly a wife going beyond the call of duty. Ibn Qudāma has already played on his audience's assumptions in this regard by stating that a wife has contracted to provide her husband with sex rather than "watering his livestock or harvesting his crops"; dispute was evidently possible only in the case of housework. If ordinary wives need not go so far in their supererogatory efforts as Asmāʾ, however, neither should they limit themselves to their strict contractual obligations. Not only is a wife who declines to tend her home acting in defiance of custom but in practical terms she impairs the good order and well-being of the household. Furthermore, if the wife is technically entitled to limit herself to her strict contractual obligations, then so is the husband; on this basis she is guaranteed no more than basic clothing and sustenance and will have no one to attend to tasks outside of the home.

Ibn Qudāma's assumption that wives both should and do perform household labor is evident at various points in the *Mughnī*.[11] His reasoning about the wife's lack of any obligation to do housework is thus clearly an argument about the way the law of marriage works, not about how actual marital households work. Like al-Sarakhsī, he addresses this disparity in part by invoking a plane of moral and social propriety separate from that of legal obligation. Indeed, his argument that a wife's abstention from housework could rightfully be met by the husband's abstention from all but the minimum of maintenance echoes al-Sarakhsī's quite directly. However, unlike al-Sarakhsī's case, Ibn Qudāma's analysis of this issue excludes moral considerations from a direct role in his legal reasoning.

If Ibn Qudāma affirms that all wives are in principle exempt from a duty to do housework, in keeping with established Ḥanbalī doctrine, he sees only some of them as being affirmatively entitled to have domestic labor provided on their behalf. He states that a wife is entitled to the services of a servant "if she is a person who does not serve herself because she is of high status (*min dhawī al-aqdār*)"—as well as, of course, if illness prevents her from working. In support of this rule he invokes Qur'an 4:19, which instructs husbands to treat their wives according to "*al-maʿrūf*," here clearly understood in terms of social custom.[12] He further notes,

> If she says, "I will serve myself and take the wages of the servant," the husband is not obliged to accept that because he is responsible for paying the wage and thus the selection of the servant is his prerogative, and [also] because providing her with service makes her available for his needs, provides her with leisure, and raises her status—and [all of] that is lost by her serving herself. If the husband says, "I will serve you myself," she is not obliged [to accept] because she feels ashamed in front of him and it impairs her prestige (*fīhi ghaḍāḍa ʿalayhā*), because her husband is a servant. There is another view (*fīhi wajh ākhar*) that she must accept it because her needs are met by it.[13]

In this passage, Ibn Qudāma justifies an elite woman's entitlement to domestic service by acknowledging the normative force of a basic form of social hierarchy, the distinction between people who serve themselves and those who are more appropriately served by others. His deference to social values in this area is based on Qur'anic wording that he (like many other jurists and exegetes) understands to demand that husbands must treat their wives according to the dictates of custom.[14] It is nevertheless notable that he assigns each spouse the option of forfeiting the prerogatives of high status by choosing to do domestic work themselves, although subject to the other partner's consent.

Strikingly, Ibn Qudāma's wording implies that an elite wife could potentially contract to receive wages to do housework herself. Although her husband is not compelled to acquiesce in this arrangement (because it defies the objectives for which she is understood to be entitled to service in the first place), if he did accept, the deal would be valid and she would receive the wage.[15] Indeed, in another passage Ibn Qudāma makes this implication explicit. Ibn Qudāma's most extensive comments on a wife's entitlement to contract for compensation for domestic work occur in the context of his discussion of wet-nursing. The base text on which Ibn Qudāma comments in the *Mughnī*, the *Mukhtaṣar* of al-Khiraqī (d. 334/946), states on this subject: "It is the father's obligation to hire a nurse (*yastarḍiʿa*) for his child, unless the mother wants to nurse it for a fair wage (*bi-ujrat mithlihā*); she is more entitled to [nurse the child] than anyone else, regardless of whether she remains married to [the father] or is divorced."[16]

Ibn Qudāma supports this doctrine with two basic arguments. One is that "the husband is not entitled to her benefits (*manāfiʿ*) of nursing and childcare (*haḍāna*); this is proven by the fact that he cannot compel her to undertake the care of her child, and she can take compensation for it from someone else. Thus, it is permissible for her to take [compensation] from him, like the price of her property."[17]

He accurately attributes to the Shāfiʿīs the argument that the wife cannot receive compensation for nursing because she has already received compensation for her detention in the home (*ḥabs*) and her sexual availability (*istimtāʿ*).[18] Ibn Qudāma responds briskly that these entitlements of the husband are distinct from childcare; the fact that one has been paid to provide one service does not mean that one cannot receive separate compensation for another.[19] If the husband were actually entitled to nursing and childcare from the wife, Ibn Qudāma reiterates in another place, she would not be able to hire herself out for this purpose with his permission—and if he hired her out, the wages would belong to him (an idea he assumes his audience will find obviously erroneous).[20] This logic also applied to household chores; in another passage, he adds the observation that a husband cannot compel his wife to provide him with service specific to himself (*khidmatihi fīmā yakhtaṣṣ bihi*).[21] (He presumably singles out the wife's personal service to the husband—rather than to the household or herself—because, like nursing a child that belonged to the husband but not to her, it is a clear test case for her husband's entitlement to her labor.)

Ibn Qudāma thus understands the husband's entitlement to sexual access as a limited prerogative that does not infringe on the wife's continuing ownership of her other capacities. Like other jurists, he holds that to be entitled to maintenance the free woman must be at her husband's disposal at all hours of the day. Nevertheless, she owns her own labor, and Ibn Qudāma emphasizes that the sole obstacle to her contracting it out is her husband's right to *istimtāʿ*. He observes, "She is prohibited from hiring herself out to an unrelated person without [her husband's] permission only because it involves depriving him of his right to sexual access some of the time and for this reason it is valid with his permission."[22]

Ibn Qudāma's narrow interpretation of the prerogatives of the husband under the marriage contract thus entails a broad interpretation of the wife's freedom to contract her labor. Significantly, this freedom of contract extends to the couple's ability to negotiate agreements with each other. Ibn Qudāma's second major argument in support of the doctrine that a wife can receive wages from her husband for nursing the couple's child is the broad principle that "every contract that [a wife] can validly conclude with someone other than her husband, she can validly conclude with him, like [a contract of] sale."[23] This was a time-honored Ḥanbalī argument, attributed to the school in almost identical wording by ʿAbd al-Wāḥid al-Rūyānī (d. 502/1108).[24] In the absence of a doctrine of marital property, Muslim jurists universally recognized that wives and husbands could validly sell their property to each other. However, as we have seen, scholars of other schools of law generally did not extend this logic to include the wife's ability to contract her usufructs (specifically, her labor) with her spouse. The Ḥanbalīs took a uniquely broad approach to the spouses' freedom of contract and explicitly included household chores; Ibn Qudāma observes that an agreement to nurse for wages "is a contract of hire (*ʿaqd ijāra*) that is valid on the part of someone other than the husband if [the husband] gives his permission for it; thus, it is valid [if contracted] with the husband, like her hiring herself out (*ijārat nafsihā*) for sewing (*al-khiyāṭa*) or service (*al-khidma*)."[25]

As we have already seen, the position that a wife could validly contract to receive wages for nursing her own child while still married to its father was unpopular although not completely unique. It was accepted by some Mālikīs with respect to the elite wife (who, in their doctrine, had no preexisting obligation to nurse) and by the Khurāsānī sub-school of the Shāfiʿī madhhab starting in the fifth/eleventh century.[26] Nevertheless, it was unusual enough to be perceived as a distinctively Ḥanbalī position; ʿAlī ibn Sulaymān al-Mardāwī (d. 885/1480) describes it as "one of the unique positions of the school" (*min mufradāt al-madhhab*).[27] The school was not unanimous on this point. Some Ḥanbalīs subscribed to the logic (also popular, as Ibn Qudāma notes, with some Shāfiʿīs) that while the husband had no direct right to his wife's nursing or other services, her own right to them was preempted by his marital claims.[28] Others affirmed a wife's right to contract for wages to breastfeed but did not extend the same logic to domestic labor; in his manual *Al-Hidāya*, Abū'l-Khaṭṭāb al-Kalwādhānī (d. 510/1116) notes briskly, "If she says, 'I will serve myself and take what you are obligated to pay for my maidservant,' she is not entitled to do that."[29]

Despite the lack of unanimity within the school, the Ḥanbalīs' unusual receptivity to the idea that a wife could receive wages for work from her husband arguably reflects a distinctively limited vision of the scope of the marriage contract. As we have seen, despite conceptualizing the marriage contract as involving an exchange of the husband's maintenance for the wife's sexual availability, many scholars of other schools developed broader frameworks that limited the wife's control over her own labor. Al-Māwardī conceived of the husband's sexual claims as preempting the wife's ownership of her other capacities; al-Sarakhsī envisioned the wife's duties as involving a broad penumbra of moral obligations. Ibn Qudāma follows the lead of many (although not all) of his Ḥanbalī predecessors in declining to extend the reach of the marriage contract in this way.

The Ḥanbalī school's distinctive approach to marriage is also reflected in its broad acceptance (unique among the four classical Sunni schools) of binding conditions (*shurūṭ*) added to the marriage contract at the agreement of the spouses.[30] Rather than envisioning the legal structure of marriage as comprehensively determining the rights and duties of the partners, in this view it is subject to negotiation between the husband and wife as freely contracting parties. Only conditions conflicting with the core objectives of marriage are excluded; thus, a wife cannot stipulate that she will not have sex with her husband, and a husband cannot stipulate that he will not provide maintenance. Beyond this irreducible (and rather minimal) core, however, the spouses are envisioned as free agents who can craft the contours of their relationship based on mutual agreement.[31]

Ibn Qudāma explicitly treats the marriage contract as involving a strictly limited set of rights over the wife and her capacities. Thus, in one place he contrasts sale and giving in security (*rahn*), whose locus is the entirety of an enslaved person, with marriage, whose locus (like that of a contract hire) is limited. "This is why it is permissible to give a married [enslaved] woman as security [for a debt], because most of her usufructs remain [unclaimed] (*li-baqāʾ muʿẓam al-manfaʿa fīhā*)."[32]

Ibn Qudāma's doctrine reflects not only a strictly delineated view of the prerogatives of marriage but a clear distinction between the legal right to labor and the moral duties that prevail within the household. He parallels al-Sarakhsī in asserting that a wife ought to provide housework and that marriage requires both spouses to go above and beyond the technical requirements of the marriage contract. However, unlike al-Sarakhsī and other Ḥanafīs, he declines to draw any legal consequences from the existence of such ethical obligations. Specifically, as a Ḥanbalī he rejects the Ḥanafī view that the moral duties of wives preempt their right to contract their labor. This principle also applied to other duties of kinship. While (as we have seen) Ḥanafīs held that a child could not claim wages for household chores from a parent due to the preexisting moral duty of filial service, Ibn

Qudāma affirms in another work that "it is valid for [a man] to hire his child for his personal service (*li-khidmatihi*)."[33] His nephew Shams al-Dīn Ibn Qudāma elaborates, "It is valid for him to hire his child for his personal service like an unrelated person . . . and similarly all of his other relatives, without distinction, like unrelated persons."[34] Al-Mardāwī comments, "This is the opinion of the members of the school, which they held to be certain (*qaṭaʿū bihi*)."[35] Ibn Qudāma (and the Ḥanbalī school in general) is not insensitive to the issue of proper familial hierarchy and the ways in which it can be expressed (or violated) by the performance of labor.[36] Nevertheless, he does not see the nuclear family as a space inherently immured from market transactions. He does not necessarily think that children *should* demand wages from their parents or wives from their husbands, but he regards individual family members as economic free agents who in principle own their own capacities and are at liberty to contract them to each other. This overall approach emphasizes the marriage contract's resemblance to other legal contracts by defining it in terms of specific and limited entitlements and services rather than framing it as an all-encompassing and hierarchical moral relationship between the spouses.

Reframing marriage: Taqī al-Dīn Ibn Taymīya

Ibn Qudāma's interpretation of the marriage contract adhered closely to the precedents of the Ḥanbalī school while consistently selecting and reinforcing those doctrines most compatible with a narrow and reciprocal understanding of the rights and responsibilities of husbands and wives. In the early fourteenth century, this Ḥanbalī doctrine of marriage was radically reformulated by Taqī al-Dīn Ibn Taymīya, a scholar whose teachings were both deeply rooted in the Ḥanbalī school and in some ways sharply divergent from it.

Ibn Taymīya, like Ibn Qudāma, came from a Ḥanbalī family whose relocation to Damascus resulted from the political dislocations of his time. Born in Harran in Mesopotamia in 661/1263, he was brought to Damascus as a child when his family fled to escape the Mongol invasion. He descended from a family of distinguished religious scholars, including his grandfather Majd al-Dīn (whose legal manual *Al-Muḥarrar* became an authoritative source within the school), and his scholarly career commenced with his succession to his father as head of the Sukkarīya madrasa when he was still in his early twenties.[37] Ibn Taymīya's adult life unfolded in circumstances of continuing social and political disruption instigated by the recurring Mongol incursions into Syria, in which he was personally involved both as a combatant and as a participant in negotiations with the Mongol leadership.

Early in his scholarly career Ibn Taymīya adhered closely to the received legal doctrines of the Ḥanbalī *madhhab*, in which the work of Muwaffaq al-Dīn ibn Qudāma played a central role.[38] He was a student of the latter's nephew and student Shams al-Dīn, and among his early works was a commentary on Muwaffaq al-Dīn's legal manual *al-ʿUmda*, the shortest of three abridgments he produced of his own magnum opus *al-Mughnī*.[39] Probably written when Ibn Taymīya was in his early thirties, the commentary "illustrates [his] early conformity to Hanbali law."[40] Henri Laoust writes that he "had an excellent personal knowledge of the work of Muwaffaq al-dīn, whom he did not stint in praising, declaring that no jurist in Syria since al-Awzāʿī had left a legal treatise comparable to the *Mughnī*." Ultimately, however, Ibn Taymīya would refuse to be constrained by this legal heritage; his "neo-Ḥanbalism, which refused to accept as a source of law *ijmāʿ* understood as the unanimous agreement of contemporary jurisconsults, was reacting against the codification of the doctrine that Muwwaffaq al-Dīn had succeeded in imposing through the influence that he exercised over the authorities of the judiciary and the universities."[41]

Ibn Taymīya's later intellectual career was devoted to the reform of Islamic thought and practice through the repudiation of partisan loyalty to the doctrines of established legal and theological schools and a renewed adherence to the authority of the Qur'an and sunna. While he attracted a fervent following, his interpretive independence exposed him to bitter intellectual and religious opposition, to recurring legal prosecution, and to repeated bouts of imprisonment.[42] He was initially accused of theological deviance (particularly of holding anthropomorphic conceptions of God, *tajsīm*), but his final trials revolved around his dissident legal interpretations. In particular, he was condemned for his denial of the irrevocable nature of a triple divorce pronounced on a single occasion, a stance that abandoned the consensus of the four Sunni schools in favor of an opinion attributed to the Prophet's Companion Ibn ʿAbbās. Having repeatedly refused to cease issuing fatwas on this subject, Ibn Taymīya died in detention in 728/1328.[43]

In his mature work, Ibn Taymīya provides an overall account of the marital relationship that in some ways diverges strikingly from the received doctrine of his school. The most salient overall themes of his analysis are an emphasis on the authority of community norms and an equally pervasive insistence on the wife's direct and personal dependence on (and subjection to) her husband. This approach de-emphasizes the view of marriage as a contract involving the reciprocal exchange of concrete and limited entitlements and obligations. Instead Ibn Taymīya envisions the marital relationship as simultaneously comprehensive and fluid, governed primarily by the shared norms of the Muslim community and the moral obligations resulting from the husband's sweeping authority over his wife.

Ibn Taymīya's most sustained analysis of the marital relationship appears in a long excursus appended to a fatwa responding to several questions regarding maintenance (*nafaqa*). While expanding on the central point that *nafaqa* is not set at a specific level but varies according to context and custom, the passage proceeds to review all basic aspects of the relationship between the spouses.[44] It begins by citing a series of Qur'anic verses, in each of which God describes some aspect of the marital relationship as being based on *al-maʿrūf*, "what is known," understood both as what is customary and as what is morally right (although the salience of these two factors varies with context).[45] He concludes his survey by observing,

> Thus, [God] mentioned that mutual agreement [on the selection of marriage partners] is according to *al-maʿrūf*; the retention [of a wife] is according to *al-maʿrūf*; the dismissal [of a divorced woman] is according to *al-maʿrūf*; companionship [between spouses] is according to *al-maʿrūf*; and the rights and duties [of wives] are according to *al-maʿrūf*, just as He said that "they are entitled to their sustenance and clothing according to *al-maʿrūf*" (verse 2:233).[46] This [*maʿrūf*] that is mentioned in the Qur'an is what is obligatory and just with respect to everything having to do with marriage.[47]

He goes on to argue that with respect to a woman's food and clothing *al-maʿrūf* means

> the custom (*al-ʿurf*) that people are familiar with (*yaʿrifuhu al-nās*) with respect to [people of] the two [spouses'] condition, in terms of kind, quantity and quality, even if that varies according to their state of wealth or poverty, and

> according to time such as winter and summer, night and day, and according to place; in every locality he feeds her whatever the people of that locality ordinarily eat, which is the custom among them. Similarly, [with respect to] the sexual enjoyment and companionship she is entitled to from him, he must spend the night with her and have intercourse with her as is customary (*bi'l-maʿrūf*), and that varies based on her condition and his.[48]

Ibn Taymīya supports the argument that a husband's maintenance of his wife is based on context and custom rather than fixed quantitative standards with hadith texts. Some of these specify that a wife is entitled to maintenance *bi'l-maʿrūf*, while others counsel the husband to feed his wife when he himself eats, and clothe her when (and implicitly, perhaps, as well as) he clothes himself. There are thus two sunna-based standards, neither of them quantitative: one refers the husband to custom, and the other urges direct personal sharing (*al-muwāsāt*) with his wife. Ibn Taymīya points out that these two approaches directly parallel the advice attributed to the Prophet on the maintenance of slaves. In one report, the Prophet declares, "They are your brothers and your servants; God placed them in your possession. So whoever has his brother in his possession, let him feed him what he [himself eats], and let him clothe him in what he [himself] wears."[49] Ibn Taymīya concludes,

> [The Prophet's] command with respect to the wife and the slave is the same: sometimes he mentions that it is obligatory to provide food and clothing as is customary (*bi'l-maʿrūf*), and sometimes he directs personal sharing with them (*muwāsātihim bi'l-nafs*). Some scholars have understood that which is customary to be what is obligatory, and personal sharing to be recommended. One might also argue that one of them clarifies the other.[50]

Ibn Taymīya emphasizes that maintenance should be understood as the direct provision of sustenance rather than the transfer of ownership of an economic asset. Paying a wife monetary maintenance is not *maʿrūf*, he declares;

> rather, the custom of the Prophet (peace be upon him!) and of the Muslims up to our day is that a man brings food to his home, and he, his wife, and his slave eat, sometimes together and sometimes separately. Sometimes there is food left over

> and they save it. The Muslims are not familiar with [the custom] that every day he gives her possession of dirhams that she can dispose of as her own property; rather, if someone behaves in this way with his wife, they will be considered by the Muslims to have treated each other in a way that is not *maʿrūf* and that is harmful to each other. This is something that they would do to each other in case of enmity (*ʿinda al-ḍarar*), not if they were treating each other according to *al-maʿrūf*.[51]

Furthermore, the husband's obligation to his wife is in this respect the same as an owner's obligation to his slave, "and the Muslims are in agreement that it is not obligatory to give a slave possession of his maintenance."[52]

As we have seen, Ibn Taymīya also argues that the standard of what is "customary and kind" that applies to food and clothing also applies to a wife's entitlement to companionship and sex.[53] He notes that some argue that her entitlement specifically amounts to a night of companionship out of every four and an act of intercourse every four months, while others are of the opinion "that what is obligatory is to have sex with her as is customary (*bi'l-maʿrūf*), so that it may be less or more according to her needs and his powers, just like [her] food."[54]

As for the wife's obligations to her husband, Ibn Taymīya describes them as comprising a personal obedience and subjection equivalent to that of a prisoner or a slave, citing the Prophet's statement that wives "are captives (*ʿawānin*) in your care."[55] Thus, she must live with him wherever he moves, unless she stipulates a condition excluding this from her marriage contract. She cannot travel or leave his house without his permission unless compelled by necessity and must provide sex on demand. However, "all of that is based on what is *maʿrūf* and not *munkar*; he cannot have sex with her in a way that harms her, or make her dwell in a dwelling that harms her, or confine her in a way that harms her."[56] In this passage, the direct contrasting of *maʿrūf* with *munkar* (etymologically "what is unfamiliar," but semantically "what is wrong, evil") suggests that here *al-maʿrūf* should be understood as what is right or kind.

The combined principles of personal subjection and customary practice similarly define a wife's obligation to do housework. Ibn Taymīya observes,

> The ulama have disagreed about whether [a wife] is obligated to serve [her husband] in tasks such as [spreading] the bedding (*firāsh*) of the household, serving

> food, drink, and bread, grinding [grain], and [preparing] food for his slaves and his livestock. . . . Some of them have stated that [such] service is not obligatory; this opinion is weak, like that of those who say that [the husband] is not obligated to [give her] companionship and intercourse. That [i.e., withholding housework] is not giving him "kind/customary companionship" [cf. Q 4:19] (*laysa muʿāshara lahu biʾl-maʿrūf*). Indeed, even a traveling companion who is a person's peer and shares his dwelling would not have treated him as is customary and kind if he refused to help him with one of his needs! It has also been said—and this is the correct [opinion]—that it is obligatory [for her to provide] service because the husband is her master (*sayyiduhā*) in the Book of God, and she is a captive in his care (*ʿāniya ʿindahu*) in the *sunna* of the Messenger of God (peace be upon him!); and a captive or a slave is obligated to provide service. [It is also obligatory for the wife to serve her husband] because that is what is customary (*maʿrūf*). Then, some [of those who have held that the wife must serve her husband] have said that [only] light service is obligatory [upon her], and others have said that it is obligatory [for her] to serve [him] as is customary (*biʾl-maʿrūf*); that is the correct [opinion]. She is obligated to serve him as is customary for someone like her [to serve] someone like him; that varies according to circumstances. The service of a Bedouin woman is not like the service of a [sedentary] village woman, and the service of a strong woman is not like the service of a weak one.[57]

Throughout Ibn Taymīya's discussion of the rights and duties of the spouses in this extended fatwa, his discussion revolves around the concept of *al-maʿrūf.* In more than one place this term is equated with custom (*al-ʿurf,* or "what [people] are familiar with").[58] However, the significance of this focal term is not limited to a deference to social practice; *al-maʿrūf* is also pervasively associated with what is right, kind, and free from harm and thus takes on a strong ethical coloring. Most fundamentally, Ibn Taymīya equates the *maʿrūf* that the Qur'an persistently associates with the rights and duties of the spouses with "justice (*ʿadl*) in everything relating to marriage . . . and the rights of the two spouses."[59] He similarly describes his doctrine regarding *nafaqa* as being "what is indicated by the Book, the Sunna, and reasoning based on justice" (*al-iʿtibār al-mabnī ʿalā al-ʿadl*).[60] His re-envisioning of the rights and duties involved in the marriage contract reflects an overall framework in which the spouses fairly and kindly fulfill each other's needs, albeit within a starkly hierarchical relationship.

When Ibn Taymīya states that those who deny either a wife's obligation to provide domestic labor or a husband's obligation to provide sexual intercourse are wrong, he is rejecting the majority views of the legal tradition up to his time. It is true that all jurists provided for judicial separation if a husband formally vowed (*īlāʾ*) to abstain from sexual intercourse for a period exceeding four months, but this provision did not cover ordinary cases of sexual abandonment or neglect.[61] Even before Ibn Taymīya's intervention, however, Ḥanbalīs had begun to display a distinctive concern for the sexual obligations of the husband; both Ibn Taymīya's grandfather Majd al-Dīn ibn Taymīya and Muwaffaq al-Dīn Ibn Qudāma held that a husband was obligated to have intercourse with his wife at least once every four months.[62] In citing the doctrine that a husband was obligated to spend one night out of four with his wife and have intercourse with her at least once every four months, Ibn Taymīya is thus reproducing the doctrines of his most immediate Ḥanbalī predecessors (although not of Aḥmad ibn Ḥanbal or the older historical doctrine of the school).[63]

However, Ibn Taymīya goes beyond this limited doctrine to propose that the husband is obligated to provide his wife with sex *bi'l-maʿrūf*, just as he provides her with sustenance. Although he does not state so explicitly in this particular fatwa, this is in fact his own doctrine, one that was sufficiently distinctive to be discussed at length in a compilation of his legal preferences (*ikhtiyārāt*). There he is quoted as stating that "it is incumbent on the husband to have sex with his wife as much as she requires, as long as this does not exhaust his body or distract him from earning a living; it is not set at [a minimum of once in] four months as in the case of an enslaved woman. If they have a dispute over this [in front of a judge], the judge must impose it on the husband like maintenance."[64] He goes on to declare that "the occurrence of harm to the wife through [the husband's] refraining from sex entails the annulment (*faskh*) of the marriage [by a judge] in all cases, regardless of whether [the harm] was intentional on the part of the husband or not intentional, and regardless of whether he is capable or incapable [of having sex], as is the case with maintenance and a fortiori."[65]

In the fatwa at hand, Ibn Taymīya signals the importance of the issue of the husband's obligation to provide company and sex by declaring that he has demonstrated it "with more than ten proofs," presumably in another work which he does not name.[66] Indeed, beyond the inherent significance of this issue, it is a lynchpin of a fundamental reframing of the underlying structure of marriage as a legal construct. His interpretation of the marital relationship in terms of a comprehensive ethic of care in which the husband is expansively responsible for the needs of his wife minimizes attention to the concrete mutual obligations the spouses are exchanging as parties to the marriage contract. No longer is the marriage contract understood as a limited exchange between female sexual availability and male monetary compensation. Rather, the husband must provide sex as well as food because he is obligated meet his wife's needs *bi'l-maʿrūf*, and she must do the housework as well as remain available for sex because she is his subordinate and dependent.

This model leaves little scope for direct questions about the legal ownership of the woman's labor capacity. With respect to the form in which food is delivered to the wife, Ibn Taymīya observes that "if the custom of [the local community] is for him to give her grain and for her to grind it at home, he does that. If [it is customary] for it to be ground at a mill and made into bread at home, he does that. . . . And if [it is customary] for him to buy bread from the market, he does that."[67] These comments contrast with Ibn Qudāma's contention that a husband may not provide his wife with unprocessed grain in the place of bread; he assumes that she is never obligated to grind or bake it herself.[68] In Ibn Taymīya's fatwa on *nafaqa*, in contrast, a wife's labor obligations are defined by community custom, on the one hand, and on her comprehensive subordination to her husband, on the other.

Ibn Taymīya provides another, briefer, and more concentrated summary of the rights and duties of marriage in his monograph on Islamic statecraft, *Al-Siyāsa al-sharʿīya*. This work, produced sometime between 1310 and 1313, appears to have been composed as a manual of advice—solicited or unsolicited—for the amīr Āqūsh al-Manṣūrī.[69] Its first section deals with the various forms of public trust or authority (*amānāt*, *wilāyāt*); the second focuses on the just adjudication of interpersonal rights or claims (*ḥuqūq*) on both the public and the private levels. Among the private claims discussed in this second section are those of a sexual nature (literally, claims relating to the genitals, *abḍāʿ*), beginning with the rights and duties of marriage.[70] As we shall see, the content of this passage parallels the emphases and concerns of the fatwa on *nafaqa* discussed above closely enough to suggest that the two works may date from the same stage of Ibn Taymīya's life. Despite the passage's lack of substantively new ideas, its context in the work as a whole gives a sense of how Ibn Taymīya's vision of marriage fits into his larger vision of the Muslim polity as well as into his broader ethico-legal project. He writes:

> Among the claims (*ḥuqūq*) [that individual persons owe to one another] are sexual claims (*al-abḍāʿ*). It is obligatory to adjudicate between spouses according to what God has commanded of [the husband's] "retaining [his wife] according to *al-maʿrūf* or dismissing [her] with kindness" [cf. Q 2:229], and she is obligated to obey him and to protect his private affairs relating to herself and his property, as God commanded [cf. Q 4:34]. It is obligatory for each of the two spouses to render to the other his or her rights willingly and gladly.[71]

Here Ibn Taymīya offers a terse but thorough rereading of the reciprocal and gendered rights and obligations of the spouses, based directly on the wording of the Qur'an rather than on the conventions of received *fiqh*. The husband's obligations comprise benevolent use of his privileges over marriage and divorce, as stipulated in verse 2:229 of the Qur'an; the wife's, in a tacit reference to verse 4:34, involve obedience and protection of the husband's private affairs. He continues:

> A wife has claims over the husband with respect to his wealth and his body. As for [her claims with respect to his] wealth, they are dower (*ṣadāq*) and maintenance according to what is customary (*al-maʿrūf*).[72] . . . As for her claim with respect to his body, it [comprises] two things: companionship (*ʿishra*) and sexual enjoyment (*mutʿa*).[73] . . . *ʿIshra* (which is allocating her a share of nights that he spends with her, *al-qasm ibtidāʾan*), and sexual enjoyment (which is intercourse, *al-waṭʾ*) is obligatory for him, as is indicated by the Qurʾān, the Sunna, and basic legal principles (*al-uṣūl*); nay, it is the objective of marriage. [The fact that intercourse] is required by the human constitution (*iqtiḍāʾ al-ṭabʿ*) does not negate its being obligatory, just as it does not negate the obligatoriness of eating and drinking. The Prophet (peace be upon him!) said to ʿAbd Allāh ibn ʿAmr (may God be pleased with both of them!) when he saw him fasting continually, "Your wife has a claim on you."[74] If she were not entitled to intercourse, she would not have the power to annul the marriage on the basis of his inability to have intercourse or refusing to do so.[75]

Noting the opinion that the husband is obligated to have intercourse only once every four months based on the maximum period of foreswearing (*īlāʾ*),

he presents the opposing opinion that "it is obligatory to have intercourse with her according to what is customary and kind (*bi'l-maʿrūf*) based on his powers and her needs, just as it is obligatory to provide maintenance based according to what is customary and kind, and just as he is entitled to what [she] is obligated [to provide] for him according to what is customary and kind based on her powers and his needs." He concludes resoundingly that "the second [opinion] is more in conformity with the Qur'an, the Sunna, the principles [of law], and the welfare of humankind; it is the only way that the needs of people can be fulfilled and harm can be averted."[76]

Proceeding to the husband's claims upon his wife, he presents a series of hadith emphasizing her subjugation to him. He concludes that "the husband is entitled to enjoy her sexually whenever he likes as long as he does not harm her or prevent her from engaging in an obligatory [task], and she is obligated to make herself available to him for that and not leave his house without his permission or the permission of the [divine] Legislator"—although he should not forbid her from visiting the mosque without good reason. He closes by asking, "Does he have a claim on her body in terms of housework (*al-khidma*), such as spreading [bedding], sweeping, cooking, and the like? The jurists have differed on this; some say that she is obligated to do it, others that she is not obligated, and [yet] others that she is obligated to do light [housework] as is dictated by custom, which differs according to people's lifeways (*ʿādāt*)."[77]

In this brief overview of the marital relationship, there are two points on which Ibn Taymīya advocates unacknowledged but significant revisions to the received majority view of the marriage contract. The husband's obligation is to provide for all of the wife's physical needs, including sex as well as food and clothing; although Ibn Taymīya is less conclusive on the issue of housework here than elsewhere, the wife's obligations appear to be correspondingly comprehensive. He creates an effect of symmetry by stating that a wife has rights with respect to her husband's body (*badan*)—specifically, regular sex—and by then framing the husband's possible entitlement to her labor as his having "a right with respect her body in service" (*ḥaqq fī badanihā min al-khidma*).[78] In another verbal parallelism that emphasizes the text's overarching theme of equity and fairness, he states that the wife is entitled to maintenance and sex "based on his abilities and her needs," while the husband's entitlements to the wife (implicitly including labor) are similarly (and reciprocally) "based on her abilities and his needs."[79] The themes of justice and of conformity to community mores are combined in the focal concept of *al-maʿrūf.*

Ibn Taymīya also overtly problematizes the idea that the reciprocal duties of the spouses are a transaction of exchange similar to hire or sale, pointing out that scholars of the various *madhhabs* have differed on the question of whether a wife's *nafaqa* is a need-based obligatory gift (*ṣila*) like that of indigent relatives or a countervalue (*muʿāwaḍa*) like the dower or a wage.[80] While he does not take an explicit stand on this issue, overall he posits a different kind of reciprocity and balance, which is not the exchange of considerations under an aleatory contract but the balance of justice and fairness. Most striking is his overall framing of the rights and duties of the marriage contract within the Qur'anic ethical standards of compliance with community mores (*maʿrūf*) and of kindness (*iḥsān*). The ethical coloring of the passage is deepened by his highlighting of the subjective attitudes of the spouses, who must render their marital duties wholeheartedly rather than grudgingly.[81] Ibn Taymīya's account of the ethico-legal structure of the marital relationship thus resonates with Ovamir Anjum's observation that "a reader familiar with medieval Sunni literature is likely to be struck by the remarkable emphasis Ibn Taymiyya places on justice (*ʿadl*). It is the guiding virtue for Ibn Taymiyya in law, ethics, and, most of all, politics."[82]

This vision of the marital bond as a comprehensive ethical relationship headed by a benevolent male provider fits harmoniously into Ibn Taymīya's overall project in this work of statecraft (*siyāsa*), which constructs a similar vision of the Muslim polity as a whole. He occasionally draws an explicit parallel between the ruler and the husband/patriarch, as when he supports an argument in favor of the ruler's broad right to impose discretionary punishments by pointing to a husband's Qur'anically stipulated right to discipline his wife (cf. Q 4:34).[83] He similarly argues that a ruler must impose Qur'anic punishments in a spirit of compassion rather than of anger or desire for domination, just as a father disciplines his child.[84] The parallel between husband and ruler was not new to Islamic thought; as Karen Bauer has observed in her study of medieval Qur'anic exegesis, "interpreters sought to frame marriage within the context of common notions of just rulership."[85] However, this parallel had until this point not been used as a productive element of legal reasoning in *fiqh* texts; Ibn Taymīya's integration of this motif into his legal analysis of the marital relationship is thus novel.

It is worth emphasizing that in *al-Siyāsa al-sharʿīya* Ibn Taymīya frames both leaders and male heads of household within a model in which rightful authority is exercised through the development and modeling of proper ethical dispositions. As discussed in the introduction, the development of ethical dispositions has become a central theme in contemporary academic accounts of premodern Islamic law but has appeared strikingly rarely in the *fiqh* texts consulted so far in this study. Ibn Taymīya, unlike most of his predecessors, ambitiously promotes the idea of a fully Sharia-based sociopolitical order that is not only regulated by the legal guidelines of *fiqh* but saturated with Islamic ethical content.[86] Indeed, he understands the raison d'être of governmental authority in general as being the enjoining of the right (*al-maʿrūf*) and the forbidding of evil (*al-munkar*).[87] In particular, Caterina Bori notes that "ruling with equity, fairness or 'justice' is the lynchpin of the second part of the treatise and a crucial component of Ibn Taymiyya's concept of 'just *siyāsa*.'"[88] In his view of governance as well as of marriage, there is no gap between what is legally required and what is morally right.

Providing for the needs of one's subordinates is, in this view, inseparable from the project of fostering their moral growth: "[A man] ought to facilitate the path of goodness and obedience, aid [his dependents] in following it, and encourage it in every way possible, such as providing for his child, or his spouse, or his household what will encourage them to pursue virtuous action, whether wealth, or praise, or anything else."[89]

In this vision, the provision of material sustenance is not merely a pragmatic duty that fulfills the physical needs of subordinates or secures their loyalty and obedience but a component of the larger project of enabling and incentivizing those subordinates' pursuit of religious virtue. Ibn Taymīya similarly relates marital sex to the moral leadership and the self-formation of the husband. Stressing the importance of the happy mean (*al-ʿadāla*) in the constitution of moral virtue, he cites hadith texts emphasizing the religious merit of having sex with one's wife and of every morsel of food one places in her mouth.[90] This larger vision helps to explain Ibn Taymīya's distinctive view of the obligations of marriage, in which sex as well as material sustenance are understood as components of the husband's ethical care for his wife.

Ibn Taymīya's views of marriage are presented in a form that is simultaneously highly fragmented and richly (if unevenly) developed. Despite the disparity of the contexts where he picks up the topic, his underlying model is consistent in its broad outlines. He understands marriage in terms of an analogy with slavery that is far more comprehensive than the "ownership of the vulva (*buḍʿ*)" envisioned by early Muslim jurists. Rather than a contractual exchange of the husband's maintenance for the wife's usufruct of sexual availability, he envisions a comprehensive relationship of both subordination and nurture. Ibn Taymīya's husband-father is a benevolent proprietor whose control over his household and responsibilities toward them are all-encompassing, tempered only by community mores and by a broad ethical standard of non-harm. The relationship between husband and wife, like that between father and child or between ruler and subject, is not a balanced contractual exchange of specific entitlements but a comprehensive relationship of benevolent dominance and submissive service (limited only by the boundaries of compassion and custom). The husband provides maintenance not as a countervalue for a limited claim upon his wife but as a form of care for one who is completely dependent. In this context, it is inevitable that the wife provide labor to her husband and unacceptable that she demand wages to do so.

Ibn Taymīya's reframing of marriage on the model of an enslaved person's comprehensive dependency on, and obedience to, an owner radically revises traditional Islamic legal understandings of the reciprocal rights and duties of the marriage contract. As Kecia Ali has demonstrated in detail, the model of slavery served as a frame of reference for the elaboration of the *fiqh* of marriage in the formative period.[91] However, at this earlier stage both the parallels and the distinctions between the statuses of wives and enslaved women were approached in terms of limited analogies applied to specific legal scenarios. In contrast, Ibn Taymīya treats the parallel dyads of husband and wife, enslaver and enslaved, as overall moral relationships with sweeping legal implications. He correspondingly de-emphasizes the degree to which the marriage contract should be understood as one of balanced exchange (*muʿāwaḍa*).

Although Ḥanbalīs generally held the required quantity of *nafaqa* to depend on the wife's needs, they nevertheless understood it as direct compensation (*ʿiwaḍ*) for her sexual availability (and thus implicitly not for other services such as housework). This point was repeatedly emphasized by Ibn Qudāma.[92] In contrast, Ibn Taymīya is strongly opposed to construing any aspect of the marital relationship in terms of payment to retain the wife for any specific form of service. The most direct expression of Ibn Taymīya's aversion to the quantification or monetization of spousal rights and duties is the case of breastfeeding. As we have seen, leading Ḥanbalī authorities argued that even a mother who remained married to the father of her child could at least hypothetically demand a standard wage (*ujrat al-mithl*) for nursing. In a lengthy discussion that is framed as a single-subject essay rather than as a response to a legal inquiry (perhaps indicating his personal interest in the subject), Ibn Taymīya directly refutes this doctrine.[93] Although he nominally references the possibility that the spouses could negotiate a wage for the wife's nursing, his larger argument seems to be that a wife is never entitled to a wage specifically corresponding to the time or effort she expends in nursing or caring for her child; rather, her entitlements are exhausted by her general dependency on her husband, who must directly provide for her needs.[94] Ibn Taymīya did affirm the established Ḥanbalī doctrine that stipulations added to their marriage contracts were valid as long as they did not conflict with the objectives of marriage.[95] However, he appears to have considered the commercialization of relations between the spouses to so conflict; in addition to denying that a wife could negotiate wages for breastfeeding, he at least entertained the idea that spouses could not validly hire each other for any purpose.[96]

Ibn Taymīya does occasionally use commercial analogies in his analysis of specific issues relating to marriage. However, he does so in ways that diverge from the common model in which the wife "sells" her sexual availability to her husband. At one point in his fatwa on *nafaqa* he notes that the marriage contract partakes of the character of an *ʿaqd muʿāwaḍa*. Unusually for a premodern scholar, he then introduces another model by arguing that the marriage contract also partakes of the character of a partnership (*mushāraka*).[97] He does so, however, not to highlight the egalitarian or reciprocal nature of the relationship but to substantiate the claim that a husband is given the role of a trustee (*muʾtamin*) over the maintenance he expends on his wife, just as an agent or partner in a business venture or a sharecropping agreement is given a role of trust over any funds he has expended on the assets of the partnership. Thus, a husband's claim to have provided past maintenance should be accepted over his wife's claim to the contrary; like the partner or agent of a business, he is given the authority to administer its assets and enjoys legal deference to his testimony about them. In this analogy the wife is implicitly likened not to a fellow member of the business partnership but to the partnership's asset (whether commercial goods or agricultural land) on which wealth is expended in the course of business or cultivation.[98]

Ibn Taymīya makes a similar, if more elaborate, analogy in his argument against a wife's claim for wages in exchange for nursing. Here he analyzes the father's duty to physically sustain mother and child through an elaborate organic analogy illustrating his view that "the child belongs to the father, not to the mother, and for this reason [the father] is responsible for maintaining it during pregnancy and for its nursing fees."[99] He writes:

> If the father is the one who maintains [the child] when it is a fetus and a nursling, and the mother is a vessel (*wiʿāʾ*), then the child is [like] a crop (*zarʿ*) belonging to the father. God said, "Your wives are a tillage for you, so go to your tillage as you like" (Q 2:223), so the woman is the cultivated land, and what is planted in it belongs to the father. . . . The crop that is in the land has been earned by the cultivator who planted it, watered it, and paid the rent on the land. [Similarly], the husband gave the wife the *mahr*, which is the wages for intercourse (*ajr al-waṭʾ*), as God said: "there is no fault in you to marry them when you have given them their wages" [Q 60:10]. . . . So the mother is the tillage, which is the land where [the child] was planted, and the father hired her (*istaʾjarahā*) with the *mahr* as land is rented [by the cultivator] and maintained the crop by maintaining [her] when she was pregnant, then supported the nursling, just as the renter [of land] pays the expenses of the crop and the fruit when it is hidden [in the earth] and when it comes forth.[100]

Here again, the wife and mother is envisioned not as a party to a contract of sale or hire but as agricultural property on which the husband expends wealth in the course of cultivating it. This scenario, which is perhaps more of an extended metaphor than a strict juristic analogy, both parallels and diverges from the model in which al-Māwardī envisioned the wife as the proprietor of a house (her body) that was maintained by its renter (her husband). In both cases, the husband's payment of *nafaqa* is likened to the expenses incurred by a renter tending to the property that he has leased. However, while al-Māwardī casts the wife as a commercial actor selling a specific usufruct (sexual availability) of her commodified body, Ibn Taymīya casts the wife and all of her capacities (for sexual enjoyment, labor, and reproduction) in the role of the leased agricultural soil. By equating the situations before and after birth, Ibn Taymīya assimilates the mother's work in feeding and caring for the nursling to the biological processes that grow the fetus within her body. Such a model left no room for the wife's labor to be considered a separate asset that she could either retain (by declining to work) or contract to her husband for compensation.

Building on the Teachings of Ibn Taymīya: Ibn Qayyim al-Jawzīya

Ibn Taymīya's views on wives' domestic labor were most fully developed by his student Ibn Qayyim al-Jawzīya, whose association with Ibn Taymīya began in 713/1313 and culminated in his imprisonment in the citadel of Damascus when his mentor was incarcerated there in 726/1326; he was released only after Ibn Taymīya's death two years later. While he diverged from Ibn Taymīya's opinions on individual issues, in general he was the central exponent of his teacher's thought.[101] On the issue of wives' obligation to provide housework, he both adopts Ibn Taymīya's doctrine and elaborates on it in new ways. Ibn al-Qayyim sets forth his views on wives' domestic labor primarily in a single extended passage of his major ethico-legal work *Zād al-maʿād* ("Provisions for the Afterlife"), which elaborates on the Prophet's normative practice in all areas of life. In his "Chapter on the Prophet's Judgment Regarding a Wife's Serving Her Husband," he writes:

> Ibn Ḥabīb said in the *Wāḍiḥa*:[102] The Prophet (peace be upon him!) adjudicated between ʿAlī ibn Abī Ṭālib and his wife Fāṭima when the two of them complained to him about work (*al-khidma*); he ruled that Fāṭima was responsible for the indoor work, [that is,] the housework (*al-khidma al-bāṭina khidmat al-bayt*), and that ʿAlī was responsible for the outside work. Then Ibn Ḥabīb said: Indoor work includes kneading [bread], cooking, spreading [the bedding], sweeping the house, drawing water, and all of the housework. In the two *Ṣaḥīḥ*s [of al-Bukhārī and Muslim] [it is reported] that Fāṭima (may God be satisfied with her!) came to the Prophet (peace be upon him!) complaining of the effect of the millstone on her hands and asking him for a servant . . . and [that] he said, "Shall I guide you to something that is better for the two of you than what you have asked for? When you go to your beds, say 'Glory be to God!' thirty-three times." . . . It is also reported in an authentic hadith from Asmāʾ [bint Abī Bakr] that she said: I used to do all of the housework for al-Zubayr. He had a horse and I used to take care

of it; I would gather hay for it and look after it. It is also stated in an authentic report from her that she used to give fodder to his horse, draw water, sew the [leather] bucket, make bread, and carry date pits on her head from some land he owned two-thirds of a parasang away.[103]

The jurists held different opinions about that. A group of the early and later [jurists] held it to be obligatory for [the wife] to serve [her husband] in the needs of the household. Abū Thawr said: She is obligated to serve her husband in every way (*fī kull shayʾ*). Another group denied that she was obligated to serve him in any way. Among those who held that opinion were Mālik, Shāfiʿī, Abū Ḥanīfa, and the Ẓāhirīs. They said: [This is because] the marriage contract entails only sexual enjoyment [of the wife], not use of [the wife] for service and the disposal of her capacities (*badhl al-manāfiʿ*). They said: The aforementioned hadiths simply indicate voluntary [service] and noble morals (*makārim al-akhlāq*), and what does this have to do with [legal] obligation?

Those who held service to be obligatory [for the wife] argued that this is what was customary (*maʿrūf*) among those whom God Most High addressed with His speech. As for giving the woman a life of leisure and having the husband serve, sweep, grind flour, knead [dough], do the washing, spread [the bedding], and take care of the housework, this was considered objectionable (lit.: "unknown," *munkar*). God Most High says, "[Women] have rights corresponding to their obligations, according to what is *maʿrūf*" (Q 2:228). He [also] said, "Men are in authority over women" (*al-rijāl qawwāmūn ʿalā al-nisāʾ*, Q 4:34). If the woman does not serve him, but he is the one who serves her, then she is the one who is in authority over him!

In addition, the dower (*mahr*) is in exchange for sexual access [*al-buḍʿ*, lit. "the vulva"], and each of the two spouses achieves his or her desire from the other; God the Exalted only made it obligatory for him to provide her maintenance, clothing, and shelter in exchange for her sexual availability, her service, and that which is customary for spouses (*wa-mā jarat bihi ʿādat al-azwāj*). In addition, contracts without conditions[104] are interpreted according to custom, and the custom is that a woman serves [her husband] and takes care of the interior affairs of the house.

Their argument that Fāṭima and Asmā's service was a voluntary act and a good deed is refuted by the fact that Fāṭima was complaining about the service she was performing, and [the Prophet] did not say to ʿAlī, "No service is obligatory for her; rather, it is obligatory for you." [The Prophet] did not favor anyone in his verdicts. And when he saw Asmāʾ with fodder on her head, and al-Zubayr was

> with him, he did not say to him, "She is not obligated to do any service!" or that this is oppression of her; rather, he [tacitly] endorsed his using her for service, and he endorsed the rest of his Companions' using their wives for service despite his knowledge that among [the wives] there were those who were unwilling as well as those who were willing; this is something about which there is no doubt.
>
> There is no valid distinction between a noble woman and a lowly one, a rich woman and a poor one; this [i.e., Fāṭima] is the noblest woman in the universe who used to serve her husband and came to [the Prophet] (peace be upon him!) complaining of the work, and he did not respond to her complaint. In an authentic hadith the Prophet called the wife a captive, saying, "Fear God with respect to your wives, for they are captives to you";[105] a captive is a prisoner, and the station of a prisoner is to serve the person in whose possession he is. There is no doubt that marriage is a kind of slavery; one of the early Muslims has said, "Marriage is slavery, so let one of you look [well] to whom he is enslaving his daughter."[106] The preponderant one of the two opinions [about women's obligation to do housework] and the stronger of the two proofs will not be hidden from any fair person.[107]

In this passage Ibn al-Qayyim acknowledges that the eponymous founders of three of the four classical Sunni schools of law categorically denied that wives were obligated to perform housework; he omits any mention that, as noted by Ibn Qudāma, this doctrine was attributed to the founder of his own school as well. He represents the arguments in favor of this position as twofold. One line of reasoning holds that, while there are reported instances of wives performing difficult domestic labor with the knowledge and apparent approval of the Prophet, the exemplary early Muslim wives in question did so as a supererogatory act of virtue. Ibn al-Qayyim dismisses this argument not, as his teacher Ibn Taymīya had done, by collapsing the distinction between legal and ethical guidelines but by arguing that the precedents in question fall on the legal side of this distinction: Fāṭima's labor, in particular, appears to have been less than willing. Although Ibn al-Qayyim is in many ways just as interested as his mentor in highlighting the congruence between Islamic law and ethics, it is not the emphasis in this passage.

The second argument that Ibn al-Qayyim addresses is that the woman's labor is not an object of the marriage contract; the husband has purchased the right to his wife's sexual availability, not to her service. He rejects this analysis on the grounds that the spouses benefit equally from their sexual enjoyment of each other; thus, the husband must be entitled to something additional in exchange for his material support of the wife.[108] Ibn al-Qayyim's argument gains force from his distinctive view of marital sex; like Ibn Taymīya, he emphatically affirms the wife's entitlement to regular intercourse, if not to sex on demand.[109] His understanding of the greater (if far from perfect) reciprocity of the spouses' sexual rights clears the way for him to frame labor as a central element of the wife's obligations arising as a result of her husband's economic support.

Having parried the arguments of his opponents, Ibn al-Qayyim builds his positive argument largely on an appeal to *al-maʿrūf.* In this passage, *al-maʿrūf* functions quite straightforwardly as an equivalent of "social custom" (*al-ʿurf*) rather than carrying a strong ethical connotation. The wife's provision of domestic labor is implied in the marriage contract, in his view, because contracts are always interpreted in light of the customary expectations of the parties. In this particular case, he sees wives' domestic labor as an immemorial custom predating, and tacitly endorsed by, the Prophet Muḥammad. In another work he explicitly states that the Prophet "endorsed (*taqrīr*) men in using [their wives] for service such as grinding [grain], washing, cooking, kneading [bread], giving fodder to horses and taking care of the needs of the household; he never said to the men, 'You are allowed to do that only if you help them or persuade them to relinquish wages [for their work].' "[110]

Nevertheless, Ibn al-Qayyim does not see the assignment of domestic labor to the wife as a merely contingent, if historically deeply rooted, feature of existing Muslim societies. Rather, it is an integral part of the moral order of marriage because God has stipulated that husbands have authority over wives, and personal service is inherently an expression of subordination. Thus, it would be an unacceptable inversion of the proper gender order for the husband to perform domestic labor, which is assumed to constitute a degrading form of "service." In another passage, Ibn al-Qayyim argues that if a woman's husband had to do errands and chores for her, "he would be the one who was subservient,[111] captive, and enslaved, and she would be the owner who ruled over him."[112] In emphasizing the central role of domestic labor in the performance of gender hierarchy within marriage, Ibn al-Qayyim erases the social hierarchies emphasized by earlier (and, indeed, many later) jurists. Whereas for centuries jurists had argued that *al-maʿrūf* required the provision of servants for wives whose social station rendered it inappropriate for them to do housework, here Ibn al-Qayyim flattens social distinctions among women in favor of a uniform gendered hierarchy between husbands and wives.

Like his mentor Ibn Taymīya, he repeatedly likens marriage to slavery and uses this model as the basis for various concrete inferences about the marital relationship, particularly in terms of asserting the wife's direct and utter material dependence on her husband.[113] As Yossef Rapoport has argued, for Ibn al-Qayyim, "slavery, rather than being a contemptible institution, was the exemplary patriarchal model, with the bond between a master and his slave the organizing principle of the military elite. . . . The absence of wages shields the supposed mutual loyalty and love between a master and his slave from the disharmonious market economy. The same should hold true, ideally, for the relations between husband and wife."[114]

Indeed, Ibn al-Qayyim argues that for a judge to accept a wife's claim for unpaid monetary maintenance "is the source of enmity and hatred between the spouses, which is the opposite of the affection and compassion that God placed between them [cf. Q 30:21]."[115] In this view, it is precisely the dependence and subordination of the wife that secures the loving mutuality of the marriage. In making this argument he echoes his teacher Ibn Taymīya, who in a passage cited above characterizes the monetization of the wife's maintenance as something that would constitute "enmity" and "harm" between the spouses.[116] In a manner that in some ways foreshadows the early modern European framing of the family as a private sphere governed by relations of sharing rather than of exchange, Ibn Taymīya and Ibn al-Qayyim regard the recognition of quantifiable economic transfers between the spouses as corrosive to the proper moral and affective character of marriage.[117]

Given the frequency with which Ibn al-Qayyim has recourse to the Qur'an in his various discussions of marriage, it is striking that he cites with equal frequency those verses that are regarded by modern Muslim feminists as most hierarchical in their implications (most notably verse 4:34) and those that are now seen as most egalitarian (such as 30:21). His easy assumption of the compatibility of these two sets of Qur'anic references reinforces the arguments of Aysha Hidayatullah, who argues that

> In the premodern context of the Qur'an's revelation, equality may not have been understood as a premise of loving, caring relationships; relationships of

male-female dominance may not have necessarily offended ideals of mercy and tranquility. Classical and premodern views of love and sexuality exhibited a range of attitudes on the relationship between mutuality and hierarchy, including ones that saw possession, passivity, and submission as natural to loving relationships.[118]

The causes and legacy of Ibn Taymīya's and Ibn al-Qayyim's intervention

What might have motivated Ibn Taymīya's and Ibn al-Qayyim's development of a vision of the marital relationship that so systematically diverged from the received Ḥanbalī views discussed by Ibn Qudāma? One explanation would point to very concrete shifts in legal practice that occurred in their lifetimes in the Mamluk domains. As demonstrated by Yossef Rapoport, while jurists had traditionally assumed that spousal maintenance would be delivered in kind, the fourteenth century saw a shift toward the doctrinal acceptance and the actual practice of husband's paying their wives cash stipends. This development elicited acute disapproval and dismay from both Ibn Taymīya and Ibn al-Qayyim not only because it problematically monetized the marital relationship but because it raised the awful (and apparently genuine) possibility of a disgruntled wife's successfully suing her husband for unpaid maintenance and having him thrown in jail, despite his having fed and clothed her for the duration of their marriage.[119]

Their alarmed response to the rise of cash maintenance explains their rejection of the traditional Ḥanbalī positions affirming that *nafaqa* once delivered was an economic asset in the wife's possession (that she could therefore gift or trade) and allowing her to claim back maintenance. It does not, of course, directly explain their distinctive and vigorously argued new positions on domestic labor and marital sex. However, it is possible that a perceived shift in the power relations of between contemporary spouses evoked broader concerns about proper hierarchy within marriage. Rapoport also argues that there is a direct "link between the monetization of marriage and the frequency of divorce," which might have helped to stimulate the two scholars' reflections on the sources of marital love and cohesion.[120] However, given the difficulty of identifying the causes of marital breakdown, it is important not to uncritically accept our elite male sources' assumption that gains in the bargaining power or financial independence of wives were corrosive to the stability of marriages.[121]

Rapoport's discussion also suggests a more direct way in which contemporary social concerns might have informed Ibn Taymīya's reinterpretation of wives' legal obligation for housework. In Ibn Taymīya's lengthy and celebrated fatwa on the impermissibility of *taḥlīl*, he laments the various stratagems that a discontented wife can use to coerce her husband into divorce.[122] He writes that one of these is that

> she can go to extremes in demanding her full entitlements from him and refraining from [voluntary] kindness (*iḥsān*) to him. I don't mean that she refrains from an obligation that she considers to be obligatory or commits a forbidden act that she believes to be forbidden, but something else, such as . . . that she may demand that he provide her with a home of her own that is appropriate to her [station] and a servant, or similar entitlements that may be burdensome for him, and that she refuses to help him in the household by cooking, making beds, sweeping, washing, and the like, all of this so that he will separate from her.[123]

Ibn Taymīya emphasizes that the scenario he is concerned with is of a wife doing such a thing without any actual violation of the Sharia. In this case, what matters is the wife's motivation: "if the wife . . . does not mind doing the housework (*khidma*) that is customary, but is merely objecting to it in order to pressure her husband so that he will divorce her," then she is committing a sin due to the harm (*ḍarar*) inflicted on her husband and her preemption of his choice to divorce or remain married.[124] Here Ibn Taymīya's concern is with the exploitation of the gap between social practice and legal doctrine. Of course, presumably a wife could go on strike from housework even if it was deemed a legal obligation; but she could do so only at the expense of both the moral and the legal high ground, a factor that might matter in the disposition of a divorce case.

One can also place these two scholars' attitudes toward wives' domestic labor in the context of evolving social attitudes toward domesticity as a component of ideal Muslim womanhood, particularly with respect to the elite women who had been most explicitly exempt from such labor in classical law. It has been noted by scholars that the thirteenth and fourteenth centuries saw a rise in expressions of admiration for the domestic labor and skills of elite Syrian women. Louis Pouzet observes that the wives of prominent and prosperous scholars in seventh/thirteenth-century Damascus were lauded as ideal women by virtue of their domestic labor as well as their piety. For instance, Sibṭ Ibn al-Jawzī eulogized his wife Zaynab bint Abī'l-Qāsim (d. 644/1246–1247) with praise for her delicious cooked dishes and pastries.[125] In a remarkably intimate and artless poem of considerable length, the jurist and historian Abū Shāma (d. 665/1268) praises his wife in part by describing how she takes care of all of the affairs of the household. Her domestic attainments range from embroidery, sewing, and spinning to sweeping, cooking, and washing. Significantly, he notes that this is not for lack of female help with such tasks; rather, due to her high standards, she chooses to do the work herself.[126]

This trend was sustained in the following period. Both Pouzet and Rapoport note the laudatory references to women's domestic skills in the work of the Damascene historian Ibn al-Jazarī (d. 833/1429). He eulogizes his prematurely deceased niece Fāṭima as "an upstanding woman who used to embroider, sew, cook various kinds [of food], take care of all of the needs of her home, and serve her husband (*taqūm bi-khidmat zawjihā*)."[127] He describes her sister Ṣāliḥa, who also went to an early grave, as having been "virtuous [*ṣāliḥa*] like her name, engaging much in prayer, fasting, embroidery, cooking, and all kinds of housework (*jamīʿ ashghāl al-bayt*)."[128] He praises the daughter of a goldsmith (*ṣāʾigh*), Zayn al-Nisāʾ bint ʿImād al-Dīn Ibn Mulham, for her service (*khidma*) as well as for her honor (*muruwwa*). He specifically notes her skill in cooking, sewing, embroidery, and weaving, domestic accomplishments that appear parallel to her religious virtues and her good-natured and unpretentious character.[129]

As we saw in the introduction, flattering depictions of elite domesticity were not completely new; Badīʿ al-Zamān al-Hamadhānī produced such a vignette (fictional but sociologically precise) as early as the fourth/tenth century. However, one would be hard pressed to find such a depiction in the biographical dictionaries of earlier centuries, which generally limited themselves to the scholarly accomplishments or the pious practices of the women they covered. It is difficult to determine whether this shift primarily reflects shifts in social values or in genre conventions; Mamluk-era biographical dictionaries are notoriously rich in personal details and outright gossip that might have scandalized scholars of earlier ages. Furthermore, the newfound interest in middle- and upper-class women's housekeeping skills was not uniform. Muḥammad al-Sakhāwī (d. 902/1497) included in his own *ṭabaqāt* work a full volume on women that is one of the richest sources of women's history for this period.[130] Unlike Ibn al-Jazarī, however (and despite his own proclivity for juicy personal details), he does not mention the domestic accomplishments of his female subjects. His only reference to housekeeping regards his own enslaved servant who used to "keep our house in order" (*kānat ḍābiṭa li-baytinā*).[131] He occasionally mentions a woman's skill in sewing or embroidery, but only if there is a reason why it is notable (in one case because the woman in question had a deformed hand, in another because she taught embroidery to the neighborhood children).[132] Several women are described as prudent or as good managers (*mudabbira*), but this general attribute is not explicitly associated with the household.[133] Pending further evidence, it is difficult to disentangle the factors of time and place from the personal proclivities of individual authors. Nevertheless, there appears to be some reason to believe that in Damascus in this period there was an enhanced appreciation for the domestic skills and the personal service of women of all classes, including those who surely had servants.

If there is some reason to believe that the novel view of Ibn Taymīya and Ibn al-Qayyim were informed by the Damascene social mores of their time, there is also evidence that their arguments reflect a longer-term shift in scholarly opinion. As discussed by Karen Bauer in a study of Qur'anic exegesis, by the eighth/fourteenth century the argument that wives were obligated to perform housework was a familiar idea associated with Qur'anic commentators hailing from a variety of different locales, including al-Zamakhsharī (d. 538/1144) and Fakhr al-Dīn Rāzī (d. 606/1209).[134] Bauer also discusses how exegetes interpreting Qur'anic verses on the marital relationship "sought to frame marriage within the context of just rulership." In particular, "the exegetes' description of marriage as a hierarchy was predicated on the idealized vision that the stronger party (the man) should treat the weaker party (the woman) within acceptable bounds of propriety."[135] These elements of the exegetical tradition on marriage offer clear precedents for the analyses of Ibn Taymīya and Ibn al-Qayyim. In this sense, the interpretations they advanced in legal contexts were less new in substance than new to the religious discipline in which they were writing; their innovation was in part to import premises and motifs from the *tafsīr* tradition into their arguments about enforceable legal claims.[136]

Of course, as we have seen, the opinion that wives were obligated to do housework was not completely new to *fiqh*; as demonstrated by Ibn al-Qayyim's invocation of Ibn Ḥabīb, the two scholars in part evinced an unusual willingness to stretch *madhhab* boundaries. However, there are grounds to believe that the fourteenth century saw a shift in legal attitudes on the issue of wives' domestic labor that went beyond inter-*madhhab* borrowing by a pair of scholars with an unusual resistance to the constraints of school precedent. While the idea that any wife had an affirmative legal obligation to provide household labor was a minority opinion in classical Mālikī *fiqh*, in the fourteenth century it was canonized as the prevalent school doctrine. In his *Mukhtaṣar* (which both summarized existing school doctrine and served as an authoritative reference for it in subsequent centuries), Khalīl ibn Isḥāq al-Jundī (d. ca. 776/1374) describes a wife's maintenance as generally being "according to custom, proportionately to [her husband's] means and her needs"; she may be entitled to a servant, but "otherwise, she is obligated to do the housework (*al-khidma al-bāṭina*) including kneading dough, sweeping, and making beds (*farsh*), unlike weaving and spinning [which she is not obliged to do]."[137] The same doctrine was articulated by the fourteenth-century Granadan Mālikī Ibn Juzayy, suggesting that by this period, school doctrine had shifted on a broad transregional level.[138] It seems likely that such articulations of prevalent school doctrine are a "lagging indicator" of preexisting shifts in opinion.

Substantively, then, the doctrines of Ibn Taymīya and Ibn al-Qayyim on wives' domestic labor are not completely new or unique. Ultimately, what is most distinctive about their arguments on this subject is less that they assert a truly novel connection between housework and proper Muslim wifehood than that they cross disciplinary boundaries to collapse the established distinction between legal and ethical obligation. One may compare their views on the household obligations of wives to those of Muḥyī al-Dīn al-Nawawī (d. 676/1277), a Damascene Shāfiʿī of the generation between Ibn Qudāma and Ibn Taymīya. Al-Nawawī addresses the issue of wives' domestic labor most directly in his commentary on the canonical hadith collection *Ṣaḥīḥ Muslim*. After enumerating the various forms of labor the prominent female Companion of the Prophet Asmāʾ bint Abī Bakr is reported to have performed for her husband, al-Nawawī declares:

> All of this is in the category of right and customary action (*al-maʿrūf*) and honorable forms of conduct (*al-murūʾāt*) that people are unanimous in following. That is that a woman serves her husband by performing the aforementioned tasks and

> similar ones, such as baking bread, cooking, washing clothes, and other things. All of that is a voluntary act (*tabarruʿ*) and a good deed (*iḥsān*) on the part of the woman toward her husband, a form of kindly companionship (*ḥusn muʿāshara*) and a right and customary act (*fiʿl maʿrūf*) with respect to him. None of that is obligatory for her; rather, if she refused to do any of this, she would not commit a sin, and he would be required to provide these things for her. It is not permissible for him to compel her to do any of these things. The woman does it only as a voluntary act; it is a goodly custom (*ʿāda jamīla*) that women have continued to follow from the earliest times until now. The only things that are obligatory on a wife are two: making herself [sexually] available to her husband and remaining in his house.[139]

In this passage, the fervency of al-Nawawī's conviction that it is good and proper for wives to provide labor to their households is matched only by the clarity of his acknowledgment that they have no legal obligation to do so. His understanding of the marital household as a social reality and as a religious ideal coexists with a legal model in which the marriage contract is an exchange between the husband's material support and the wife's sexual availability. In his legal manuals *Rawḍat al-ṭālibīn* and *Minhāj al-ṭālibīn*, in contrast, al-Nawawī confines himself to questions of *fiqh*; in these works he affirms that elite wives are entitled to servants and prefers the doctrine that a wife can validly receive wages for nursing or housework from her husband.[140] A wife *ought* to be willing to work for free, but she legally *can* contract for wages for cooking.[141] The primary difference between al-Nawawī's views and those of Ibn Taymīya and Ibn al-Qayyim is thus not that the latter believe that wives should provide domestic labor (a point on which all three scholars concur) but that they make this view of the moral obligations of marriage central to their reasoning about its legal obligations.

While Ibn Taymīya's writings discussed here are now included in his "collected fatwas," these particular texts are not fatwas in the strict sense of narrowly tailored responses to questions of legal interpretation; rather, they are broad ethico-legal syntheses.[142] While one of them is technically a fatwa in the sense that it responds to a set concrete legal inquiries about the law of *nafaqa*, Ibn Taymīya chooses to extend his response into a survey of the rights and duties of marriage that carries it beyond the conventional boundaries of the genre. Scholars have debated the genre designation appropriate to the other major work discussed above in which he laid forth his views of marriage, the monograph *Al-Siyāsa al-sharʿīya*. Mona Hassan notes that "*Al-Siyāsa al-sharʿiyya* is not a legal manual, a book of jurisprudence," but "a composition designed to advise the ruling elite and elevate their moral standards of governance."[143] Hassan emphasizes this work's continuity with the genre of "mirrors for princes," while Ovamir Anjum argues for its formal novelty: "The raw material of which Ibn Taymiyya's political tracts like *Siyāsa* . . . are constructed is entirely scriptural, but its deployment and construction by Ibn Taymiyya do not resemble any classical discourse."[144] In this view, the work is legal in that it is an exposition of the Sharia, but Ibn Taymīya has radically expanded the scope of *sharʿī* discourse to include far more than conventional *fiqh*. These views converge in the shared recognition that Ibn Taymīya's works extend and repurpose preexisting genre conventions.[145] Ibn Taymīya at the very least stretches received genre boundaries, and his textual strategy is a direct function of a project to reimagine the role and purview of Islamic law.

* * *

Ibn Taymīya is not completely novel in incorporating ethical discourse into his legal writing. As we have seen, on the topic of wives' domestic labor al-Sarakhsī highlights the issue of moral obligation while making careful distinctions between ethical and legal claims; Ibn Qudāma similarly incorporates discussion of the wife's ethical obligations into his *fiqh* manual, although without any apparent implications for the legal doctrine he expounds. The legal argumentation of jurists such as Ibn Qudāma and al-Nawawī is certainly not hermetically sealed from ethical discourses. For instance, in *al-Mughnī* Ibn Qudāma discusses in passing the issue of proper marital jealousy (*ghayra*), and al-Nawawī includes in the *Rawḍa* a discussion of "kind companionship" (*al-muʿāshara bi'l-maʿrūf*) that extends it to a general ethic of reciprocity and consideration between the spouses.[146] However, neither of them uses such ethical considerations as grounds to modify received school doctrine on marriage.

Ibn Taymīya's analysis of marriage thus produces an unprecedented synthesis of legal and ethical discourses. It is important to note that his ethical discourse is one emphatically based in Qur'an and hadith, rather than in *falsafa*. Greek ideas about "household management" (*tadbīr al-manzil*) had long since filtered into the broader religious discourse. Ibn Taymīya's twelfth-century Ḥanbalī predecessor, the Baghdadi preacher Ibn al-Jawzī, includes in his work *Ṣayd al-khāṭir* a chapter that is in its entirety a detailed summary of Bryson's work on *Tadbīr al-manzil* (albeit one that is not identified as such), including reference to a wife's role in household management.[147] Ibn Taymīya, for his part, saw no value in Greek practical ethics, including the science of household management; he declared with asperity that anything Greek philosophers had to offer in the areas of "the management of moral characteristics, households and polities (*siyāsat al-akhlāq wa'l-manzil wa'l-madāʾin*)" was inferior to the guidance of revealed religions.[148] His approach was to build ethical principles inductively from the wording of revealed texts, in this case focusing centrally on the Qur'anic concept of *al-maʿrūf.*

Ibn Taymīya's concrete doctrines on wives' domestic labor were to some extent incorporated into the legal manuals of the Ḥanbalī madhhab, but they did not prevail as school doctrine.[149] As Christopher Melchert has shown, this is typical of his clear but limited contribution to the *furūʿ* literature of the Ḥanbalī school overall in the centuries following his death. For his part, Ibn al-Qayyim is rarely cited in later legal compendia at all.[150] As we shall see in the conclusion, the full impact of Ibn Taymīya and Ibn al-Qayyim's new ethico-legal synthesis of marriage would be delayed until their rediscovery in the modern period.

Conclusion

THUS FAR, WE have explored a series of Muslim jurists' approaches to the issue of wives' domestic labor on their own terms and within their own historical contexts. This conclusion takes a brief look at developments subsequent to the period covered in the body of the book, with a particular focus on the ways in which the doctrines and texts examined there have been reappropriated and reframed in subsequent centuries. It begins by briefly illustrating that the abiding gap between the *fiqh* of wives' domestic labor and the prevailing social and religious norms persisted, giving rise to sporadic but ongoing reflection on the relationship between Islamic law and ethics. In the second section, it examines the significant doctrinal shifts that took place beginning in the late nineteenth century, showing that this period's ideology of domesticity showed both significant continuities and genuine departures from the patterns of earlier centuries. It then takes a brief look at contemporary developments in which modern Muslims have selectively and creatively drawn on the doctrinal repertories of earlier eras. Finally, it revisits the larger question of the relationship between Islamic law and ethics as it has been envisioned in the existing secondary literature, suggesting that rather than ushering in an unprecedented bifurcation of law and ethics the modern period has seen the reconfiguration of an already complex Islamic normative landscape.

The *fiqh* and ethics of domestic labor in the fourteenth–nineteenth centuries

As we have seen, the idea that "Islamic law does not require wives to do housework" requires some modification, particularly for the postclassical period. Despite the interventions of scholars like Ibn Taymīya, however, there remained a perplexing gap between *fiqh* doctrines largely denying that wives were obligated to provide domestic labor and widespread mores demanding that they do so. As discussed in chapter 4, in the fourteenth century there were some shifts in scholarly opinion beyond the intervention of Ibn Taymīya. Most notably in terms of mainstream *madhhab* doctrines, the Mālikī Khalīl ibn Isḥāq (d. ca. AH 776/1374 CE) articulated an affirmative duty for non-elite wives to cook and clean that for the first time became canonical for a major school of law.[1] Nevertheless, in Sunni *fiqh* overall, rationales for such a duty remained ill-articulated and the authority of earlier school teachings persisted. Meanwhile, the perception that various forms of quotidian labor were customarily performed by (and demanded of) wives remained pervasive. This perceived disjunction, which raised the specter of women's exploitation, continued to provoke intermittent expressions of moral concern. Neither was the tension merely one between theory and practice; rather, *fiqh* continued to coexist with other religious discourses emphasizing housework as a defining function of a virtuous Muslim wife.

In the literature of ethical edification and admonishment, the religious merit of wives' engagement in housework continued to be extolled with little emphasis on their legal privilege to decline it. A marriage manual probably dating to the ninth/fifteenth century incorporates a text in which the Prophet Muḥammad admonishes his daughter Fāṭima with a long series of exhortations on her marital duties, including cooking, spinning, and washing clothes.[2] Fulsome reports in praise of women's household labor circulated in works that, while sometimes attracting the wrath of religious scholars, achieved wide and lasting dissemination. One of these is the fifteenth-century preacher's manual *Nuzhat al-majālis wa-muntakhab al-nafāʾis* of ʿAbd al-Raḥmān al-Ṣaffūrī, which contains such pseudo-hadith as "If a woman washes her husband's clothes, God records for her a thousand good deeds and forgives for her a thousand sins; everything the sun shines on asks forgiveness for her, and she is raised a thousand degrees."[3] This work's disrepute was such that an inquiry to the Egyptian polymath ʿAbd al-Raḥmān al-Suyūṭī suggested that all copies should be destroyed. Nevertheless, it was clearly popular; the questioner notes that it is being read and dictated for copying from "preacher's seats and pulpits" (*al-karāsī wa'l-manābir*).[4]

Sometimes the discrepancy between pious traditions celebrating wives' domestic work and legal doctrines denying the husband any entitlement to it was manifest within a single work. In a treatise on the religious virtue of various kinds of human activity, the fourteenth-century Yemeni scholar Muḥammad al-Waṣṣābī al-Ḥubayshī (d. 782/1380–1381) introduces a litany of precedents for wives' performance of household labor with the observation that "the wives of the Prophet and of his Companions used to care for their children, serve their husbands, and subject themselves to labor (*yamtahinna anfusahunna*)."[5] Having exhausted every possible example of Muslim foremothers engaging in household chores, he concludes that "these are explicit proof texts (*dalāʾil muṣarraḥa*) that [the Prophet's and Companions'] wives used to employ themselves with housework (*khidma*); and they are the best women of the Umma."[6] There follows a chapter of largely dubious hadith texts on the vast otherworldly merits of women's spinning, including such declarations as "No woman cooks for her husband but that God gives her the reward of a martyr; when she heats the oven God sends her a thousand angels to ask forgiveness for her. Any woman who arises and makes bread for her husband and the heat of the [oven's] fire hurts her face and hands, God makes her face forbidden to the Fire. A woman's service to her husband is better than this world and all that is in it."[7] Nevertheless, in enumerating a husband's duties to his wife, al-Ḥubayshī remarks laconically that "he should not make her serve him, as it is not obligatory for her."[8]

Not all authors shared al-Ḥubayshī's apparent disinterest in the mismatch between his lavish citation of texts exalting a wife's domestic labor and his grudging acknowledgment that she had no legal obligation to provide it. For some, the discrepancy was the cause for genuine concern. In the early sixteenth century CE, the prominent Shāfiʿī jurist, Sufi, and preacher ʿAlī ibn ʿAṭīya al-Ḥamawī, known as Shaykh ʿAlwān (d. 936/1530), apostrophized his listeners in the Syrian city of Hama about their domestic relations:

> Woe to you, o heedless one! It is obligatory for you to provide service for your wife; you disobey God Most High by using her for service. She owes you neither

> cooking nor blowing [on the fire], neither kneading nor washing, neither [baking] bread nor [making] clothes, neither sewing nor cutting out [of garments]. Everything she does for you is purely an act of kindness on her part, even suckling your infant and tending to it. If she were to demand wages for her work from you, you would know [the value of] her good deed and favor. Give thanks to God for having made her subject to you (*sakhkharahā laka*) and made her serve you while you sit like a prince, ordering and forbidding, chiding and rebuking, insulting and cursing, not knowing the value of what God has blessed you with.[9]

Shaykh ʿAlwān's comments emphasize that, legally speaking, a woman has no obligation to provide domestic service to her husband; hypothetically—although he clearly considers this a provocative counterfactual scenario—she would be entitled to demand monetary compensation for her labor. As a matter of de facto custom, in contrast, he represents husbands as bossing and bullying their wives as the women wait on them hand and foot. Despite the asperity of the scholar's exhortation, he does not demand that his listeners relieve their wives of household tasks; rather, he urges them to recognize the moral debt they owe in exchange for their wives' supererogatory labor. The remedy for the exploitation Shaykh ʿAlwān deplores is not a fundamental reallocation of household work but simply gratitude to God and the husband's manifestation of humility (*tawāḍuʿ*, as he puts it later in this passage[10]) by helping his wife with her chores.

A more technically legal (and less morally edifying) comment on the same disconnect between legal doctrine and prevalent mores was offered by another Shāfiʿī more than a century later. In his commentary on the Shāfiʿī legal manual *Nihāyat al-muḥtāj*, the Egyptian scholar ʿAlī ibn ʿAlī al-Shubrāmallisī (d. 1087/1686) interrupts his impersonal exposition of *madhhab* doctrine to recount a spontaneous exchange that occurred in his teaching circle (presumably at Al-Azhar in Cairo, where he both studied and taught):

> A question was raised in the lesson: Is a man obligated to inform his wife that she is not obligated to serve him in the customary way, such as cooking, sweeping, and the like, as women customarily do, or not? We answered that the most probable doctrine (*al-ẓāhir*) is the former [i.e., that he is obligated to inform her], because if she does not know that that is not obligatory, she will imagine that it is obligatory and that she is not entitled to maintenance (*nafaqa*) or clothing

(*kiswa*) if she does not do it. She will then in effect be coerced (*fa-ṣārat ka'annahā mukraha*) into doing it. Nevertheless, if she does it and does not know [that it is not obligatory for her], it is possible that she will not be entitled to wages for doing so because she has been negligent in failing to investigate and ask about that.[11]

With its awkward repetition of the reference to prevailing custom, this question may reflect the incredulity of a student newly encountering a legal doctrine at odds with social expectations. Implicitly acknowledging the likelihood that women are unaware of their legal rights in this area, al-Shubrāmallisī points to the problematic implications of this situation: if wives' domestic labor is not contractually required, neither is it truly voluntary. Hovering behind this observation is the inference (soon after voiced only to deny it) that a wife thus coerced into service may be entitled to a fair wage. In the context of al-Shubrāmallisī's legal analysis, unlike that of Shaykh ʿAlwān's pastoral exhortation, the wife's possible entitlement to wages looms as a potential material liability rather than simply a moral claim. Rather than insisting that wives be informed of the law, however, al-Shubrāmallisī ultimately minimizes the ethical and legal implications of keeping them in ignorance. A wife's failure to pursue the relevant knowledge, he hopefully concludes, may negate the claims arising from her unwilling contribution of her labor. Al-Shubrāmallisī's answer also suggests a folk interpretation of the gendered obligations of the marriage contract; rather than understanding their economic maintenance as compensation for their sexual availability (as classical *fiqh* doctrine would suggest), he suggests that many wives may have assumed it to compensate them for housework.[12]

While the social context and the concrete details of wives' domestic labor must have changed in myriad ways, the points of principle raised in al-Shubrāmallisī's study circle in seventeenth-century Cairo closely parallel the concerns addressed seven centuries earlier in the fatwa attributed to Ibn Abī Zayd al-Qayrawānī (discussed in chapter 1). The lack of a clear legal obligation for wives to provide housework was a relic of early Islamic thought that had posed at least a latent conundrum for much of the history of Islamic law. Over the centuries, at least some elite women knew and exercised their entitlement to maintain a servant at their husbands' expense; this is visible through contractual provisions modeled in notarial manuals and in legal discussions of their enforceability.[13] Anecdotal evidence suggests that even in the absence of a contractual provision, an elite urban wife (but not a humble or rural one) might successfully petition a judge to instruct her husband to provide a servant.[14] Nevertheless, the scattered evidence available suggests that the lack of any strong legal basis for wives' general responsibility to do housework remained both unfamiliar and jarring to many Muslims of both sexes. The question of what women knew (or were entitled to know) was thus of particular concern.

To the extent that this issue is visible in our sources, it appears that prior to the late-nineteenth-century scholars often shied away from asserting that women must be informed of the law on this point. The only exception I am aware of suggests the radical implications of affirming women's right to know. The West African revivalist ʿUthmān dan Fodio (d. AH 1817), wrote,

> Muslim women—Do not listen to the speech of those who are misguided and who sow the seed of error in the heart of another; they deceive you when they stress obedience to your husbands without telling you of obedience to God and to his Messenger. . . . They seek only their own satisfaction, and that is why they impose upon you tasks which the Law of God and that of his Prophet have never especially assigned to you. Such are—the preparation of foodstuffs, the washing of clothes, and other duties which they like to impose upon you, while they neglect to teach you what God and the Prophet have prescribed for you.[15]

Even in this case, framed as part of a fundamental challenge to the religious legitimacy of the existing social order, it is unclear that the force of the remark is to advocate women's actual abandonment of domestic tasks. Rather, it emphasizes the importance of religious knowledge and the primacy of divinely mandated duties over those that merely serve the interests of other human beings.

Doctrinal shifts of the late nineteenth and twentieth centuries

As has been widely noted in the secondary literature, the late nineteenth century saw fundamental transformations in attitudes toward domesticity among Muslims in the Middle East and beyond. Influenced by and in confrontation with European discourses and practices, they directed unprecedented attention to homemaking as a female calling with its own exacting standards.[16] This ideal of modern domesticity, which was disseminated in part through periodicals aimed at middle-class women, also found expression in contemporary discussions of Islamic legal doctrine on wives' domestic labor. The Egyptian reformer Rashīd Riḍā (d. 1935) addresses this theme in his commentary on verse 2:228 of the Qur'an, which states that "the rights of wives [with regard to their husbands] are equal to the [husbands'] rights with regard to them, although men have precedence over them."[17] Like Shaykh ʿAlwān, Riḍā laments Muslim men's abuse of their wives' services. However, perhaps reflecting the enhanced religious knowledge then available to the educated layperson, he assumes that it occurs in full knowledge of the applicable *fiqh*:

> If you wish to know the vast distance between what most Muslims do and what they believe about their Sharia, look at how they treat their wives. You will find that . . . nothing but weakness restrains one of them from oppressing his wife, and they impose on them burdens that [the women] can bear only with effort and strain. . . . If you were to ask them about their beliefs regarding what [their wives] owe them, they will say what most of their religious scholars say: They owe us no service, cooking, cleaning, sweeping, spreading [of bedding], nursing or upbringing of a child, or supervision of the servants that we employ for those purposes; all they are obligated to do is to remain in the home and make themselves available for [sexual] enjoyment.[18]

Riḍā places his critique explicitly within a context where Muslims' gender norms are subject to disingenuous scrutiny from Western observers. He notes with anguish that "these Europeans whose civilization falls short of our Sharia in raising women's status . . . have come to accuse us of barbarity in the treatment of women," and may see Islam itself as the cause.[19] As we have seen in the introduction, by this period some Muslims cited wives' exemption from housework under the Sharia as a debating point in the confrontation with colonial feminism.[20] Riḍā's response, in contrast, charts a middle path by critiquing both the religiously unwarranted exploitation of wives and the (for him) equally problematic specter of liberated women abandoning their household duties.

The problem, in his eyes, is not merely that husbands misuse their wives but that wives misuse their growing freedoms. Riḍā continues:

> [However], those two things [required from wives by the marriage contract] are non-existent—that is, refraining from leaving the home without permission, and

> refraining from objecting to [sexual] enjoyment. The implication is that [wives] are obligated to do nothing for their husbands at all . . . I say that this is an exaggeration in exempting [wives] from the duties that are incumbent upon them according to the religious law and to custom, and a corresponding exaggeration in placing [extraneous] duties upon them in practice.[21]

The solution, Riḍā argues, requires fundamental reconsideration of the relevant legal doctrines. While acknowledging the majority doctrine of the four classical Sunni schools of law, which denies that wives are obligated to provide housework, he himself thus endorses the doctrine advanced by Ibn Taymīya and Ibn Qayyim al-Jawzīya: based on the Prophet Muḥammad's directive to his own daughter Fāṭima and her husband, ʿAlī, wives are indeed responsible for the care of the home.[22] Riḍā's critique of his contemporaries' approach to the Islamic law of marriage is thus a double one: on the one hand they hypocritically flout the received *fiqh* rules to which they pay lip service, and on the other they adhere to an archaic *fiqh* that fails to capture the spirit of the divine guidance for marriage.

Riḍā further suggests that the issue is more than merely a pragmatic or technically legal question. Rather, he sees the Prophet's allocation of duties between his daughter and son-in-law as manifesting "what is required by the *fiṭra* of God Most High, which is the distribution of tasks between the two spouses: the woman is responsible for managing the household (*tadbīr al-manzil*) and undertaking the tasks within it, and the man is responsible for laboring and earning outside of it."[23] The Qur'anic term *fiṭra* (cf. Q 30:30), which literally means "mode of creation," refers to a person's divinely endowed innate nature.[24] In this interpretation, men's and women's appointed tasks reflect not merely a mutually beneficial exchange formalized by the marriage contract but the immutable and inborn nature of the two sexes. Riḍā concedes that spouses may help each other with their distinctive tasks or hire help if they have the means; nevertheless, he reiterates, the allocation of housework to wives and of remunerative outside labor to husbands "is the default and the *fiṭrī* division [of labor] by which people's welfare is ensured."[25]

The gendering of the concept of *fiṭra* appears to be a modern phenomenon reflecting a newly biologized and essentialized understanding of the gender binary.[26] It takes us into a quite different discursive world from the premodern *fiqh* discussions of the marriage contract, in which the propriety of engaging in household chores is most strongly associated with social status. Even the arguments of Ibn Taymīya and Ibn al-Qayyim, although they generalize the obligation of housework to wives regardless of status, emphasize proper gender hierarchy within marriage rather than any innate affinity between women and housework: women (like children and servants) serve because they are subordinate, not because they are feminine. Riḍā's discussion also reflects the emergence of home economics as a field of expertise understood to require women's education and qualify them as nurturers of the nation. He notes the increasing knowledge needed to run a modern household, particularly if it is a wealthy one. For instance, nursing ailing family members used to be a simple matter, but now it requires a significant amount of competence and training.[27]

This brief reconstruction of modern shifts in Islamic legal discussions surrounding wives' domestic labor both reinforces the general arguments of the existing literature on late-nineteenth-century domesticity in the Muslim Middle East and suggests some qualifications. On the one hand, as several authors have already observed, a clear transition is visible, both in terms of the growing prominence of arguments in favor of wives' obligation to do housework and in terms of this duty's elaboration as a demanding managerial task that justifies women's education even as it exemplifies their innate femininity. On the other hand, this study shows that there were premodern precursors to some central aspects of the modern ideal of domesticity, including a pervasive association between women and "indoor" labor, a widespread acknowledgment that wives were customarily expected to perform household tasks appropriate to their status and milieu, and the religious exaltation of women's performance of chores for their families.[28] Consequently, one cannot posit a sharp dichotomy between "the precolonial exemption of women from housework" and a new "ideal of domesticity."[29] It is the technicalization of housework, its consequent linkage with education, and its mobilization for the production and reproduction of the nation that are genuinely new.[30]

Contemporary developments

On the issue of wives' domestic labor among many others, the opinions of Ibn Taymīya and Ibn al-Qayyim attained a newfound influence over the course of the twentieth century.[31] Riḍā's invocation of gendered *fiṭra* has also been widely disseminated.[32] The question of wives' obligation to do housework is a subject on which some leading modern scholars have been strikingly willing to abandon the majority doctrine of classical *fiqh*. The influential Egyptian scholar Yūsuf al-Qaraḍāwī (b. 1926) opens his fatwa on the subject with the frank statement that the exemption of wives from domestic labor "is an opinion of some legal scholars, and not everything the legal scholars have said is 100% right; they are mujtahids who may err or be correct."[33] In other cases, scholars appear to willfully misrepresent the historical record; the senior Saudi establishment scholar Muḥammad ibn Muḥammad al-Mukhtār al-Shanqīṭī (1942–2019) claims legal consensus (*ijmāʿ*) on wives' obligation to serve their husbands and describes the opposing view as isolated (*shādhdh*).[34]

Contemporary *fiqh* discussions suggest that the denial of a wifely obligation to do housework is often unfamiliar and shocking to Muslim laypeople. Al-Qaraḍāwī's fatwa responds to the query of "Aḥmad" from Qatar, who has been told about the classical doctrine in the mosque and asks incredulously, "Is this true religiously? . . . If it is correct, this will embolden women against men and wreak chaos (*yuqallib al-awḍāʿ*) in homes and societies."[35] The prominent Saudi scholar ʿAbd Allāh ibn Jibrīn (1933–2009) responds to a questioner who has read in the paper that wives are not contractually obligated to provide housework but only to be sexually available; he asks plaintively, "Is this correct? If it is not correct, I praise God that this newspaper is not widely circulated; otherwise, some husbands will become single when some women read this fatwa!"[36] (Ibn Jibrīn duly reassures him that it is incorrect and that the wives of the Companions of the Prophet did chores.)

As we have seen, the dissonance on this point between classical doctrine and popular practice is itself far from new; neither is the disapproval and incredulity of laypeople newly exposed to the relevant *fiqh*. The more novel factor is the awareness that *fiqh* discussions now circulate in forums readily accessible to ordinary women. Such awareness is also suggested by a scenario addressed by the senior Saudi authority Ibn ʿUthaymīn (1929–2001) in his commentary on the Ḥanbalī legal manual *Zād al-mustanqiʿ*: "If the husband were to say [to his wife], 'Make food; I have men with me [as guests],' and she were to say, 'I won't do it! I married only for [sexual] enjoyment, not to serve you,' is she obliged to do it or not?"[37]

Here the wife's retort should probably be interpreted not as an assertion of hedonism but as a manifestation of Saudi women's enhanced exposure to formal religious knowledge: she is aware that her contractual obligation as a wife is limited to sexual availability. Ibn ʿUthaymīn responds, "Yes; she is obliged to do it, because that is what is required by custom, and what is consistently done according to custom is tantamount to an explicit [contractual] condition."[38]

Even as some religious authorities of the late twentieth century amplified the minority opinion that wives are obligated to provide domestic labor, other Muslims cited the majority classical doctrine denying this obligation in support of legislation enhancing the financial rights of divorced and widowed women.[39] While the debates surrounding such legislation were not purely *fiqh*-based, *fiqh* doctrines served to provide legitimate precolonial precedents for substantive legal change.

The country in which legislation in this area appears to have evoked the most extensive debates over Islamic legal precedent is Morocco, where Article 49 of the 2004 personal status law (Mudawwanat al-Usra) provides that if spouses have not reached a formal agreement about the allocation of wealth amassed over the course of their marriage, it will be divided based on "the labor of each spouse, the efforts s/he exerted and the burdens s/he bore to increase the wealth of the family."[40] A clarification issued in the same year by the Moroccan Ministry of Justice explains that "the fact that the burdens and contributions borne by the wife within the household are not explicitly mentioned does not mean that they are not included."[41]

The 2004 legislation was both preceded and followed by widespread debate over the relevant provisions of Mālikī law. This discussion focused centrally on the distinctive legal heritage of Berber regions of the country, where custom had long dictated that agricultural products included in an estate be distributed among heirs in proportion to the labor they had contributed to their production. While conservative scholars argued that this precedent was applicable only to wives' direct participation in agricultural production in the specific regions of Morocco where this practice was historically customary, proponents of the new provision pointed to wives' general exemption from household labor as grounds for their entitlement to a portion of household wealth acquired over the course of the marriage.[42] Given that classical Mālikī doctrine explicitly allowed wives to make economic claims based on their labor in producing crafts such as yarn and carpets, much of the discussion of the relevant *fiqh* precedents revolved around the question of whether routine domestic labor was economically "productive."[43] Participants in the debate also differed in their representations of Mālikī doctrine on wives' obligation to do housework, with supporters of the new property regime emphasizing the absence of such an obligation and critics emphasizing the precedents requiring indoor labor commensurate with the wife's background and status.[44]

Awareness of *fiqh* (and of *fiqh*-influenced legislation in Muslim-majority countries) can also inform the transactions of Muslims living in countries, like the United States, where Islamic legal principles are not incorporated into state law. The Shariawiz website, "an online portal that offers legal forms and information about Islamic wills and Sharī'a rules of inheritance" founded by American lawyer Abed Awad, addresses the concerns of a husband who wishes to leave his wife more than the Qur'anically stipulated fraction of his estate. One of its proposed Sharia-compliant solutions to this problem is that

> you may acknowledge a moral debt to your devoted wife based on your marriage contract. Strong Sharī'a authority finds a marriage contract does not require a wife to be responsible for the domestic chores for the family and her husband. . . . Based on this authority, a husband may be required to hire domestic help to provide for these domestic services. If his wife provides those domestic chores—which includes preparing food, caring for the children, and cleaning the home—the husband may be required to financially compensate his wife for all of the domestic services she provided for him and the family.[45]

Awareness of Islamic precedents can also inform a pious individual's willingness to take advantage of the provisions of secular law. As one American Muslim divorcée informed the scholar Zahra Ayubi, she was originally reluctant to request a settlement from her ex-husband because of the lack of a marital joint property regime in *fiqh*. However, she ultimately decided to do so because she had provided household labor that was not required by her Muslim marriage contract; the recognition of material claims based on such labor in Moroccan law reinforced her conclusion that they were Islamically legitimate.[46]

Individual women may also negotiate Islamic marriage contracts incorporating the idea that husbands are obligated to provide household help. The American lawyer Asma T. Uddin describes her own contract as stipulating, among other things, that "as long as he can afford it, [her husband] needs to pay for housekeeping and childcare."[47] This provision was based not merely on her personal negotiation with her husband-to-be but on the conviction (grounded in the teachings of American Muslim scholars Hamza Yusuf and Nuh Ha Mim Keller) that, in Islamic law, "a wife is not required to cook and clean, the husband must inform her of this privilege, and if the wife decides to cook and clean for her husband 'as an act of charity,' he's required to *pay her wages* for doing this work."[48]

Islamic law and ethics

As discussed in the introduction, over the last two decades the Western academic discussion of Islamic law has been dominated by Talal Asad's argument that it was only in the colonial context of the late nineteenth century that Muslims came to envision "separate domains for state-administered law and religiously derived morality," a "separation [that] presupposes a very different conception of ethics from the one embedded in the classical sharīʿa."[49] Similarly, Wael Hallaq has influentially argued that "the distinction between—and the segregation of—the legal and the moral" in the nineteenth-century colonial context displaced a premodern Sharia order in which " 'law' . . . not only seamlessly meshed with morality but depended on morality for enforcement."[50] The prevalent view of premodern Sharia is that it functioned within a harmonious overall fusion of personal ethical formation, social custom, and enforceable law, in Hallaq's words, bringing together "theistic teleology, eschatology, socially grounded moral gain, status, honor, shame, and much else of a similar type" in a synthesis that was ruptured only in modernity.[51] Both Asad and Hallaq emphasize the degree to which the classical Sharia functions as a framework for the cultivation of embodied virtues that are inculcated centrally through the ritual duties (*ʿibādāt*) that are such a central topic of premodern *fiqh* (and so anomalous to modern Western construals of "law").[52]

Asad's proposals are grounded in deep readings of selected texts from the late nineteenth and early twentieth centuries and have been extremely fruitful in generating deeper analyses of developments in the colonial period and beyond. However, only more recently have scholars begun to juxtapose these modern developments with serious inquiry into the premodern sources.[53] To what extent does the material examined here support Asad's views of the premodern status quo? And based on this conclusion's limited sample of modern developments, what might the example of wives' domestic labor contribute to our understanding of the reconfiguration of law and morality in the colonial and post-colonial periods? Given the salience of family law as a modern instantiation of the Sharia and the centrality of marital roles to both classical and modern conceptions of religiously proper gendered selfhood, the question of wives' marital obligations offers a very appropriate test case for these questions.

On one level, premodern Islamic normative discourses around quotidian household labor fit Asad's schema very well. They assume a model of ethics that is interpersonal, pedagogical, and embodied. *Khidma* (as we have seen, the larger ethico-legal category with which wives' domestic labor has historically been associated) is practiced relationally within groups (the household, the Sufi lodge) and dyadically in relationships of discipleship and fealty. It is widely understood as an ethical practice that is cultivated through the body and that performatively produces and expresses the virtue of humility (*tawāḍuʿ*), a virtue that is continuous with the moral dispositions that are produced by the *ʿibādāt* (particularly prayer).

However, this model is distinct from the *fiqh* framework of the marriage contract, which also regulates issues of household labor but from a very different vantage point and to very different ends. Whereas the currently prevalent model envisions premodern Islamic normativity as a seamless whole, the premodern textual sources reflect a plurality of discourses that pursue different objectives and address different concerns. These findings support those of Zahra Ayubi, who has interrogated the relationship between Islamic law and ethics from the vantage point of the *akhlāq* literature rather than of *fiqh*.[54]

As we have seen, historically the issue of wives' domestic labor was often approached by Muslim scholars as a legal matter that could be treated largely in isolation from concerns about ethical self-formation. Although the widely cited system of five legal statuses (*al-aḥkām al-khamsa*) offers a framework in which *fiqh* can address cases of nonobligatory virtuous action, it is notable that wives' domestic labor is rarely identified as being recommended (*mandūb, mustaḥabb*). Rather, those scholars like al-Sarakhsī who incorporated it into their legal schemas did so by arguing that it was obligatory in a different, ethico-religious mode (*diyānatan*). Legal obligation was distinctively characterized by the possibility that its performance could, at least notionally, be compelled against a person's will (*ijbār, ikrāh*); in al-Sarakhsī's words, a wife's lack of obligation to provide labor as a matter of legal verdict is indicated by the fact that "she is not forced to do it as a matter of compulsion (*lā tujbar ʿalayhi kurhan*)."[55] This is worth noting in view of the currently widespread view that the premodern Sharia as a whole was a framework for the cultivation of personal virtue without a systematic division between matters of moral pedagogy and those of at least potential governmental coercion.[56] As noted in the introduction, the almost complete absence of the categories of "recommended" and "reprehensible" from the *fiqh* discussion on our topic reflects the fact that the marital relationship was analyzed under the rubric of contract law. Based on this contractual framework, the animating concerns of the discussion are what entitlements the parties could demand in court and what contracts (such as an agreement for the wife to receive wages for housework) would be legally valid and binding.

The legal model of the marriage contract produced by Muslim scholars in the formative period was a largely autonomous construct whose field-specific premises coexisted with quite different frameworks in the fields of ascetic piety and philosophical ethics. In some cases, scholars perceived a painful disjuncture between the contractual parameters of the marital relationship and what they understood to be the demands of personal virtue. This finding parallels those of Baber Johansen, who has highlighted the fact that Ḥanafī scholars developed terminology distinguishing ethical obligations from enforceable legal ones.[57] However, the historical debate over wives' domestic labor suggests that the nature and implications of the distinction between law and ethics were variable and contested. The development of Ḥanafī terminology addressing these distinctions did not reflect a uniform or abiding response to the relevant questions. Sometimes the divergent frameworks and objectives of multiple Islamic discourses were simply confined to works of different genres. This is true of the formative-period texts discussed in chapter 1, where anecdotes in the *zuhd* literature emphasizing the virtues of men's performance of menial chores (and of wives' eschewal of servants) coexisted with rulings in the *fiqh* literature emphasizing wives' entitlement to domestic help. It is also true in the case of al-Māwardī (discussed in chapter 2), who approached the goals and parameters of marriage very differently in his works of law and *akhlāq*. At other times legal and ethical discourses were manifest within individual works of *fiqh*, as when al-Juwaynī affirmed the legal right of elite men and women to protect their social capital while expressing in passing his moral deprecation of such values. Sometimes nonbinding ethical obligations were incorporated into legal works as a distinct if subordinate element, as in the case of al-Sarakhsī discussed in chapter 3.

In the broadest chronological frame, the general trajectory has been toward greater integration between the two fields. A greater interpenetration between religious fields is visible from the fifth/eleventh century, when the moral ideal of humble service to superiors permeated realms from political thought to legal reasoning to Sufi piety. In the eighth/fourteenth century, Ibn Taymīya and his disciple Ibn Qayyim al-Jawzīya attempted a seamless synthesis of law and ethics on the issue of domestic labor, replacing the gendered contractual exchange of the classical *fiqh* of marriage with a vision of the Muslim family fully integrated into their ideals of personal and social virtue. Nevertheless, wives' domestic labor was still not incorporated into a project of ethical self-fashioning; it expressed the proper ethico-legal hierarchy between the spouses but did not necessarily morally shape or transform wives.

At least on a discursive level, housework as an issue of *fiqh* has been even more fully integrated into ethics in the modern period. Not only did the model proposed by Ibn Taymīya and Ibn Qayyim al-Jawzīya receive an unprecedented degree of acceptance and circulation among twentieth-century Sunnis but it was supplemented with a newly gendered concept of *fiṭra*, in which a wife's performance of housework was understood as the actualization of a gendered mode of being centered on nurture and care. Although feminine *fiṭra* is envisioned as being divinely implanted and innate, it must also be cultivated through a personal commitment to prescribed gender roles. It is thus a moral project as well as an inbred and quasi-biological fact. With this model, the fault line between *fiqh* and ethics is completely closed. This fusion is expressed in al-Qaraḍāwī's observation at the end of his fatwa that "a truly Muslim woman will serve her husband and her home by virtue of her innate nature," while "a woman who is rebellious or malicious . . . will not care for the opinion of any of the Muslim jurists (*fuqahāʾ*)."[58] Here adherence to the law is both enabled and rendered otiose by the personal goodness that results from harmonious development of the *fiṭra*.

This idea is elaborated at length by al-Shanqīṭī. He opens his discussion of the issue with the premise that "God Most High formed (*faṭara*) and created woman and placed within her qualities conducive to the conduct and management of the affairs of the home." For al-Shanqīṭī, the key issue is not who actually performs domestic labor but the internal dispositions manifested by the wife. It is thus acceptable for her to request a servant, as Fāṭima did, if there is a legitimate need; however, she violates the *fiṭra* if she does so "out of desire for leisure, or arrogance, or her false fancy (*ẓann*) that she was not created for that." A woman can recognize and cultivate the dictates of her *fiṭra* in the face of conflicting custom and practice only by praying for divine support and nurturing within herself the necessary "psychological factors" (*al-ʿawāmil al-nafsīya*) to maintain the faith that she is divinely mandated to obey and serve her husband. She must also recognize that the recompense for her actions comes from God and not from her husband; here the reciprocal exchange of the marriage contract is displaced by the vertical relationship between the woman and God. Only when a wife comes to feel that subjection to her husband is a perfection and not a defect will she truly embrace her *fiṭra* and come to experience it with serenity. She can help to create the conditions for this by reading about the lives of exemplary early Muslim women and by contemplating the positive fruits of compliance in this world and the next.[59]

In al-Shanqīṭī's account, housework assumes a central place in a comprehensive project of pious self-fashioning for women. The centrality and moral weight given to housework are in themselves not completely new or distinctively modern; as we have seen in chapter 1, as early as the ninth century CE, Ibn Ḥabīb wrote lyrically and at length about the lavish divine rewards awaiting wives who diligently worked for their households, and the tradition of philosophical ethics rooted in the philosophy of Bryson portrayed household management as the central function of a good wife. Nevertheless, to affirm that wives' domestic labor is religiously meritorious or morally good is not to frame it as a project of ethical self-cultivation of the kind suggested by al-Shanqīṭī. A wife who devoted herself to service of her husband might gain entrance to paradise, but premodern sources did not frame this idea in terms of the kind of escalating self-refinement that the ethicists envisioned for men. Al-Shanqīṭī's more open-ended and transformational model, which envisions housework as an integral part of a program to realize a woman's innate femininity, is thus a significant departure from the patterns set prior to the late nineteenth century.

A wife's internalization of a naturalized model of feminine nurture and support is not the only form in which the *fiqhī* allocation of domestic labor can be reframed as an ethical project. Asma Uddin understands the exemption of wives from domestic labor as reflecting the broader principle that the Islamic law of marriage requires men to "nurture [the] divine element" in women.[60] Just as importantly, Islamic law provides for spouses to negotiate the terms of their own marriage; Uddin writes, "I negotiated because my religion told me not only that I could negotiate, but that I *should* negotiate. As clichéd as this may sound, my religion empowered me."[61] Here the Islamic law of marriage is once again envisioned as morally formative. On the one hand, its basic principles provide for the material and spiritual elevation of wives; on the other, it encourages a process of negotiation that is in itself an ethical practice, contributing to the formation of a mature and empowered self. The allocation of housework plays a central role on both of these levels.

If the twentieth and twenty-first centuries have seen the emergence of models that merge the *fiqh* of marriage and domestic labor with Islamic ethics in newly comprehensive ways, what may have caused this development? In part, it may reflect the belated integration of women into a long-standing model of moral self-fashioning. As Zahra Ayubi has demonstrated, premodern Islamic philosophical ethics treated women's domestic labor as purely instrumental to men's ethical self-cultivation (which required that elite men be relieved of time-consuming daily tasks).[62] Despite their sharply divergent gender politics and interpretations of *fiqh*, al-Shanqīṭī and Uddin both respond to a situation in which Muslim women must be addressed as ethico-religious actors in their own right. (Of course, the apparent novelty of this situation may be in part a function of the minimal representation of premodern women's perspectives in the surviving written record.) Nevertheless, the shift is not merely a function of the enhanced visibility of women to (and in) modern Islamic discourses; as we have seen, premodern texts do not seamlessly synthesize the moral and legal aspects of quotidian household labor for men either. For a man as well as a woman, declining to engage in such work can be simultaneously a legal right and a moral failing.

In addition to the greater development of discourses focusing on the ethical self-cultivation of women, one may also place modern Muslim discourses on domestic labor in the context of the emergence of "family law" as a distinct category. Janet Halley writes of the United States that "in the early nineteenth century, there was no family law. The law of husband and wife and the law of parent and child were separate, parallel, and closely related legal topics, but they were equally proximate to . . . the law of master and servant. . . . The wife, the child, and the servant were not just subordinate; they were similarly subordinate."[63]

In contrast, "By the 1860s, the consensus view, even among early opponents of the idea, was that marriage was not contract. Instead it became *status*." This shift, which de-emphasized contractual relationships within the family in favor of fixed and comprehensive roles, involved in part the "separation of the law of familial intimacy from the law of productive labor."[64] One long-term legal implication of this development was the reframing of wives' domestic duties from an entitlement of the husband based on his ownership of her labor to a matter of domestic sentiment and devotion. When in the later nineteenth century wives gained the right to claim their own wages earned outside of the home, housework and care work were recategorized as expressions of familial love that could not be subject to contract between husband and wife or made contingent on financial benefits.[65]

Halley's categories of "contract" and "status" are derived from the thought of Sir Henry Maine (d. 1888), who posited that the primitive family was characterized by the all-encompassing authority of a "despotic pater-familias" and that, historically, this pattern was gradually supplanted by one in which contractual relationships between individuals prevailed over kinship relations.[66] Maine's analysis used a questionable analysis of Roman law in the service of a prejudicial interpretation of society in India, in whose colonial governance he was personally involved. Nevertheless, it has been retained (or revived) as a useful heuristic by legal historians, with the additional observation that "the transition is not as complete or as unidirectional" as Maine suggested; in particular, in the modern era "one can discern a direction moving in a significant degree from contract to status."[67] In Halley's analysis, the modern emergence of family law constitutes a return to "status" in the sense that it posits familial roles and duties that are not subject to contractual negotiation between the parties.

The contrast between "contract" and "status" can also be a useful heuristic for historical developments in the *fiqh* of marriage. Among the *fiqh* models examined in this book, the "contract" end of the spectrum would be represented by Ibn Qudāma's pervasive affirmation of the two spouses' entitlement to freely negotiate many parameters of their relationship (including the wife's labor). Here the Islamic marriage contract is approached as an agreement under which the two parties exchange certain specific considerations while retaining the right to contract with each other in other areas. At the "status" end of the spectrum is the model advanced by Ibn Taymīya, which envisions the ethico-legal roles of husband and wife as all-encompassing and divinely decreed, with an overwhelming emphasis on the authority of the husband. No scholar advances a model that is purely either "status" or "contract," but to the extent that there is a longue-durée chronological development, it would be the rise to prominence of Ibn Taymīya's status-dominated model in the twentieth and twenty-first centuries.

At a more structural level, the application of the new category of "family law" in Muslim-majority regions in the colonial period had several implications for Muslim legal analyses of marriage. On the one hand, colonial authorities strove to disentangle the law of marriage and divorce from the property issues with which it was traditionally embedded, thus de-emphasizing the model of sale-like exchange historically underlying the *fiqh* of marriage.[68] Although this development directly involved the institutions of the colonial-era state, it seems likely that over time the legal culture of many Muslims also gradually came to envision family law as a field separate from commercial law and distinctively associated with sentiment and moral obligation. On the other hand, fatwas on marriage and divorce issued by ulama to ordinary believers increasingly foregrounded the ethical issues that could not be adjudicated by state courts that lacked religious legitimacy. While this development can be seen as creating a "widening gap between ethics and law," it can also be seen as creating a new synthesis between law and ethics within the discourses of the ulama.[69] Whereas a jurist like al-Sarakhsī was centrally interested in defining the claims that could be enforced in a court of law and distinguishing these from non-enforceable moral imperatives, by the late nineteenth century many ulama (sidelined from the project of judicial enforcement) could address the religious validity of a marriage or divorce and its ethical implications in a single package of religious guidance for interested laypeople.

While modern discussions of the *fiqh* of marriage may incorporate ethical concerns to an unprecedented extent, the point here is thus not simply to invert the model proposed by Asad and Hallaq to assert that premodern discursive fragmentation was succeeded by modern synthesis. The diversity of Islamic ethico-religious discourses persists, although its content and configurations have changed. Thus, even as domestic labor within marriage was reframed in ways that melded Islamic law with ethics, *khidma* in the sense of service—sometimes (but not always) including the kinds of quotidian chores that make up "housework"—has continued to be a muted but ubiquitous feature of modern Muslim piety in contexts far beyond the marital household.[70] It plays a prominent role in the pious practices of more than one major modern Islamic movement, where it has undergone extensive transformations.[71]

Overall, rather than transitioning from a holistic synthesis in which *fiqh* crystallized the social, embodied, and ethically formative aspects of Islamic ethics to a novel bifurcation between law and ethics starting in the colonial period, the examples examined in this study suggest that we should envision a more complex constellation of autonomous yet overlapping normative Islamic discourses that were reconfigured and redistributed in modernity. Among these, even in the premodern sources rules that were envisioned as being enforceable by a judge were a marked category distinctively associated with the core mission of *fiqh*. Without denying that the dislocations of the colonial period were both qualitatively and quantitatively unique, we should not imagine premodern Islam as a monolithic synthesis that was disturbed only by outside interference. Rather, as we have seen in the analysis of individual authors, the interface between *fiqh* and other normative discourses was a fluid and dynamic one that accommodated quite diverse scholarly projects.

The material examined here also helps to modulate the idea, prevalent since Leila Ahmed's landmark study *Women and Gender in Islam*, that "the egalitarian conception of gender inhering in the ethical vision of Islam existed in tension with the hierarchical relation between the sexes encoded into the marriage structure instituted by Islam."[72] In discussions of wives' domestic labor, ethics—whether in a Greek-derived philosophical framework or in the form of basic religious ideals of personal humility—often valorized selfless service in ways that disadvantaged wives and other structural subordinates.[73] Even as it advanced an asymmetrical and hierarchical vision of marriage, *fiqh* posited wives' entitlement to make demands that were—at least in principle—contractually enforceable even when they were morally suboptimal. In Islamic legal discussions as in U.S. law, framing marriage as an arena for women's moral and affective cultivation could be a means of denying justified material claims. Nevertheless, this dynamic should not detract from the genuine ethical value that domestic labor can carry. As the authors of one modern empirical study report, "One of the surprises in our study that we did not anticipate and about which we asked no direct questions was the emergence of a spiritual dimension of housework."[74] Despite the gendered and classed biases that may permeate historical and current discussions of the ethico-religious valence of household chores, the sources examined in this study also suggest that mundane daily labor may be invested with genuine resonance and value for the religious agents who engage in it.

If the material examined in this book demonstrates one thing, it is that the *fiqh* of marriage must be understood in the context of a much broader set of religious frameworks with which it coexists and with which it is in dialog—sometimes explicitly and at other times implicitly. Only by recognizing the larger discursive landscape in which Muslim jurists operated can we understand how their arguments operated in a multidimensional ethical and religious world.

Notes

Introduction

1. *Mürüvvetten* (Arabic *muruwwatan*). Mübeccel Kızıltan, ed., *Fatma Aliye Hanım: Yaşamı, Sanatı, Yapıtları; ve-Nisvan-ı Islam* (Istanbul: Mutlu Yayıncılık, 1993), 140.
2. Fatma Aliye, "Nisvan-ı Islam," in Kızıltan, *Fatma Aliye Hanım*, 140–141; Arabic translation in Zaynab bint ʿAlī Fawwāz, *Al-Durr al-manthūr fī ṭabaqāt rabbāt al-khudūr*, ed. Muḥammad Amīn Ḍannāwī (Beirut: Dār al-Kutub al-ʿIlmīya, AH 1420/1999 CE), 2:246. My translation diverges somewhat from that of Fawwāz.
3. Elif Ekin Akşit, "Fatma Aliye's Stories: Ottoman Marriages Beyond the Harem," *Journal of Family History* 25, no. 3 (2010): 208. See also Carter Vaughn Findley, "Fatma Aliye: First Ottoman Woman Novelist, Pioneer Feminist," in *Histoire économique et sociale de l'Empire ottoman et de la Turquie (1326–1960): Actes du Congrès international tenu à Aix-en-Provence . . . 1994*, ed. D. Panzac (Paris: Peeters, 1995), 783–794; and Carter Vaughn Findley, "La soumise, la subversive: Fatma Aliye, romancière et féministe," *Turcica* 27 (1995): 153–176.
4. Azizah Y. al-Hibri, "An Introduction to Muslim Women's Rights," in *Windows of Faith: Muslim Women Scholar-Activists in North America*, ed. Gisela Webb (Syracuse, N.Y.: Syracuse University Press, 2000), 63.
5. Asifa Quraishi-Landes, "A Meditation on *Mahr*, Modernity, and Muslim Marriage Contract Law," in *Feminism, Law, and Religion*, ed. by Marie A. Failinger, Elizabeth R. Schiltz, and Susan J. Stabile (Farnham, Surrey: Ashgate, 2013), 176.
6. Al-Hibri, "Introduction," 63. See also Asifa Quraishi and Najeeba Syeed-Miller, "No Altars: A Survey of Islamic Family Law in the United States," in *Women's Rights and Islamic Family Law: Perspectives on Reform*, ed. Lynn Welchman (London: Zed, 2004), 198.
7. Quraishi-Landes, "Meditation," 176.

8. For a discussion of these pieces of legislation and sources related to them, see the conclusion to this book.
9. Quraishi-Landes, "Meditation," 176.
10. Kecia Ali, "Progressive Muslims and Islamic Jurisprudence," in *Progressive Muslims: On Justice, Gender, and Pluralism*, ed. Omid Safi (Oxford: Oneworld, 2003), 165.
11. Ali, "Progressive Muslims," 169; Kecia Ali, *Marriage and Slavery in Early Islam* (Cambridge, Mass.: Harvard University Press, 2010), 6, and passim. Intisar Rabb has raised questions about the meaning of the word *milk* in this context, arguing that the *fiqh* rules relating to *milk al-yamīn* "render the validation of master-slave sexual relations more akin to family law under the rubric of contract law than to slave law under the rubric of property law." See Intisar A. Rabb, *Doubt in Islamic Law: A History of Legal Maxims, Interpretation and Islamic Criminal Law* (New York: Cambridge University Press, 2015), 151–152n78.
12. Ali, "Progressive Muslims," 170; see also Ali, *Marriage and Slavery*, 71, 75–76.
13. Ali, "Progressive Muslims," 179.
14. Ingrid Mattson, "A Believing Slave Is Better Than an Unbeliever: Status and Community in Early Islamic Society and Law" (Ph.D. diss., University of Chicago, 1999), 231–232.
15. Mattson, "Believing Slave," 198.
16. Mattson, "Believing Slave," 205.
17. Karen Bauer, *Gender Hierarchy in the Qurʾān: Medieval Interpretations, Modern Responses* (Cambridge: Cambridge University Press, 2015), 164.
18. Ẓahīr al-Dīn ʿAbd al-Rashīd ibn Abī Ḥanīfa al-Walwālijī, *Al-Fatāwā al-Walwālijīya*, ed. Miqdād ibn Mūsā Furaywī (Beirut: Dār al-Kutub al-ʿIlmīya, AH 1424/2003 CE), 1:383.
19. While the word *service* is not used for housework in contemporary English (and those who do it professionally are now rarely referred to as "servants"), the link with quotidian household labor remains, whether in offices where the paradigmatic form of subordinating labor is making coffee, in academic departments where administrative busywork is often referred to as "housekeeping," or in congregations where soup kitchens are often the central form of direct service.
20. Reva Siegel, "The Modernization of Marital Status Law," *Georgetown Law Journal* 82 (1993–1994): 2210.
21. Reva Siegel, "Home as Work: The First Women's Rights Claims Concerning Wives' Domestic Labor, 1850–1880," *Yale Law Journal* 103 (1993–1994): 1082.
22. Siegel, "Home as Work," 1084.
23. Siegel, "Modernization," 2139–2140.
24. Katharine Silbaugh, "Turning Labor into Love: Housework and the Law," *Northwestern University Law Review* 91 (1996): 2.
25. See Sara L. Zeigler, "Wifely Duties: Marriage, Labor, and the Common Law in Nineteenth-Century America," *Social Science History* 20, no. 1 (Spring 1996): 63–96.
26. *Fiqh* (literally "understanding") is the term historically used to designate the Islamic scholarly discipline of law, as contrasted with Sharia, Islamic law in the abstract (i.e., as known to God).
27. See Khaled Abou El Fadl, *Rebellion and Violence in Islamic Law* (Cambridge: Cambridge University Press, 2001); Ali, *Marriage and Slavery*; Hina Azam, *Sexual*

Violation in Islamic Law: Substance, Evidence, and Procedure (New York: Cambridge University Press, 2015); Behnam Sadeghi, *The Logic of Law-Making in Islam: Women and Prayer in the Legal Tradition* (Cambridge: Cambridge University Press, 2013); Mairaj Syed, *Coercion and Responsibility in Islam: A Study in Ethics and Law* (Oxford: Oxford University Press, 2016); and Nurit Tsafrir, *Collective Liability in Islam: The ʿĀqila and Blood-Money Payments* (Cambridge: Cambridge University Press, 2020).

28. Syed, *Coercion and Responsibility*, 12.
29. Michael Chamberlain, *Knowledge and Practice in Medieval Damascus, 1190–1350* (Cambridge: Cambridge University Press, 1994). Chamberlain argues of the biographical dictionaries that represent a disproportionate share of our source base for the social life of the ulama class that "to the extent that [their] language was formulaic it is something of an advantage, as through it we can glimpse at how our subjects imagined the social universe and plotted their movements within it." Chamberlain, *Knowledge and Practice*, 19.
30. Ali, *Marriage and Slavery*, 5.
31. Even *qasam* (division of time between cowives) is a potentially litigable issue (since the husband could be subject to a court order if his wife objected to his division of time).
32. Dates are given with AH (*anno Hegirae*, or "in the year of [Muhammad's] Hijra") first followed by CE (of the Common Era). On al-Samarqandī and his works, see Fuat Sezgin, *Geschichte des arabischen Schrifttums* (Leiden: Brill, 1967), 1:445–450; Joseph Schacht, "Abū 'l-Layth al-Samarḳandī," in *Encyclopaedia of Islam*, 2nd ed. (hereafter, *EI2*), ed. by P. Bearman, Th. Bianquis, C. E. Bosworth, E. van Donzel, and W. P. Heinrichs (Leiden: Brill, 1960–2005).
33. Abdur-Rahman Mangera, "A Critical Edition of Abū 'l-Layth al-Samarqandī's Nawāzil" (Ph.D. thesis, School of Oriental and African Studies, University of London, 2013), 325. The book published as Abū'l-Layth al-Samarqandī, *Fatāwā al-nawāzil*, ed. Al-Sayyid Yūsuf Aḥmad (Beirut: Dār al-Kutub al-ʿIlmīya, AH 1425/2004 CE) is not, in fact, the *Fatāwā* of al-Samarqandī; see Mangera, "Critical Edition," 8–10. I thank Samy Ayoub for bringing this fact to my attention.
34. Maḥmūd ibn Ismāʿīl al-Khayrmītī, *Al-Durra al-gharrāʾ fī naṣīḥat al-salāṭīn wa'l-quḍāt wa'l-umarāʾ*, ed. Aḥmad al-Zaʿbī (Beirut: Ibn al-Azraq Center for Political Heritage Studies, AH 1433/2012 CE), 305–306 (this chapter is presented as a verbatim reproduction of material collected by al-Samarqandī; see al-Khayrmītī, *Durra*, 293).
35. Abū'l-Layth al-Samarqandī, *ʿUyūn al-masāʾil fī furūʿ al-ḥanafīya*, ed. Sayyid Muḥammad Muhannā (Beirut: Dār al-Kutub al-ʿIlmīya, AH 1419/1998 CE), 216.
36. Abū'l-Layth al-Samarqandī, *Tanbīh al-ghāfilīn*, ed. al-Sayyid al-ʿArabī (Cairo: Maktabat al-Īmān, AH 1415/1994 CE), 404–405.
37. Vincent Cornell, *Realm of the Saint: Power and Authority in Moroccan Sufism* (Austin: University of Texas Press, 1998), 69–70. Original text in Yūsuf ibn Yaḥyā al-Tādilī, known as Ibn al-Zayyāt, *al-Tashawwuf ilā rijāl al-taṣawwuf wa-akhbār Abī ʿAbbās al-Sabtī*, ed. Aḥmad al-Tawfīq (Rabat: Manshūrāt Kullīyat al-Ādāb wa'l-ʿUlūm al-Insānīya, AH 1404/1984 CE), 219.
38. Abū Ḥāmid al-Ghazālī, *Iḥyāʾ ʿulūm al-dīn* (Beirut: Dār al-Fikr, AH 1414/1994 CE), 3:111.

39. Abū Ḥāmid al-Ghazālī, *Al-Wasīṭ fī'l-madhhab*, ed. Muḥammad Muḥammad Tāmir (Cairo: Dār al-Salām, AH 1417/1997 CE), 6:208. As used in Islamic ethical literature, the concept of *ḥaya'* designates not mere personal embarrassment but a morally grounded sense of propriety. See Marion Holmes Katz, "Shame (*Ḥayā'*) as an Affective Disposition in Islamic Legal Thought," *Journal of Law, Religion and State* 3 (2014): 139–169.
40. Robert W. Hefner, "Shari'a Law and the Quest for a Modern Muslim Ethics," in *Shari'a Law and Modern Muslim Ethics*, ed. Robert W. Hefner (Bloomington: Indiana University Press, 2016), 4. Emphasis in original.
41. Samuli Schielke, "Being Good in Ramadan: Ambivalence, Fragmentation, and the Moral Self in the Lives of Young Egyptians," *Journal of the Royal Anthropological Institute* 15, no. s1 (2009): S30.
42. Schielke, "Being Good," S30.
43. Schielke, "Being Good," S29.
44. Lara Deeb and Mona Harb, *Leisurely Islam: Negotiating Geography and Morality in Shi'ite South Beirut* (Princeton, N.J.: Princeton University Press, 2013), 19.
45. Deeb and Harb, *Leisurely Islam*, 21.
46. While the overlapping moral registers invoked by the scholars presumably coexisted in their lived reality with values that were not articulated in religious terms, the focus here is exclusively on the values articulated in works of Islamic normativity.
47. Schielke, "Being Good," S26.
48. See Shahab Ahmed, *What Is Islam? The Importance of Being Islamic* (Princeton, N.J.: Princeton University Press, 2017), 117–129.
49. Ahmed, *What Is Islam?*, 123.
50. Italics in original. See Ahmed, *What Is Islam?*, 31.
51. Sally Engle Merry, *Getting Justice and Getting Even: Legal Consciousness Among Working-Class Americans* (Chicago: University of Chicago Press, 1990), 10.
52. Ann Swidler, *Talk of Love: How Culture Matters* (Chicago: University of Chicago Press, 2001), 146. I thank Jeff Guhin for bringing this book to my attention.
53. Zahra Ayubi, *Gendered Morality: Classical Islamic Ethics of the Self, Family, and Society* (New York: Columbia University Press, 2019), 35.
54. Ayubi, *Gendered Morality*, 36.
55. My claim here is not that Sufism in general is continuous with *zuhd* but that the two trends share a common set of tropes on the specific subject of domestic labor. For contrasting views of the relationship between asceticism and Sufism, see Christopher Melchert, "The Transition from Asceticism to Mysticism in the Middle of the Ninth Century C.E.," *Studia Islamica* 83 (1996): 51–70; Alexander Knysh, *Islamic Mysticism: A Short History* (Leiden: Brill, 2000), 20n41; and Nile Green, *Sufism: A Global History* (Chichester, U.K.: Wiley-Blackwell, 2012), 19–21.
56. The term *aḥkām* has also been translated as "judgments" (the most literal translation), as "categorizations" (Bernard Weiss, *The Search for God's Law: Islamic Jurisprudence in the Writings of Sayf al-Dīn al-Āmidī* [Salt Lake City: University of Utah Press, 1992], 1), or as "values" (Mohammad Hashim Kamali, *Principles of Islamic Jurisprudence*, rev. ed. [Cambridge: Islamic Texts Society, 1989], 34). For a

summary and discussion of one classical rendition of the five *aḥkām*, see Weiss, *Search for God's Law*, 93–111.

57. Weiss, *Search for God's Law*, 2; and A. Kevin Reinhart, "Islamic Law as Islamic Ethics," *Journal of Religious Ethics* 11, no. 2 (Fall 1983): 194–195.
58. A. Kevin Reinhart, "Law," in *Key Themes for the Study of Islam*, ed. by Jamal Elias (Oxford: Oneworld Publications, 2010), 225. See also 226, 227, 233.
59. Reinhart, "Law," 227.
60. Wael Hallaq notes that "a contract concluded in a lawful transaction, say one of hire, is not subject to classification in accordance with the five norms governing acts. While the act of hiring is itself classifiable, the contract itself is not, and can be deemed either valid or invalid." Wael Hallaq, *A History of Islamic Legal Theories* (Cambridge: Cambridge University Press, 1997), 41–42.
61. See Weiss, *Search for God's Law*, 2; and Reinhart, "Islamic Law as Islamic Ethics," 193–194.
62. On the use of *jāʾiz* as a *ḥukm waḍʿī*, see, for instance, Muḥammad ibn al-Ḥasan al-Shaybānī, *Al-Aṣl*, ed. Muḥammad Boynukalın (Qatar: Wizārat al-Awqāf wa'l-Shuʾūn al-Islāmīya, AH 1433/2012 CE), editor's introduction, 1:271.
63. On the meanings of this term in early Islamic literature, see Leah Kinberg, "What Is Meant by *Zuhd*," *Studia Islamica* 61 (1985): 27–44.
64. See R. Walzer and H. A. R. Gibb, "Akhlāḳ," in *EI2*; Peter Adamson, "Ethics in Philosophy," in *Encyclopaedia of Islam*, 3rd ed. (hereafter, *EI3*), ed. by Kate Fleet, Gudrun Krämer, Denis Matringe, John Nawas, and Everett Rowson (Leiden: Brill, 2007).
65. Ayubi, *Gendered Morality*, 29.
66. Ayubi, *Gendered Morality*, 41.
67. Ayubi, *Gendered Morality*, 45.
68. Ayubi, *Gendered Morality*, 124, 130.
69. Based on the magnitude and complexity of the holdings the text implies, Simon Swain translates the work's title as *Management of the Estate*. See Simon Swain, *Economy, Family, and Society from Rome to Islam: A Critical Edition, English Translation, and Study of Bryson's "Management of the Estate"* (Cambridge: Cambridge University Press, 2013), 36. Here I will follow the more obvious meaning of the Arabic phrase, which was used by scholars who drew on Bryson to apply to elite households of various sizes rather than exclusively to large landed estates. Swain suggests that Bryson is "certainly a *nom de plume*." Swain, *Economy, Family, and Society*, 34.
70. Hefner, "Shari'a Law," 4.
71. It is the word translated as "good character" in the quotation from Fatma Aliye at the beginning of this introduction. On the semantic range and historical development of this term, see B. Farès and Ed., "Murūʾa," in *EI2*; and Nadia Jamil, *Ethics and Poetry in Sixth-Century Arabia* (Cambridge: Gibb Memorial Trust, 2017), 3–24. On its gendered aspects, see Ayubi, *Gendered Morality*, 43, 45.
72. See, for instance, Ṣāliḥ ibn Junāḥ, *Kitāb al-adab wa'l-murūʾa*, in ʿAlī, *Rasāʾil al-bulaghāʾ*, ed. Muḥammad Kurd (Cairo: Dār al-Kutub al-ʿArabīya al-Kubrā, AH 1331/1913 CE), 302–314; and Muḥammad ibn Khalaf Ibn al-Marzubān, *al-Murūʾa*, ed. Muḥammad Khayr Ramaḍān Yūsuf (Beirut: Dār Ibn Ḥazm, AH 1420/1999 CE).

73. Ibn Marzubān, *Murūʾa*, 42, 45, 51, 57, 80.
74. Ibn Marzubān, *Murūʾa*, 39–40.
75. Ibn Marzubān, *Murūʾa*, 58, 71.
76. ʿAlī ibn ʿAbd al-Raḥmān Ibn Hudhayl, *ʿAyn al-adab wa'l-siyāsa wa-zayn al-ḥasab wa'l-riyāsa* (Cairo: Al-Maṭbaʿa al-Iʿlāmīya, AH 1302/[1884–1885] CE), 115 (attributed to Yaḥyā ibn Khālid, perhaps al-Barmakī). In the same vein, an early epistle on *murūʾa* advised that the frequent host should employ a skillful cook and supervise him vigilantly. Ṣāliḥ ibn Junāḥ, "Kitāb al-adab wa'l-murūʾa," in *Rasāʾil al-bulaghāʾ*, ed Muḥammad Kurd ʿAlī (Cairo: Muṣṭafā al-Bābī al-Ḥalabī wa-Akhawayhi, AH 1331/1913 CE), 306.
77. Ibn Hudhayl, *ʿAyn al-adab*, 116.
78. Ibn Hudhayl, *ʿAyn al-adab*, 116.
79. See, for instance, ʿAbd al-Malik ibn ʿAbd Allāh al-Juwaynī, *Nihāyat al-maṭlab fī dirāyat al-madhhab*, ed. ʿAbd al-ʿAẓīm Maḥmūd al-Dīb (Jadda: Dār al-Minhāj, AH 1428/2007 CE), 14:558, 15:427.
80. Of course, Kant's views of religion and law represent only one strand of Enlightenment-era thought on this subject. For a discussion of how "enlightened *philosophes*" incorporated the figure of Muḥammad as lawgiver into their model of "civil religion," see Guy G. Stroumsa, *A New Science: The Discovery of Religion in the Age of Reason* (Cambridge, Mass.: Harvard University Press, 2010), 142.
81. Immanuel Kant, *Religion Within the Boundaries of Mere Reason and Other Writings*, eds. Allen Wood and George di Giovanni (Cambridge: Cambridge University Press, 1998), 131; see also 174.
82. Thus, he admits that the payment of obligatory alms mandated by the Sharia could be understood as a "means of grace" if only "it occurred from a truly virtuous and at the same time religious disposition to human duty" rather than being subject to coercive extraction. Kant, *Religion Within Boundaries*, 185.
83. G. A. Lipton, "Secular Sufism: Neoliberalism, Ethnoracism, and the Reformation of the Muslim Other," *Muslim World* 101, no. 3 (2011): 429.
84. Lipton, "Secular Sufism," 431.
85. See Tomoko Masuzawa, "Islam: A Semitic Religion," in *The Invention of World Religions: Or, How European Universalism Was Preserved in the Language of Pluralism* (Chicago: University of Chicago Press, 2005).
86. Cornelis Tiele, "Religions," in *Encyclopædia Britannica*, 9th ed., vol. 20 (Edinburgh: Adam and Charles Black, 1886), 379. On Tiele's schema see Arie L. Molendijk, "Religious Development: C. P. Tiele's Paradigm of Science of Religion," *Numen* 51 (2004): 321–351.
87. Tiele, "Religions," 381. See also Tiele, "Religions," 380; and Cornelis Tiele, *Elements of the Science of Religion* (Edinburgh: William Blackwood and Sons, 1897), 1:127.
88. Baber Johansen, "The Muslim *Fiqh* as a Sacred Law: Religion, Law and Ethics in a Normative System," in *Contingency in a Sacred Law: Legal and Ethical Norms in the Muslim* Fiqh (Leiden: Brill, 1999), 42–43.
89. Johansen, "Muslim *Fiqh* as a Sacred Law," 42–43.
90. Joseph Schacht, *Introduction to Islamic Law* (London: Oxford University Press, 1964), 1; see discussion in Johansen, "Muslim *Fiqh* as a Sacred Law," 59–60.

91. Johansen, "Muslim *Fiqh* as a Sacred Law," 60.
92. Baber Johansen, "Die sündige, gesunde Amme. Moral und gestzliche Bestimmung (*ḥukm*) im islamischen Recht," in *Contingency*, 173. English translation mine.
93. Johansen, "Sündige, gesunde Amme," 177.
94. Johansen, "Sündige, gesunde Amme," 178.
95. Johansen, "Sündige, gesunde Amme," 182–183.
96. Johansen, "Sündige, gesunde Amme," 178–179.
97. Johansen, "Sündige, gesunde Amme," 179–180.
98. Johansen, "Sündige, gesunde Amme," 181–182.
99. Johansen, "Sündige, gesunde Amme," 184–185.
100. Johansen, "Muslim *Fiqh* as a Sacred Law," 46–47.
101. Talal Asad, *Formations of the Secular: Christianity, Islam, Modernity* (Stanford, Calif.: Stanford University Press, 2003), 250.
102. Asad, *Formations of the Secular*, 206, 235–236. For a similar argument, see Samira Haj, *Reconfiguring Islamic Tradition: Reform, Rationality, and Modernity* (Stanford, Calif.: Stanford University Press, 2008), 38: "The ascendance of such currents [i.e., those separating the domains of *uṣūl al-dīn* and *uṣūl al-fiqh*] stripped the shariʿa of its moral character and created a tradition in which usul al-fiqh came to be regarded instead as a formal code of particular precepts and practices that were detached from the inner or spiritual foundation of the din."
103. Asad states that he will address premodern sources only "briefly—and then only in order to draw certain contrasts." Asad, *Formations of the Secular*, 206.
104. Khaled Fahmy, *In Quest of Justice: Islamic Law and Forensic Medicine in Modern Egypt* (Oakland: University of California Press, 2018), 24. Asad does engage with Johansen's arguments about classical Ḥanafī law, critiquing his discussion of the *ẓāhir/bāṭin* distinction on the basis that his use of the term *conscience* (which, Asad observes, "refers to something at once modern and Christian"). Asad, *Formations of the Secular*, 245; see also Junaid Quadri, "Moral Habituation in the Law: Rethinking the Ethics of the Sharīʿa," *Islamic Law and Society* 26 (2019): 196n17. While Asad's (and Quadri's) scrutiny of Johansen's terminology is justified, it does not directly address the terminology or assumptions of his primary sources.
105. Wael B. Hallaq, *Sharīʿa: Theory, Practice, Transformations* (Cambridge: Cambridge University Press, 2009), 173.
106. Hallaq, *Sharīʿa*, 169.
107. Hallaq, *Sharīʿa*, 226.
108. Wael B. Hallaq, *The Impossible State: Islam, Politics, and Modernity's Moral Predicament* (New York: Columbia University Press, 2013), 112, 113.
109. Craig Perry, "The Daily Life of Slaves and the Global Reach of Slavery in Medieval Egypt, 969–1250 CE" (Ph.D. diss., Emory University, 2014), 82.
110. Torsten Wollina, *Zwanzig Jahre Alltag: Lebens-,Welt- und Selbstbild im Journal des Aḥmad ibn Ṭawq* (Goettingen: V&R unipress, 2014), 100. Translation mine.
111. Abū'l-Faḍl Aḥmad ibn al-Ḥusayn al-Hamadhānī, *Maqāmāt Badīʿ al-Zamān al-Hamadhānī*, ed. Muḥammad ʿAbduh (Beirut: Dār al-Kutub al-ʿIlmīya, AH 1426/2005 CE), 124–125. For a discussion of this *maqāma*, see Fadwa Malti-Douglas,

"*Maqāmāt* and *Adab*: 'al-Maqāma al-Maḍīriyya' of al-Hamadhānī," in *Power, Marginality, and the Body in Medieval Islam* (Aldershot: Ashgate Variorum, 2001), xii.

112. Hamadhānī, *Maqāmāt*, 131.
113. Mattson, "A Believing Slave," 189.
114. See Paulina Lewicka, *Food and Foodways of Medieval Cairenes: Aspects of Life in an Islamic Metropolis of the Eastern Mediterranean* (Leiden: Brill, 2011), 88–100, and sources cited there.
115. Lewicka, *Food and Foodways*, 99, 99n112, 100; Yossef Rapoport, *Marriage, Money and Divorce in Medieval Islamic Society* (Cambridge: Cambridge University Press, 2005), 59–60; and Shirley Guthrie, *Arab Women in the Middle Ages: Private Lives and Public Roles* (London: Saqi Books, 2001), 93–94. The dubious quality and purity of street food meant that families with the necessary resources preferred to produce their own bread and food at home (Lewicka, *Food and Foodways*, 115); for Abbasid Baghdad, see also Nawal Nasrallah, *Annals of the Caliphs' Kitchens: Ibn Sayyār al-Warrāq's Tenth-Century Baghdadi Cookbook* (Leiden: Brill, 2007), 34–35. However, such households often also had enslaved servants to do the cooking. Thus, Lewicka concludes that "women of the family did not cook in Cairo" (Lewicka, *Food and Foodways*, 122).
116. Nasrallah, *Annals of the Caliphs' Kitchens*, 32.
117. Lewicka, *Food and Foodways*, 120–122.
118. Compare Gillian Clark's observation that, with respect to the Late Antique world, "It is difficult to discover what houses at any social level were like in terms of spaces and surfaces, rooms and their uses, and what needed doing to keep them presentable." Gillian Clark, *Women in Late Antiquity: Pagan and Christian Life-Styles* (Oxford: Clarendon, 1993), 95.
119. Azam, *Sexual Violation*, 117.
120. See, for instance, Mālik ibn Anas al-Aṣbaḥī, *al-Mudawwana al-kubrā, riwāyat al-imām Saḥnūn ibn Saʿīd al-Tanūkhī*, ed. Zakarīyā ʿUmayrāt (Beirut: Dār al-Kutub al-ʿIlmīya, AH 1426/2005 CE), 2:188; and Ibn Abī Zayd al-Qayrawānī, *Al-Nawādir wa'l-ziyādāt ʿalā mā fī'l-Mudawwana min ghayrihā min al-ummahāt*, ed. Muḥammad Ḥijjī (Beirut: Dār al-Gharb al-Islāmī, 1999), 4:610.
121. For a discussion of the difficulty of theorizing "domestic labor" as a category, written from a Marxist perspective, see Lise Vogel, "Domestic Labor Revisited," *Science & Society* 64, no. 2 (Summer 2000): 151–170; on the unarticulated (and problematic) assumptions informing empirical research, see Margrit Eichler and Patrizia Albanese, "What Is Household Work? A Critique of Assumptions Underlying Empirical Studies of Housework and an Alternative Approach," *Canadian Journal of Sociology/Cahiers canadiens de sociologie* 32, no. 2 (2007): 227–258.
122. Eichler and Albanese, "What Is Household Work?" 231.
123. Eichler and Albanese, "What Is Household Work?" 231 (citing Helen J. Mederer), and 232.
124. See, for instance, Vogel's opening definitions of domestic labor as "the *unwaged* labor of housework, childbearing, and childrearing," and as "women's *unpaid* family work" (Vogel, "Domestic Labor Revisited," 151, emphases added).
125. Eichler and Albanese, "What Is Household Work?" 230.

126. The comparative weight given daily chores versus personal service could vary. The Shāfiʿī jurist Abū'l-Faraj al-Zāz (d. AH 494/1101 CE) reportedly argued that the *khidma* a husband is obligated to provide for an elite wife comprised cooking, laundry, and the like; for her to demand to be waited on was merely frivolity. In contrast, al-Baghawī (probably Abū Muḥammad, d. AH 516/1122 CE) argued that it was precisely personal service such as having her water carried to the bathroom that the husband was obligated to finance by supporting her servant; cooking and cleaning were the responsibility of neither the wife nor her servant. See Yaḥyā ibn Sharaf al-Nawawī, *Rawḍat al-ṭālibīn*, eds. ʿĀdil Aḥmad ʿAbd al-Mawjūd and ʿAlī Muḥammad Muʿawwaḍ (Riyadh: Dār ʿĀlam al-Kutub, AH 1423/2003 CE), 6:455.
127. Siegel, "Home as Work," 1085.
128. For a critical overview of the longer-term historical emergence of "separate spheres" in England, emphasizing the localized and negotiable nature of the gendered division of labor and space, see Amanda J. Flather, "Space, Place, and Gender: The Sexual and Spatial Division of Labor in the Early Modern Household," *History and Theory* 52 (October 2013): 344–360.
129. Rapoport, *Marriage, Money and Divorce*, 33. Nevertheless, jurists sometimes explicitly acknowledge the possibility of a husband's providing free paid domestic help for his wife. The Mamluk period is from the mid-thirteenth through the early sixteenth century CE and in the region of Egypt and Greater Syria.
130. See J. P. Goldberg, "Life and Death: The Ages of Man," in *A Social History of England: 1200–1500*, ed. by Rosemary Horrox and W. Mark Ormrod (Cambridge: Cambridge University Press, 2006), 419–421. However, legal sources from other times and places emphasize that a husband may provide his elite wife with domestic service by employing a free (and implicitly female) servant. See, for instance, al-Juwaynī, *Nihāyat al-maṭlab*, 15:426.
131. See, for instance, the mystical "recipe" of the early Muslim renunciant Dhakkāra in Abū ʿAbd al-Raḥmān Muḥammad ibn al-Ḥusayn al-Sulamī, *Ṭabaqāt al-ṣūfīya wa-yalīhi Dhikr al-niswa al-mutaʿabbidāt al-ṣūfīyāt. Ed. Muṣṭafā ʿAbd al-Qādir ʿAṭā* (Beirut: Dār al-Kutub al-ʿIlmīya, AH 1424/2003 CE), 409. For a comparable example from the Late Antique Christian monastic tradition see Clark, *Women in Late Antiquity*, 101–102.
132. See Rkia Cornell's comments in the introduction to Abū ʿAbd al-Raḥmān al-Sulamī, *Early Sufi Women: Dhikr an-niswa al-mutaʿabbidāt aṣ-Ṣūfiyyāt*, ed. and trans. Rkia Elaroui Cornell (Louisville: Fons Vitae, 1999), 67.
133. Richard Maxwell Eaton, *Sufis of Bijapur, 1300–1700: Social Roles of Sufis in Medieval India* (Princeton, N.J.: Princeton University Press, 1978), 157; also see Annemarie Schimmel, *My Soul Is a Woman: The Feminine in Islam*, trans. Susan H. Ray (New York: Continuum, 1997), 120–124; and Karen G. Ruffle, *Gender, Sainthood, and Everyday Practice in South Asian Shi'ism* (Chapel Hill: University of North Carolina Press, 2011), 73.
134. Even within the realm of male-authored texts, to the best of my knowledge there is no direct equivalent of the late medieval European devotional works that, Glenn Burger argues, aim to show how "the good wife can equal, or even excel, the virgin nun in her excellence as a fully formed ethical subject"—although

even there, household chores appear as an obstacle to, rather than a medium for, the wife's spiritual development. Glenn D. Burger, *Conduct Becoming: Good Wives and Husbands in the Later Middle Ages* (Philadelphia: University of Pennsylvania Press, 2018), 7, 64.

1. Domestic Labor in the Literature of *Zuhd* (Renunciation) and in Early Mālikī Texts

1. Dates are given with AH (*anno Hegirae*, or "in the year of [Muhammad's] Hijra") first followed by CE (of the Common Era).
2. "*Lā yazāl al-ʿabd min Allāh wa-huwa minhu mā lam yukhdam, fa-idhā khudima, wajaba ʿalayhi al-ḥisāb.*" *Mā lam yukhdam* could also be translated "as long as he is not given a servant."
3. ʿAbd al-Razzāq ibn Hammām al-Ṣanʿānī, *Al-Musannaf*, ed. Ḥabīb al-Raḥmān al-Aʿẓamī ([Beirut]: al-Majlis al-ʿIlmī, n.d.), 11:97.
4. See Shams al-Dīn al-Sarakhsī, *Kitāb al-Mabsūṭ* (Beirut: Dār al-Maʿrifa, AH 1409/1989 CE), 5:181. The question of whether a husband must provide a slave for his wife or simply support one she already possesses is discussed below.
5. For an overview of the scholarly discussion of the attribution of this work, see Waqar Akbar Cheema, "Al-Jāmi' of Ma'mar bin Rāshid: Extinct or Extant?" *Journal of Islamic Sciences* 3, no. 1 (2015): 9–14. Harald Motzki makes a case for the broad authenticity of the larger compilation in which this text is preserved, the *Musannaf* of ʿAbd al-Razzāq al-Ṣanʿānī, in Harald Motzki, *The Origins of Islamic Jurisprudence: Meccan Fiqh Before the Classical Schools*, trans. Marion Holmes Katz (Leiden: Brill, 2002).
6. Ṣanʿānī, *Musannaf*, 10:421.
7. Ṣanʿānī, *Musannaf*, 10:393.
8. Ṣanʿānī, *Muṣannaf*, 11:25.
9. Ṣanʿānī, *Musannaf*, 11:33–34.
10. [Muslim ibn al-Ḥajjāj], *Ṣaḥīḥ Muslim* (Vaduz, Liechtenstein: Thesaurus Islamicus Foundation, 2000), 1:333 (*Kitāb al-Jumʿa, Bāb Wujūb ghusl al-jumʿa*); see also [Muḥammad ibn Ismāʿīl al-Bukhārī], *Ṣaḥīḥ al-Bukhārī* (Vaduz, Liechtenstein: Thesaurus Islamicus Foundation, 2000), 1:170 (*Kitāb al-jumʿa, Bāb Waqt al-jumʿa idhā zālat al-shams*).
11. Ingrid Mattson, "A Believing Slave Is Better Than an Unbeliever: Status and Community in Early Islamic Society and Law" (PhD diss., University of Chicago, 1999), 159–60 (the source is Ibn Shabba, vol. 2, 724–725).
12. Mattson, "Believing Slave," 192.
13. See Mattson, "Believing Slave," 107, 192.
14. *Mawlāt lanā taṣaddaqat ʿalaynā bi-khidmatihā.* ʿAbd Allāh ibn Muḥammad Ibn Abī'l-Dunyā, *Kitāb al-Zuhd* (Beirut: Dār Ibn Kathīr, AH 1999/1420 CE), 60. See also Aḥmad ibn Ḥanbal, *Al-Zuhd*, ed. Muḥammad ʿAbd al-Salām Shāhīn (Beirut: Dār al-Kutub al-ʿIlmīya, AH 1420/1999 CE), 91–92 (Abū Bakr bequeaths a slave in an

otherwise minimal set of possessions); Hannād ibn al-Sirrī, *Kitāb al-Zuhd*, ed. ʿAbd al-Raḥmān ibn ʿAbd al-Jabbār al-Faryawāʾī (al-Ṣabāḥīya, Kuwait: Dār al-Khulafāʾ li'l-Kitāb al-Islāmī, AH 1406/1985 CE), 1:325–326 (Masrūq declares that he is never more serene that when his servant tells him that he possesses neither a bushel of wheat nor a dirham); and Abū Nuʿaym al-Iṣfahānī, *Ḥilyat al-awliyāʾ wa-ṭabaqāt al-aṣfiyāʾ* (Beirut: Dār al-Fikr/Cairo: Maktabat al-Khānjī, AH 1416/1996 CE), 10:129 (Abū Umāma al-Bāhilī insists on giving away everything he has, but has a servant girl who prepares his food, tends his lamp, and spreads his bedding).

15. Abū Nuʿaym, *Ḥilyat al-awliyāʾ*, 6:270 (cited in Christopher Melchert, "Asceticism," *Encyclopaedia of Islam*, 3rd ed. (hereafter, *EI3*), ed. by Kate Fleet, Gudrun Krämer, Denis Matringe, John Nawas, and Everett Rowson (Leiden: Brill, 2007).
16. As Leah Kinberg has demonstrated, the term *zuhd* as used in early Islamic sources is not the ethic of a splinter group of renunciants but "the philosophy of life inherent in Islam according to which any Muslim who considers himself pious—no matter what religious current he thinks he belongs to—must behave." Leah Kinberg, "What Is Meant by *Zuhd*," *Studia Islamica* 61 (1985): 29. While accepting Kinberg's argument that *zuhd* involves broad ethical principles that are applicable to all Muslims rather than be associated with some narrow class of "ascetics" or "mystics," however, I still see *zuhd* works as reflecting (although not being exhausted by) a distinctive emphasis on symbolic or substantive renunciation.
17. ʿAbd Allāh ibn ʿAbd al-Ḥakam, *Sīrat ʿUmar ibn ʿAbd al-ʿAzīz*, ed. by Aḥmad ʿUbayd (n.p.: ʿĀlam al-Kutub, AH 1404/1984 CE), 43–44 (the caliph ʿUmar ibn ʿAbd al-ʿAzīz).
18. Wakīʿ ibn al-Jarrāḥ, *Kitāb al-zuhd*, ed. ʿAbd al-Raḥmān ʿAbd al-Jabbār al-Faryawāʾī (Medina: Maktabat al-Dār, AH 1404/1984 CE), 3:802. Another anecdote has al-Rabīʿ (probably the same figure) declare to his servant, "I'll do half of the work and you'll do half, and I'll sweep the hut" (Ibn Ḥanbal, *Zuhd*, 268).
19. Wakīʿ, *Zuhd*, 3:807; and Bukhārī, *Ṣaḥīḥ*, 1:130 (*Kitāb al-Ādhān, Bāb Man kāna fī ḥājat ahlihi fa-uqīmat al-ṣalāt fa-kharaja*). Al-Bukhārī glosses *mihnat ahlihi* as *khidmat ahlihi*.
20. Ibn Saʿd, *Al-Ṭabaqāt al-kubrā* (Beirut: Dār Iḥyāʾ al-Turāth al-ʿArabī, n.d.), 1:176; see also Hannād ibn al-Sirrī, *Kitāb al-Zuhd*, 2:408; and Aḥmad ibn Ḥanbal, *Musnad al-Imām Aḥmad Ibn Ḥanbal*, ed. Shuʿayb al-Aranaʾūṭ et al (Beirut: Mu'assasat al-Risāla, AH 1421/2001 CE), 41:390.
21. Ibn Saʿd, *Ṭabaqāt*, 1:243–244.
22. Abū Nuʿaym, *Ḥilyat al-awliyāʾ*, 6:212. On Kahmas ibn al-Ḥasan, see Shams al-Dīn al-Dhahabī, *Siyar aʿlām al-nubalāʾ*, ed. by Shuʿayb al-Arnaʾūṭ, vol. 6, ed. Ḥusayn al-Asad (Beirut: Muʾassasat al-Risāla, AH 1417/1996 CE), 316–317.
23. ʿAbd Allāh ibn al-Mubārak, *Kitāb al-Zuhd wa-yalīhi Kitāb al-Raqāʾiq*, ed. Ḥabīb al-Raḥmān al-Aʿẓamī (Beirut: Dār al-Kutub al-ʿIlmīya, AH 1425/2004 CE), 352. The same behavior is attributed to the caliph ʿUthmān. See Ibn Ḥanbal, *Al-Zuhd*, 104, 105; and 'Abd Allāh ibn Muḥammad Ibn Abī Shayba, *Muṣannaf Ibn Abī Shayba fī'l-aḥādīth wa'l-āthār*, ed. Saʿīd al-Laḥḥām (Beirut: Dār al-Fikr, AH 1428–1429/2008

CE), 1:222. See also Ibn Abī'l-Dunyā, *Kitāb al-Qanāʿa wa'l-taʿaffuf*, ed. by Muṣṭafā ʿAbd al-Qādir ʿAṭā (Beirut: Muʾassasat al-Kutub al-Thaqāfīya, AH 1413/1993 CE), 19, where it is said that an early figure "would not ask his servant to give him water to drink, or to bring him [water] to perform *wuḍūʾ*."

24. Ibn ʿAbd al-Ḥakam, *Sīrat ʿUmar ibn ʿAbd al-ʿAzīz*, 43.
25. Abū Nuʿaym, *Ḥilyat al-awliyāʾ*, 7:394.
26. Ibn al-Mubārak, *Kitāb al-Jihād*, ed. Nazīh Ḥammād (Jedda: Dār al-Maṭbūʿāt al-Ḥadītha, n.d.), 177–179. On this work and its relationship to *zuhd*, see Christopher Melchert, "Ibn al-Mubārak's *Kitāb al-Jihād* and Early Renunciant Literature," in *Violence in Islamic Thought from the Qur'an to the Mongols*, ed. by Robert Gleave and István T. Kristó-Nagy (Edinburgh: Edinburgh University Press, 2015), 49–69. On the themes of service and companionship in it, see Michael Bonner, *Aristocratic Violence and Holy War* (New Haven, Conn.: American Oriental Society, 1996), 121, 128.
27. Ibn al-Mubārak, *Kitāb al-Jihād*, 177; and Hannād ibn al-Sirrī, *Kitāb al-Zuhd*, 2:407.
28. Ibn al-Mubārak, *Kitāb al-Jihād*, 177–179; Ibn al-Mubārak, *Kitāb al-Zuhd*, 260, 261; Aḥmad ibn Ḥanbal, *Zuhd*, 158; Ibn Abī'l-Dunyā, *Kitāb al-Tahajjud wa-qiyām al-layl*, ed. Musʿad ʿAbd al-Ḥamīd al-Saʿdanī (Cairo: Maktabat al-Qurʾān, n.d.), 76; and Hannād ibn al-Sirrī, *Kitāb al-zuhd*, 2:380.
29. Maʿmar ibn Rāshid, *The Expeditions: An Early Biography of Muhammad*, trans. Sean Anthony (New York: New York University Press, 2015), xxvi.
30. Ibn Abī'l-Dunyā, "Kitāb Mujābū al-daʿwa," in *Mawsūʿat rasāʾil Ibn Abī al-Dunyā*, vol. 4, ed. by Ziyād Ḥamdān (Beirut: Muʾassasat al-Kutub al-Thaqāfīya, AH 1414/1993 CE), 67. In the edition of Ibn Abī'l-Dunyā, he takes off his own cloak and shoes. In the parallel text in Abū Nuʿaym, *Ḥilyat al-awliyāʾ* (2:129–130) the verb is in the feminine, which makes more sense in the context of the story.
31. See Dhahabī, *Siyar aʿlām al-nubalāʾ*, 8:174–175.
32. Abū al-Faraj Ibn al-Jawzī, *Ṣifat al-ṣafwa*, ed. Khālid Ṭarṭūsī (Beirut: Dar al-Kitāb al-ʿArabī, AH 1433/2012 CE), 717.
33. Aḥmad ibn Muḥammad al-Ṭaḥāwī, *Mukhtaṣar Ikhtilāf al-ʿulamāʾ*, abridged by Aḥmad ibn ʿAlī al-Jaṣṣāṣ, ed. ʿAbd Allāh Nadhīr Aḥmad (Beirut: Dār al-Bashāʾir, AH 1417/1996 CE), 2:371.
34. Abū Bakr Muḥammad ibn Ibrāhīm Ibn al-Mundhir, *Al-Ishrāf ʿalā madhāhib al-ʿulamāʾ*, ed. Abū Ḥammād Ṣaghīr Aḥmad al-Anṣārī (Raʾs al-Khayma, UAE: Maktabat Makka al-Thaqāfīya, AH 1426/2005 CE), 5:157–158.
35. Ibn al-Mundhir, *Ishrāf*, 5:158.
36. See, for instance, al-Shāfiʿī's observation that verse 4:3 of the Qur'an (which references the husband's duty to support his wives) "is a clear statement (*bayān*) that the husband is obligated [to provide] whatever is indispensable for his wife, including maintenance, clothing and shelter—and service (*khidma*), in the case that she is not able to perform work that is necessary for her physical wellbeing." Muḥammad ibn Idrīs al-Shāfiʿī, *Al-Umm* (Beirut: Dār al-Maʿrifa, [1973]), 5:87.
37. al-Shāfiʿī's statements on this topic are complex and apparently contradictory; he states variously that a husband must finance a servant for his wife only if she is ill or disabled, that he must do so if her social status makes it inappropriate for her to do the work herself, and that he must pay for the processing of

her food even if she lacks a servant. See Shāfiʿī, *Umm*, 5:87, 88, 107. Within the school, his final doctrine was understood to be that the elite wife was entitled to a servant. See *Mukhtaṣar al-Muzanī* (published as unnumbered final volume of Shafi'i, *Umm*), 230–231.

38. Ibn al-Mundhir, *Al-Iqnāʿ*, ed. ʿAbd Allāh ibn ʿAbd al-ʿAzīz al-Jabrīn (Riyadh: Maṭābiʿ al-Farazdaq al-Tijārīya, AH 1408), 1:313.
39. Karen Bauer, *Gender Hierarchy in the Qurʾān: Medieval Interpretations, Modern Responses* (New York: Cambridge University Press, 2015), 161–162. Early scholars did occasionally address the possibility that the wife possessed no servant.
40. ʿUmar ibn ʿAbd al-ʿAzīz ibn Māza, known as al-Ṣadr al-Shahīd, *Sharḥ Adab al-qāḍī li'l-Khaṣṣāf*, ed. Muḥyī Hilāl al-Sarḥān (Baghdad: al-Dār al-ʿArabīya li'l-Ṭibāʿa, AH 1398/1978 CE), 4:236. The version in al-Khaṣṣāf's *Adab al-qāḍī* with the commentary of al-Jaṣṣāṣ states less vividly that "if she receives wheat or flour, she is entitled to refuse to grind the wheat or make the flour into bread." Abū Bakr Aḥmad ibn ʿAmr al-Shaybānī al-maʿrūf bi'l-Khaṣṣāf, *Kitāb Adab al-qāḍī*, sharḥ Abī Bakr Aḥmad ibn ʿAlī al-Rāzī al-maʿrūf bi'l-Jaṣṣāṣ, ed. Farhat Ziadeh (Cairo: American University in Cairo Press, 1978), 647.
41. On this figure and his *Mudawwana*, see M. Talbi, "Saḥnūn," in *Encyclopaedia of Islam*, 2nd ed. (hereafter, *EI2*), ed. by P. Bearman, Th. Bianquis, C. E. Bosworth, E. van Donzel, and W. P. Heinrichs (Leiden: Brill, 1960–2005); and Jonathan E. Brockopp, "Saḥnūn b. Saʿīd (d. 240/854)," in *Islamic Legal Thought: A Compendium of Muslim Jurists*, ed. by David Powers, Oussama Arabi, and Susan Spectorsky (Leiden: Brill, 2013), 65–84.
42. Jonathan Brockopp notes that in some passages of the *Mudawwana*, "Saḥnūn was not concerned to make the connection to Ibn al-Qāsim explicit, and . . . it was later generations of students who added interpolative remarks to make this attribution clear." Jonathan Brockopp, "Saḥnūn's *Mudawwana* and the Piety of the '*Sharīʿah*-minded,'" in *Islamic Law in Theory: Studies in Jurisprudence in Honor of Bernard Weiss*, ed. by A Kevin Reinhart and Robert Gleave (Leiden: Brill, 2014), 136. In this particular passage, the attribution to Ibn al-Qāsim is an inference based on the traditional account of the genesis of the *Mudawwana*, which is generally supported by Brockopp's scholarship.
43. *Laysa ʿalayhā min khidmatihā wa-lā min khidmat baytihā shayʾ*. Mālik ibn Anas al-Aṣbaḥī, *Al-Mudawwana al-kubrā, riwāyat al-imām Saḥnūn ibn Saʿīd al-Tanūkhī* (hereafter, Saḥnūn, *Mudawwana*), ed. Zakarīyā ʿUmayrāt (Beirut: Dār al-Kutub al-ʿIlmīya, AH 1426/2005 CE), 2:188.
44. Saḥnūn, *Mudawwana*, 2:266.
45. *Innahumā yataʿāwanān ʿalā al-khidma*. I am reading *yukhdimahā* (form IV) since the subject ("*ammā al-khādim*") is domestic servants and their maintenance.
46. Saḥnūn, *Mudawwana*, 2:184. The word I am translating as "means" is *quwwa*. I am interpreting *quwwa* as "[economic] means" rather than as bodily strength because the word *quwwa* is used in this way elsewhere in this section of the *Mudawwana* (cf. 2:180). In itself, the wording is ambiguous.
47. Saḥnūn, *Mudawwana*, 2:184.
48. Saḥnūn, *Mudawwana*, 2:264 (but compare 1:342–343, where a debtor may be forced to sell a slave and replace it with a less valuable one that fills his needs).

There is no indication that this obligation is contingent on the father's being sick or disabled; the implication seems to be that any free adult requires someone to provide basic domestic work.

49. Saḥnūn, *Mudawwana*, 1:342–343, 344, 593. On this theme, see Ingrid Mattson, "Status-Based Definitions of Need in Early Islamic *Zakat* and Maintenance Laws," in *Poverty and Charity in Middle Eastern Contexts*, ed. by Michael Bonner (Albany: State University of New York Press, 2003), 31–51.
50. *Al-khādim allatī takuff wajh ahl al-bayt* (Saḥnūn, *Mudawwana*, 1:593).
51. Saḥnūn, *Mudawwana*, 2:111–112.
52. Jonathan Brockopp notes that "both the Qur'ān and early law seem to maintain a distinction between use of male slaves in agriculture and commerce, and use of female slaves for household tasks and sex." Jonathan Brockopp, *Early Mālikī Law: Ibn ʿAbd Al-Hakam and His Major Compendium of Jurisprudence* (Leiden: Brill, 2000), 158. See also Kecia Ali, *Marriage and Slavery in Early Islam* (Cambridge, Mass.: Harvard University Press, 2010), 7.
53. Saḥnūn, *Mudawwana*, 3:331–332; see also 4:608 (value of a male slave is enhanced if he can weave brocade).
54. Abū'l-Walīd Ibn Rushd al-Qurṭubī, *Al-Bayān wa'l-taḥṣīl wa'l-sharḥ wa'l-tawjīh wa'l-taʿlīl fī masāʾil al-Mustakhraja*, ed. Saʿīd Aʿrāb (Beirut: Dār al-Gharb al-Islāmī, AH 1404/1984 CE, 2nd printing AH 1408/1988 CE), 7:183. The word I have translated here as "embroidery" is *raqm*. The verb *raqama* can mean "to write," but in this passage *raqm* is explicitly contrasted with reading and writing, which are declared not to be commercially relevant skills of enslaved women. *Raqama* can also mean to add stripes or figures to a textile.
55. See J. Schacht, "Umm al-walad," *EI2*. The doctrine that the owner of an *umm walad* may not exploit her labor is independently recorded in another very early witness of Mālikī doctrine, the *Mukhtaṣar* of Ibn ʿAbd al-Ḥakam (d. AH 214/829 CE). ʿAbd Allāh ibn ʿAbd al-Ḥakam, *al-Mukhtaṣar al-kabīr*, ed. Aḥmad ibn ʿAbd al-Karīm Najīb (Dublin: Manshūrāt Markaz Najībawayh, AH 1432/2011 CE), 460; translated in Brockopp, *Early Mālikī Law*, 277.
56. Mattson, "Believing Slave," 126.
57. Saḥnūn, *Mudawwwana*, 2:539; see also 3:446.
58. See Abū al-Walīd Ibn Rushd, *Al-Muqaddamāt al-mumahhadāt*, ed. Muḥammad Ḥujjī (Beirut: Dār al-Gharb al-Islāmī, 1408/1988), 3:199.
59. Saḥnūn, *Mudawwana*, 2:540 (see also 2:541).
60. Saḥnūn, *Mudawwana*, 2:202–203; 2:537; 2:555; 2:556–557.
61. Shāfiʿī, *Umm*, 5:102, 6:251. Al-Shāfiʿī holds that the service expected from an *umm walad* depends on her and her enslaver's social status: "she must work for him as her peers work for his peers" *(taʿmal lahu mā yaʿmal mithluhā li-mithlihi)*" (in discussion of the case of a Christian *umm walad*; *Umm*, 6:102).
62. Muḥammad ibn al-Ḥasan al-Shaybānī, *Al-Aṣl*, ed. Muḥammad Boynukalın (Qatar: Wizārat al-Awqāf wa al-Shuʾūn al-Islāmīya, AH 1433/2012 CE): 5:143, 10:337.
63. Saḥnūn, *Mudawwana*, 2:440 (*lahu ʿalayhi qīmat khidmatihi*) and 4:608–609. However, the owner is exempt from paying the market value of the service if he

continues to deny having manumitted the slave (even if it is proven against him); see also 4:516.

64. Saḥnūn, *Mudawwana*, 4:340–341 (*li'anna ʿitqahu iyyāhā hibatun minhu lahā khidmatahā*).
65. See *Al-Mawsūʿa al-fiqhīya* (Kuwayt: Wizārat al-Awqāf wa'l-Shuʾūn al-Islāmīya, AH 1404–1427/1983–2006 CE), s.v. *riqq*, para. 13–15, vol. 23:20–21.
66. Cf. Saḥnūn, *Mudawwana*, 4:342, 345.
67. Saḥnūn, *Mudawwana*, 4:344.
68. Ibn Manẓūr, *Lisān al-ʿarab* (Beirut: Dār Ṣādir, AH 1410/1990 CE), 8:14 (s.v. *b-ḍ-ʿ*).
69. The reconstruction of this model and its multifarious implications for the law of marriage and divorce is the central theme of Ali, *Marriage and Slavery.*
70. Saḥnūn, *Mudawwana*, 2:172; see translation and discussion of this passage in Ali, *Marriage and Slavery*, 68–70.
71. On the history of wet-nursing, see Avner Giladi, *Infants, Parent and Wet Nurses: Medieval Islamic Views on Breastfeeding and Their Social Implications* (Leiden: Brill, 1999).
72. Saḥnūn, *Mudawwana*, 2:304.
73. Saḥnūn, *Mudawwana*, 2:304–305.
74. Saḥnūn, *Mudawwana*, 3:456.
75. Saḥnūn, *Mudawwana*, 3:456.
76. Saḥnūn, *Mudawwana*, 3:440.
77. Saḥnūn, *Mudawwana*, 4:73.
78. Ibn Rushd, *Al-Bayān wa'l-Taḥṣīl*, 14:179; for passages articulating the same principle see also Ḥakam, *Al-Mukhtaṣar al-kabīr*, 299; and Ibn Abī Zayd al-Qayrawānī, *Al-Nawādir wa'l-ziyādāt ʿalā mā fī al-Mudawwana min ghayrihā min al-ummahāt*, ed. Muḥammad Ḥujjī (Beirut: Dār al-Gharb al-Islāmī, 1999), 4:618. On the *Mustakhraja* of Muḥammad ibn Aḥmad al-ʿUtbī, which collected material primarily from Ibn al-Qāsim, see Fuat Sezgin, *Geschichte des arabischen Schrifttums* (Leiden: Brill, 1967), 1:472; and Miklos Muranyi, *Materialien zur mālikitischen Rechtsliteratur* (Wiesbaden: Otto Harrassowitz, 1984), 50–65. According to Muranyi, in North Africa and Spain the work enjoyed an authority second only to that of Ibn Ḥabīb's *Wāḍiḥa*. Muranyi, *Materialien*, 54.
79. See Maya Shatzmiller, *Labour in the Medieval Islamic World* (Leiden: Brill, 1994), 351.
80. Ibn Rushd, *Al-Bayān wa'l-taḥṣīl*, 7:183.
81. *Naʾkul min ghazlī wa-ʿamal yadī wa-kasbī.*
82. Ibn Rushd, *Al-Bayān wa'l-taḥṣīl*, 3:240.
83. On this work and its surviving fragments, see Muranyi, *Materialien*, 14–29.
84. Qayrawānī, *Nawādir*, 4:610–611. See also ʿAlī ibn Khalaf Ibn Baṭṭāl, *Sharḥ Ibn Baṭṭāl ʿalā Ṣaḥīḥ al-Bukhārī*, ed. Muṣṭafā ʿAbd al-Qādir ʿAṭā (Beirut: Dār al-Kutub al-ʿIlmīya, AH 1424/2003 CE), 7:284, 7:433; al-Qāḍī ʿIyāḍ ibn Mūsā al-Yaḥṣubī, *Al-Tanbīhāt al-mustanbaṭa ʿalā'l-kutub al-Mudawwana wa'l-Mukhtaliṭa*, ed. Muḥammad al-Wathīq (Beirut: Dār Ibn Ḥazm, AH 1432/2011 CE), 2:646–647; Ibn Rushd, *Al-Bayān wa'l-taḥṣīl*, 5:426; and Sulaymān ibn Khalaf al-Bājī, *Al-Muntaqā sharḥ al-Muwaṭṭa,'* ed. Muḥammad ʿAbd al-Qādir ʿAṭā (Beirut: Dār al-Kutub al-ʿIlmīya, AH 1420/1999 CE), 5:442–443.

85. On this figure, see al-Qāḍī ʿIyāḍ ibn Mūsā al-Yaḥṣubī, *Tartīb al-madārik wa-taqrīb al-masālik li-maʿrifat aʿlām madhhab Mālik* (Rabat: Wizārat al-Awqāf wa'l-Shuʾūn al-Islāmīya, AH 1403/1983 CE), 3:136–144; and Muranyi, *Materialien*, 26.
86. On this figure, see ʿIyāḍ ibn Mūsā, *Tartīb al-madārik*, 4:17–22; and Muranyi, *Materialien*, 55–57.
87. Ibn Rushd, *Al-Bayān wa'l-taḥṣīl*, 2:509–510.
88. ʿIyāḍ ibn Mūsā, *Tanbīhāt*, 2:647. For ʿAbd Allāh Ibn Nāfiʿ, see ʿIyāḍ ibn Mūsā, *Tartīb al-madārik*, 3:128–130; for Muḥammad Ibn Maslama, see ʿIyāḍ ibn Mūsā, *Tartīb al-madārik*, 3:131–132. Reading *taqumma* (sweep) rather than *taqūma* (stand up), as in the text.
89. Ibn Baṭṭāl, *Sharḥ*, 7:433. See also Muḥammad ibn Faraj al-Qurṭubī, *Aqḍiyat rasūl Allāh ṣallā Allāhu ʿalayhī wa-sallam* (Aleppo: Dār al-Waʿy, AH 1396/[1976] CE), 73.
90. An early Shi'ite version of this report emphasizes the dimension of modesty by having Fāṭima declare that she is delighted with the verdict because she need not mix with men. ʿAbd Allāh ibn Jaʿfar al-Ḥimyarī, *Qurb al-isnād* (Beirut: Muʾassasat Āl al-Bayt li-Iḥyāʾ al-Turāth, AH 1413/1993 CE), 52.
91. Ibn Abī Shayba, *Muṣannaf Ibn Abī Shayba*, ed. Saʿīd al-Laḥḥām (Beirut: Dār al-Fikr), AH 1428–1429/2008 CE), 7:8, 8:157; and Abū Nuʿaym, *Ḥilyat al-awliyāʾ*, 6:104. Both Ibn Abī Shayba and al-Qurṭubī include the anecdote in collections of the Prophet's legal verdicts (*aqḍiya*).
92. Ibn Baṭṭāl (d. AH 444/1052–1053 CE or AH 449/1057 CE) notes, "One of my teachers said, 'We do not know that [it is stated] in any of the well-authenticated reports (*al-akhbār al-thābita*) that the Prophet ruled that Fāṭima was responsible for the indoor work.'" Ibn Baṭṭāl, *Sharḥ*, 7:433.
93. ʿAbd al-Malik ibn Ḥabīb, *Kitāb Adab al-nisāʾ al-mawsūm bi-Kitāb al-Ghāya wa'l-nihāya*, ed. ʿAbd al-Majīd Turkī (Beirut: Dār al-Gharb al-Islāmī, AH 1412/1992 CE), introduction, 7–22. Turkī argues that the book reflects a stage in the development of hadith transmission compatible with a date in the early third century AH and formally resembles Ibn Ḥabīb's other preserved works.
94. *Lahā ajr wa-iḥsān.*
95. *Lā tukallaf an taʿmal illā mā khaffa ʿalayhā.*
96. The phrasing here suggests that the contract might validly contain a provision regarding housework. Turkī suggests based on a reference by al-Wansharīsī that Ibn Ḥabīb addressed this issue. See Ibn Ḥabīb, *Adab al-nisāʾ*, introduction, 86, referring to Aḥmad al-Wansharīsī, *Al-Miʿyār al-muʿrib*, ed. Muḥammad Ḥijjī (Rabat: Wizārat al-Awqāf wa'l-Shuʾūn al-Islāmīya, AH 1401/1981 CE), 3:106. However, my own reading of the passage suggests that Ibn Ḥabīb is used as the source of an analogous ruling on *nafaqa*.
97. *Ahl al-ḍaʿf.* This phrase seems to have been unclear to copyists. Al-Qāḍī ʿIyāḍ attributes parallel wording to the *Mabsūṭ* of Ismāʿīl ibn Isḥāq (d. AH 282/895–896 CE), rendering the corresponding phrase as *ahl al-ṣuffa* (the People of the Bench), which is graphically similar. ʿIyāḍ ibn Mūsā, *Tanbīhāt*, 1:646; and ʿIyāḍ ibn Mūsā al-Yaḥṣubī, *Ikmāl al-muʿlim bi-fawāʾid Muslim*, ed. Yaḥyā Ismāʿīl (al-Manṣūra: Dār al-Wafāʾ, AH 1419/1998 CE), 7:76. The People of the Bench were a group of the Companions of the Prophet Muḥammad who lived in the portico of the mosque because they lacked homes and property. See R. Tottoli, "Ahl al-Ṣuffa," *EI3*. In

either case, the underlying idea is that a wife must do housework if the only alternative would be for her to hire herself out.

98. Ibn Ḥabīb, *Adab al-nisāʾ*, 281. I am emending the sentence slightly differently than the editor, reading "*allatī in lam taṭḥan li-zawjihā ṭaḥanat li-ghayrihi*"; the editor amends instead "*allatī lam taṭḥan lizawjihā wa-qad ṭaḥanat li-ghayrihi.*"

99. See Ibn Ḥabīb, *Adab al-nisāʾ*, 281–282, 291–294.

100. ʿAbd al-Majīd Turkī infers that Jaʿfar ibn Muḥammad is Jaʿfar al-Ṣādiq (d. AH 148/765 CE), from whom Ibn Ḥabīb could not have transmitted directly, and amends the name to ʿAlī ibn Jaʿfar ibn Muḥammad (from whom Ibn Ḥabīb is said to have transmitted). See Ibn Ḥabīb, *Adab al-nisāʾ*, 291n1.

101. Ibn Ḥabīb, *Adab al-nisāʾ*, 291–292. This material seems to have no direct parallels in the classical hadith literature, although similar reports seem to have been in circulation at least by the tenth century CE; see, for instance, Abū Shujāʿ Shīrawayh al-Daylamī, *Al-Firdaws bi-maʾthūr al-khiṭāb* (Beirut: Dār al-Kutub al-ʿIlmīya, AH 1406/1986 CE), 1:332, 2:399. A strikingly similar series of statements was later incorporated into a story in which the Prophet admonishes his daughter Fāṭima with a series of exhortations beginning "Yā Fāṭima!" (O Fatima!). See Jalāl al-Dīn al-Suyūṭī [attributed], *Nuzhat al-mutaʾammil wa-murshid al-mutaʾahhil*, ed. Muḥammad al-Tūnajī (Beirut: Dār Amwāj, 1989), 69–72.

102. Ibn Ḥabīb, *Adab al-nisāʾ*, 161–162.

103. Ṣanʿānī, *Muṣannaf*, 11:33–34.

104. Bukhārī, *Ṣaḥīḥ*, 3:1123 (*Kitāb al-Nafaqāt, Bāb ʿAmal al-marʾa fī bayt zawjihā*), 3:1286 (*Kitāb al-Daʿawāt, Bāb al-Takbīr wa'l-tasbīḥ ʿinda al-manām).*

105. For the range of versions of this report see, for instance, Ibn Abī Shayba, *Muṣannaf*, 7:38, 52–3; and Ibn Ḥanbal, *Musnad*, 2:140–141, 288, 435–436.

106. Ibn Ḥabīb, *Adab al-nisāʾ*, 281–282. The editor can find no textual support for these reports. See Ibn Ḥabīb, *Adab al-nisāʾ*, 481, 492. A version of this lengthy text had been provided with an *isnād* (if a weak one) by the first third of the fourth/tenth century (the *isnād* states that it was transmitted by dictation (*imlāʾ*) in the year AH 337/948–949 CE), suggesting that the text was drawn into at least the margins of formal hadith culture. See Abū'l-Ḥasan al-Mubārak ibn ʿAbd al-Jabbār al-Ṭuyūrī, *Al-Ṭuyūrīyāt*, selected by Abū Ṭāhir Aḥmad ibn Muḥammad al-Silafī al-Iṣbahānī, eds. Dasmān Yaḥyā Maʿālī and ʿAbbās Ṣakhr al-Ḥasan (Riyadh: Maktabat Aḍwāʾ al-Salaf, AH 1425/2004 CE), 6:550–552; and Ibn al-ʿAdīm, *Bughyat al-ṭalab fī taʾrīkh Ḥalab*, ed. Suhayl Zakkār (Beirut: [Dār al-Fikr], 1988), 5:2182–2183. The editors of *Al-Ṭuyūrīyāt* note (6:551n1) that the text contains grammatical errors. The wording closely parallels that in *Adab al-nisāʾ*, but the differences are sufficient to suggest that the two texts are not directly related to each other.

107. Ibn Saḥnūn, Muḥammad ibn ʿAbd al-Salām ibn Saʿīd al-Tanūkhī, *Fatāwā Ibn Saḥnūn*, ed. Muṣṭafā Maḥmūd al-Azharī (Riyadh: Dār Ibn al-Qayyim li'l-Nashr wa'l-Tawzīʿ/Cairo: Dār Ibn ʿAffān, AH 1432/2011 CE), editor's introduction, 23. The discussion of wives' labor is on 124–129. On Muḥammad ibn Saḥnūn, see Sezgin, *Geschichte*, 1:472–473; and Miklos Muranyi, *Beiträge zur Geschichte der Ḥadīṯ- und Rechtsgelehrsamkeit der Mālikiyya in Nordafrika bis zum 5. Jh. D.H.* (Wiesbaden: Harrassowitz Verlag, 1997), 56–59. Muranyi considers the attribution of this

work to Ibn Saḥnūn to be tenuous. See Muranyi, *Beiträge*, 57; also see Muranyi, *Materialien*, 48–49.

108. *Ḥakama ʿalā*.
109. The word I am translating as "tending" is *taʿmīr*; the exact meaning is unclear to me. The editor's note (124n9) indicates that different manuscripts have a range of different words here, suggesting that there may have been confusion among copyists as well.
110. *Qaḍā ʿalā*.
111. Ibn Saḥnūn, *Fatāwā*, 124. The report uses two different verbs that I have translated as "ruled," *ḥakama ʿalā* and *qaḍā ʿalā*.
112. See Ibn Saḥnūn, *Fatāwā*, editor's introduction, 23.
113. See Muranyi, *Beiträge*, 56.
114. Lit., "Their livers are hungry."
115. Ibn Saḥnūn, *Fatāwā*, 125–126.
116. The ʿUkkāsha incident is recounted in a long narrative hadith transmitted in Sulaymān ibn Aḥmad al-Ṭabarānī, *Al-Muʿjam al-kabīr*, ed. Ḥamdī ʿAbd al-Majīd al-Silafī (Cairo: Maktabat Ibn Taymīya, n.d.), 3:53–61; and in Abū Nuʿaym, *Ḥilyat al-awliyāʾ*, 4:73–79. In this story, the Prophet is forewarned of his death and gives a sermon in which he implores the community to inform him of any grievances against him. The only person who comes forward is an old man named ʿUkkāsha, whom the Prophet accidentally hit with a switch during a military campaign. The Prophet sends Bilāl to fetch the switch from Fāṭima; ʿUkkāsha, offered the opportunity to hit the Prophet's exposed stomach, kisses it instead. The version transmitted by al-Ṭabarānī and Abū Nuʿaym does not mention Fāṭima's grinding barley.
117. Ibn Saḥnūn, *Fatāwā*, 126.
118. Translation from Muhammad Asad, *The Message of the Qurʾān* (Bristol, Engl.: Book Foundation, 2003), 127.
119. Ibn Saḥnūn, *Fatāwā*, 126.
120. On probity as a requirement for prayer leadership, legal testimony, and other functions, see *Al-Mawsūʿa al-fiqhīya*, s.v. "ʿadl," para. 1–18 (30:5–13).
121. Ibn Saḥnūn, *Fatāwā*, 126–127.
122. Another response in the published text states that if a woman wants to spin or weave and keep the proceeds for herself (or for her children from another marriage), her husband may forbid her from doing so; the proceeds of any work she does before he forbids her, however, accrue to her. This exchange, however, is in a final chapter appended to only one manuscript of the work and does not seem to be attributed to Ibn Saḥnūn. See Ibn Saḥnūn, *Fatāwā*, 540 (on the supplementary chapter see Ibn Saḥnūn, *Fatāwā*, 538n1).
123. Ibn Saḥnūn, *Fatāwā*, 127.
124. Ibn Saḥnūn, *Fatāwā*, 127–128.
125. On the issue of indeterminacy as a factor that may invalidate a contract, see *Al-Mawsūʿa al-fiqhīya*, s.v. "gharar" (31:149–167).
126. Ibn Saḥnūn, *Fatāwā*, 128–129.
127. Ibn Saḥnūn, *Fatāwā*, 129.

128. Ibn Saḥnūn's attitudes should not be understood in the context of a strict urban/rural dichotomy; Saḥnūn himself (although born and raised in Qayrawan) is said to have owned and worked a farm. See Brockopp, "Saḥnūn b. Saʿīd," 70–71). Presumably, however, the distinction is between the lifestyle of a learned urban-based landowner and that of the peasants.
129. On Ibn Abī Zayd al-Qayrawānī, see Muranyi, *Beiträge*, 234–264. ʿAbd al-Majīd Turkī treats the fatwas preserved in the *Miʿyār* of al-Wansharīsī (d. AH 914/508 CE) as a viable source for the legal thought of Ibn Abī Zayd; see Ibn Abī Zayd al-Qayrawānī, *Kitāb al-Jāmiʿ*, ed. ʿAbd al-Majīd Turkī (Beirut: Dār al-Gharb al-Islāmī, 1990), introduction, 70.
130. The fatwas attributed to Ibn Abī Zayd have been collected by Ḥamīd Muḥammad Laḥmar in his book *Fatāwā Ibn Abī Zayd al-Qayrawānī* (Beirut: Dār al-Gharb al-Islāmī, 2004; revised version published as *Fatāwā Ibn Abī Zayd al-Qayrawānī (Mālik al-Ṣaghīr)* (Cairo: Dār al-Laṭāʾif, 2012). The fatwa discussed here appears in *Fatāwā Ibn Abī Zayd al-Qayrawānī*, 151–152, and in *Fatāwā Mālik al-Ṣaghīr*, 1:212–213. In both editions of the book, Dr. Laḥmar ends the fatwa with the words "*fa-qawl Ibn Mājishūn yubīḥ*" ("Thus, Ibn al-Mājishūn's opinion permits"). The rationale for this editorial decision is not clear to me; because the later parts of the discussion refer back to the opening passage (and al-Rāshidī explicitly attributes material from the later parts of the text to Ibn Abī Zayd), it seems to be a unified composition.

    I am indebted to Dr. Laḥmar for his references to other sources for this text. The sources consulted for this discussion are Abū'l-Qāsim ibn Aḥmad al-Balawī al-Burzulī, *Fatāwā al-Burzulī: Jāmiʿ masāʾil al-aḥkām li-mā nazala min al-qaḍāyā bi'l-muftīn wa'l-ḥukkām*, ed. Muḥammad al-Ḥabīb al-Hīla (Beirut: Dār al-Gharb al-Islāmī, 2002), 2:357–359; Muḥammad ibn Muḥammad ibn ʿAbd al-Nūr al-Ḥimyarī, *Al-Ḥāwī jumalan min al-fatāwī*, ed. Muṣṭafā Maḥmūd ʿAlī Shaḥāta (Damascus: Dār al-ʿAṣmāʾ, 1441/2020), 540–545; and ʿAbd al-Raḥmān ibn ʿAbd al-Qādir al-Rāshidī, *Al-Taʿrīj wa'l-tabrīj fī dhikr aḥkām al-mughārasa wa'l-taṣyīr wa'l-tawlīj*, ed. Khālid Bū Shamma (Beirut: Dār Ibn Ḥazm, AH 1426/2005 CE), 519. Al-Burzulī and al-Ḥimyarī both present the full text, which is fully consistent on a sentence-by-sentence level but contains a large number of divergences ranging from individual words to full phrases.
131. Ḥimyarī, *Al-Ḥāwī*, 544.
132. Ḥimyarī, *Ḥāwī*, p. 541; and Burzulī, *Fatāwā*, 2:358.
133. Ḥimyarī, *Al-Ḥāwī*, 540, has "*Laysa ʿalayhā min khidmat al-bayt qalīl wa-lā kathīr*"; Burzulī (*Fatāwā*, 2:357) has "*laysa ʿalayhā min khidmat baytihā shayʾ albattata*." Both versions of the fatwa here insert "if [the husband] is prosperous," which both diverges from the content of the *Mudawwana* and makes no sense in context; in al-Ḥimyarī's text it is immediately followed by the observation, "Ibn al-Mājashūn and Aṣbagh said: "That is only if he is prosperous . . ."
134. Ḥimyarī, *Al-Ḥāwī*, 540–541 (*fa-fī qawl Ibn al-Mājishūn . . . hādhā amr fasīḥ*); Burzulī (*Fatāwā*, 2:358) has *yubīḥ*. The doctrines reviewed in this opening passage correspond closely to those presented by Ibn Abī Zayd al-Qayrawānī in *Nawādir*, 4:610–611.

135. Ḥimyarī, *Al-Ḥāwī*, 541; and Burzulī, *Fatāwā*, 2:358.
136. Ḥimyarī, *Al-Ḥāwī*, 541; and Burzulī, *Fatāwā*, 2:358. It is notable that *Adab al-nisā᾿* assumes such a contractual condition to be permissible (Ibn Ḥabīb, *Adab al-nisā᾿*, 281). The repeated discussion of this issue, if only in passing, suggests that adding the wife's labor to the marriage contract was one approach pursued by people who objected to the default legal doctrine that she was not responsible for housework.
137. I am reading "*yubālī*" rather than "*tubālī*" for the sense.
138. Ḥimyarī, *Al-Ḥāwī*, 541; and Burzulī, *Fatāwā*, 2:358.
139. Ḥimyarī, *Al-Ḥāwī*, 544; and Burzulī, *Fatāwā*, 2:359.
140. Ḥimyarī, *Al-Ḥāwī*, 544; and Burzulī, *Fatāwā*, 2:359.
141. Ḥimyarī, *Al-Ḥāwī*, 542, has "hold" (*tumsik*); I have followed the rendition *tasūs* from Burzulī, *Fatāwā*, 2:358.
142. See Bukhārī, *Ṣaḥīḥ*, 3:1094 (*Kitāb al-Nikāḥ, Bāb al-Ghayra*); and Muslim, *Ṣaḥīḥ*, 2:946–947 (*Kitāb al-Salām, Bāb Jawāz irdāf al-mar᾿a al-ajnabīya*).
143. al-Ḥimyarī, *Al-Ḥāwī*, 541–543; and Burzulī, *Fatāwā*, 2:358.
144. Ḥimyarī, Al-*Ḥāwī*, 543–544; and Burzulī, *Fatāwā*, 2:358. A similar story is told about the Companion Salmān al-Fārisī (probably the original version, since it makes sense of an otherwise confusing reference to the wife's being from the tribe of Kinda). See Abū Nuʿaym, *Ḥilyat al-awliyā᾿*, 1:185–6; in this version, Salmān finds that his wife has maidservants and expels them from their home.
145. Ḥimyarī, *Al-Ḥāwī*, 544; and Burzulī, *Fatāwā*, 2:358.
146. Ḥimyarī, *Ḥāwī*, 544, reading "*sāqiṭ ʿanka*" instead of "*sāqiṭ ʿinda*" for the sense; the comment about Ibn Abī Zayd's own preference is missing from Burzulī, *Fatāwā*, 2:358–359.
147. See Ibn Abī Zayd, *Nawādir*, 5:254–255, which distinguishes between a husband's genuine dislike (*bughḍ*) of his wife and his manipulative mistreatment (*ẓulm*) of her.
148. See, for instance, *Mudawwana*, 2:190–191 (a man may have sex with one wife but not with the other if this is simply how his desires run, but not to inflict harm or out of partiality; nevertheless, the husband who sincerely desires a life of constant worship is demanded to give his wife sex or divorce her), 2:340 (swearing to refrain from sex for a good reason rather than to inflict harm does not constitute *īlā᾿*); Ali, *Marriage and Slavery*, 117.
149. Ali, *Marriage and Slavery*, 125.
150. See, for instance, Muḥammad ibn Aḥmad al-Qurṭubī, *Al-Jāmiʿ li-aḥkām al-Qur᾿ān*, ed. Sālim Muṣṭafā al-Badrī (Beirut: Dār al-Kutub al-ʿIlmīya, AH 1424/2004 CE), 5:114 (states that it is disputed whether a husband may physically chastise his wife to make her do housework but concludes that he may do so if she withholds "the service that she is obligated to provide the husband according to what is customary and right [*al-maʿrūf*])."
151. Note that this is the same verse cited in Ibn Saḥnūn, *Fatāwā*, 126, in support of the principle that a husband should not transgress in demanding labor from his wife.
152. *Al-Jabal.*
153. *Ya᾿khudhūnahunna bi'l-khidma.*

154. Quoted in Qurṭubī, *Jāmiʿ*, 3:102.
155. Ahmed El Shamsy, *The Canonization of Islamic Law: A Social and Intellectual History* (Cambridge: Cambridge University Press, 2013), 110–111.
156. See the discussion of Ibn Khuwayz Mandād, above.
157. This is the central argument of El Shamsy, *Canonization of Islamic Law*.
158. See Jonathan A. C. Brown, *Hadith: Muhammad's Legacy in the Medieval and Modern World* (Oxford: Oneworld, 2009), 25–26.
159. Muwaffaq al-Dīn ibn Qudāma, *Al-Mughnī* (Beirut: Dār al-Kutub al-ʿIlmīya, 2009), 8:130. For these figures, see Sezgin, *Geschichte*, 1:108–109 (Ibn Abī Shayba), 1:135 (Abū Isḥāq al-Jūzajānī). For the opinion of Abū Thawr, see ʿAlī ibn Aḥmad Ibn Ḥazm, *Al-Muḥallā bi'l-āthār*, ed. ʿAbd al-Ghaffār Sulaymān al-Bindārī (Beirut: Dār al-Kutub al-ʿIlmīya, AH 1425/2003 CE), 9:228; and Saʿdī Ḥusayn ʿAlī Jabr, *Fiqh al-imām Abī Thawr* (Beirut: Muʾassasat al-Risāla / Amman: Dār al-Furqān, AH 1403/1983 CE), 487–488, and sources cited on 487n1; for this figure's identity, see Sezgin, *Geschichte* 1:491. Abū Thawr is also reported to have held that a mother is obligated to nurse her baby "even if she is the caliph's daughter" (see Jabr, *Fiqh al-imām Abī Thawr*, 489). Elsewhere he is cited as holding that a wife is entitled to a servant if she cannot appropriately serve herself due to her status or illness, based on an analogy between domestic service and housing as components of maintenance; this argument seems less compatible with his reported position on wives' duty to do housework, unless the *khidma* to which the elite wife is entitled is personal service rather than housework. Jabr, *Fiqh al-imām Abī Thawr*, 546–547.
160. Brown, *Hadith*, 27–28.
161. See Sezgin, *Geschichte*, 1:362.
162. Brown, *Hadith*, 30; and Dhahabī, *Siyar*, 13:285–291.
163. Abū Bakr Aḥmad ibn ʿAmr al-Khaṣṣāf, *Kitāb al-Nafaqāt*, with *Sharḥ* of al-Ṣadr al-Shahīd ʿAbd al-ʿAzīz ibn ʿUmar Ibn Māza, ed. Abū'l-Wafā al-Afghānī (Bombay: al-Dār al-Salafīya, n.d.), 34.
164. Khaṣṣāf, *Nafaqāt*, 16–17.
165. Abū Bakr ʿAbd Allāh ibn Muḥammad ibn Abī'l-Dunyā, *Kitāb al-ʿIyāl*, ed. Najam ʿAbd al-Raḥmān Khalaf (Al-Dammām: Dār Ibn al-Qayyim, AH 1410/1990 CE), 2:577–83.
166. Ibn Abī'l-Dunyā, *Kitāb al-ʿIyāl*, 2:580; Ibn Abī'l-Dunyā, *Kitāb al-ʿIyāl*, 2:581; see also Muḥammad ibn Jarīr al-Ṭabarī, *Jāmiʿ al-bayān ʿan tawīl āy al-Qurʾān* (Beirut: Dār al-Fikr, AH 1408/1988 CE), 18:28 (commentary on verse 23:51); and Abū Nuʿaym, *Ḥilyat al-awliyāʾ*, 4:144.
167. The most widely cited is a report from ʿĀʾisha advising, "Do not teach [women] to read; [rather,] teach them spinning and Sūrat al-Nūr [the 24th chapter of the Qurʾān; verse 31 of this chapter instructs women in the rules of modesty]." See Sulaymān ibn Aḥmad al-Ṭabarānī, *Al-Muʿjam al-awsaṭ*, eds. Ṭāriq ibn ʿAwaḍ Allāh ibn Muḥammad and ʿAbd al-Muḥsin ibn Ibrāhīm al-Ḥusaynī (Cairo: Dār al-Ḥaramayn, AH 1415/1995 CE), 6:34. This advice was famously cited in a verse by the tenth-century Syrian poet Abū al-ʿAlāʾ al-Maʿarrī. See Ṭāhā Ḥusayn and Ibrāhīm al-Abyārī, *Sharḥ Luzūm mā lā yalzam* (Cairo: Dār al-Maʿārif, n.d.), 1:148. Al-Ḥākim al-Naysābūrī considered the hadith *ṣaḥīh* by the criteria of al-Bukhārī

and Muslim, but al-Dhahabī declared it forged. Muḥammad ibn ʿAbd Allāh al-Ḥākim al-Naysābūrī, *Al-Mustadrak ʿalā al-Ṣaḥīḥayn*, ed. Muṣṭafā ʿAbd al-Qādir ʿAṭā (Beirut: Dār al-Kutub al-ʿIlmīya, AH 1422/2002 CE), 2:430; ʿUmar ibn ʿAlī Ibn al-Mulaqqin, *Mukhtaṣar istidrāk al-ḥāfiẓ al-Dhahabī ʿalā Mustadrak Abī ʿAbd Allāh al-Ḥākim*, ed. ʿAbd Allāh ibn Ḥamd al-Luḥaydān (Riyadh: Dār al-ʿĀṣima, AH 1411), 2:879.

168. On Ibn Ḥanbal, see Nimrod Hurvitz, *The Formation of Hanbalism: Piety into Power* (London: Routledge, 2002), 34, 36. For Sufyān al-Thawrī, see Abū Bakr al-Bayhaqī, *Al-Madkhal ilā al-sunan al-kubrā*, ed. Muḥammad Ḍiyāʾ al-Raḥmān al-Aʿẓamī (al-Ṣabāḥīya, Kuwayt: Dār al-Khulafāʾ li'l-Kitāb al-Islāmī, n.d.), 329; and Abū Nuʿaym, *Ḥilyat al-awliyāʾ*, 7:67.
169. Abū Nuʿaym, *Ḥilyat al-awliyāʾ*, 8:353 (in the anecdote, the sister's scrupulosity is such that she consults Aḥmad ibn Ḥanbal about the licitness of spinning by the light of the governor's lamps).
170. Ibn Ḥanbal, *Musnad*, 35:372; for discussion of this anecdote, see Leor Halevi, *Muhammad's Grave: Death Rites and the Making of Islamic Society* (New York: Columbia University Press, 2007), 108–109; and Hurvitz, *The Formation of Hanbalism*, 36 ("We also know that when his family ran into financial problems, his wives would spin wool [*taghzilu ghazlan*] and sell their wares"); see also 34 (Ibn Ḥanbal asks for money from his concubine Ḥusn, who sells spun thread to obtain it).
171. *ʿAjibtu min aṣḥābinā, min ayna awjabū ʿalā al-zawj ikhdāma zawjatihi ḥattā jaʿalū dhālika ka'l-nafaqa; wa huwa ʿindī radī* (Qaḍī ʿIyāḍ, *Tartīb al-madārik*, 5:176). I owe this reference to Muḥammad al-Wathīq, who references it in his edition of the *Tanbīhāt* (ʿIyāḍ ibn Mūsā, *Tanbīhāt*, 2:647n3).
172. Qaḍī ʿIyāḍ, *Tartīb al-madārik*, 5:175.
173. Qaḍī ʿIyāḍ, *Tartīb al-madārik*, 5:177.
174. Ibn Ḥabīb, *Adab al-nisāʾ*, introduction, 11.
175. On the concept of the *mashhūr*, see Wael B. Hallaq, *Authority, Continuity and Change in Islamic Law* (Cambridge: Cambridge University Press, 2005), 152.

2. *Falsafa* and *Fiqh* in the Writings of al-Māwardī

1. Dates are given with AH (anno Hegirae, or "in the year of [Muhammad's] Hijra") first followed by CE (of the Common Era).
2. Dimitri Gutas, *Greek Thought, Arabic Culture: The Graeco-Arabic Translation Movement in Baghdad and Early ʿAbbāsid Society (2nd–4th/8th–10th Centuries)* (London: Routledge, 1998), 2.
3. For a general summary and analysis of Aristotle's ethics as expressed in this work, see Richard Kraut, "Aristotle's Ethics," *Stanford Encyclopedia of Philosophy*, Stanford University, June 15, 2019, https://plato.stanford.edu/archives/sum2018/entries/aristotle-ethics.
4. Anna A. Akasoy and Alexander Fidora, eds., *The Arabic Version of the Nicomachean Ethics*, with an introduction and annotated translation by Douglas M. Dunlop (Leiden: Brill, 2005), 6–12, 26–27.

5. Aristotle, *Nicomachean Ethics*, trans. David Ross, revised with an introduction and notes by Lesley Brown (New York: Oxford University Press, 2009), 142 (bk. VIII, para. 1).
6. Aristotle, *Nicomachean Ethics*, 144–147 (bk. VIII, para. 3–4).
7. Aristotle, *Nicomachean Ethics*, 150, 155 (bk. VIII, para. 7, 10).
8. Aristotle, *Nicomachean Ethics*, 159 (bk. VIII, para. 12).
9. On the dating of Bryson, see Simon Swain, *Economy, Family, and Society from Rome to Islam: A Critical Edition, English Translation, and Study of Bryson's Management of the Estate* (Cambridge: Cambridge University Press, 2013), 33. On the date of the Arabic translation he notes that "we . . . find [Bryson] being used about the 920s by Qudāma ibn Jaʿfar and in the middle of the century by Ibn al-Jazzār." Swain, *Economy, Family, and Society*, 54. On this work and its influence on Islamic literature see also Mauro Zonta, "Bryson," in *Encyclopaedia of Islam*, 3rd ed. (hereafter, *EI3*), ed. by Kate Fleet, Gudrun Krämer, Denis Matringe, John Nawas, and Everett Rowson (Leiden: Brill, 2007); Yassine Essid, *A Critique of the Origins of Islamic Economic Thought* (Leiden: Brill, 1995), part 3 (179–219); W. Heffening and G. Endress, "Tadbīr al-manzil," in *Encyclopaedia of Islam*, 2nd ed. (hereafter, *EI2*), ed. by P. Bearman, Th. Bianquis, C. E. Bosworth, E. van Donzel, and W. P. Heinrichs (Leiden: Brill, 1960–2005).
10. Swain, *Economy, Family, and Society*, 465.
11. Swain, *Economy, Family, and Society*, 467.
12. Swain, *Economy, Family, and Society*, 44.
13. Swain, *Economy, Family, and Society*, 473 (original Arabic, 472; see also 470); see also 332.
14. See M. Arkoun, "Miskawayh," *EI2*.
15. On Miskawayh's *Tahdhīb al-akhlāq* and its relationship to Bryson see Swain, *Economy, Family, and Society*, 100, 352–353.
16. Abū ʿAlī Aḥmad ibn Muḥammad "Miskawayh," *Tahdhīb al-akhlāq wa-taṭhīr al-aʿrāq*, with an introduction by Ḥasan Tamīm (Beirut: Manshūrāt Dār Maktabat al-Ḥayāt, n.d.), 125–127.
17. Miskawayh, *Tahdhīb*, 125.
18. Constantine K. Zurayk, *The Refinement of Character: A Translation from the Arabic of Aḥmad ibn Muḥammad Miskawayh's "Tahdhīb al-Akhlāq"* (Beirut: American University of Beirut, 1968), 129 (original text in Miskawayh, *Tahdhīb*, 130; see quotation and discussion in Swain, *Economy, Family, and Society*, 352–353.
19. On the "Brysonian terminology," see Swain, *Economy, Family, and Society*, 353.
20. On his life and works see A. M. Goichon, "Ibn Sīnā," *EI2*.
21. Swain, *Economy, Family, and Society*, 83.
22. Swain notes of the attribution of this book that "it is accepted as genuine by most Western and Eastern . . . scholars of Avicenna" (*Economy, Family, and Society*, 99), while Hümeyra Özturan notes that it "might not be authentic" in "The Practical Philosophy of al-Fārābī and Avicenna: A Comparison," *Nazariyat* 5, no. 1 (May 2019): 26. For the interchangeable use of *siyāsa* and *tadbīr*, see Abū ʿAlī Ibn Sīnā, *Kitāb al-Siyāsa*, ed. ʿAlī Muḥammad Isbar (Jableh, Syria: Bidāyāt, 2007), 59. For an English translation of this work, see Jon McGinnis and David C. Reisman, *Classical Arabic Philosophy: An Anthology of Sources* (Indianapolis: Hackett, 2007), 224–237.

23. Ibn Sīnā, *Siyāsa*, 59.
24. Ibn Sīnā, *Siyāsa*, 61–63.
25. Ibn Sīnā, *Siyāsa*, 62.
26. Ibn Sīnā, *Siyāsa*, 79 (compare the slightly different translation in McGinnis and Reisman, *Classical Arabic Philosophy*, 232).
27. Ibn Sīnā, *Siyāsa*, 79 (compare the slightly different translation in McGinnis and Reisman, *Classical Arabic Philosophy*, 232).
28. Ibn Sīnā, *Siyāsa*, 79–80.
29. Ibn Sīnā, *Siyāsa*, 80.
30. McGinnis and Reisman, *Classical Arabic Philosophy*, 233 (Ibn Sīnā, *Siyāsa*, 81). Swain argues that Ibn Sīnā's overall approach to the wife is very different from Bryson's, on the grounds that "the property is not joint: it is his only; and the tone of the three matrimonial parameters is decidedly more oppressive than anything in the Greek tradition. There is nothing on love and affection." Swain, *Economy, Family, and Society*, 359–60. However, he also notes that Ibn Sīnā characterizes the wife as a partner and manager and references her role in managing servants.
31. Muḥammad ibn Yūsuf al-ʿĀmirī, *al-Saʿāda wa'l-isʿād fī'l-sīra al-insānīya*, ed. Aḥmad ʿAbd al-Ḥalīm ʿAṭīya (Cairo: Dār al-Thaqāfa li 'l-Nashr wa 'l-Tawzīʿ, [1991]), 372. Compare also the statement attributed to Pythagorus, which urges the wife to "exert herself in serving [to ensure] a prosperous life" (*tastakidda nafsahā fī'l-khidma fī ṣalāḥ al-ʿaysh*), 372, and another referring to "the duty that she serve him" and "the duty that she aid him in [securing] a prosperous life," 373. For a discussion of these passages, see Swain, *Economy, Family, and Society*, 353–354. The attribution of this work to al-ʿĀmirī (d. AH 381/992 CE) is contested; see Swain, *Economy, Family, and Society*, 353; and Everett Rowson, "al-ʿĀmirī," *EI2*.
32. Swain, *Economy, Family, and Society*, 353.
33. For instance, a hadith declares that "each of you is a shepherd, and each of you is responsible for his flock," going on to specify that "a wife is a shepherd over her husband's house and children." This widely cited report appears multiple times in Bukhārī, suggesting its wide application in his *fiqh*. See [Muḥammad ibn Ismāʿīl al-Bukhārī], *Ṣaḥīḥ al-Bukhārī* (Vaduz, Liechtenstein: Thesaurus Islamicus Foundation, 2000), 1:169 (*Kitāb al-Jumʿa, Bāb al-Jumʿa fī'l-qurā wa'l-mudun*); 1:450 (*Kitāb fī'l-Istiqrāḍ wa-adāʾ al-duyūn, Bāb al-ʿAbd rāʿ fī māl sayyidihi wa-lā yaʿmal illā bi-idhnihi*); 1:480 (*Kitāb al-ʿItq, Bāb Karāhīyat al-taṭāwul ʿalā al-raqīq*); 2:533 (*Kitāb al-Waṣāyā, Bāb Taʾwīl qawl Allāh taʿāla [min baʿd waṣīya yūṣā bihā aw dayn]*); 3:1085 (*Kitāb al-Nikāḥ, Bāb [qū anfusakum wa-ahlīkum nāran]*); 3:1090 (*Kitāb al-Nikāḥ, Bāb al-Marʾa rāʿiya fī bayt zawjihā*); 3:1441 (*Kitāb al-Aḥkām, Bāb [Aṭīʿū Allāh wa-aṭīʿū al-rasūl wa-ūlī al-amr minkum]*). See also Swain, *Economy, Family, and Society*, 349. Similarly suggesting a managerial role for at least some wives, the *Mudawwana* of Saḥnūn (see chapter 1) presents the opinion (implicitly attributed to Ibn al-Qāsim) that a man who is embarking on a journey may select the wife of his choice to accompany him because "he may have a wife . . . who is the one in charge of his wealth (*ṣāḥibat mālihi*) and the manager of his estate (*mudabbirat ḍayʿatihi*)," so he would incur losses if he took her with him. Mālik ibn Anas

al-Aṣbaḥī, *Al-Mudawwana al-kubrā, riwāyat al-imām Saḥnūn ibn Saʿīd al-Tanūkhī*, ed. Zakarīyā ʿUmayrāt (Beirut: Dār al-Kutub al-ʿIlmīya, AH 1426/2005 CE), 2:190.

34. Christopher Melchert, "Māwardī, Abū Yaʿlā, and the Sunni Revival," in *Prosperity and Stagnation: Some Cultural and Social Aspects of the Abbasid Period (750–1258)*, ed. Krzystof Kościelniak (Kraców: UNUM, 2010), 46.
35. See Henri Laoust, "La pensée et l'action politiques d'al-Māwardī (364–450/974–1058)," *Revue des Études Islamiques* 36, no. 1 (1968): 13–14. Melchert notes, "The famous *Mukhtaṣar* of al-Qudūrī (d. Baghdad, 428/1037) is its Ḥanafī counterpart, while ʿAbd al-Wahhāb al-Thaʿlabī (d. Cairo, 422/1031) prepared an epitome of Māliki law, probably *al-Talqīn*." Christopher Melchert, "Māwardī's Legal Thinking," *Al-ʿUṣūr al-Wusṭā* 23 (2015): 71.
36. See Melchert, "Māwardī's Legal Thinking," 70.
37. Melchert, "Māwardī, Abū Yaʿlā, and the Sunni Revival," 47.
38. See Ovamir Anjum, *Politics Law, and Community in Islamic Thought* (New York: Cambridge University Press, 2012), 254; and Mona Hassan, *Longing for the Lost Caliphate: A Transregional History* (Princeton, N.J.: Princeton University Press, 2017), 304n76.
39. Melchert, "Māwardī, Abū Yaʿlā, and the Sunni Revival," 47.
40. See Kecia Ali, *Marriage and Slavery in Early Islam* (Cambridge, Mass.: Harvard University Press, 2010).
41. See Abū al-Ḥasan ʿAlī ibn Muḥammad ibn Ḥabīb al-Māwardī, *Al-Ḥāwī al-kabīr fī fiqh madhhab al-imām al-Shāfiʿī*, eds. ʿAlī Muḥammad Muʿawwaḍ and ʿĀdil Aḥmad ʿAbd al-Mawjūd (Beirut: Dār al-Kutub al-ʿIlmīya, AH 1419/1999 CE), 9:77, 395, 471, 482, 483; 10:87; 11:461, 462.
42. See, for instance, Māwardī, *Ḥāwī*, 3:354 ("Marriage is a contract by which usufruct is made licit," *al-nikāḥ ʿaqd yustabāḥ bi al-manfaʿa*); 7:164 ("The usufructs of the vulva are equivalent to property, because they are acquired for a countervalue in marriage," *manāfiʿ al-buḍʿ tajrī majrā al-amwāl li'annahā tumlak bi-ʿiwaḍ fī al-nikāḥ*). On the husband's sexual rights in marriage as usufructory rights, see Hina Azam, *Sexual Violation in Islamic Law: Substance, Evidence, and Procedure* (New York: Cambridge University Press, 2015), 86, 120, 121.
43. Māwardī, *Ḥāwī*, 11:423.
44. Māwardī, *Ḥāwī*, 11:445.
45. Māwardī, *Ḥāwī*, 11:428. The text reads "The husband is equivalent" (*jarā al-zawj*); I have emended it to "the wife" for the sense.
46. See, for instance, Māwardī, *Ḥāwī*, 11:422 (*nafaqat al-zawja muʿāwaḍa fī muqābalat al-istimtāʿ bihā*, "The wife's maintenance is a countervalue in exchange for [access to] sexual enjoyment of her"). As we shall see, there were inter-*madhhab* debates over whether *nafaqa* was a countervalue (*ʿiwaḍ*) or not. For comparable inter-*madhhab* debates on whether the dower (*mahr/ṣadāq*) is a countervalue, see Azam, *Sexual Violation*, 121, 137–138.
47. Māwardī, *Ḥāwī*, 11:426.
48. Māwardī, *Ḥāwī*, 11:423–425.
49. Māwardī, *Ḥāwī*, 11:454–456.

50. For the concept of *manfaʿa* in classical *fiqh* see *Al-Mawsūʿa al-fiqhīya* (Kuwayt: Wizārat al-Awqāf wa'l-Shuʾūn al-Islāmīya, AH1404–1427/1983–2006 CE), s.v. "Manfaʿa" (39:101–111); and Azam, *Sexual Violation*, 119.
51. Māwardī, *Ḥāwī*, 10:491.
52. See, for instance, Māwardī, *Ḥāwī*, 7:160–162; and Muḥammad ibn Idrīs al-Shāfiʿī, *al-Umm* (Beirut: Dār al-Maʿrifa, [1973]), 4:261. On the divergences among *madhhabs* in conceptualizing *manfaʿa*, see Mahmoud A. El-Gamal, *Islamic Finance: Law, Economics, and Practice* (Cambridge: Cambridge University Press, 2006), 37.
53. See Shāfiʿī, *Umm*, 5:59; and Mawardī, *Ḥāwī*, 9:410–411.
54. On the Ḥanafī view of *manāfiʿ* as lacking independent legal existence absent a contract of hire, see Shams al-Dīn al-Sarakhsī, *Kitāb al-Mabsūṭ* (Beirut: Dār al-Maʿrifa, AH 1409/1989 CE), 7:83, 11:78–79; and Māwardī, *Ḥāwī*, 9:410. On the use of the husband's labor as dower, see Muḥammad ibn al-Ḥasan al-Shaybānī, *Al-Jāmiʿ al-ṣaghīr maʿa sharḥihi al-Nāfiʿ al-kabīr* (Karachi: Idārat al-Qurʾān wa'l-ʿUlūm al-Islāmīya, AH 1411/1990 CE), 83–184; and Sarakhsī, *Mabsūṭ*, 5:106. The dispute on this point between the Ḥanafīs and the Shāfiʿīs is analyzed in Aḥmad ibn Muḥammad al-Qudūrī, *Al-Tajrīd*, eds. Muḥammad Aḥmad Sarrāj and ʿAlī Jumʿa Muḥammad (Madīnat Naṣr, Egypt: Dār al-Salām, AH 1424/2004 CE), 9:4635–4639; and Jār Allāh Maḥmūd ibn ʿUmar al-Zamakhsharī, *Ruʾūs al-masāʾil*, ed. ʿAbd Allāh Nadhīr Aḥmad (Beirut: Dār al-Bashāʾir al-Islāmīya, AH 1407/1987 CE), 400–401.
55. See, for instance, the discussion in Māwardī, *Ḥāwī*, 8:219–226, where al-Māwardī's detailed discussion of this issue consistently identifies the enslaved person's *manfaʿa* with his *khidma* (service), which corresponds to the slave's labor capacity in general, including any wage-bearing labor (*kasb*). He sometimes uses the plural (*manāfiʿ*), presumably to refer to the various specific skills a man may possess or kinds of work that he may perform.
56. Māwardī, *Ḥāwī*, 6:214; 7:160, 9:67, 9:109.
57. On this point see Baber Johansen, "The Valorization of the Human Body in Muslim Sunni Law," *Princeton Papers: Interdisciplinary Journal of Middle Eastern Studies* 4 (1996): 83–4; and Ali, *Marriage and Slavery*, 12–13.
58. Māwardī, *Ḥāwī*, 9:399.
59. Māwardī, *Ḥāwī*, 9:109; for other examples, see 7:401 and 7:160.
60. For an analysis of the tenuous connection between stated legal methodology and substantive legal doctrine in the area of ritual law, see Behnam Sadeghi, *The Logic of Law-Making in Islam: Women and Prayer in the Legal Tradition* (Cambridge: Cambridge University Press, 2013).
61. See Māwardī, *Ḥāwī*, 9:66–67.
62. Māwardī, *Ḥāwī*, 10:492; see also 4:125.
63. Al-Māwardī seems to see concubines (that is, enslaved women taken as sexual partners by their owners) as a somewhat anomalous subset contrasted with the ordinary run of female slaves, who are used for their labor. He distinguishes between enslaved women used for labor (*jawārī al-khidma*) and those used as concubines (*jawārī al-tasarrī*). Māwardī, *Ḥāwī*, 11:529. On the conventions relating to enslaved concubines, see Māwardī, *Ḥāwī*, 15:408–409.
64. Al-Māwardī reiterates the statement that the objective of the marriage is sexual enjoyment in *Ḥāwī*, 4:125, 9:106 and 9:137.

65. Māwardī, *Ḥāwī*, 11:428; see also 11:429. Avner Giladi notes that "the Shāfiʿīs . . . tended to charge the husband with all the expenses involved in his sexual life and its consequences, including hiring a midwife." Avner Giladi, *Muslim Midwives: The Craft of Birthing in the Premodern Middle East* (Cambridge: Cambridge University Press, 2015), 133.
66. Māwardī, *Ḥāwī*, 11:432–433.
67. Māwardī, *Ḥāwī*, 9:154–155.
68. Māwardī, *Ḥāwī*, 9:80; see also 9:345. On this point, see Azam, *Sexual Violation*, 120: "A husband did not own his wife's physical body, but rather only the usufructory right to her sexuality (*buḍʿ*), while a slave owner actually owned his concubine's physical body, including her sexuality."
69. Māwardī, *Ḥāwī*, 11:445–446. On the distinction between day as the time for work and night as the time for sexual enjoyment, see also Māwardī, *Ḥāwī*, 9:76, 9:83–84. If an owner allows his male slave to marry, al-Māwardī notes that he is entitled to use the slave for labor (*istikhdām*) during the daytime, while the slave is entitled to spend the night with his wife because it is the time of *istimtāʿ*. He also notes that some occupations are nocturnal, in which case the time for sexual enjoyment would be during the day. Māwardī, *Ḥāwī*, 9:84.
70. Māwardī, *Ḥāwī*, 11:446.
71. Māwardī, *Ḥāwī*, 11:446. Al-Māwardī also notes here that if a woman entered into a contract of hire before the marriage and the husband was not aware of this fact, "he has the choice between upholding the marriage and annulling it, because the nullification of [his entitlement to] sexual enjoyment during the daytime is a defect [in the wife]" (11:446). See also 9:175.
72. If the wife's entitlement to maintenance results from the husband's right to keep her present and available for his sexual needs, al-Māwardī also acknowledges the converse: the husband's right to control his wife's time and movements is contingent on his provision of maintenance. If he fails to provide the minimum of necessary maintenance, she is entitled to go out during the daytime in order to earn her living or to beg. Due to his failure to maintain her, the right to control her movements has reverted to her. If he wants to have sex during the day, she is justified in refusing him because it is work time (*zaman al-iktisāb*), apparently even if she is in fact at home. Māwardī, *Ḥāwī*, 11:460; see also Kecia Ali, *Marriage and Slavery*, 91.
73. Māwardī, *Ḥāwī*, 11:494.
74. Māwardī, *Ḥāwī*, 11:495.
75. Māwardī, *Ḥāwī*, 11:495.
76. Māwardī, *Ḥāwī*, 11:324.
77. Māwardī, *Ḥāwī*, 11:495–496.
78. The Ḥanafīs define *istiḥqāq* as the establishment that something is an entitlement owed to another party (*ẓuhūr kawn al-shayʾ ḥaqqan wājiban li'l-ghayr*), and Shāfiʿīs (while not articulating a formal definition) also use it in this technical sense. *Al-Mawsūʿa al-fiqhīya*, s.v. "Istiḥqāq," para. 1 (3:219).
79. In another passage he writes, "If they are [still] married, she is not entitled to nurse [the infant] for a wage, because by virtue of his ownership of sexual enjoyment of her he has the right to prevent her from hiring herself out [to someone

else] as a nurse, so she is not entitled to compensation for nursing." Māwardī, *Ḥāwī*, 10:69. Here the wife's right to receive wages from her husband is assumed to parallel her right to hire herself out to a third party. This argument seems problematic since (for instance) working for a third party might involve leaving the home; nursing the couple's own child presumably would occur within the home and occupy no more of the wife's time than nursing the baby for free.

80. Māwardī, *Ḥāwī*, 11:417.
81. Māwardī, *Ḥāwī*, 11:423; and Sarakhsī, *Mabsūṭ*, 5:181.
82. Māwardī, *Ḥāwī*, 11:446.
83. Māwardī, *Ḥāwī*, 9:175.
84. Māwardī, *Ḥāwī*, 9:72; see also 9:131.
85. Māwardī, *Ḥāwī*, 6:352. Although al-Māwardī does not use the phrase *tadbīr al-manāzil*, his references to *tadbīr khadamihā* (management of her servants) and *tadbīr mā yatawallāhu al-nisāʾ min umūr al-manāzil* (management of what women administer of household affairs) evoke the terminology relating to women and households in the *akhlāq* literature.
86. On this term, see Toshihiko Izutsu, *Ethico-Religious Concepts in the Qurʾān* (Montreal: McGill-Queen's University Press, 2002), 213–215; Kevin Reinhart, "What We Know About Maʿrūf," *Journal of Islamic Ethics* 1 (2017): 51–82; and Ingrid Mattson, "Status-Based Definitions of Need in Early Islamic *Zakat* and Maintenance Laws," in *Poverty and Charity in Middle Eastern Contexts*, ed. Michael Bonner (Albany: State University of New York Press, 2003), 42, 45.
87. Reading *li-qiyāmihā* instead of *li-qiyāsihā* for the sense.
88. Māwardī, *Ḥāwī*, 11:418.
89. Māwardī, *Ḥāwī*, 11:426.
90. Māwardī, *Ḥāwī*, 11:418. For an analysis of this passage, see Mattson, "Status-Based Definitions of Need," 45–46.
91. Māwardī, *Ḥāwī*, 11:418.
92. Māwardī, *Ḥāwī*, 11:419.
93. Neither does possession of a servant help her case if she lacks the requisite rank; if a woman whose social status does not warrant service nevertheless in fact owns a servant, she is herself responsible for the servant's maintenance. Māwardī, *Ḥāwī*, 3:355–356, reading *fa-ʿalayhā [rather than ʿalayhi] nafaqatuhu wa-zakāt fiṭrihi dūna al-zawj* for the sense.
94. Māwardī, *Ḥāwī*, 3:356, 11:419.
95. Abū Isḥāq Ibrāhīm ibn Aḥmad al-Marwazī (d. AH 340/951–952 CE) was a student of Ibn Surayj; see Shams al-Dīn al-Dhahabī, *Siyar aʿlām al-nubalāʾ*, ed. Shuʿayb al-Arnaʾūṭ (Beirut: Muʾassasat al-Risāla, AH 1402/1982 CE), 15:429–430.
96. Abū ʿAlī al-Ḥasan ibn al-Ḥusayn Ibn Abī Hurayra (d. AH 345/956–957 CE) was a student of both Ibn Surayj and Abū Isḥāq al-Marwazī; see al-Dhahabī, *Siyar aʿlām al-nubalāʾ*, 15:430.
97. Māwardī, *Ḥāwī*, 11:419–420; see also Māwardī, *Ḥāwī*, 3:356.
98. Māwardī, *Ḥāwī*, 11:420.
99. On this legal point, see Māwardī, *Ḥāwī*, 7:317–318.
100. Māwardī, *Ḥāwī*, 3:355–356.

101. Discussing Ḥanafī law, Baber Johansen observes that the "circulation of a good or a person as a commodity or as an appropriated good implies, according to the jurists, its 'profanation' (*ibtiḏāl*), a term which is defined by the jurists through its opposition to protection, conservation and chastity (*ṣawn* or *ṣiyāna*), and to *ḥurma*, inviolability and sacred status. It implies the idea of use and abuse by everybody." Johansen, "Valorization of the Body," 74.
102. Al-Zabīdī notes that "*ibtidhāl* is the opposite of *ṣiyāna*" and defines the verb *ibtadhala* as "to abase/demean" (*ahāna*). The primary association is with worn-out work clothes. The active participle *mubtadhil* may refer to someone who wears worn-out garments but can also mean "a person who does his own work" (*al-ladhī yalī ʿamal nafsihi*). Murtaḍā al-Zabīdī, *Tāj al-ʿarūs min jawāhir al-Qāmūs*, eds. ʿAbd al-Munʿim Khalīl Ibrāhīm and Karīm Sayyid Muḥammad Maḥmūd (Beirut: Dār al-Kutub al-ʿIlmīya, AH 1428/2007 CE), 28:40.
103. Māwardī, *Ḥāwī*, 16:274.
104. Māwardī, *Ḥāwī*, 13:232, 330 (both referring to the rationale for the *ḥadd* punishment of sexual slander).
105. For invocations of *ṣiyāna* as an ideal for girls or women, see Māwardī, *Ḥāwī*, 14:115 (women are exempted from jihad because it is necessary to protect (*ṣawn*) them from the *bidhla* of war); 3:61 (a female corpse should be modestly covered for the sake of *ṣiyāna*); 13:203 (a woman being stoned for adultery is buried up to her chest because it is *astar wa-aṣwan*); 11:508 (a girl in custody of mother should be kept indoors "so she becomes accustomed to *ṣiyāna*"); 11:511 (an unmarried adult woman should be encouraged to live with parents for the sake of *ṣiyāna*).
106. Māwardī, *Ḥāwī*, 2:455.
107. Māwardī, *Ḥāwī*, 11:529. One of the multiple folk etymologies al-Māwardī offers for the term *sirrīya* (concubine) is that it is derived from the word *satr*, "coverage, modesty," because a concubine is secluded after having been exposed to the common gaze (*baʿd al-bidhla*). Māwardī, *Ḥāwī*, 15:409.
108. Māwardī, *Ḥāwī*, 9:547, 548.
109. See Māwardī, *Ḥāwī*, 3:23, 16:86, 16:301, 16:320–321, 17:151, 17:300.
110. See Māwardī, *Ḥāwī*, 3:492, 493 (a man making an *iʿtikāf* retreat in the mosque may go home to eat and relieve himself to avoid the *bidhla* of doing so in public); 6:495 (a person may choose to transact business through an agent [*wakīl*] "to protect himself from being cheapened" [*ṣiyānatan li-nafsihi min al-bidhla*]).
111. See Māwardī, *Ḥāwī*, 16:42 (a judge should avoid personally engaging in trade); 16:44 (a judge may decline to attend banquets); 16:174–175 (a judge accused of miscarriage of justice shielded from public exposure for sake of *ṣiyāna*).
112. On this concept, see Farhat J. Ziadeh, "Equality (*Kafāʾah*) in the Muslim Law of Marriage," *American Journal of Comparative* Law 6 (1957): 504–517; Amalia Zomeño, "Kafāʾa in the Mālikī School: A fatwā from Fifteenth-Century Fez," in *Islamic Law: Theory and Practice*, ed. by Robert Gleave and Eugenia Kermeli (London: I. B. Tauris, 2001), 87–106; and *Al-Mawsūʿa al-fiqhīya*, s.v. "kafāʾa," 34:266–287.
113. The relative ranks and merits of different forms of livelihood was a topic to which al-Māwardī devoted recurring attention; in addition to the passage under consideration, see Māwardī, *Ḥāwī*, 5:11–13, 15:153.

114. Māwardī, *Ḥāwī*, 9:105.
115. Māwardī, *Ḥāwī*, 9:105. On the stigmatization of weavers (and the hadith texts identifying it as bar to marriage equality), see Robert Brunschvig, "Métiers vils en Islam," *Studia Islamica* 16 (1962): 46, 52–54; and Louise Marlow, *Hierarchy and Egalitarianism in Islamic Thought* (Cambridge: Cambridge University Press, 1997), 33, 163. On the illicitness of the earnings of the cupper and its basis in hadith, see Māwardī, *Ḥāwī*, 15:152–156; Brunschvig, "Métiers vils," 46–50; and Marlow, *Hierarchy and Egalitarianism*, 33, 163.
116. Bukhārī, *Ṣaḥīḥ*, 3:1067 (*Kitāb al-Nikāḥ, Bāb al-Akfāʾ fī'l-dīn*); and Muslim, *Ṣaḥīḥ*, 1:606 (*Kitāb al-Raḍāʿ, Bāb Istiḥbāb nikāḥ dhāt al-dīn*).
117. For this hadith, its authenticity and its interpretation, see Zayn al-Dīn ʿAbd al-Raḥīm ibn al-Ḥusayn al-ʿIrāqī and Abū Zurʿa al-ʿIrāqī, *Tarḥ al-tathrīb fī sharḥ al-Taqrīb* (Beirut: Dār Iḥyāʾ al-Turāth al-ʿArabī, n.d.), 7:19–20.
118. Māwardī, *Ḥāwī*, 9:105–106.
119. "Choose the pious one, darn you!" (*ʿalayka bi-dhāt al-dīn taribat yadāk*). See Bukhārī, *Ṣaḥīḥ*, 3:1067 (*Kitāb al-Nikāḥ, Bāb al-Akfāʾ fī'l-dīn*); and Muslim, *Ṣaḥīḥ*, 1:606 (*Kitāb al-Nikāḥ, Bāb Istiḥbāb nikāḥ dhāt al-dīn*).
120. See, for instance, Muḥammad ibn Jarīr al-Ṭabarī, *Jāmiʿ al-bayān ʿan taʾwīl āy al-Qurʾān* (Beirut: Dār al-Fikr, AH 1408/1988 CE), 30:279.
121. Māwardī, *Ḥāwī*, 9:106.
122. The term *muwāṣala* can refer to sexual as well as social intercourse, but in this context is explicitly contrasted with sex.
123. Māwardī, *Ḥāwī*, 9:173; see also 9:394. In context, this claim is a rationalization of the Shāfiʿī legal doctrine that a man can marry a slave woman only to provide himself with a licit sexual outlet (see *Ḥāwī*, 9:233).
124. Māwardī, *Ḥāwī*, 9:350.
125. Māwardī, *Ḥāwī*, 9:488–489.
126. Māwardī, *Ḥāwī*, 9:342. He similarly rationalizes the doctrine that a woman's eloquence enhances her fair dower with the observation that "eloquence of speech contributes to sexual enjoyment" (9:490).
127. Māwardī, *Ḥāwī*, 9:32.
128. See Geneviève Gobillot, "Celibacy," *EI3*.
129. Māwardī, *Ḥāwī*, 9:31.
130. Māwardī, *Ḥāwī*, 9:32.
131. Mohammed Arkoun, "L'Éthique musulmane d'après Māwardī," *Revue des Études Islamiques* 31 (1963): 5, 10. Translations mine.
132. Arkoun, "L'Éthique musulmane," 3, 6–7. Al-Māwardī frames the book in his introduction as drawing on the Qur'an, the sunna of the Prophet, "the maxims of the sages (*amthāl al-ḥukamāʾ*), the answers of the eloquent, and the sayings of the poets." Abū'l-Ḥasan ʿAlī ibn Muḥammad ibn Ḥabīb al-Māwardī, *Adab al-dunyā wa'l-dīn*, ed. Muḥammad Jāsim al-Ḥadīthī (Baghdad: Manshūrāt al-Majmaʿ al-ʿIlmī, AH 1429/2008 CE), 1:51–52. The term *sage* (*ḥakīm*) was often used to refer to the Greek philosophers, and while al-Māwardī rarely cites them by name, concepts and premises drawn from *falsafa* are central to the work.
133. Arkoun, "L'Éthique musulmane," 6–8.
134. Arkoun, "L'Éthique musulmane," 3.

135. Arkoun, "L'Éthique musulmane," 12.
136. Māwardī, *Adab al-dunyā wa'l-dīn*, 1:271.
137. Māwardī, *Adab al-dunyā wa'l-dīn*, 1:301.
138. Māwardī, *Adab al-dunyā wa'l-dīn*, 1:316.
139. Māwardī, *Adab al-dunyā wa'l-dīn*, 1:316, 318.
140. Māwardī, *Adab al-dunyā wa'l-dīn*, 1:319.
141. Māwardī, *Adab al-dunyā wa'l-dīn*, 1:319–320.
142. Māwardī, *Adab al-dunyā wa'l-dīn*, 1:321.
143. Māwardī, *Adab al-dunyā wa'l-dīn*, 1:321.
144. Māwardī, *Adab al-dunyā wa'l-dīn*, 1:322.
145. Māwardī, *Adab al-dunyā wa'l-dīn*, 1:323–327.
146. Māwardī, *Adab al-dunyā wa'l-dīn*, 1:327–328.
147. Lit., "of the two conditions"; *laysa bi-alzam ḥālatay al-nisāʾ*.
148. Māwardī, *Adab al-dunyā wa'l-dīn*, 1:329.
149. The printed text has *istibdāl* (substitution); I have emended it to *istibdhāl* for the sense.
150. Māwardī, *Adab al-dunyā wa'l-dīn*, 1:329.
151. Māwardī, *Adab al-dunyā wa'l-dīn*, 1:329–330.
152. My interpretation diverges here from that of Simon Swain, who argues that Māwardī's de-emphasis on sexual pleasure "chimes well with the growing influence of the mystical movement, which, at its early ascetic stage, was marked by a negative attitude to sexuality." Swain, *Economy, Family, and Society*, 356.
153. For the Platonic tripartite soul and its role in Islamic ethics see Peter Adamson, "Ethics in Philosophy," *EI3*.
154. Māwardī, *Ḥāwī*, 11:529.
155. Al-Māwardā, *Adab al-dunyā wa'l-dīn*, 1:448–450; see also Marlow, *Hierarchy and Egalitarianism*, 158–159.
156. Melchert, "Māwardī, Abū Yaʿlā and the Sunni Revival," 43.
157. See Fachrizal A. Halim, *Legal Authority in Premodern Islam: Yaḥyā ibn Sharaf al-Nawawī in the Shāfiʿī School of Law* (London: Routledge, 2015), 58.
158. Abū Isḥāq al-Shīrāzī, *Al-Muhadhdhab fī fiqh al-imām al-Shāfiʿī*, ed. Muḥammad al-Zuḥaylī (Damascus: Dār al-Qalam/Beirut: Al-Dār al-Shāmīya, AH 1417/1996 CE), 4:236.
159. For a useful overview of the opinions on this point within the four classical Sunni schools of law, see ʿAbd Allāh b. Mubārak Āl Sayf, "Idhā istaʾjara imraʾtahu li-raḍāʿ waladihi," Shabakat al-Alūka al-Sharʿīya, accessed June 12, 2020, https://www.alukah.net/sharia/0/84431/.
160. See Abū Isḥāq al-Shīrāzī, *Muhadhdhab*, 4:635; and ʿAbd al-Wāḥid ibn Ismāʿīl al-Rūyānī, *Baḥr al-madhhab fī furūʿ madhhab al-imām al-Shāfiʿī*, ed. Aḥmad ʿIzz and ʿInāya al-Dimashqī (Beirut: Dār Iḥyāʾ al-Turāth al-ʿArabī, AH 1423/2002 CE), 9:304 (arguing that a wife cannot receive compensation from her husband for nursing because she is already being compensated for *istimtāʿ* and *tamkīn*). On al-Isfarāyinī as the focal figure of the Iraqi *ṭarīqa*, see Halim, *Legal Authority*, 60.
161. Quoted from al-Rūyānī's work *al-Tajriba* in Aḥmad ibn Ḥamdān al-Adhruʿī, *Qūt al-muḥtāj fī sharḥ al-Minhāj*, ed. by ʿĪd Muḥammad ʿAbd al-Ḥamīd (Beirut: Dār al-Kutub al-ʿIlmīya, AH 1437/2015 CE), 3:426. On al-Rūyānī, see Tāj al-Dīn

al-Subkī, *Ṭabaqāt al-shāfiʿīya al-kubrā*, ed. Maḥmūd Muḥammad al-Ṭināḥī and ʿAbd al-Fattāḥ Muḥammad al-Ḥilw (Cairo: Fayṣal ʿĪsā al-Bābī al-Ḥalabī/Dār Iḥyāʾ al-Kutub al-ʿArabīya, AH 1383/1964 CE), 7:195.

162. ʿAbd al-Malik ibn ʿAbd Allāh al-Juwaynī, *Nihāyat al-maṭlab fī dirāyat al-madhhab*, ed. ʿAbd al-ʿAẓīm Maḥmūd al-Dīb (Jedda: Dār al-Minhāj, AH 1428/2007 CE), 8:80.
163. Najm al-Dīn Aḥmad ibn Muḥammad Ibn al-Rifʿa, *Kifāyat al-nabīh sharḥ al-Tanbīh fī fiqh al-imām al-Shāfiʿī*, ed. Majdī Muḥammad Surūr Bāssalūm (Beirut: Dār al-Kutub al-ʿIlmīya, 2009), 15:262.
164. ʿAbd al-Karīm ibn Muḥammad al-Rāfiʿī, *Al-ʿAzīz sharḥ al-Wajīz al-maʿrūf bi'l-Sharḥ al-kabīr*, eds. ʿAlī Muḥammad Muʿawwaḍ and ʿĀdil Aḥmad ʿAbd al-Mawjūd (Beirut: Dār al-Kutub al-ʿIlmīya, AH 1417/1997 CE), 6:101 (text from al-Wajīz), 102 (comment by al-Rāfiʿī). See also Shīrāzī, *Muhadhdhab*, 4:635 (one Shāfiʿī opinion states that she can contract for wages for nursing just as she could for weaving).
165. Juwaynī, *Nihāyat al-maṭlab*, 8:80.
166. Juwaynī, *Nihāyat al-maṭlab*, 8:198.
167. Mariam Sheibani, personal communication; see her forthcoming book, *Islamic Legal Philosophy: ʿIzz al-Dīn Ibn ʿAbd al-Salām and the Ethical Turn in Medieval Islamic Law.*
168. Rūyānī, *Baḥr al-madhhab*, 9:304.
169. Juwaynī, *Nihāyat al-maṭlab*, 15:425.
170. Juwaynī, *Nihāyat al-maṭlab*, 15:427.
171. Juwaynī, *Nihāyat al-maṭlab*, 14:558 (see also 15:425–426). The issue is that a person who is not able to free a slave may fast instead (cf. Q 4:92; 58:3–4).
172. On the emphasis on preserving the social status quo in Shāfiʿī doctrine of this period on entitlement to *zakat*, see Mattson, "Status-Based Definitions of Need," 42–43.
173. Juwaynī, *Nihāyat al-maṭlab*, 14:460.
174. Juwaynī, *Nihāyat al-maṭlab*, 12:153.
175. Reading *ḥaṭṭ* instead of *ḥaẓẓ* for the meaning.
176. Juwaynī, *Nihāyat al-maṭlab*, 12:154.
177. Ovamir Anjum, *Politics Law, and Community*, 254; and Hassan, *Longing for the Lost Caliphate*, 304n76.
178. Anjum, *Politics Law, and Community*, 254.

3. Legal and Ethical Obligation in the *Mabsūṭ* of al-Sarakhsī

1. Dates are given with AH (anno Hegirae, or "in the year of [Muhammad's] Hijra") first followed by CE (of the Common Era).
2. See Margaret Malamud, "Sufi Organizations and Structures of Authority in Medieval Nishapur," *International Journal of Middle East Studies* 26, no. 3 (1994): 427–442; Antonio Jurado Aceituno, "La 'ḫidma' selyuqí: La red de relaciones de dependencia mutua, la dinámica del poder y las formas de obtención de los beneficios" (Ph.D. diss., Universidad Autónoma, 1995); Jürgen Paul, "*Khidma* in the Social

History of Pre-Mongol Iran," *Journal of the Economic and Social History of the Orient* 57 (2014): 392–422; Marina Rustow, "Formal and Informal Patronage Among Jews in the Islamic East: Evidence from the Cairo Geniza," *Al-Qanṭara* 29, no. 2 (2008): 341–382; and Eve Krakowski, *Coming of Age in Medieval Egypt: Female Adolescence, Jewish Law, and Ordinary Culture* (Princeton, N.J.: Princeton University Press, 2017), 59. I have not been able to consult Aceituno's dissertation directly.

3. See Rustow, "Formal and Informal Patronage," 355–357.
4. Krakowski, *Coming of Age*, 59.
5. Krakowski, *Coming of Age*, 13.
6. Krakowski, *Coming of Age*, 15.
7. ʿAbd al-Ghāfir ibn Ismāʿīl al-Fārisī, *Al-Muntakhab min al-Siyāq li-taʾrīkh Naysābūr*, selected by Ibrāhīm ibn Muḥammad al-Ṣarīfīnī, ed. Muḥammad Aḥmad ʿAbd al-ʿAzīz (Beirut: Dār al-Kutub al-ʿIlmīya, AH 1409/1989 CE), 321. See also 145, where an aged hadith transmitter is said to be "served by grandees (*al-akābir*) because of the dignity of his age."
8. Fārisī, *Muntakhab*, 246, 299, 317, 318, 417, 440, 468, 488. 491. It is sometimes difficult to distinguish between service of a hadith teacher and discipleship of a Sufi master, particularly since some individuals were known as both; see, for instance, Fārisī, *Muntakhab*, 111, 317, 462 (here the teacher/mentor is the subject's father), 486.
9. On *khidma* as a central part of spiritual discipleship, see Fārisī, *Muntakhab*, 53, 70–71, 76, 116, 118, 221, 238, 241, 254, 281, 282, 284, 318, 349, 353, 392, 434, 455, 457, 484. On men involved in political life, see Fārisī, *Muntakhab*, 72, 153, 160, 165, 166, 171, 470.
10. Fārisī, *Muntakhab*, 333. Of another it is stated that he served in the study circle (*majlis*) of the Shāfiʿī jurist Abū al-Ṭayyib Sahl al-Ṣuʿlūkī "in his childhood and his youth" (*fī ṣibāhu wa-shabābihi*). Fārisī, *Muntakhab*, 488.
11. To the extent that political *khidma* involved concrete personal duties, Paul identifies these as including letter writing and gift giving; there was also a component in which the "servant" personally attended upon the ruler and ritually stepped upon his carpet. Paul, "*Khidma*," 408–409.
12. On the "systematization of the Sufi tradition" under way in Khurasan in this period, see Alexander Knysh, *Islamic Mysticism: A Short History* (Leiden: Brill, 2000), 116–149.
13. For contrasting views of the relationship between asceticism and Sufism, see Christopher Melchert, "The Transition from Asceticism to Mysticism in the Middle of the Ninth Century C.E.," *Studia Islamica* 83 (1996): 51–70; Knysh, *Islamic Mysticism*, 20n41; and Nile Green, *Sufism: A Global History* (Chichester, U.K.: Wiley-Blackwell, 2012), 19–21.
14. Margaret Malamud, "Gender and Spiritual Self-Fashioning: The Master-Disciple Relationship in Classical Sufism," *Journal of the American Academy of Religion* 64, no. 1 (1996): 90.
15. On al-Sulamī, see Gerhardt Böwering, "al-Sulamī," in *Encyclopaedia of Islam*, 2nd ed. (hereafter, *EI2*), ed. by P. Bearman, Th. Bianquis, C. E. Bosworth, E. van Donzel, and W. P. Heinrichs (Leiden: Brill, 1960–2005).

16. On the structure of al-Sulamī's *Ṭabaqāt* and the authenticity of the materials presented in it, see Jawid A. Mojaddedi, *The Biographical Tradition in Sufism: The Tabaqāt Genre from al-Sulamī to Jāmī* (Richmond, Surrey: Curzon, 2001), 9–39.
17. See, for instance, Abū ʿAbd al-Raḥmān Muḥammad ibn al-Ḥusayn al-Sulamī, *Ṭabaqāt al-ṣūfīya wa-yalīhi Dhikr al-niswa al-mutaʿabbidāt al-ṣūfīyāt*, ed. Muṣṭafā ʿAbd al-Qādir ʿAṭā (Beirut: Dār al-Kutub al-ʿIlmīya, AH 1424/2003 CE), 94, where *khidma* appears parallel with *ʿibāda* (see also 389).
18. Sulamī, *Ṭabaqāt*, 346; for similar sayings, see also 211, 281, 369.
19. Sulamī, *Ṭabaqāt*, 96, 202, 211, 244, 246, 281, 291, 305, 332, 340, 369, 380.
20. See, for instance, Sulamī, *Ṭabaqāt*, 389, 390, 391, 392, 393, 395, 397, 398, 403, 404, 405, 406, 407, 408, 413, 420, 423, 424.
21. See, for instance, Sulamī, *Ṭabaqāt*, 390, 407, 413.
22. Abū ʿAbd al-Raḥmān al-Sulamī, *Early Sufi Women*, edited and translated by Rkia Elaroui Cornell (Louisville: Fons Vitae, 1999), 67–68. For references to women acting as servants, see, for instance, Sulamī, *Ṭabaqāt*, 389, 393, 395, 403, 404, 406, 423. While early male Sufis are frequently characterized as engaging in *khidma*, they seem less likely to be described as the "servant" of a specific figure. Maria Dakake has pointed more broadly to the prominence of "metaphors of female domesticity" in reports about early Sufi women. Maria Dakake, " 'Guest of the Innermost Heart': Conceptions of the Divine Beloved Among Early Sufi Women," *Comparative Islamic Studies* 3, no. 1 (2007): 82. She points to the marriage-like qualities of their relationship with God, in which female devotees may "display the traditional wifely virtue of contentment with the provisions they have been given by their divine 'spouse' and 'provider' " and emphasize the permanence, stability and intimacy of their bond with God over ecstatic moments of union with the divine (76, 80). She also notes the centrality of the home as the spatial locus of women's piety (84–85).
23. Sulamī, *Early Sufi Women*, 54, 67.
24. Sulamī, *Ṭabaqāt*, 404.
25. Sulamī, *Early Sufi Women*, 316–317 (my translation diverges slightly from Cornell's).
26. Abū al-Qāsim al-Qushayrī, *Al-Risāla al-Qushayrīya fī ʿilm al-taṣawwuf* (Beirut: Dār al-Jīl, n.d.), 99 (a man draws water for his mother). In another anecdote from Ibn al-Jawzī's *Ṣifat al-ṣafwa* compiled by Cornell, a female devotee describes how her son used to prepare firewood and keep a brazier burning to warm her as she worshiped in winter. Sulamī, *Early Sufi Women*, 272–273.
27. On the distinctively prominent role of service in the piety of Abū Saʿīd, see H. Ritter, "Abū Saʿīd Faḍl Allāh b. Abi 'l-K̲h̲ayr," *EI2*; and Terry Graham, "Abū Saʿīd Ibn Abī'l-Khayr and the School of Khurāsān," in *The Heritage of Sufism*, vol. 1: *Classical Persian Sufism from Its Origins to Rumi (700–1300)*, ed. Leonard Lewisohn (Oxford: Oneworld, 1999), 125.
28. See Moḥmmed Ebn-e Monavvar, *The Secrets of God's Mystical Oneness or The Spiritual Stations of Shaikh Abu Sa'id*, Translated with Notes and Introduction by John O'Kane (Costa Mesa, Calif.: Mazda with Bibliotheca Persica, 1992), translator's introduction, 9.

29. Ebn-e Monavvar, *Secrets*, 92; and Mohammad b. Monavvar, *Asrār al-Tawḥīd fī maqāmāt al-shaykh Abī Saʿīd*, ed. Mohammad Rezā Shāfi'ī Kadkanī (Tehran: Muʾassaseh-ye Enteshārāt-e Āgāh, 2nd printing, AH 1367/[1989 CE]), 1:27. In drawing on this source, I have used the English translation and checked the relevant passages against the Persian original.
30. Ebn-e Monavvar, *Secrets*, 98, 99; and Persian *Asrār*, 1:31.
31. Ebn-e Monavvar, *Secrets*, 117–118; and Persian *Asrār*, 1:45.
32. H. Ritter argues that "already at this time [i.e., before the age of forty] the social motive of sūfism, the 'service of the poor' (*khidmat-i darwīshān*) begins to assume importance for him. . . . This 'service of the poor,' conceived principally for self-abasement at first, came ever more to the fore in the course of his life." See H. Ritter, "Abū Saʿīd Faḍl Allāh b. Abi 'l-Kh̲ayr," *EI2*. However, I would argue that Abū Saʿīd's reported trajectory resembles that which Shahzad Bashir identifies among somewhat later Sufis, where accomplished Sufi masters "work" by attracting food and prosperity through their personal holiness, rather than through the physical toil that characterized their earlier years of ascetic striving. See Shahzad Bashir, *Sufi Bodies: Religion and Society in Medieval Islam* (New York: Columbia University Press, 2011), 164–166. It is also worth considering to what extent Abū Saʿīd's service was aimed at "the poor" in the socio-economic sense.
33. Ebn-e Monavvar, *Secrets*, 141, 147–149, 163; and Persian *Asrār*, 1:63, 68–71, 82.
34. Ebn-e Monavvar, *Secrets*, 219; and Persian *Asrār*, 1:127.
35. One story involves a devotee from a noble household who has not set foot outside of her home for years; she has a maidservant to do her errands. See Ebn-e Monavvar, *Secrets*, 152; and Persian *Asrār*, 1:73.
36. On the *khidma* of sultans, see Abū Ḥāmid al-Ghazālī, *Iḥyāʾ ʿulūm al-dīn* (Beirut: Dār al-Fikr, AH 1414/1994 CE), 1:70. On children offering *khidma* to parents, see Ghazālī, *Iḥyāʾ*, 3:351.
37. Ghazālī, *Iḥyāʾ*, 1:63; see also 1:64; 3:350; 3:363; 3:367.
38. See, for instance, Ghazālī, *Iḥyāʾ*, 2:281. However, he argues that in his own day the practice of "humbling oneself through service" (*al-tawāḍuʿ bi'l-khidma*) has become a means of seeking disciples and money (Ghazālī, *Iḥyāʾ*, 2:260; see also 2:273). It is possible that in his time the earlier model of personal engagement in menial tasks had been replaced by a more institutionalized (and potentially lucrative) practice of fund-raising through public begging.
39. Ghazālī, *Iḥyāʾ*, 3:376; see also 2:389, 2:412.
40. Ghazālī, *Iḥyāʾ*, 3:374.
41. Ghazālī, *Iḥyāʾ*, 1:63, 2:9–10, 2:20, 2:262, 2:264, 3:374–375.
42. Zahra Ayubi, *Gendered Morality: Classical Islamic Ethics of the Self, Family, and Society* (New York: Columbia University Press, 2019), 111, 115, 116, 123–4, 130–131.
43. See Ayubi, *Gendered Morality*, 130–131; and Kenneth Cuno, *Modernizing Marriage: Family, Ideology, and Law in Nineteenth- and Early Twentieth-Century Egypt* (New York: Syracuse University Press, 2015), 86. For a similar point see Lev Weitz, "Al-Ghazālī, Bar Hebraeus, and the 'Good Wife,'" *Journal of the American Oriental Society* 134, no. 2 (2014): 210.

44. Ghazālī, *Iḥyāʾ*, 2:35; see also 2:27, 2:67. Zahra Ayubi translates and discusses a parallel passage from Ghazālī's Persian work *Kimyā'-ye sa'ādat* in *Gendered Morality*, 130–131.
45. See Ghazālī, *Iḥyāʾ*, 2:66.
46. As we have seen in chapter 2, the most important of these works was the *Tadbīr al-manzil* attributed to the otherwise obscure Greek philosopher Bryson. Simon Swain notes that "whether the influence was direct or indirect, it cannot be doubted that the concept of *tadbīr al-manzil* as used by Ghazālī descends from Bryson." Simon Swain, *Economy, Family, and Society from Rome to Islam: A Critical Edition, English Translation, and Study of Bryson's Management of the Estate* (Cambridge: Cambridge University Press, 2013), 359.
47. Swain, *Economy, Family, and Society*, 357–359.
48. Ayubi, *Gendered Morality*, 66, 111.
49. Ayubi, *Gendered Morality*, 7.
50. Ghazālī, *Iḥyāʾ*, 3:251.
51. Ghazālī, *Iḥyāʾ*, 2:178.
52. Ghazālī, *Iḥyāʾ*, 1:152.
53. Ghazālī, *Iḥyāʾ*, 4:253–254; see also 3:301.
54. See, for instance, Abū Ḥāmid al-Ghazālī, *Al-Wajīz fī fiqh al-imām al-Shāfiʿī*, ed. ʿAlī Muʿawwaḍ and ʿĀdil ʿAbd al-Mawjūd (Beirut: Dār al-Arqam ibn Abī al-Arqam, AH 1418/1997 CE), 2:114.
55. Ayubi notes that "the ever-practical ethicists recognized that marriage facilitated the exchange of a wife's domestic labor for the ability to attend to a man's loftier goals, even though, as Kecia Ali has shown, the marital arrangement in *fiqh* required furnishing the wife with financial support and household services due to the wife in exchange for her sexual availability." Ayubi, *Gendered Morality*, 131.
56. Ghazālī, *Iḥyāʾ*, 3:111.
57. On the boundaries and history of this region, see C. E. Bosworth, "Mā Warāʾ al-Nahr," *EI2*.
58. For an overview of al-Sarakhsī's life and works, see N. Calder, "Al-Sarakhsī," *EI2*; Osman Taştan, "Al-Sarakhsī (D. 483/1090)," in *Islamic Legal Thought: A Compendium of Muslim Jurists*, ed. by David Powers, Susan Spectorsky, and Oussama Arabi (Leiden: Brill, 2013), 239–251. On al-Marwazī, see Fuat Sezgin, *Geschichte des arabischen Schrifttums* (Leiden: Brill, 1967), 1:443–444; and ʿAbd al-Ḥayy al-Laknawī, *Al-Fawāʾid al-bahīya fī tarājim al-ḥanafīya* (Cairo: Maṭbaʿat al-Saʿāda, AH 1324), 185–186. The work commented by al-Sarakhsī is known as *Al-Mukhtaṣar al-kāfī* (sometimes referred to simply as *Al-Mukhtaṣar* or *Al-Kāfī*); see Muḥammad ibn al-Ḥasan al-Shaybānī, *Al-Aṣl*, ed. Mehmet Boynukalın (Qatar: Wizārat al-Awqāf and Beirut: Dār Ibn Ḥazm, 2012), editor's introduction (published as a separate volume), 119–121.
59. See Shams al-Dīn al-Sarakhsī, *Kitāb al-Mabsūṭ* (Beirut: Dār al-Maʿrifa, [AH 1409/1989 CE]), 5:41; 5:64; 5:78; 5:93; 5:184. Establishing and analyzing this model is the central theme of Kecia Ali, *Marriage and Slavery in Early Islam* (Cambridge, Mass.: Harvard University Press, 2010); see discussion of that work in the introduction to this book.

60. Sarakhsī, *Mabsūṭ*, 5:62; 5:78; 7:83.
61. Sarakhsī, *Mabsūṭ*, 5:122; see also 5:61 (doctrine of al-Karkhī; al-Sarakhsī objects to his reasoning that one can thus conclude a marriage contract with the terminology of hire rather than of purchase). Similarly, regarding a slave woman, al-Sarakhsī notes that "having sexual intercourse while [the woman] is in [his] possession is equivalent to using her for service because on a literal level (*min ḥaythu al-ḥaqīqa*) having sex is merely availing oneself of a benefit (*manfaʿa*); the distinction between [sex and labor] is made only as a legal matter (*min ṭarīq al-ḥukm*), specifically in cases where [the woman] is not in the possession [of the man]; when [she is in his] possession, having sex remains similar to using her for service." Sarakhsī, *Mabsūṭ*, 7:86.
62. Sarakhsī, *Mabsūṭ*, 13:96–97.
63. Sarakhsī, *Mabsūṭ*, 7:83.
64. Sarakhsī, *Mabsūṭ*, 5:184.
65. For the definition of *ṣila*, see Baber Johansen, "Secular and Religious Elements in Hanafite Law: Function and Limits of the Absolute Character of Government Authority," in *Contingency in a Sacred Law: Legal and Ethical Norms in the Muslim Fiqh* (Leiden: Brill, 1999), 204; and *Al-Mawsūʿa al-fiqhīya*, s.v. "arḥām," para. 3–10 (3:82–85); s.v. "ṣila," (27:357–359). Ḥanafīs also considered the dower to be a *ṣila*, on the ground that the *buḍʿ* was not a commodity with monetary value (*māl mutaqawwim*). See Sarakhsī, *Mabsūṭ*, 5:74, 2:168, 3:41.
66. See *Al-Mabsūṭ*, 5:181. This is an early Ḥanafī doctrine articulated by Muḥammad ibn al-Ḥasan al-Shaybānī in *Aṣl*, 10:327; see also 10:325, 326.
67. Sarakhsī, *Mabsūṭ*, 5:181.
68. Sarakhsī, *Mabsūṭ*, 5:223.
69. Sarakhsī, *Mabsūṭ*, 5:185; see also 4:193, 5:223.
70. Sarakhsī, *Mabsūṭ*, 5:181.
71. See, for instance, Sarakhsī, *Mabsūṭ*, 4:158, 16:37.
72. See Sarakhsī, *Mabsūṭ*, 4:158: "Contracts of hire for acts of obedience [to God, *ṭāʿāt*] that cannot validly be performed by a non-believer are not valid according to us [i.e., the Ḥanafīs]," and the parallel statement on 16:37.
73. Sarakhsī, *Mabsūṭ*, 1:140; 16:102.
74. Sarakhsī, *Mabsūṭ*, 1:140.
75. See Sarakhsī, *Mabsūṭ*, 5:186, 5:187, 5:192, 5:195, 5:199, 5:223.
76. Sarakhsī, *Mabsūṭ*, 1:140, 3:18.
77. Sarakhsī, *Mabsūṭ*, 4:159. See also Sarakhsī, *Mabsūṭ*, 22:20, 22:63 (working partner in a commenda contract is entitled to a stipend to support him on basis of analogy with a wife).
78. Māwardī, *Ḥāwī*, 11:417.
79. Sarakhsī, *Mabsūṭ*, 5:186. For a discussion of this passage, see Avner Giladi, *Infants, Parents and Wet Nurses: Medieval Islamic Views on Breastfeeding and Their Social Implications* (Leiden: Brill, 1999), 103–104.
80. Sarakhsī, *Mabsūṭ*, 16:55.
81. Sarakhsī, *Mabsūṭ*, 5:187, 192, 195, 199, 204. The terms *khidma* and *al-qiyām bi-maṣāliḥihi* (here with respect to a baby) also appear parallel to each other in the context of al-Sarakhsī's discussion of wet-nursing; see *Mabsūṭ*, 15:118.

82. Sarakhsī, *Mabsūṭ*, 2:22.
83. Sarakhsī, *Mabsūṭ*, 5:210; see also 6:169.
84. Sarakhsī, *Mabsūṭ*, 16:55.
85. Sarakhsī, *Mabsūṭ*, 5:208–209.
86. *Al-maʿnā*, here equivalent to *al-ʿilla*.
87. Sarakhsī, *Mabsūṭ*, 15:128.
88. For a parallel instance of the *dīn/dayn* pairing, see Sarakhsī, *Mabsūṭ*, 11:33. This distinction has been discussed by Baber Johansen in "Die sündige, gesunde Amme: Moral und gesetzliche Bestimmung (*hukm*) im islamischen Recht," in *Contingency in a Sacred Law: Legal and Ethical Norms in the Muslim Fiqh* (Leiden: Brill, 1999), 172–188.
89. The literature on this subject is large; for several contrasting examples see Talal Asad, "The Construction of Religion as an Anthropological Category," in *Genealogies of Religion: Discipline and Reasons of Power in Christianity and Islam* (Baltimore: Johns Hopkins University Press, 1993), 27–54; Guy Stroumsa, *A New Science: The Discovery of Religion in the Age of Reason* (Cambridge, Mass.: Harvard University Press, 2010); and Brent Nongbri, *Before Religion: A History of a Modern Concept* (New Haven, Conn.: Yale University Press, 2013).
90. Rushain Abbasi, "Did Premodern Muslims Distinguish the Religious and Secular? The *Dīn-Dunyā* Binary in Medieval Islamic Thought," *Journal of Islamic Studies* 31, no. 2 (2020): 191.
91. Junaid Quadri, *Transformations of Tradition: Islamic Law in Colonial Modernity* (Oxford: Oxford University Press, 2021), 184. On this subject, see also Ahmet T. Karamustafa, "Islamic *Dīn* as an Alternative to Western Models of 'Religion,'" in *Religion, Theory, Critique: Classic and Contemporary Approaches and Methodologies*, ed. by Richard King (New York: Columbia University Press, 2017), 163–171.
92. Quadri, *Transformations*, 185. Quadri is here citing the wording of José Casanova.
93. Shaybānī, *Aṣl*, editor's introduction, 284.
94. In the case examined by Quadri, the ritual issues designated as *umūr dīnīya* can nevertheless involve the intervention of judges; as he observes, it is only in the modern context that they are reinterpreted as "religious" in the sense of being private and exempt from judicial intervention. Quadri, *Transformations*, 186, 194.
95. On this distinction see Baber Johansen, "Die sündige, gesunde Amme," especially 184–186.
96. Sarakhsī, *Mabsūṭ*, 15:21.
97. Sarakhsī, *Mabsūṭ*, 10:96–97.
98. Sarakhsī, *Mabsūṭ*, 10:95 (for another example, see *Mabsūṭ*, 20:30).
99. Sarakhsī, *Mabsūṭ*, 16:86.
100. This is also a Ḥanbalī doctrine. See *Al-Mawsūʿa al-fiqhīya*, s.v. "ijāra," para. 109–110 (1:291).
101. Sarakhsī, *Mabsūṭ*, 16:39; for another example see *Mabsūṭ*, 16:40.
102. Sarakhsī, *Mabsūṭ*, 30:204.
103. Literally "for kissing or touching" (*al-taqbīl wa'l-lams*), which leaves it open whether the wife is the agent or the object of the action; I have translated these verbal nouns with the wife as the subject because in context the subject is actions performed by the wife.

104. Sarakhsī, *Mabsūṭ*, 15:128.
105. Sarakhsī, *Mabsūṭ*, 16:55.
106. See the discussion of reports claiming that the Prophet assigned the housework to Fāṭima in chapter 1, in the sections on Ibn Ḥabīb and Muḥammad ibn Saḥnūn.
107. See ʿAlāʾ al-Dīn al-Kāsānī, *Badāʾiʿ al-ṣanāʾiʿ fī tartīb al-sharāʾiʿ*, eds. ʿAlī Muḥammad Muʿawwaḍ and ʿĀdil Aḥmad ʿAbd al-Mawjūd (Beirut: Dār al-Kutub al-ʿIlmīya, 1424/2003) 5:150, 6:15; and Zayn al-Dīn Ibn Nujaym, *al-Baḥr al-rāʾiq sharḥ Kanz al-daqāʾiq*, ed. Zakarīyā ʿUmayrāt (Beirut: Dār al-Kutub al-ʿIlmīya, AH 1418/1997 CE), 4:311.
108. Behnam Sadeghi, *The Logic of Law-Making in Islam: Women and Prayer in the Legal Tradition* (Cambridge: Cambridge University Press, 2012), 67–69.
109. See Muḥammad ibn al-Ḥasan al-Shaybānī, *Al-Jāmiʿ al-ṣaghīr maʿa sharḥihi al-Nāfiʿ al-kabīr liʾl-ʿallāma al-shahīr Abīʾl-Ḥasanāt ʿAbd al-Ḥayy al-Laknawī* (Karachi, Pakistan: Idārat al-Qurʾān waʾl-ʿUlūm al-Islāmīya, AH 1411/1990 CE), 183–184. Al-Shaybānī's text states that the free husband pays a standard dower in place of the service, rather than that he has the option to do so.
110. Sarakhsī, *Mabsūṭ*, 16:55.
111. Sarakhsī, *Mabsūṭ*, 5:106.
112. Sarakhsī, *Mabsūṭ*, 16:55–56.
113. Sarakhsī, *Mabsūṭ*, 16:56.
114. Sarakhsī, *Mabsūṭ*, 16:56.
115. Note that this sphere is defined by a series of bilateral kinship ties; it is not equivalent to the family (*ʿāʾila/usra*) that emerges in the late nineteenth century as the basic building block of modern society. See Talal Asad, *Formations of the Secular: Christianity, Islam, Modernity* (Stanford, Calif.: Stanford University Press, 2003), 227–232.
116. See Sarakhsī, *Mabsūt*, 5:23, 30:258. A version of this hadith is in [Muḥammad ibn ʿĪsā al-Tirmidhī], *Sunan al-Tirmidhī* (Vaduz, Liecht.: Thesaurus Islamicus Foundation, 2000), 2:581 (*Kitāb al-fitan*, Bāb 67, hadith 2420); [Muḥammad ibn Yazīd Ibn Māja], *Sunan Ibn Māja* (Vaduz, Liecht.: Thesaurus Islamicus Foundation, 2000), 582 (*Kitab al-fitan*, Bāb 21, hadith 4152). In context, this hadith warns the believer against humiliation through being exposed to tribulations too great to be borne.
117. See, for instance, Sarakhsī, *Mabsūt*, 9:56, where he argues that for a nonbeliever to use a Muslim for service degrades the Muslims.
118. Sarakhsī, *Mabsūt*, 16:56.
119. Al-Sarakhsī does argue elsewhere that certain family members (including adult children, siblings, and even parents) are not entitled a reward (*juʿl*) for a one-time task such as returning an escaped slave if they are economic dependents of the beneficiary. The rationale is that "customarily (*ʿādatan*) it is a man's dependents who look for his escaped slave." See Sarakhsī, *Mabsūṭ*, 11:33.
120. Sarakhsī, *Mabsūṭ*, 16:56.
121. Sarakhsī, *Mabsūṭ*, 11:202.
122. Shaybānī, *Aṣl*, 4:42.
123. Sarakhsī, *Mabsūṭ*, 16:52, 16:55.
124. The obligation to provide *khidma* to infants and young children might appear to violate the correlation between relative status and obligations for service,

but in this context *khidma* clearly denotes "care" rather than "service." See Sarakhsī, *Mabsūṭ*, 15:118, 15:121 (on the duties of wet nurses).

125. Although al-Sarakhsī references licit female professions such as wet-nursing, in principle he regards women as categorically incapable of supporting themselves; thus, a father is responsible for the maintenance of his adult son only if the latter is physically or mentally disabled but for an adult daughter as long as she is unmarried. Sarakhsī, *Mabsūṭ*, 5:223; see also 5:185.
126. See Maḥmūd ibn Aḥmad Ibn Māza, *Al-Muḥīṭ al-burhānī fī al-fiqh al-nuʿmānī*, ed. ʿAbd al-Karīm Sāmī al-Jundī (Beirut: Dār al-Kutub al-ʿIlmīya, AH 1424/2004 CE), 3:530 (also briefly referenced at 3:172).
127. See Ṭāhir ibn Aḥmad al-Bukhārī, *Al-Khulāṣa*, ms. al-Maktaba al-Azharīya, khāṣṣ 1950, ʿāmm 26789, https://www.alukah.net/sharia/0/78944/ on 9/14/2021, folio 78a; Muḥammad ibn ʿAbd al-Wāḥid al-Sīwāsī, known as Ibn al-Humām, *Sharḥ Fatḥ al-qadīr*, ed. ʿAbd al-Razzāq Ghālib al-Mahdī (Beirut: Dār al-Kutub al-ʿIlmīya, AH 1424/2003 CE), 4:349; and Zayn al-Dīn ibn Nujaym, *Al-Baḥr al-rāʾiq, sharḥ Kanz al-daqāʾiq*, ed. Zakarīyā ʿUmayrāt (Beirut: Dār al-Kutub al-ʿIlmīya, AH 1418/1997 CE), 4:311.
128. Sarakhsī, *Mabsūṭ*, 5:23. Similarly, in justifying the ailing (and thus sexually unavailable) wife's entitlement to maintenance, Muḥammad al-Marwazī (d. AH 334/946 CE, the author of the base text on which al-Sarakhsī is commenting) states that "marriage is contracted for the sake of companionship and affection" (*al-nikāḥ yuʿqad li'l-ṣuḥba wa'l-ulfa*). Sarakhsī, *Mabsūṭ*, 5:192. On another level, al-Sarakhsī argues that the objective of marriage is to preserve life by ensuring reproduction and securing the support of children. Sarakhsī, *Mabsūṭ*, 4:212; 4:236; 5:48.
129. Sarakhsī, *Mabsūṭ*, 5:60.
130. This is only if the property in question is located in a place other than their shared home, as one of the conditions of the amputation penalty is that the property be stolen from a place that is secure from the thief (*ḥirz*); see Sarakhsī, *Mabsūṭ*, 9:189. For the Shāfiʿī view, see also Māwardī, *Ḥāwī*, 13:345–347.
131. Sarakhsī, *Mabsūṭ*, 9:189.
132. The text has "he is"; I have amended it to fit the meaning.
133. *Lā yuqāla hādhā al-ittiḥād baynahumā fī ḥuqūq al-nikāḥ khāṣṣatan*. Here and elsewhere, based on context, I have interpreted the term "*nikāḥ*" to refer specifically to the marriage contract (rather than to marriage in general).
134. Sarakhsī, *Mabsūṭ*, 16:123.
135. Sarakhsī, *Mabsūṭ*, 15:128.
136. Sarakhsī, *Mabsūṭ*, 11:33.
137. Michael Bonner notes that in the "Book of Livelihood" (*Kitāb al-kasb*) of the *Mabsūṭ*, "Sarakhsī uses language and ideas that derive from this Bryson tradition, if not from Bryson himself." Michael Bonner, "The *Kitāb al-kasb* Attributed to al-Shaybānī: Poverty, Surplus, and the Circulation of Wealth," *Journal of the American Oriental Society* 121, no. 3 (2001): 422.
138. Swain, *Economy, Family, and Society*, 465.
139. Swain, *Economy, Family, and Society*, 467 (with minor editing).
140. Swain, *Economy, Family, and Society*, 352; see also Ayubi, *Gendered Morality*, 145.

141. Swain, *Economy, Family, and Society*, 334.
142. See Sarakhsī, *Mabsūṭ* 4:192; 16:123.
143. This is a section in al-Sarakhsī's "Book of Livelihood" (*Kitāb al-kasb*) reproducing Bryson's argument that humans are materially interdependent because their sustenance requires too many different crafts for an individual to master in a lifetime (Bonner, "*Kitāb al-kasb*," 423). Swain understands references to *maṣlaḥat al-maʿāsh* or to *iṣlāḥ* in Arabic texts deriving from Bryson as allusions to the Aristotelian ideal of the "good life" (Swain, *Economy, Family, and Society*, 354, 359). However, it is not clear to me that this connotation attaches to al-Sarakhsī's use of parallel language.
144. Sarakhsī, *Mabsūṭ*, 16:123.
145. Sarakhsī, *Mabsūṭ*, 5:48.
146. See, for instance, Junaid Quadri, "Moral Habituation in the Law: Rethinking the Ethics of the Sharīʿa," *Islamic Law and Society* 26 (2019): 191–226; for a contrasting view, see Marion Holmes Katz, "Shame (*Ḥayāʾ*) as an Affective Disposition in Islamic Legal Thought," *Journal of Law, Religion and State* 3 (2014): 139–169.
147. Swain, *Economy, Family, and Society*, 39–40, 53.
148. In his discussion of the custody of the daughters of separated parents, al-Sarakhsī both notes that a girl "needs to learn how to spin, cook, and wash clothes, and the mother is more capable [of teaching her these skills]" and that a daughter is more likely to retain her modesty (*ḥayāʾ*) in the company of women. However, he does not explicit associate housework itself with the cultivation of virtues such as humility. Sarakhsī, *Mabsūṭ*, 5:207–208.
149. Ibn Māza, *Muḥīṭ*, 3:172. Ibn Māza cites this statement from the *Muntaqā*, a well-regarded (but no longer extent) work of Muḥammad al-Marwazī, the author of the base text on which al-Sarakhsī is commenting in *Al-Mabsūṭ*. For this book, see Laknawī, *Fawāʾid*, 185–186 (it is not mentioned in the entry on al-Marwazī in Sezgin, *Geschichte*, 1:443–444).
150. Ibn Māza, *Muḥīṭ*, 3:172 (also citing from *Al-Muntaqā*).
151. Shaybānī, *Aṣl*, 10:325–326; Aḥmad ibn Muḥammad al-Ṭaḥāwī, *Mukhtaṣar Ikhtilāf al-ʿulamāʾ*, abridged by Aḥmad ibn ʿAlī al-Jaṣṣāṣ, ed. ʿAbd Allāh Nadhīr Aḥmad (Beirut: Dār al-Bashāʾir, 1416/1995), 2:371; and Abū Jaʿfar Aḥmad ibn Muḥammad al-Ṭaḥāwī, *Mukhtaṣar al-Ṭaḥāwī*, ed. Abū al-Wafā al-Afghānī (Hayderabad: Lajnat Iḥyāʾ al-Maʿārif al-Nuʿmānīya, n.d.), 223.
152. ʿUmar ibn ʿAbd al-ʿAzīz Ibn Māza, known as al-Ṣadr al-Shahīd, *Sharḥ Adab al-qāḍī li'l-Khaṣṣāf*, ed. Muḥyī Hilāl al-Sarḥān (Baghdad: al-Dār al-ʿArabīya li'l-Ṭibāʿa, 1398/1978), 4:236; and Abū Bakr Aḥmad ibn ʿAmr al-Shaybānī, known as al-Jaṣṣāṣ, *Adab al-qāḍī, wa-sharḥ Abī Bakr Aḥmad ibn ʿAlī al-Rāzī, known as al-Jaṣṣāṣ*, ed. Farhat Ziadeh (Cairo: American University in Cairo Press, 1978), 647. The difference in wording between the two commentaries suggest that they do not reproduce al-Khaṣṣāf's base text verbatim, but the substantive content is the same. On al-Khaṣṣāf and his position within the Ḥanafī school, see F. J. Ziadeh, "Al-Khaṣṣāf," *EI2*; and Peter C. Hennigan, "Al-Khaṣṣāf (D. 261/874)," in *Islamic Legal Thought: A Compendium of Muslim Jurists*, ed. by David Powers, Susan Spectorsky, and Oussama Arabi (Leiden: Brill, 2013), 107–110.

153. Abdur-Rahman Mangera, "A Critical Edition of Abū 'l-Layth al-Samarqandī's Nawāzil," (PhD thesis, School of Oriental and African Studies, University of London, 2013), 325. The book published as Abū al-Layth al-Samarqandī, *Fatāwā al-nawāzil*, ed. Al-Sayyid Yūsuf Aḥmad (Beirut: Dār al-Kutub al-ʿIlmīya, AH 1425/2004 CE) is not, in fact, the *fatāwā* of al-Samarqandī; see Luʾayy ʿAbd al-Raʾūf al-Khalīlī, *Laʾālī al-muḥār fī takhrīj maṣādir Ibn ʿĀbidīn fī ḥāshiyatihi Radd al-Muḥtār* (Amman: Dār al-Fatḥ, AH 1431/2010 CE), 1:403. I thank Samy Ayoub for this reference.
154. Maḥmūd ibn Ismāʿīl al-Khayrmītī, *Al-Durra al-gharrāʾ fī naṣīḥat all-salāṭīn wa al-quḍāt wa al-umarāʾ*, ed. Aḥmad al-Zaʿbī (Beirut: Ibn al-Azraq Center for Political Heritage Studies, AH 1433/2012 CE), 305–306. This chapter is presented as a verbatim reproduction of material collected by al-Samarqandī; see al-Khayrmītī, *Durra*, 293.
155. Abū'l-Layth al-Samarqandī, *ʿUyūn al-masāʾil fī furūʿ al-ḥanafīya*, ed. Sayyid Muḥammad Muhannā (Beirut: Dār al-Kutub al-ʿIlmīya, AH 1419/1998 CE), 216. Abū Ḥanīfa's student Abū Yūsuf is said to have held a different doctrine, arguing that if a wife spins cotton that her the husband has bought and left in the house, "it belongs exclusively to her and she owes nothing [to him]. It is equivalent to food that he put in his house, and she ate it." See Ibn Māza, *Muḥīṭ*, 3:169 (citing from al-Marwazī's *Muntaqā*). In this view, raw materials for spinning are likened to the other things the husband contributes to the home in his role as provider.
156. For al-Samarqandī's articulation of this implied logic see Samarqandī, *ʿUyūn al-masāʾil*, 216; for the general rule that a usurper who transforms the usurped substance (for instance, by grinding grain or sewing cloth) owns the resulting product but must reimburse the original owner for the usurped raw material see, for instance, Shaybānī, *Aṣl*, 8:16.
157. Samarqandī, *ʿUyūn al-masāʾil*, 216; and Ibn Māza, *Muḥīṭ*, 3:169 (ending "because this [i.e., spinning] is included in the housework, so she is working for the husband" [*l'anna hādhā min jumlat khidmat al-bayt, fa-kānat ʿāmila li'l-zawj*]). Ibn Māza also cites Abū'l-Layth as stating that, in contrast, if the wife sells the thread and uses the proceeds to buy goods for herself, the goods belong to her because she has transacted the sale on her own behalf. (Ibn Māza, *Muḥīṭ*, 3:168, citing the chapter on sales in al-Samarqandī's *Fatāwā*.) However, this conclusion seems to emerge from her execution of the sale rather than from the idea that she owns the fruits of her labor in the first place.
158. Cited in Ibn Māza, *Muḥīṭ*, 3:168.
159. Ibn Māza, *Muḥīṭ*, 7:457. The author of the *Fatāwā al-ẓahīrīya* comments on this doctrine: "It has also been said that this is questionable (*fīhi naẓar*), and it should be valid [for her to charge rent]; because allowing him to live in her house is obligatory on her neither as a legal verdict nor as a religious matter, so it is as if she hired herself [to him] for something other than household chores [*aʿmāl al-bayt*], which is valid." See Ẓahīr al-Dīn al-Ḥasan ibn ʿAlī al-Marghīnānī, *Al-Fatāwā al-Ẓahīrīya*, ms. Universitätsbiliothek Leipzig, B. or. 006-1, folio 204a, https://www.islamic-manuscripts.net/receive/IslamHSBook_islamhs_00000501; last accessed

10/1/2021; Badr al-Dīn Maḥmūd ibn Aḥmad al-ʿAynī, *Al-Masāʾil al-badrīya al-muntakhaba min al-Fatāwā al-ẓahīrīya*, ed. Sulaymān ibn ʿAbd Allāh ibn Ḥamūd Abā ʾl-Khayl (Riyadh: Dār al-ʿĀṣima, AH 1435/2014 CE), 2:718. *Al-Fatāwā al-ẓahīrīya* is variously attributed to Ẓahīr al-Dīn al-Ḥasan ibn ʿAlī al-Marghinānī, to his father Ẓahīr al-Dīn ʿAlī ibn ʿAbd al-ʿAzīz, or to al-Ḥasan ibn ʿAlī's student Ẓahīr al-Dīn Muḥammad ibn Aḥmad al-Bukhārī; see Laknawī, *Fawāʾid*, 156–157.

Historically, it appears that in some cases wives did charge their husbands rent for the privilege of living with them in their houses and that jurists upheld this; see Yossef Rapoport, *Marriage, Money and Divorce in Medieval Islamic Society* (Cambridge: Cambridge University Press, 2005), 62–63. For the Mālikī debate over the same issue, see Maya Shatzmiller, *Her Day in Court: Women's Property Rights in Fifteenth-Century Granada* (Cambridge, Mass.: Harvard University Press, 2007), 53–55.

160. Nurit Tsafrir, *Collective Liability in Islam: The ʿĀqila and Blood-Money Payments* (Cambridge: Cambridge University Press, 2020).
161. Tsafrir, *Collective Liability*, 102.
162. See E. Ashtor, "Ḳuṭn," *EI2*. For relevant fatwas using the term *jūzaqa*, see Mukhtār ibn Maḥmūd al-Zāhidī al-Ghazmīnī, *Qunyat al-munya li-tatmīm al-Ghunya*, ms. Jāmiʿat al-Malik Suʿūd, al-raqam al-ʿām 7382, raqam al-ṣinf 217.4 qāf j, folio 52a, https://makhtota.ksu.edu.sa/makhtota/7824/65#.XtpuA0RKiYk.
163. Tsafrir, *Collective Liability*, 109.
164. Bukhārī, *Khulāṣa*, folio 193a–b. The manuscript states that "al-Shaykh al-Imām Ẓahīr al-Dīn al-Marghīnānī wrote this legal issue (*masʾala*) in his own handwriting and sent it to me." This is presumably his maternal uncle and teacher, Ẓahīr al-Dīn al-Ḥasan ibn ʿAlī al-Marghīnānī (see Laknawī, *Al-Fawāʾid al-bahīya*, 84). A very similar (and equally lengthy) discussion of the problems of ownership raised by wives' spinning their husband's cotton is presented in *al-Fatāwā al-ẓahīrīya*, whose authorship is disputed (see above, note 159) but which in any case originated from the immediate circle of Ẓahīr al-Dīn al-Ḥasan ibn ʿAlī al-Marghīnānī. See Marghīnānī, *Al-Fatāwā al-Ẓahīrīya*, folio 75b; and ʿAynī, *Masāʾil*, 1:276–277.
165. Bukhārī, *Khulāṣa*, folio 193a–b; compare ʿAynī, *Masāʾil*, 1:276.
166. See, for instance, ʿAbd al-Rashīd ibn Abī Ḥanīfa al-Walwālijī, *Al-Fatāwā al-Walwālijīya*, ed. Miqdād ibn Mūsā Furaywī (Beirut: Dār al-Kutub al-ʿIlmīya, AH 1424/2003 CE), 1:385–386; Sirāj al-Dīn ʿAlī ibn ʿUthmān al-Ūshī, *Al-Fatāwā al-Sirājīya*, ed. Muḥammad ʿUthmān al-Bustawī (Lenasia, Johannesburg, S.A.: Dār al-ʿUlūm Zakarīya, AH 1432/2011 CE), 211; Muḥammad ibn Yūsuf al-Ḥusaynī al-Samarqandī, *Al-Multaqaṭ fī fatāwā al-ḥanafīya*, eds. Maḥmūd Naṣṣār and al-Sayyid Yūsuf Aḥmad (Beirut: Dār al-Kutub al-ʿIlmīya, 1420/2000), 107–108; al-Ḥasan ibn Manṣūr, known as Qāḍī Khān, *Fatāwā Qāḍī Khān fī madhhab al-imām al-aʿẓam Abī Ḥanīfa al-Nuʿmān* (Beirut: Dār al-Kutub al-ʿIlmīya, 2009), 1:368; ʿAlī ibn Abī Bakr al-Marghīnānī, *Mukhtārāt al-nawāzil fiʾl-fiqh al-ḥanafī*, ed. Imtithāl Ṣalāḥ al-Dīn al-Ṣaghīr (Damascus and Beirut: Dār al-Muqatabas, AH 1440/2019 CE), 2:864; Ibn Māza, *Muḥīṭ*, 3:530 (see also 3:172); and ʿAynī, *Masāʾil*, 1:217.
167. Tsafrir, *Collective Liability*, 117.

168. Marghīnānī, *Al-Fatāwā al-ẓahīrīya*, folio 203b; and ʿAynī, *Masāʾil*, 2:718 (with slight difference in word order).
169. al-Ṣadr al-Shahīd, *Sharḥ Adab al-qāḍī*, 4:239. This passage immediately follows the one in which al-Khaṣṣāf famously states that a wife may decline to cook or bake if her husband provides her with unprocessed foodstuffs; al-Ṣadr al-Shahīd modifies this with Abū'l-Layth's statement that this applies only to wives who are noble or disabled (4:236–237).
170. Shaybānī, *Aṣl*, editor's introduction (published as separate volume), 284.
171. Shaybānī, *Aṣl*, 4:43; and Ibn Māza, *Muḥīṭ*, 7:451. Al-Shaybānī similarly specifies that a wife cannot contract to receive wages from her husband for nursing their child (although she also cannot be compelled to nurse). Shaybānī, *Aṣl*, 10:349.
172. Shaybānī, *Aṣl*, 4:43.
173. Shaybānī, *Aṣl*, 9:379. Al-Sarakhsī follows the same logic with respect to the reward for returning an escaped slave; see Sarakhsī, *Mabsūṭ*, 11:33.
174. He states that a child can contract to receive wages from a parent for pasturing livestock or caring for an estate but not for household service; conversely, it is unseemly (*lā yanbaghī*) for a parent to serve a child. Shaybānī, *Aṣl*, 4:43–44.
175. See Ibn al-Humām, *Sharḥ Fatḥ al-qadīr*, 4:349; and Ibn Nujaym, *Al-Baḥr al-rāʾiq*, 4:311.
176. Qāḍī Khān, *Fatāwā*, 2:216.
177. The more difficult question was whether she or her husband controlled her time. Some jurists opined that a husband could forbid his wife from spinning (presumably for her own profit); see Qāḍī Khān, *Fatāwā*, 1:382; Ibn Māza, *Muḥīṭ*, 3:171 (citing "*Fatāwā ahl Samarqand*"); Marghīnānī, *Al-Fatāwā al-Ẓahīrīya*, folio 65b; and ʿAynī, *Masāʾil*, 1:223. In contrast, Ṭāhir al-Bukhārī states that "a husband is not entitled to prevent his wife from spinning her own cotton, for herself or for someone else for a wage, except at times when he is in need of her." Bukhārī, *Khulāṣa*, 77b.
178. Johansen, "Die sündige, gesunde Amme," 176 (translation mine).
179. Johansen, "Secular and Religious Elements," 191.
180. Johansen distinguishes between "commercial exchange," in which women have equal legal capacity to engage in transactions under Ḥanafī law, and marriage as a paradigmatic "social exchange," in which they have limited legal capacity. Our focus here is not on the contracting of the marriage itself, but on the wife's ongoing ability to contractually dispose of an economic asset, her labor. See Johansen, "Valorization of the Human Body," 71–73.

4. Marriage Reimagined: The Work of Ibn Qudāma and Ibn Taymīya

1. Dates are given with AH (anno Hegirae, or "in the year of [Muhammad's] Hijra") first followed by CE (of the Common Era).
2. See Rodrigo Adem, "The Intellectual Genealogy of Ibn Taymīya" (Ph.D. diss., University of Chicago, 2015), 21–25. I thank Mariam Sheibani for directing me to this work.

3. See Adem, "Intellectual Genealogy," 43–48.
4. On the career of Muwaffaq al-Dīn ibn Qudāma, see Adem, "Intellectual Genealogy," 49–55.
5. Henri Laoust, *Le Précis de Droit d'Ibn Qudāma* (Beirut: Institut Français de Damas, 1950), xxviii.
6. Laoust, *Précis de Droit*, xi. English translation mine.
7. Muwaffaq al-Dīn ʿAbd Allāh ibn Aḥmad Ibn Qudāma, *Al-Mughnī* (Beirut: Dār al-Kutub al-ʿIlmīya, n.d.), 8:130. I have not been able to locate a statement to this effect attributed to Ibn Ḥanbal in an early source, although Ibn Qudāma's wording suggests that he is citing an explicit statement rather than merely an inference from Ibn Ḥanbal's legal methodology.
8. Ibn Qudāma, *Mughnī*, 8:130. He further cites al-Jūzajānī as adducing a hadith declaring that a wife would be obligated to carry things "from a black mountain to a red mountain" or the reverse if her husband so directed her; al-Jūzajānī reasons, "That is obedience with respect to something that has no benefit, so what of the tasks of [the husband's] daily life?" Finally, al-Jūzajānī is quoted as adducing a report in which the Prophet avails himself of his wife ʿĀʾisha's labor. For Ibn Abī Shayba and al-Jūzajānī, see Fuat Sezgin, *Geschichte des arabischen Schrifttums* (Leiden: Brill, 1967), 1:108–109 (Ibn Abī Shayba), 1:135 (Abū Isḥāq al-Jūzajānī). Ibn Abī Shayba transmits a report that "the Messenger of God ruled that his daughter Fāṭima was responsible for the housework (*khidmat al-bayt*), and that ʿAlī was responsible for the work (*khidma*) that was outside of the house." Ibn Abī Shayba, *Muṣannaf Ibn Abī Shayba*, ed. Saʿīd Muḥammad al-Laḥḥām (Beirut: Dār al-Fikr), AH 1428–1429/2008 CE), 7:8.
9. Ibn Qudāma, *Mughnī*, 8:131.
10. For an exhaustive analysis of this underlying structure of the marriage contract in Islamic legal texts of the formative period, see Kecia Ali, *Marriage and Slavery in Early Islam* (Cambridge, Mass.: Harvard University Press, 2010); and Hina Azam, *Sexual Violation in Islamic Law* (Cambridge: Cambridge University Press, 2015), 84–88.
11. See Ibn Qudāma, *Mughnī*, 7:396 (a mentally incompetent man may need a wife for either sex or service); 9:303 (a young girl must be trained in skills such as spinning and cooking); 4:523 (a girl's financial competence is tested with tasks of "the mistress of a household (*rabbat al-bayt*), such as hiring women to spin, appointing an agent to buy flax, and the like").
12. Ibn Qudāma, *Mughnī*, 9:237.
13. Ibn Qudāma, *Mughnī*, 9:238.
14. See, for instance, Qur'an verses 4:19 and 4:25.
15. Arguably, the wife would not be receiving a wage for her own work but pocketing the wage of a servant while meeting her own needs by doing the work herself; however, the distinction here seems to be immaterial.
16. Abu'l-Ḥasan ʿUmar ibn al-Ḥusayn al-Khiraqī, *Mukhtaṣar al-Khiraqī*, ed. Muhammad Zuhayr Shāwīsh (Damascus: Muʾassasat al-Salām li'l-Ṭabāʿa wa'l-Nashr, AH 1378/1958–1959), 173.
17. Ibn Qudāma, *Mughnī*, 6:76; see also 9:313.

18. This accurately reflects the position of at least some Shāfiʿīs; see, for instance, ʿAbd al-Wāḥid ibn Ismāʿīl al-Rūyānī, *Baḥr al-madhhab fī furūʿ madhhab al-imām al-Shāfiʿī*, eds. Aḥmad ʿIzz and ʿInāya al-Dimashqī (Beirut: Dār Iḥyāʾ al-Turāth al-ʿArabī, AH 1423/2002 CE), 9:304. Al-Rūyānī also reports a (minority?) Shāfiʿī line of reasoning stating that if a wife hires herself out to nurse for a third party, the contract is valid pending nullification by the husband because "the contract deals with a locus other than that which is dealt with by the contract of marriage, because [the husband] does not own her service or her nursing." Rūyānī, *Baḥr*, 9:304.
19. Ibn Qudāma, *Mughnī*, 6:76.
20. Ibn Qudāma, *Mughnī*, 9:313.
21. Ibn Qudāma, *Mughnī*, 9:312.
22. Ibn Qudāma, *Mughnī*, 9:313.
23. Ibn Qudāma, *Mughnī*, 6:76; see also 9:313.
24. Rūyānī, *Baḥr*, 9:304.
25. Ibn Qudāma, *Mughnī*, 9:313.
26. For the Mālikī doctrine, see the discussion of the *Mudawwana* of Saḥnūn in chapter 1; for Shāfiʿī views, see the section "Al-Māwardī in the context of the Shāfiʿī school" in chapter 2.
27. ʿAlī ibn Sulaymān al-Mardāwī, *Al-Inṣāf fī maʿrifat al-rājiḥ min al-khilāf ʿalā madhhab al-imām al-mubajjal Aḥmad ibn Ḥanbal*, ed. Muḥammad Ḥāmid al-Fiqī (Cairo: Maṭbaʿat al-Sunna al-Muḥammadīya, AH 1374–1377/1955–1958 CE), 9:406; see also 6:29.
28. Al-Mardāwī attributes to ʿAbd al-Wahhāb al-Shīrāzī (d. AH 536/1142 CE) the argument that such a contract "is not valid, because he is [already] entitled to her benefit (*nafʿahā*), just as if he were to hire her for a month for service (*li'l-khidma*), then [additionally] hired her during that month to build [something]." Mardāwī, *Inṣāf*, 9:406.
29. Abū'l-Khaṭṭāb Maḥfūẓ b. Aḥmad al-Kalwadhānī, *Al-Hidāya ʿalā madhhab al-imām Abī ʿAbd Allāh Aḥmad ibn Muḥammad Ibn Ḥanbal al-Shaybānī*, eds. ʿAbd al-Laṭīf Humayyim and Māhir Yāsīn al-Faḥl (Kuwait: Ghirās, AH 1425/2004 CE), 495. Al-Kalwadhānī affirms the wife's ability to contract with her husband for wages in exchange for nursing and childcare (299). Ibn Qudāma and al-Mardāwī also state that such a contract was rejected by "the judge" (*al-qāḍī*). See Ibn Qudāma, *Mughnī*, 6:76; and Mardāwī, *Inṣāf*, 6:29. This title would ordinarily refer to Abū Yaʿlā al-Farrāʾ (d. AH 458/1131 CE); however, in currently available works he acknowledges the acceptance of such contracts as school doctrine. See al-Qāḍī Abū Yaʿlā Muḥammad ibn al-Ḥusayn al-Farrāʾ, *Al-Jāmiʿ al-ṣaghīr fi'l-fiqh ʿalā madhhab al-imām Aḥmad ibn Muḥammad ibn Ḥanbal*, ed. Nāṣir ibn Suʿūd ibn ʿAbd Allāh al-Salāma (Riyadh: Dar Aṭlas li'l-Nashr wa'l-Tawzīʿ, AH 1421/2000 CE), 195; and al-Qāḍī Abū Yaʿlā Muḥammad ibn al-Ḥusayn al-Farrāʾ, *Sharḥ Mukhtaṣar al-Khiraqī*, ed. Nāṣir ibn Suʿūd ibn ʿAbd Allāh al-Salāma (Riyadh: Dār Aṭlas al-Khaḍrāʾ, AH 1439/2018 CE), 2:279–280.
30. This Ḥanbalī doctrine on stipulations in marriage contracts is merely one manifestation of the school's distinctively expansive approach to freedom of contract in general. See *Al-Mawsūʿa al-fiqhīya*, s.v. "sharṭ," para. 18–27, 26:10–16; and

Oussama Arabi, "Contract Stipulations (*Shurūṭ*) in Islamic Law: The Ottoman *Majalla* and Ibn Taymiyya," *International Journal of Middle East Studies* 30 (1998): 29–50.

31. Ibn Qudāma, *Mughnī*, 7:448–452.
32. Ibn Qudāma, *Mughnī*, 4:402.
33. Muwaffaq al-Dīn Ibn Qudāma, *Al-Muqniʿ*, ed. ʿAbd Allāh ibn ʿAbd al-Muḥsin al-Turkī (Giza: Hajar, AH 1415/1995 CE), 14:325.
34. Shams al-Din 'Abd al-Rahman ibn Muhammad Ibn Qudāma al-Maqdisī, *Al-Sharḥ al-kabīr*, published with Muwaffaq al-Dīn ibn Qudāma, *Muqniʿ*, ed. ʿAbd Allāh ibn ʿAbd al-Muḥsin al-Turkī (Giza: Hajar, AH 1415/1995 CE), 14:325–26.
35. Mardāwī, *Inṣāf*, 6:29.
36. See, for instance, Ibn Qudāma, *Mughnī*, 5:360, 6:138–139. Al-Mardāwī editorializes on the school doctrine that a child can validly contract for wages to serve his parent, "But this seems distasteful" (*wa-fī 'l-nafs minhu shayʾ*). Mardāwī, *Inṣāf*, 6:29.
37. On the Banū Taymīya and their role in the Ḥanbalī intellectual life of Harran, see Adem, "Intellectual Genealogy," 422–446; on the *Muḥarrar*, see Adem, "Intellectual Genealogy," 438–439.
38. He was also well-versed in the Harranian Ḥanbalī tradition as conveyed from his grandfather through his father; see Adem, "Intellectual Genealogy," 458.
39. On his studies, see Laoust, *Précis de Droit*, xlviii.
40. John Hoover, *Ibn Taymiyya* (London: Oneworld Academic, 2019), 8; see also Abdul Hakim I. al-Matroudi, *The Ḥanbalī School of Law and Ibn Taymiyyah: Conflict or Conciliation* (London: Routledge, 2006), 25. Ibn Taymīya's commentary covers only the sections devoted to matters of ritual, so it does not address the specific issues of interest here.
41. Laoust, *Précis de Droit*, xlix. English translation mine.
42. His scholarly partisans seem to have been limited in number, if intense in their loyalty; at the same time, he enjoyed great popularity and repute among the Muslim masses. See Caterina Bori, "Ibn Taymiyya *wa-Jamāʿatuhu* Authority, Conflict and Consensus in Ibn Taymiyya's Circle," in *Ibn Taymiyya and His Times*, ed. by Yossef Rapoport and Shahab Ahmed (Princeton, N.J.: Princeton University Press, 2010), 24–52.
43. For overviews of Ibn Taymīya's life and work, see Henri Laoust, "Ibn Taymiyya," in *Encyclopaedia of Islam*, 2nd ed. (hereafter *EI2*), ed. P. Bearman, Th. Bianquis, C. E. Bosworth, E. van Donzel, and W. P. Heinrichs (Leiden: Brill, 1960–2005); Al-Matroudi, *Ḥanbalī School*, 13–30; and Hoover, *Ibn Taymiyya*, 5–39. On his general legal views, see (in addition to Al-Matroudi) Yossef Rapoport, "Ibn Taymiyya's Radical Legal Thought: Rationalism, Pluralism and the Primacy of Intention," in *Ibn Taymiyya and His Times*, ed. by Yossef Rapoport and Shahab Ahmed (Oxford: Oxford University Press, 2010), 191–226.
44. Ibn Qudāma similarly held that *nafaqa* was situationally dependent rather than set at a fixed quantity, although this seems to have been debated within the school; see Ibn Qudāma, *Mughnī*, 9:231–232.
45. Q 2:228–229; 2:231, 2:232, 4:19, 65:2. On the semantic field of the Qur'anic term *maʿrūf* see Toshihiko Izutsu, *Ethico-Religious Concepts in the Qur'ān* (Montreal:

McGill-Queen's University Press, 2002), 213–215. Izutsu notes that "it is [a] characteristic feature of the word *maʿrūf* that it tends to be used most appropriately in the legislative portions of the Book, particularly where regulations concerning moral duties in family relations, between husband and wife, parents and children, or among near kinsfolk, are in question" (214–215).

46. This could also be a reference to a hadith paralleling the wording of this Qur'anic verse; see [Muslim ibn al-Ḥajjāj], *Ṣaḥīḥ* (Vaduz, Liect.: Thesaurus Islamicus Foundation, 2000), 1:500 (*Kitāb al-Ḥajj, Bāb Ḥijjat al-Nabī ṣallā 'llāhu ʿalayhi wa-sallam*).
47. Taqī al-Dīn Aḥmad ibn ʿAbd al-Ḥalīm Ibn Taymīya, *Majmūʿ al-fatāwā*, ed. Muṣṭafā ʿAbd al-Qādir ʿAṭā (Beirut: Dār al-Kutub al-ʿIlmīya, AH 1421/2000 CE), 34:46.
48. Ibn Taymīya, *Majmūʿ al-fatāwā*, 34:46.
49. Ibn Taymīya, *Majmūʿ al-fatāwā*, 34:47.
50. Ibn Taymīya, *Majmūʿ al-fatāwā*, 34:47.
51. Ibn Taymīya, *Majmūʿ al-fatāwā*, 34:48; see also 34:43–44.
52. Ibn Taymīya, *Majmūʿ al-fatāwā*, 34:48; see also 34:43–44.
53. Ibn Taymīya, *Majmūʿ al-fatāwā*, 34:46.
54. Ibn Taymīya, *Majmūʿ al-fatāwā*, 34:48.
55. For this hadith, see [Muḥammad ibn ʿĪsā Al-Tirmidhī,] *Sunan al-Tirmidhī* (Vaduz, Liecht.: Thesaurus Islamicus Foundation, 2000), 1:314 (*Kitāb al-Raḍāʿ, Bāb Mā jāʾa fī ḥaqq al-marʾa ʿalā zawjihā*); and [Ibn Māja, Muḥammad ibn Yazīd], *Sunan Ibn Māja* (Vaduz, Liecht.: Thesaurus Islamicus Foundation, 2000), 269 (*Kitāb al-Nikāḥ, Bāb Ḥaqq al-marʾa ʿalā zawjihā*).
56. Ibn Taymīya, *Majmūʿ al-fatāwā*, 34:48.
57. Ibn Taymīya, *Majmūʿ al-fatāwā*, 34:49.
58. Ibn Taymīya, *Majmūʿ al-fatāwā*, 34:46, 49.
59. Ibn Taymīya, *Majmūʿ al-fatāwā*, 34:46.
60. Ibn Taymīya, *Majmūʿ al-fatāwā*, 34:45.
61. See *Al-Mawsūʿa al-fiqhīya*, s.v. "Īlāʾ," 7:221–240, especially 221; and Ali, *Marriage and Slavery*, 121–124.
62. See Majd al-Dīn Abū al-Barakāt [Ibn Taymīya], *Al-Muḥarrar fī al-fiqh ʿalā madhhab al-imām Ahmad ibn Hanbal* (Maṭbaʿat al-Sunna al-Muḥammadīya, AH 1369/1950 CE), 2:41 (explicitly stating that the husband's failure to do so is grounds for judicial separation); and Ibn Qudāma, *Mughnī*, 8:141–142.
63. See Ibn Taymīya, *Muḥarrar*, 2:41; Ibn Qudāma, *Mughnī*, 8:140; and Susan A. Spectorsky, *Chapters on Marriage and Divorce: Responses of Ibn Ḥanbal and Ibn Rāhwayh* (Austin: University of Texas Press, 1993), 154, 233–234.
64. ʿAlī ibn Muḥammad al-Baʿlī, *Al-Akhbār al-ʿilmīya min al-ikhtiyārāt al-fiqhīya li-shaykh al-islām Ibn Taymīya*, ed. Aḥmad ibn Muḥammad ibn Ḥasan al-Khalīl (Riyadh: Dār al-ʿĀṣima, 1998), 354.
65. Al-Baʿlī, *Al-Akhbār al-ʿilmīya*, 355.
66. Ibn Taymīya, *Majmūʿ al-fatāwā*, 34:48.
67. Ibn Taymīya, *Majmūʿ al-fatāwā*, 34:47.
68. Ibn Qudāma, *Mughnī*, 9:232–233.
69. Ibn Taymīya, *Al-Siyāsa al-sharʿīya fī iṣlāḥ al-rāʿī wa al-raʿīya*, ed. ʿAlī ibn Muḥammad al-ʿImrān (Mecca: Dār ʿĀlam al-Fawāʾid, AH 1329), introduction, 20–21; but compare Caterina Bori, "One or Two Versions of al-Siyāsa al-Sharʿiyya of Ibn

Taymiyya? What Do They Tell Us?" ASK Working Paper 26 (Bonn, December 2016): 11 and 11n64. As discussed by al-ʿImrān and Bori, this work exists in two distinct versions: a more extensive original version (represented in the manuscript edited by al-ʿImrān) and an abbreviated version that is included in *Majmūʿ al-fatāwā*, 28:111–179, and has been published multiple times as a freestanding work.

70. For general overviews of this work see Hoover, *Ibn Taymiyya*, 98–105; and Bori, "One or Two Versions," esp. 6.
71. Ibn Taymīya, *Siyāsa*, 210–211; compare *Majmūʿ al-fatāwā*, 28:173.
72. Ibn Taymīya, *Siyāsa*, 211; compare *Majmūʿ al-fatāwā*, 28:173.
73. Ibn Taymīya, *Siyāsa*, 213.
74. For this hadith, see Bukhārī, *Ṣaḥīḥ*, 1:369 (*Kitāb al-Ṣawm, Bāb Ḥaqq al-jism fī 'l-ṣawm*), 3:1090 (*Kitāb al-Nikāḥ, Bāb Li-zawjika ʿalayka ḥaqq*).
75. Ibn Taymīya, *Siyāsa*, 214; compare *Majmūʿ al-fatāwā*, 28:173. I am not sure of the significance of the final words of the sentence, "*bi'l-dīn*."
76. Ibn Taymīya, *Siyāsa*, 214; compare *Majmūʿ al-fatāwā*, 28:174.
77. Ibn Taymīya, *Siyāsa*, 216; compare *Majmūʿ al-fatāwā*, 28:174.
78. Ibn Taymīya, *Siyāsa*, 216.
79. Ibn Taymīya, *Siyāsa*, 214.
80. Ibn Taymīya, *Siyāsa*, 213.
81. Ibn Taymīya, *Siyāsa*, 210–211; and *Majmūʿ al-fatāwā*, 28:173.
82. Ovamir Anjum, *Politics Law, and Community in Islamic Thought* (New York: Cambridge University Press, 2012), 241.
83. Ibn Taymīya, *Siyāsa*, 114; and Ibn Taymīya, *Majmūʿ al-fatāwā*, 28:145.
84. Ibn Taymīya, *Siyāsa*, 125; and Ibn Taymīya, *Majmūʿ al-fatāwā*, 28:149.
85. Karen Bauer, *Gender Hierarchy in the Qur'an: Medieval Interpretations, Modern Responses* (New York: Cambridge University Press, 2015), 166.
86. See Michael Cook, *Commanding Right and Forbidding Wrong in Islamic Thought* (Cambridge: Cambridge University Press, 2004), 156–157.
87. Ibn Taymīya, *Siyāsa*, 94; and *Majmūʿ al-fatāwā*, 28:138. On the Qur'anic obligation of *al-amr bi'l-maʿrūf*, see Cook, *Commanding*, 13–17; on Ibn Taymīya's distinctive approach to this duty, see Cook, *Commanding*, 151–155.
88. See Bori, "One or Two Versions?" 6.
89. Ibn Taymīya, *Siyāsa*, 181; and *Majmūʿ al-fatāwā*, 28:167.
90. Ibn Taymīya, *Siyāsa*, 180; and *Majmūʿ al-fatāwā*, 28:167.
91. Ali, *Marriage and Slavery in Early Islam.*
92. See, for instance, Ibn Qudāma, *Mughnī*, 9:240, 9:249–250.
93. Ibn Taymīya, *Majmūʿ al-fatāwā*, 34:34–41 (refutation of Abū Yaʿlā at 34:35); see also Baʿlī, *Al-Akhbār al-ʿilmīya*, 412–413.
94. Ibn Taymīya, *Majmūʿ al-fatāwā*, 34:38–40.
95. See Baʿlī, *Al-Akhbār al-ʿilmīya*, 314–317.
96. See Baʿlī, *Al-Akhbār al-ʿilmīya*, 328.
97. For a modern proposal along these lines, see Asifa Quraishi-Landes, "A Meditation on *Mahr*, Modernity, and Muslim Marriage Contract Law," in *Feminism, Law, and Religion*, ed. by Marie A. Failinger, Elizabeth R. Schiltz, and Susan J. Stabile (Farnham, Surrey: Ashgate, 2013), 174, 187–193.

98. Ibn Taymīya, *Majmūʿ al-fatāwā*, 34:44.
99. Ibn Taymīya, *Majmūʿ al-fatāwā*, 34:36.
100. Ibn Taymīya, *Majmūʿ al-fatāwā*, 34:36–37.
101. On Ibn al-Qayyim and his relationship to Ibn Taymīya, see Henri Laoust, "Ibn Ḳayyim al-Djawziyya," *EI2*; and Al-Matroudi, *Ḥanbalī School*, 131–136.
102. Ibn Ḥabīb was an Andalusian Mālikī scholar; his compilation *al-Wāḍiḥa*, which combined hadith with *fiqh*, is preserved only in fragments. See Sezgin, *Geschichte*, 1:362. See the discussion of his opinions on wives' domestic labor in chapter 1.
103. A parasang (*farsakh*) is a Persian unit of distance corresponding to approximately six kilometers. See W. Hinz, "Farsakh," *EI2*.
104. *Al-ʿuqūd al-muṭlaqa*.
105. See note 55 above.
106. The status of this statement as a hadith of the Prophet is disputed; it is also transmitted as a statement of the Companion Asmāʾ bint Abī Bakr. See Aḥmad ibn al-Ḥusayn al-Bayhaqī, *Al-Sunan al-kabīr*, ed. ʿAbd Allāh ibn ʿAbd al-Muḥsin al-Turkī (Cairo: Markaz Hajar li-'l-Buḥūth wa 'l-Dirāsāt al-ʿArabīya wa 'l-Islāmīya, AH 1432/2011 CE), 14:14.
107. Ibn Qayyim al-Jawzīya, *Zād al-maʿād fī hady khayr al-ʿibād*, ed. Muḥammad al-Anwar Aḥmad al-Baltājī (Ṣaydā/Beirut: al-Maktaba al-ʿAṣrīya, AH 1428/2007 CE), vol. 5, part 1, 188–190.
108. He makes a similar argument in Ibn al-Qayyim, *Zād al-maʿād*, vol. 5, part 2, 531, where he argues that the wife is entitled only to direct feeding and care from her husband rather than to a monetary maintenance because "each of the two spouses receives the same amount of sexual enjoyment as the other."
109. See Ibn Qayyim al-Jawzīya, *Rawḍat al-muḥibbīn wa-nuzhat al-mushtāqīn*, ed. Muḥammad ʿUzayr Shams (Jedda: Majmaʿ al-Fiqh al-Islāmī, n.d.), 314–315. His argument on this point revolves in part on the Qur'anic concept *al-maʿrūf*, here clearly understood primarily as "kindness."
110. Ibn Qayyim al-Jawzīya, *Iʿlām al-muwaqqiʿīn ʿan rabb al-ʿālamīn*, ed. Muḥammad ʿAbd al-Salām Ibrāhīm (Beirut: Dār al-Kutub al-ʿIlmīya, AH 1417/1996 CE), 2:280.
111. Following the textual variant *ʿānī* rather than *muʿāshar*. See Ibn Qayyim al-Jawzīya, *Ighāthat al-lahfān fī maṣāyid al-shayṭān*, ed. Muḥammad ʿUzayr Shams (Dār ʿĀlam al-Fawāʾid, n.d.), 2:744n2.
112. Ibn al-Qayyim, *Ighāthat al-lahfān*, 2:744.
113. See, for instance, Ibn al-Qayyim, *Zād al-maʿād*, vol. 5, part 2, 531.
114. Rapoport, *Marriage, Money and Divorce*, 52.
115. Ibn al-Qayyim, *Zād al-maʿād*, vol. 5, part 2, 531.
116. See Ibn Taymīya, *Majmūʿ al-fatāwā*, 34:48.
117. On this point see Yossef Rapoport, *Marriage, Money and Divorce*, 52, and further discussion of his arguments point below.
118. Aysha A. Hidayatullah, *Feminist Edges of the Qur'an* (Oxford: Oxford University Press, 2014), 165.
119. Rapoport, *Marriage, Money and Divorce*, 59–61.
120. Rapoport, *Marriage, Money and Divorce*, 64.
121. Rapoport's analysis of the rapid successive marriages and divorces of a manumitted slave woman in fourteenth-century Jerusalem (*Marriage, Money and*

Divorce, 64–66) suggests that the financial benefits of marriage motivated her hasty remarriages; it does not, however, necessarily explain why her marriages collapsed in the first place. Even if she does not appear to have received her marriage gifts in full, we have no reason to assume that she was not fed, clothed, or sheltered by her successive husbands.

122. *Taḥlīl* is the practice of an irrevocably divorced wife's entering into a nominal marriage with the sole intention of becoming eligible to remarry her ex-husband (cf. Q 2:230).
123. Ibn Taymīya, *Bayān al-dalīl ʿalā buṭlān al-taḥlīl*, ed. Ḥamdī ʿAbd al-Majīd al-Silafī ([Beirut]: al-Maktab al-Islāmī, [AH 1418/1998 CE]), 460; see Rapoport, *Marriage, Money and Divorce*, 73.
124. Ibn Taymīya, *Bayān al-dalīl*, 461.
125. Louis Pouzet, *Damas au VIKe/XIIIe siècle: Vie et structures religieuses d'une métropole islamique* (Beirut: Dar el-Machreq, 1988), 401. For original passage, see Yūsuf ibn Qizʾūghlī, known as Sibṭ ibn al-Jawzī, *Mirʾāt al-zamān fī tārīkh al-aʿyān*, ed. Kāmil Salmān al-Jabūrī (Beirut: Dār al-Kutub al-ʿIlmīya, AH 1434/2013 CE), 15:148.
126. Shihāb al-Dīn ʿAbd al-Raḥmān ibn Ismāʿīl, known as Abū Shāma al-Maqdisī, *Tarājim rijāl al-qarnayn al-sādis wa'l-sābi'* (Cairo: Dār al-Kutub al-Malikīya, AH 1366/1947 CE), 196–197; discussed in Louis Pouzet, *Damas*, 402.
127. Muḥammad ibn Ibrāhīm Ibn al-Jazarī, *Taʾrīkh ḥawādith al-zamān wa-anbāʾihi wa-wafayāt al-akābir wa-l'-aʿyān min abnāʾihi al-ma'rūf bi-Ta'rīkh Ibn al-Jazarī*, ed. ʿUmar ʿAbd al-Salām Tadmurī (Ṣaydā, Beirut: Al-Maktaba al-'Aṣrīya, AH 1419/1998 CE), 3:980 (mentioned in Rapoport, *Marriage, Money and Divorce*, 34).
128. Ibn al-Jazarī, *Taʾrīkh ḥawādith al-zamān*, 3:976 (mentioned in Rapoport, *Marriage, Money and Divorce*, 34).
129. Ibn al-Jazarī, *Taʾrīkh ḥawādith al-zamān*, 3:827–828 (mentioned in Rapoport, *Marriage, Money and Divorce*, 34).
130. See Huda Lutfi, "Al-Sakhāwī's *Kitāb al-nisāʾ* as a Source for the Social and Economic History of Muslim Women During the Fifteenth Century A.D.," *Muslim World* 71, no. 2 (1981): 104–124. On al-Sakhāwī's predilection for gossip in this source, see Rapoport, *Marriage, Money and Divorce*, 82.
131. Shams al-Dīn Muḥammad ibn ʿAbd al-Raḥmān al-Sakhāwī, *al-Ḍawʾ al-lāmiʿ li-ahl al-qarn al-tāsiʿ* (Beirut: Dār al-Jīl, [AH 1412/1992 CE]), 12:5.
132. Sakhāwī, *Ḍawʾ*, 12:94, 102.
133. Cf. Sakhāwī, *Ḍawʾ*, 12:43, 44, 71.
134. Bauer, *Gender Hierarchy*, 164.
135. Bauer, *Gender Hierarchy*, 166.
136. In her study of Ibn al-Qayyim's *Aḥkām ahl al-dhimma*, Antonia Bosanquet demonstrates how his originality often lay not in originating a given doctrine but in drawing it from another genre (such as advice literature, *naṣīḥa*) into the sphere of *fiqh*. See, for instance, Antonia Bosanquet, *Minding Their Place: Space and Religious Hierarchy in Ibn al-Qayyim's* Aḥkām ahl al-dhimma (Leiden: Brill, 2020), 19.
137. Khalīl ibn Isḥāq al-Mālikī, *Mukhtaṣar al-ʿallāma Khalīl*, ed. Aḥmad Jād (Cairo: Dār al-Ḥadīth, AH 1426/2005 CE), 136.

138. Muḥammad ibn Aḥmad Ibn Juzayy, *Al-Qawānīn al-fiqhīya*, ed. Muḥammad Mawhūb ibn Ḥusayn (ʿAyn Malīla, Algeria: Dār al-Hudā, 2000), 230; see also Maya Shatzmiller, *Her Day in Court: Women's Property Rights in Fifteenth-Century Granada* (Cambridge, Mass.: Harvard University Press, 2007), 100.
139. Yaḥyā ibn Sharaf al-Nawawī, *Ṣaḥīḥ Muslim bi-sharḥ al-imām Muḥyī al-Dīn al-Nawawī al-musammā al-Minhāj bi-sharḥ Ṣaḥīḥ Muslim ibn al-Ḥajjāj*, ed. Khalīl Maʾmūn Shīḥā (Beirut: Dār al-Maʿrifa, AH 1414/1994 CE), 14:388.
140. See Yaḥyā ibn Sharaf al-Nawawī, *Minhāj al-ṭālibīn wa-ʿumdat al-muftīn*, ed. Muḥammad Muḥammad Ṭāhir Shaʿbān (Jedda: Dār al-Minhāj, AH 1426/2005 CE), 459–460, 464; and Yaḥyā ibn Sharaf al-Nawawī, *Rawḍat al-ṭālibīn*, eds. ʿĀdil Aḥmad ʿAbd al-Mawjūd and ʿAlī Muḥammad Muʿawwaḍ (Riyadh: Dār ʿĀlam al-Kutub, AH 1423/2003 CE), 4:261, 6:453–455.
141. Nawawī, *Rawḍa*, 4:261 (endorses opinion that she can contract for wages for cooking).
142. Emphasizing how the legal writings of both Ibn Taymīya and Ibn Qayyim diverge from genre conventions in that they "often interweave theological and ethical reasoning," Birgit Krawietz refers to the collection known as *Majmūʿ al-fatāwā* as "Ibn Taymiyya's so-called fatwa collection." Birgit Krawietz, "Transgressive Creativity in the Making: Ibn Qayyim al-Ǧawziyyah's Reframing Within Ḥanbalī Legal Methodology," in *A Scholar in the Shadow: Essays in the Legal and Theological Thought of Ibn Qayyim al-Ǧawziyyah*, ed. by Caterina Bori and Livnat Holtzman (Rome: Istituto per l'Oriente C. A. Nallino, 2010), 47, 48. Similarly, see Bosanquet's discussion of the genre of Ibn al-Qayyim's *Aḥkām ahl al-dhimma* in *Minding Their Place*, 123.
143. Mona Hassan, "Modern Interpretations and Misinterpretations of a Medieval Scholar: Apprehending the Political Thought of Ibn Taymiyya," in *Ibn Taymiyya and His Times*, ed. by Yossef Rapoport and Shahab Ahmed (Oxford: Oxford University Press, 2010), 346, 347.
144. Anjum, *Politics, Law and Community*, 253. Also see Hassan's response in Mona Hassan, *Longing for the Lost Caliphate: A Transregional History* (Princeton, N.J.: Princeton University Press, 2017), 304n76.
145. Birgit Krawietz speaks of the "genre fluidity" of the work of both Ibn Taymiyya and Ibn al-Qayyim; see Krawietz, "Transgressive Creativity," 47.
146. Ibn Qudāma, *Mughnī*, 8:137; and Nawawī, *Rawḍa*, 5:657.
147. Abū al-Faraj Ibn al-Jawzī, *Ṣayd al-khāṭir*, ed. ʿAbd al-Qādir Aḥmad ʿAṭā (Beirut: Dār al-Kutub al-ʿIlmīya, AH 1412/1992 CE), 239–242. The summary incorporates explicitly Islamic elements that suggest either that Ibn al-Jawzī adapted the work's content for his own purposes or that he was working with an intermediary source.
148. Ibn Taymīya, *Al-Jawāb al-ṣaḥīḥ li-man baddala dīn al-masīḥ*, ed. ʿAlī ibn Ḥasan ibn Nāṣir, ʿAbd al-ʿAzīz ibn Ibrāhīm al-ʿAskar and Ḥamdān ibn Muḥammad al-Ḥamdān (Riyadh: Dār al-ʿĀṣima, AH 1419/1999 CE), 5:138.
149. Particularly, but not exclusively, the denial that a wife could validly contract for wages for nursing from her husband. See Mardāwī, *Inṣāf*, 6:29, 8:230, 9:406; Muḥammad Ibn Mufliḥ al-Maqdisī, *Kitāb al-furūʿ*, ed. ʿAbd Allāh b. ʿAbd al-Muḥsīn

al-Turkī (Muʾassasat al-Risāla / Dār al-Muʾayyad, AH 1424/2003 CE), 8:398; 9:297, 319–20.

150. See Christopher Melchert, "The Relation of Ibn Taymiyya and Ibn Qayyim al-Jawziyya to the Ḥanbalī School of Law," in *Islamic Theology, Philosophy and Law: Debating Ibn Taymiyya and Ibn Qayyim al-Jawziyya*, ed. Birgit Krawietz and Georges Tamer, in collaboration with Alina Kokoschka (Berlin: De Gruyter, 2013), 146–161.

Conclusion

1. Dates are given with AH (anno Hegirae, or "in the year of [Muhammad's] Hijra") first followed by CE (of the Common Era).
2. See Jalāl al-Dīn al-Suyūṭī [attributed], *Nuzhat al-mutaʾammil wa-nuzhat al-mutaʾahhil fī ʿl-khāṭib waʾl-mutazawwij*, ed. Muḥammad al-Tūnajī (Beirut: Dār Amwāj, 1989), 68–72; and Jalāl al-Dīn al-Suyūṭī and Muḥammad Quṭb al-Iznīqī, *Nuzhat al-mutaʾammil wa-nuzhat al-mutaʾahhil*, ed. Jūrj Kadar (Beirut: Aṭlas li'l-Nashr wa'l-Intāj al-Thaqāfī, 2012), 103–109. This work was variously attributed to Jalāl al-Dīn al-Suyūṭī and to Muḥammad ibn Muḥammad al-Iznīqī (d. AH 885/1480 CE); one of the manuscripts used by Jūrj Kadar was copied in AH 926/1520 CE (see editor's introduction, 26). This passage closely parallels material that had appeared in Ibn Ḥabīb's *Adab al-nisāʾ* centuries before; see discussion in chapter 1.
3. ʿAbd al-Raḥmān al-Ṣaffūrī, *Nuzhat al-majālis wa-muntakhab al-nafāʾis* (Cairo: Maktabat al-Qāhira, 1991), 2:28.
4. ʿAbd al-Raḥmān ibn Abī Bakr al-Suyūṭī, *Al-Ḥāwī liʾl-fatāwā*, ed. ʿAbd al-Laṭīf Ḥasan ʿAbd al-Raḥmān (Beirut: Dār al-Kutub al-ʿIlmīya, AH 1421/2000 CE), 2:45. The original inquiry (*istiftāʾ*) includes two texts on domestic labor (including the one cited here, 2:36), but al-Suyūṭī does not appear to comment on them individually in his response.
5. Abū ʿAbd Allāh Muḥammad ibn ʿAbd al-Raḥmān al-Waṣṣābī al-Ḥubayshī, *Al-Baraka fī faḍl al-saʿy waʾl-ḥaraka* (n.p., n.d.), 53.
6. Ḥubayshī, *Baraka*, 55.
7. Ḥubayshī, *Baraka*, 57–59.
8. Ḥubayshī, *Baraka*, 60. Al-Ḥubayshī's discussion of this topic received sufficient dissemination over time and space that it is extensively reproduced (without attribution) in Rifāʿa al-Ṭahṭāwī's nineteenth-century didactic manual *Al-Murshid al-amīn liʾl-banāt waʾl-banīn*, ed. Munā Aḥmad Abū Zayd (Cairo: Dār al-Kitāb al-Miṣrī / Beirut: Dār al-Kitāb al-Lubnānī, AH 1433/2012 CE), 592–595, 600.
9. ʿAlī ibn ʿAṭīya al-Hītī, known as Shaykh ʿAlwān, *Nasamāt al-asḥār fī manāqib wa-karāmāt al-awliyāʾ al-akhyār*, ed. Aḥmad Farīd al-Mazīdī (Beirut: Dār al-Kutub al-ʿIlmīya, AH 1421/2001 CE), 346. On the life of this figure, see David Larsen, "al-Ḥamawī, ʿAlwān," in *Encyclopaedia of Islam*, 3rd ed. (hereafter, *EI3*), eds. Kate Fleet, Gudrun Krämer, Denis Matringe, John Nawas, and Everett Rowson (Leiden: Brill, 2007).

10. Shaykh ʿAlwān, *Nasamāt*, 347 (comparing the ideal husband to Moses, who humbly fetches fire for his wife's cooking).
11. Nūr al-Dīn ʿAlī ibn ʿAlī al-Shubrāmallisī, *Ḥāshiya*, in margin of Shams al-Dīn Muḥammad ibn Aḥmad al-Ramlī, *Nihāyat al-muḥtāj ilā sharḥ al-Minhāj fī'l-fiqh ʿalā madhhab al-imām al-Shāfiʿī* (Beirut: Dār al-Kutub al-ʿIlmīya, AH 1424/2003 CE), 7:190.
12. A popular belief in wives' obligation to do housework under the Sharia is similarly suggested by the remarks of the Ottoman traveler Muḥammad ʿĀlī (d. 1600), who writes of Egyptian women that "in serving their husband they do not act like the Turkish women (*Rūmīye*); . . . if they one day spread out and remove beddings and pillows themselves, saying "Thus the Divine Law prescribes it," the next time they will charge their husbands with this work and will be served by them." Andreas Tietze, *Muṣṭafā ʿĀlī's Description of Cairo of 1599: Text, Transliteration, Translation, Notes* (Vienna: Verlag der Österreichischen Akademie der Wissenschaften, 1975), 41.
13. See Christina de la Puente, "Slaves in Al-Andalus through Mālikī *Wathāʾiq* Works (4th–6th Centuries H/10th–12th Centuries CE): Marriage and Slavery as Factors of Social Categorisation," *Annales Islamologiques* 42 (2008): 195; Muḥammad ibn Aḥmad al-Umawī Ibn al-ʿAṭṭār, *Kitāb al-Wathāʾiq wa'l-sijillāt*, eds. P. Chalmeta and F. Corriente (Madrid: Academia Matritense del Notariado Instituto Hipano-Árabe de Cultura, 1983), 8; Aḥmad ibn Mughīth al-Ṭulayṭilī, *Al-Muqniʿ fī ʿilm al-shurūṭ*, ed. Francisco Javier Aguirre Sáda (Madrid: al-Majlis al-Aʿlā li al-Abḥāth al-ʿIlmīya, Maʿhad al-Taʿāwun maʿa al-ʿĀlam al-ʿArabī, 1994), 22; al-Qāḍī ʿIyāḍ ibn Mūsā al-Yaḥṣubī, *Madhāhib al-ḥukkām fī nawāzil al-aḥkām li'l-qāḍi ʿIyāḍ wa-waladihi Muḥammad*, ed. Muḥammad ibn Sharīfa (Beirut: Dār al-Gharb al-Islāmī, 1990), 265–266; and Aḥmad ibn Yaḥyā al-Wansharīsī, *Al-Minhaj al-fāʾiq wa al-manhal al-rāʾiq wa al-maʿnā al-lāʾiq bi-ādāb all-muwaththiq wa-aḥkām al-wathāʾiq*, ed. ʿAbd al-Raḥmān ibn Ḥamūd ibn ʿAbd al-Raḥmān al-Aṭram (Dubai: Dār al-Buḥūth li'l-Dirāsāt al-Islāmīya wa-Iḥyāʾ al-Turāth, AH 1426/2005 CE), 1:414–415. A real-world example from Syria at the end of the Mamluk period is provided in the diary of Aḥmad ibn Ṭawq, who describes one woman's *nafaqa* as including money to maintain her servants. Torsten Wollina, *Zwanzig Jahre Alltag: Lebens-,Welt- und Selbstbild im Journal des Aḥmad ibn Ṭawq* (Goettingen: V&R unipress, 2014), 60.
14. The Tunisian jurist Abū al-Qāsim al-Burzulī (d. AH 841/1438 CE) recounts an anecdote about a scholar two generations older who was a judge in charge of marriage cases (*qāḍī ankiḥa*). Approached by a sedentary woman (*imraʾa min ṣinf al-ḥaḍar*) complaining of her labor grinding grain, he directed her husband to purchase a servant for her; approached by a tribal woman (*badawīya*) complaining of her labors, including grinding grain and such outdoor tasks as collecting firewood, he directed her to stay with her husband and continue as she was on the grounds that this was the (implicit) condition on which she as a tribal woman had contracted her marriage. See Abū'l-Qāsim ibn Aḥmad al-Balawī, known as al-Burzulī, *Jāmiʿ masāʾil al-aḥkām li-mā nazala min al-qaḍāyā bi'l-muftīn wa'l-ḥukkām*, ed. Muḥammad al-Ḥabīb al-Hīla (Beirut: Dār al-Gharb al-Islāmī, 2002), 2:359–360.

15. Quoted from ʿUthmān dan Fodio, *Nūr al-albāb*, in *Nigerian Perspectives: A Historical Anthology*, 2nd ed., ed. by Thomas Hodgkin (Oxford: Oxford University Press, 1975), 255. On ʿUthmān dan Fodio, see Murray Last, "Fūdī, ʿUthmān," *EI3*.
16. See, among others, Afsaneh Najmabadi, "Crafting an Educated Housewife in Iran," in *Remaking Women: Feminism and Modernity in the Middle East*, ed. Lila Abu-Lughod (Princeton, N.J.: Princeton University Press, 1998), 91–125; Hoda Elsadda, "Gendered Citizenship: Discourses on Domesticity in the Second Half of the Nineteenth Century," *Hawwa* 4, no. 1 (2006): 1–28; Beth Baron, *The Women's Awakening in Egypt: Culture, Society, and the Press* (New Haven, Conn.: Yale University Press, 1994), 155–158; and Margot Badran, *Feminists, Islam and Nation* (Princeton, N.J.: Princeton University Press, 1994), 61–65.
17. Translation from Muhammad Asad, *The Message of the Qurʾān* (Bristol, Engl.: The Book Foundation, 2003), 61.
18. Muḥammad Rashīd Riḍā, *Tafsīr al-qurʾān al-ḥakīm* [*Tafsīr al-manār*], 2nd ed. (Cairo: AH 1350/[1931–1932 CE]), 2:379–380.
19. Riḍā, *Tafsīr*, 2:376.
20. For the concept of "colonial feminism," see Leila Ahmed, *Women and Gender in Islam* (New Haven, Conn.: Yale University Press, 1992), 151; compare Margot Badran's "imperial feminism" in *Feminists, Islam, and Nation*, 70.
21. Riḍā, *Tafsīr*, 2:380.
22. Riḍā, *Tafsīr*, 2:378–379.
23. Riḍā, *Tafsīr*, 2:379.
24. See Jon Hoover, "Fiṭra," *EI3*, and references there.
25. Riḍā, *Tafsīr*, 2:379.
26. Premodern discussions of *fiṭra* focused on the primordial monotheism of all human beings and the innate knowledge (whether axiomatic principles or moral intuitions) shared by humankind; see Hoover, "Fiṭra." Based on a hadith, *fiṭra* was also associated with the trimming and removal of body hair, circumcision, and other practices constituting "a natural sense of personal hygiene (*sunan al-fiṭra*)." On this topic, see Birgit Krawietz, "Body, in Law," *EI3*; Frederick Denny, "Circumcision," in *Encyclopaedia of the Qur'an*, ed. by Jane Dammen McAuliffe (Leiden: Brill, 2001–2006); [Muḥammad ibn Ismāʿīl al-Bukhārī], *Ṣaḥīḥ al-Bukhārī* (Vaduz, Liecht.: Thesaurus Islamicus Foundation, 2000), 3:1213 (*Kitāb al-Libās, Bāb Qaṣṣ al-shārib*); and Muslim ibn al-Ḥajjāj, *Ṣaḥīḥ Muslim* (Vaduz, Liecht.: Thesaurus Islamicus Foundation, 2000), 1:124–125 (*Kitāb al-Ṭahāra, Bāb Khiṣāl al-fiṭra*). As far as I have been able to determine, classical sources generally do not associate the term *fiṭra* with gendered concepts of virtue. On the gendering of the concept of *fiṭra* in *Tafsīr al-Manār*, see Omaima Abou-Bakr, "Turning the Tables: Perspectives on the Construction of 'Muslim Manhood,'" *Journal of Women of the Middle East and the Islamic World* 11 (2003): 98–100.
27. Riḍā, *Tafsīr*, 2:377–378.
28. The association between wives and housework or "indoor" tasks (*khidmat al-dākhil*) seems to be congruent with, but not merely a function of, jurists' concern with female modesty.
29. On "the precolonial exemption of women from housework," see Kenneth Cuno, *Modernizing Marriage: Family, Ideology, and Law in Nineteenth- and Early*

Twentieth-Century Egypt (New York: Syracuse University Press, 2015), 96; see also 80, 88, 95. On the "ideal of domesticity," see Cuno, *Modernizing Marriage*, 80. Despite this repeated generalization, Cuno is insightful in observing that "prior to the advent of the new family ideology, diverse aspects of family life were addressed in a variety of genres, including prose and poetry, works on proper comportment (*adab*), and juridical compendia and commentaries" (78).

30. Another example of an author who overstates the absolute nature of the transition while also providing evidence of a more nuanced development is Afsaneh Najmabadi, who observes that for Iranian reformers at the turn of the twentieth century, "Woman was now to become . . . the manager of the household (*mudabbir-i manzil*), instead of being subject to [her husband's] management." "Crafting an Educated Housewife," 102. As we have seen, the association between women and *tadbīr al-manzil* (including its managerial dimension) had a much longer history; however, Najmabadi persuasively illustrates that what is truly new is the extent to which household management was understood to require women's education, and its placement within a project of national regeneration in which women were seen as educators of the rising generation.
31. On the rediscovery and dissemination of Ibn Taymīya's works by Muslim reformers at the turn of the twentieth century, see Ahmed El Shamsy, *Rediscovering the Islamic Classics: How Editors and Print Culture Transformed an Intellectual Tradition* (Princeton, N.J.: Princeton University Press, 2020), 182–191; on Ibn Taymīya's influence on leading scholars in twentieth-century Saudi Arabia, see Abdul Hakim I. al-Matroudi, *The Ḥanbalī School of Law and Ibn Taymiyyah: Conflict or Conciliation* (London: Routledge, 2006), 162–168; on the circulation and status of the ideas of Ibn Taymīya in the intervening centuries, see Caterina Bori, "Ibn Taymiyya (14th to 17th Century): Transregional Spaces of Reading and Reception," *Muslim World* 108 (2018): 87–123.
32. For instance, Yūsuf al-Qaraḍāwī's widely cited fatwa on the subject combines extensive reproduction of Ibn al-Qayyim's arguments with an invocation of Riḍā's claim about women's *fiṭra*. See Yūsuf al-Qaraḍāwī, "Hal tajib ʿalā al-zawj khidmat zawjatihi?," Islam Online, accessed September 13, 2008, http://www.islamonline.net/servlet/Satellite?pagename=IslamOnline-Arabic-Ask_Scholar/FatwaA/FatwaA&cid=1122528600720.
33. Qaraḍāwī, "Hal tajib ʿalā al-zawj khidmat zawjatihi?"
34. Shaykh ʿAbd Allāh Ibn Jabrīn, "Wujūb khidmat al-marʾa zawjahā," Saaid, accessed May 29, 2020. http://www.saaid.net/Doat/ehsan/141.htm.
35. Qaraḍāwī, "Hal tajib ʿalā al-zawj khidmat zawjatihi?"
36. Ibn Jabrīn, "Wujūb khidmat al-marʾa zawjahā."
37. Muḥammad ibn Ṣāliḥ al-ʿUthaymīn, *Al-Sharḥ al-mumtiʿ ʿalā Zād al-mustanqiʿ* (ʿUnayza, Saudi Arabia: Dār Ibn al-Jawzī, AH 1427), 12:383. *Zād al-mustanqiʿ* is an abridgement of Ibn Qudāma's legal manual *al-Muqniʿ* by Mūsā ibn Aḥmad al-Ḥajjāwī (d. AH 968/1561 CE).
38. Ibn al-ʿUthaymīn, *Al-Sharḥ al-mumtiʿ*, 12:383 (see also 12:441, 13:461).
39. A number of Muslim-majority countries have introduced various forms of marital joint property regimes, some on the basis of secular or customary legislation and others in the context of projects of Islamic legal reform; the two can

intersect in various ways. See M. Siraj Sait, "Our Marriage, Your Property? Renegotiating Islamic Marital Property Regimes," in *Changing God's Law: The Dynamics of Middle Eastern Family Law*, ed. Nadjma Yassari (London: Routledge, 2016), 245–286; and Musawah for Equality in the Family, "Who Provides? Who Cares? Changing Dynamics in Muslim Families" accessed April 15, 2021, https://www.musawah.org/wp-content/uploads/2018/11/WhoProvidesWhoCares_En.pdf, 39, 46–48, 51–52. An early example was the Islamic Republic of Iran, which in 1992 passed a law requiring divorcing husband to pay back "wages for housework." In analyzing the controversy surrounding the enactment of this law, Mehrangiz Kar and Homa Hoodfar note that the law was initially contested by "many conservative religious leaders" who saw women's care work as a religious imperative; the law was rejected by the Assembly of Religious Experts, but its veto was overruled. Mehrangiz Kar and Homa Hoodfar, "Personal Status Law as Defined by the Islamic Republic of Iran: An Appraisal," in *Shifting Boundaries in Marriage and Divorce in Muslim Communities*, ed. Homa Hoodfar (Women Living Under Muslim Laws Special Dossier 1996), 31–33; see also Sait, "Our Marriage, Your Property," 265–266; and Musawah, "Who Provides?" 39.

40. Musawah, "Why Provides?" 39. For the original text see "Mudawwanat al-Usra," Al-Mamlaka al-Maghribīya, Wizārat al-ʿAdl, accessed September 22, 2021, https://adala.justice.gov.ma/production/legislation/ar/Nouveautes/%D9%85%D8%AF%D9%88%D9%86%D8%A9%20%D8%A7%D9%84%D8%A3%D8%B3%D8%B1%D8%A9.pdf, 20.
41. Al-Mamlaka al-Maghribīya, Wizārat al-ʿAdl, *Al-Muqtaḍayāt al-Jadīda li-Mudawwanat al-Usra* (Rabat: Manshūrāt Jamʿīyat Nashr al-Maʿlūmāt al-Qānūnīya wa 'l-Qaḍāʾīya, 2004), 98–99.
42. See Farīda Banānī, *Taqsīm al-ʿamal bayna al-zawjayn fī ḍawʾ al-qānūn al-Maghribī wa al-fiqh al-islāmī, al-jins miʿyāran* (Marrakesh: Silsilat Manshūrāt Kullīyat al-ʿUlūm al-Qānūnīya wa'l-iqtiṣādīya wa'l-ijtimāʿīya, 1993); Muḥammad al-Tāwīl, *Ishkālīyat al-amwāl al-muktasaba muddat al-zawjīya: ruʾya islāmīya* (Fez, 2006); and Al-Mīlūd Kaʿwāss, *Ḥaqq al-zawja fī al-kadd wa'l-siʿāya* (Rabat: Markaz al-Dirāsāt wa'l-Abḥāth wa-Iḥyāʾ al-Turāth, 2008).
43. Farīda Banānī uses contemporary economic data and Marxist and feminist principles to argue vigorously in favor of the idea that housework contributes to economic output and to the reproduction of the labor force (Banānī, *Taqsīm al-ʿamal bayna'l-zawjayn*, 183–192), while Muḥammad al-Tāwīl vehemently denies it (Tāwīl, *Ishkālīyat al-amwāl*, 2–3).
44. Compare, for instance, Banānī, *Taqsīm al-ʿamal*, 143–144, 148, with Kaʿwāss, *Ḥaqq al-zawja*, 73–75.
45. "My Wife and I Married a Long Time Ago . . . ," Shariawiz, accessed January 25, 2021, https://halaqa.shariawiz.com/2020/02/03/my-wife-and-i-married-a-long-time-ago-alhamdullilah-we-have-been-blessed-with-beautiful-children-and-abundant-wealth-i-know-that-under-the-sharia-inheritance-rules-my-wife-will-only-recei/. I thank Abed Awad for directing me to this resource. The current version of the website states with respect to the same issue that "some scholars agree with this opinion, but only for a wife who was accustomed to such lifestyle prior to marriage." Shariawiz, accessed February 26, 2022, https://www

.shariawiz.com/halaqa/2020/02/03/what-sharia-permissible-steps-are-available-to-make-sure-my-wife-is-financially-secure-if-i-predecease-her/.

46. Zahra Ayubi, "Negotiating Justice: American Muslim Women Navigating Islamic Divorce and Civil Law," *Journal for Islamic Studies* 30 (2010): 95 and 95n27.
47. Asma T. Uddin, *When Islam Is Not a Religion: Inside America's Fight for Religious Freedom* (New: Pegasus, 2019), 184.
48. Uddin, *When Islam Is Not a Religion*, 183; emphasis in original.
49. Talal Asad, *Formations of the Secular: Christianity, Islam, Modernity* (Stanford, Calif.: Stanford University Press, 2003), 209.
50. Wael Hallaq, *The Impossible State: Islam, Politics, and Modernity's Moral Predicament* (New York: Columbia University Press, 2013), 112.
51. Hallaq, *Impossible State*, 113.
52. Asad, *Formations*, 249; see also Hallaq, *Impossible State*, 115–135.
53. For an outstanding recent example, see Junaid Quadri, *Transformations of Tradition: Islamic Law in Colonial Modernity* (Oxford: Oxford University Press, 2021), esp. chap. 5 (165–208). Hallaq is the leading scholar of premodern *fiqh* in North America, but his recent, more theoretical work offers an interpretation of the broad structure and *longue durée* development of the Sharia rather than delving into detailed examinations of specific points of the law.
54. See Zahra Ayubi, *Gendered Morality: Classical Islamic Ethics of the Self, Family, and Society* (New York: Columbia University Press, 2019), 36.
55. Sarakhsī, *Mabsūṭ*, 15:128.
56. For an influential articulation of this model see, for instance, Hussein Ali Agrama's argument about the institution of *ḥisba* that "the [classical] *Shari'a* was characterized by interconnected techniques of moral inquiry and criticism that aimed to secure virtues fundamental to it," a function that was "legalized" in terms of public and private interests only in modernity. Hussein Ali Agrama, *Questioning Secularism: Islam, Sovereignty, and the Rule of Law in Egypt* (Chicago: University of Chicago Press, 2012), 64–65. See also Khaled Fahmy's critique of these arguments. Khaled Fahmy, *In Quest of Justice: Islamic Law and Forensic Medicine in Modern Egypt* (Berkeley: University of California Press, 2018), 181–182.
57. Baber Johansen, "Die sündige, gesunde Amme. Moral und gestzliche Bestimmung (*ḥukm*) im islamischen Recht," in *Contingency in a Sacred Law: Legal and Ethical Norms in the Muslim Fiqh* (Leiden: Brill, 1999), 173–187.
58. Qaraḍāwī, "Hal tajib ʿalā al-zawj khidmat zawjatihi?"
59. Summarized from the speech "Ḥuqūq al-zawj 1" from the series "Fiqh al-usra li'l-shaykh Muḥammad al-Shanqīṭī," Youtube, accessed May 29, 2020, https://www.youtube.com/watch?v=x38Qq-IIb5I. The first section of the passage is quoted by Shaykh ʿAbd Allāh ibn Jabrīn in a fatwa published under the title "Wujūb khidmat al-marʾa zawjahā," Saaid, accessed May 29, 2020, http://www.saaid.net/Doat/ehsan/141.htm.
60. Uddin, *When Islam Is Not a Religion*, 182.
61. Uddin, *When Islam Is Not a Religion*, 185.
62. Ayubi, *Gendered Morality*, 124, 130.
63. Janet Halley, "What Is Family Law?: A Genealogy Part I," *Yale Journal of Law & the Humanities* 23:1 (2011), 2.

64. Janet Halley, "What Is Family Law?" 2.
65. Katharine Silbaugh, "Turning Labor into Love: Housework and the Law," *Northwestern University Law Review* 91 (1996): 1–86.
66. See R. C. J. Cocks, "Maine, Sir Henry James Sumner (1822–1888)," in *Oxford Dictionary of National Biography* (Oxford: Oxford University Press, 2004).
67. See Thomas A. J. McGinn, ed., *Obligations in Roman Law: Past, Present, and Future* (Ann Arbor: University of Michigan Press, 2012), 8; and Carla Masi Doria, "Status and Contract in Ancient Rome with Some Thoughts on the 'Future of Obligations,'" in McGinn, *Obligations,* 120–124. Masi Doria herself questions whether this is a return to "status" in the sense posited by Maine.
68. See Julia Stephens, *Governing Islam: Law, Empire, and Secularism in South Asia* (New York: Cambridge University Press, 2018), 57–104.
69. See Stephens, *Governing Islam*, 80.
70. See, for instance, Zareena Grewal, *Islam Is a Foreign Country: American Muslims and the Global Crisis of Authority* (New York: New York University Press, 2014), 204–205.The English-language Sufi website Muwasala, which disseminates Sufi guidance from the spiritual masters of Hadramawt, advises its readers, "Assisting the shaykh in implementing his objectives or assisting anyone in implementing any objective which is valid in the Shariah is a type of service. Any action which requires humility is more beneficial for the soul, such as cleaning, washing and cooking." Muwasala, "What are some of the etiquettes of service (khidmah)?," Facebook, January 2, 2018, https://www.facebook.com/Muwasala/posts/1938634152832659.
71. See Jeremy Walton, "The Institutions and Discourses of Hizmat, and Their Discontents," in *Hizmet Means Service: Perspectives on an Alternative Path Within Islam*, ed. by Martin E. Marty (Berkeley: University of California Press, 2015), 41–56, esp. 44–45; Zain Abdullah, *Black Mecca: The African Muslims of Harlem* (New York: Oxford University Press, 2010), 189–190; Rosemary Corbett, *Making Moderate Islam: Sufism, Service, and the "Ground Zero Mosque" Controversy* (Stanford, Calif.: Stanford University Press, 2016), 188; Mumtaz Ahmad, "Tablīghī Jamāʿat," *The Oxford Encyclopedia of the Islamic World*, ed. by John L. Esposito (New York: Oxford University Press, 1995), 4:165–169; Barbara Metcalf, "Islam and Women: The Case of the Tablighi Jama'at," *Stanford Humanities Review*, 5, no. 1 (1995): 51–59; Halkano Abdi Wario, "Reforming Men, Refining Umma: Tablīghī Jamāʿat and Novel Visions of Islamic Masculinity," *Religion and Gender* 2, no. 2 (2012): 246; and Arsalan Khan, "Pious Masculinity, Ethical Reflexivity, and Moral Order in an Islamic Piety Movement in Pakistan," *Anthropological Quarterly* 91 (2018): 60.
72. Ahmed, *Women and Gender in Islam*, 64.
73. On this theme see Ayubi, *Gendered Morality.*
74. Margrit Eichler and Patrizia Albanese, "What Is Household Work? A Critique of Assumptions Underlying Empirical Studies of Housework and an Alternative Approach," *Canadian Journal of Sociology/Cahiers canadiens de sociologie* 32, no. 2 (2007): 242.

Bibliography

Abbasi, Rushain. "Did Premodern Muslims Distinguish the Religious and Secular? The *Dīn-Dunyā* Binary in Medieval Islamic Thought." *Journal of Islamic Studies* 31, no. 2 (2020): 185–225.

Abdullah, Zain. *Black Mecca: The African Muslims of Harlem*. New York: Oxford University Press, 2010.

Abou-Bakr, Omaima. "Turning the Tables: Perspectives on the Construction of 'Muslim Manhood.'" *Journal of Women of the Middle East and the Islamic World* 11 (2003): 89–107.

Abou El Fadl, Khaled. *Rebellion and Violence in Islamic Law*. Cambridge: Cambridge University Press, 2001.

Abū Nuʿaym al-Iṣfahānī. *Ḥilyat al-awliyāʾ*. 10 vols. Beirut: Dār al-Fikr / Cairo: Maktabat al-Khānjī, AH 1416/1996 CE.

Abū Shāma al-Maqdisī, Shihāb al-Dīn ʿAbd al-Raḥmān ibn Ismāʿīl. *Tarājim rijāl al-qarnayn al-sādis waʾl-sābiʿ*. Cairo: Dār al-Kutub al-Malikīya, AH 1366/1947 CE.

Aceituno, Antonio Jurado. "La 'ḫidma' selyuqí: La red de relaciones de dependencia mutua, la dinámica del poder y las formas de obtención de los beneficios." Ph.D. diss., Universidad Autónoma, 1995.

Adamson, Peter. "Ethics in Philosophy." In *Encyclopaedia of Islam*, 3rd ed., ed. by Kate Fleet, Gudrun Krämer, Denis Matringe, John Nawas, and Everett Rowson. Leiden: Brill, 2007.

Adem, Rodrigo. "The Intellectual Genealogy of Ibn Taymīya." Ph.D. diss., University of Chicago, 2015.

al-Adhruʿī, Aḥmad ibn Ḥamdān. *Qūt al-muḥtāj fī sharḥ al-Minhāj*, ed. by ʿĪd Muḥammad ʿAbd al-Ḥamīd. 12 vols. Beirut: Dār al-Kutub al-ʿIlmīya, AH 1437/2015 CE.

Agrama, Hussein Ali. *Questioning Secularism: Islam, Sovereignty, and the Rule of Law in Egypt*. Chicago: University of Chicago Press, 2012.

Ahmad, Mumtaz. "Tablīghī Jamāʿat." *The Oxford Encyclopedia of the Islamic World*, ed. by John L. Esposito. New York: Oxford University Press, 1995.

Ahmed, Leila. *Women and Gender in Islam*. New Haven, Conn.: Yale University Press, 1992.

Ahmed, Shahab. *What Is Islam? The Importance of Being Islamic*. Princeton, N.J.: Princeton University Press, 2017.

Akasoy, Anna A., and Alexander Fidora, eds., *The Arabic Version of the "Nicomachean Ethics."* Trans. Douglas M. Dunlop. Leiden: Brill, 2005.

Akşit, Elif Ekin. "Fatma Aliye's Stories: Ottoman Marriages Beyond the Harem." *Journal of Family History* 25, no. 3 (2010): 207–218.

Āl Sayf, Abd Allāh b. Mubārak. "Idhā istaʾjara imraʾtahu li-raḍāʿ waladihi." Shabakat al-Alūka al-Sharʿīya. Accessed June 12, 2020. https://www.alukah.net/sharia/0/84431/.

Ali, Kecia. *Marriage and Slavery in Early Islam*. Cambridge, Mass.: Harvard University Press, 2010.

——. "Progressive Muslims and Islamic Jurisprudence." In *Progressive Muslims: On Justice, Gender, and Pluralism*, ed. Omid Safi, 163–189. Oxford: Oneworld, 2003.

al-ʿĀmirī, Muḥammad ibn Yūsuf. *Al-Saʿāda wa'l-isʿād fī al-sīra al-insānīya*. Ed. Aḥmad ʿAbd al-Ḥalīm ʿAṭīya. Cairo: Dār al-Thaqāfa li 'l-Nashr wa 'l-Tawzīʿ, [1991].

Anjum, Ovamir. *Politics, Law, and Community in Islamic Thought*. New York: Cambridge University Press, 2012.

Arabi, Oussama. "Contract Stipulations (*Shurūṭ*) in Islamic Law: The Ottoman *Majalla* and Ibn Taymiyya." *International Journal of Middle East Studies* 30 (1998): 29–50.

Arkoun, Mohammed. "L'Éthique musulmane d'après Māwardī." *Revue des Études Islamiques* 31 (1963): 1–31.

——. "Miskawayh." In *Encyclopaedia of Islam*, 2nd ed., ed by P. Bearman, Th. Bianquis, C. E. Bosworth, E. van Donzel, and W. P. Heinrichs. Leiden: Brill, 1960–2005.

Aristotle. *Nicomachean Ethics*. Trans. David Ross. New York: Oxford University Press, 2009.

Asad, Muhammad. *The Message of the Qurʾān*. Bristol, Engl.: Book Foundation, 2003.

Asad, Talal. *Formations of the Secular: Christianity, Islam, Modernity*. Stanford, Calif.: Stanford University Press, 2003.

——. *Genealogies of Religion: Discipline and Reasons of Power in Christianity and Islam*. Baltimore: Johns Hopkins University Press, 1993.

Ashtor, E. "Ḳuṭn." In *Encyclopaedia of Islam*, 2nd ed., ed. by P. Bearman, Th. Bianquis, C. E. Bosworth, E. van Donzel, and W. P. Heinrichs. Leiden: Brill, 1960–2005.

al-ʿAynī, Badr al-Dīn Maḥmūd ibn Aḥmad. *Al-Masāʾil al-badrīya al-muntakhaba min al-Fatāwā al-ẓahīrīya*. Ed. Sulaymān ibn ʿAbd Allāh ibn Ḥamūd Abā 'l-Khayl. 2 vols. Riyadh: Dār al-ʿĀṣima, AH 1435/2014 CE.

Ayubi, Zahra. *Gendered Morality: Classical Islamic Ethics of the Self, Family, and Society*. New York: Columbia University Press, 2019.

——. "Negotiating Justice: American Muslim Women Navigating Islamic Divorce and Civil Law." *Journal for Islamic Studies* 30 (2010): 78–102.

Azam, Hina. *Sexual Violation in Islamic Law: Substance, Evidence, and Procedure*. Cambridge: Cambridge University Press, 2015.

Badran, Margot. *Feminists, Islam and Nation*. Princeton, N.J.: Princeton University Press, 1994.

al-Baʿlī, ʿAlī ibn Muḥammad. *Al-Akhbār al-ʿilmīya min al-ikhtiyārāt al-fiqhīya li-shaykh al-islām Ibn Taymīya*. Ed. Aḥmad ibn Muḥammad ibn Ḥasan al-Khalīl. Riyadh: Dār al-ʿĀṣima, 1998.

al-Bājī, Sulaymān ibn Khalaf. *Al-Muntaqā sharḥ al-Muwaṭṭa.'* Ed. Muḥammad ʿAbd al-Qādir ʿAṭā. 9 vols. Beirut: Dār al-Kutub al-ʿIlmīya, AH 1420/1999 CE.

Banānī, Farīda. *Taqsīm al-ʿamal bayna al-zawjayn fī ḍawʾ al-qānūn al-maghribī wa al-fiqh al-islāmī, al-jins miʿyāran*. Marrakesh: Silsilat Manshūrāt Kullīyat al-ʿUlūm al-Qānūnīya wa'l-iqtiṣādīya wa'l-ijtimāʿīya, 1993.

Baron, Beth. *The Women's Awakening in Egypt: Culture, Society, and the Press*. New Haven, Conn.: Yale University Press, 1994.

Bashir, Shahzad. *Sufi Bodies: Religion and Society in Medieval Islam*. New York: Columbia University Press, 2011.

Bauer, Karen. *Gender Hierarchy in the Qurʾān: Medieval Interpretations, Modern Responses*. Cambridge: Cambridge University Press, 2015.

al-Bayhaqī, Abū Bakr Aḥmad ibn al-Ḥusayn. *Al-Madkhal ilā al-sunan al-kubrā*. Ed. Muḥammad Ḍiyāʾ al-Raḥmān al-Aʿẓamī al-Ṣabāḥīya. Kuwait: Dār al-Khulafāʾ li'l-Kitāb al-Islāmī, n.d.

———. *Al-Sunan al-kabīr*. 24 vols. Ed. ʿAbd Allāh ibn ʿAbd al-Muḥsin al-Turkī. Cairo: Markaz Hajar li-'l-Buḥūth wa 'l-Dirāsāt al-ʿArabīya wa 'l-Islāmīya, AH 1432/2011 CE.

Bonner, Michael. *Aristocratic Violence and Holy War: Studies in the Jihad and the Arab-Byzantine Frontier*. New Haven, Conn.: American Oriental Society, 1996.

———. "The *Kitāb al-kasb* Attributed to al-Shaybānī: Poverty, Surplus, and the Circulation of Wealth." *Journal of the American Oriental Society* 121, no. 3 (2001): 410–427.

Bori, Caterina. "Ibn Taymiyya (14th to 17th Century): Transregional Spaces of Reading and Reception." *Muslim World* 108 (2018): 87–123.

———. "Ibn Taymiyya *wa-Jamāʿatuhu*. Authority, Conflict and Consensus in Ibn Taymiyya's Circle." In *Ibn Taymiyya and His* Times, ed. by Yossef Rapoport and Shahab Ahmed, 24–52. Princeton, N.J.: Princeton University Press, 2010.

———. "One or Two Versions of al-Siyāsa al-Sharʿiyya of Ibn Taymiyya? What Do They Tell Us?" ASK Working Paper 26. Bonn, December 2016.

Bosanquet, Antonia. *Minding Their Place: Space and Religious Hierarchy in Ibn al-Qayyim's* Aḥkām ahl al-dhimma. Leiden: Brill, 2020.

Bosworth, C. E. "Mā Warāʾ al-Nahr." In *Encyclopaedia of Islam*, 2nd ed., ed. by P. Bearman, Th. Bianquis, C. E. Bosworth, E. van Donzel, and W. P. Heinrichs. Leiden: Brill, 1960–2005.

Böwering, Gerhardt. "Al-Sulamī." In *Encyclopaedia of Islam*, 2nd ed. ed. by P. Bearman, Th. Bianquis, C. E. Bosworth, E. van Donzel, and W. P. Heinrichs. Leiden: Brill, 1960–2005.

Brockopp, Jonathan E. *Early Mālikī Law: Ibn ʿAbd Al-Hakam and His Major Compendium of Jurisprudence*. Leiden: Brill, 2000.

———. "Saḥnūn ibn Saʿīd (d. 240/854)." In *Islamic Legal Thought: A Compendium of Muslim Jurists*, ed. by David Powers, Oussama Arabi, and Susan Spectorsky, 65–84. Leiden: Brill, 2013.

———. "Saḥnūn's *Mudawwana* and the Piety of the '*Sharīʿah*-minded.'" In *Islamic Law in Theory: Studies in Jurisprudence in Honor of Bernard* Weiss, ed. by A. Kevin Reinhart and Robert Gleave, 129–141. Leiden: Brill, 2014.

Brown, Jonathan A. C. *Hadith: Muhammad's Legacy in the Medieval and Modern World*. Oxford: Oneworld, 2009.

Brunschvig, Robert. "Métiers vils en Islam." *Studia Islamica* 16 (1962): 41–60.

[al-Bukhārī, Muḥammad ibn Ismāʿīl]. *Ṣaḥīḥ al-Bukhārī*. 3 vols. Vaduz, Liecht.: Thesaurus Islamicus Foundation, 2000.

al-Bukhārī, Ṭāhir ibn Aḥmad. *Al-Khulāṣa*. ms. al-Maktaba al-Azharīya, khāṣṣ 1950. ʿāmm 26789. https://www.alukah.net/sharia/0/78944/.

Burger, Glenn D. *Conduct Becoming: Good Wives and Husbands in the Later Middle Ages*. Philadelphia: University of Pennsylvania Press, 2018.

al-Burzulī, Abū'l-Qāsim ibn Aḥmad al-Balawī. *Fatāwā al-Burzulī: Jāmiʿ masāʾil al-aḥkām li-mā nazala min al-qaḍāyā bi'l-muftīn wa'l-ḥukkām*. 7 vols. Ed. Muḥammad al-Ḥabīb al-Hīla. Beirut: Dār al-Gharb al-Islāmī, 2002.

Calder, Norman. "Al-Sarakhsī." In *Encyclopaedia of Islam*, 2nd ed. ed. by P. Bearman, Th. Bianquis, C. E. Bosworth, E. van Donzel, and W. P. Heinrichs. Leiden: Brill, 1960–2005.

Chamberlain, Michael. *Knowledge and Practice in Medieval Damascus, 1190–1350*. Cambridge: Cambridge University Press, 1994.

Cheema, Waqar Akbar. "Al-Jāmi' of Ma'mar bin Rāshid: Extinct or Extant?" *Journal of Islamic Sciences* 3, no. 1 (2015): 9–14.

Clark, Gillian. *Women in Late Antiquity: Pagan and Christian Life-Styles*. Oxford: Clarendon, 1993.

Cocks, R. C. J. "Maine, Sir Henry James Sumner (1822–1888)." In *Oxford Dictionary of National Biography*. Oxford: Oxford University Press, 2004.

Cook, Michael. *Commanding Right and Forbidding Wrong in Islamic Thought*. Cambridge: Cambridge University Press, 2000.

Corbett, Rosemary. *Making Moderate Islam: Sufism, Service, and the "Ground Zero Mosque" Controversy*. Stanford, Calif.: Stanford University Press, 2016.

Cornell, Vincent. *Realm of the Saint: Power and Authority in Moroccan Sufism*. Austin: University of Texas Press, 1998.

Cuno, Kenneth. *Modernizing Marriage: Family, Ideology, and Law in Nineteenth- and Early Twentieth-Century Egypt*. New York: Syracuse University Press, 2015.

Dakake, Maria. " 'Guest of the Innermost Heart': Conceptions of the Divine Beloved Among Early Sufi Women." *Comparative Islamic Studies* 3, no. 1 (2007): 72–97.

al-Daylamī, Abū Shujāʿ Shīrawayh. *Al-Firdaws bi-maʾthūr al-khiṭāb*. 6 vols. Ed. Al-Saʿīd ibn Basyūnī Zaghlūl. Beirut: Dār al-Kutub al-ʿIlmīya, AH 1406/1986 CE.

Deeb, Lara, and Mona Harb. *Leisurely Islam: Negotiating Geography and Morality in Shi'ite South Beirut*. Princeton, N.J.: Princeton University Press, 2013.

de la Puente, Christina. "Slaves in Al-Andalus through Mālikī *Wathāʾiq* Works (4th–6th Centuries H/10th–12th Centuries CE): Marriage and Slavery as Factors of Social Categorisation." *Annales Islamologiques* 42 (2008): 187–212.

Denny, Frederick. "Circumcision." In *Encyclopaedia of the Qur'an*, ed. by Jane Dammen McAuliffe. Leiden: Brill, 2001–2006.

al-Dhahabī, Shams al-Dīn. *Siyar aʿlām al-nubalāʾ*, ed. by Shuʿayb al-Arnaʾūṭ. 29 vols. Ed. Ḥusayn al-Asad. Beirut: Muʾassasat al-Risāla, AH 1417/1996 CE.

Doria, Carla Masi. "Status and Contract in Ancient Rome with Some Thoughts on the 'Future of Obligations.' " In *Obligations in Roman Law: Past, Present, and Future*, ed. by Thomas A. J. McGinn, 102–130. Ann Arbor: University of Michigan Press, 2012.

Eaton, Richard Maxwell. *Sufis of Bijapur, 1300–1700: Social Roles of Sufis in Medieval India*. Princeton, N.J.: Princeton University Press, 1978.

Eichler, Margrit, and Patrizia Albanese. "What Is Household Work? A Critique of Assumptions Underlying Empirical Studies of Housework and an Alternative Approach." *Canadian Journal of Sociology/Cahiers canadiens de sociologie* 32, no. (2007): 227–258.

El-Gamal, Mahmoud A. *Islamic Finance: Law, Economics, and Practice*. Cambridge: Cambridge University Press, 2006.

Elsadda, Hoda. "Gendered Citizenship: Discourses on Domesticity in the Second Half of the Nineteenth Century." *Hawwa* 4, no. 1 (2006): 1–28.

El Shamsy, Ahmed. *The Canonization of Islamic Law: A Social and Intellectual History*. Cambridge: Cambridge University Press, 2013.

——. *Rediscovering the Islamic Classics: How Editors and Print Culture Transformed an Intellectual Tradition*. Princeton, N.J.: Princeton University Press, 2020.

Essid, Yassine. *A Critique of the Origins of Islamic Economic Thought*. Leiden: Brill, 1995.

Fahmy, Khaled. *In Quest of Justice: Islamic Law and Forensic Medicine in Modern Egypt*. Oakland: University of California Press, 2018.

Farès, B. "Murūʾa." In *Encyclopaedia of Islam*, 2nd ed., ed. by P. Bearman, Th. Bianquis, C. E. Bosworth, E. van Donzel, and W. P. Heinrichs. Leiden: Brill, 1960–2005.

al-Fārisī, ʿAbd al-Ghāfir ibn Ismāʿīl. *Al-Muntakhab min al-Siyāq li-taʾrīkh Naysābūr*. Ed. Muḥammad Aḥmad ʿAbd al-ʿAzīz. Beirut: Dār al-Kutub al-ʿIlmīya, AH 1409/1989 CE.

al-Farrāʾ, al-Qādī Abū Yaʿlā Muḥammad ibn al-Ḥusayn. *Al-Jāmiʿ al-ṣaghīr fi'l-fiqh ʿalā madhhab al-imām Aḥmad ibn Muḥammad ibn Ḥanbal*. Ed. Nāṣir ibn Suʿūd ibn 'Abd Allāh al-Salāma. Riyadh: Dar Aṭlas li'l-Nashr wa'l-Tawzīʿ, AH 1421/2000 CE.

——. *Sharḥ Mukhtaṣar al-Khiraqī*. 2 vols. Ed. Nāṣir ibn Suʿūd ibn ʿAbd Allāh al-Salāma. Riyadh: Dār Aṭlas al-Khaḍrāʾ, AH 1439/2018 CE.

Fawwāz, Zaynab bint ʿAlī. *Al-Durr al-manthūr fī ṭabaqāt rabbāt al-khudūr*. 2 vols. Ed. Muḥammad Amīn Ḍannāwī. Beirut: Dār al-Kutub al-ʿIlmīya, AH 1420/1999 CE.

Findley, Carter Vaughn. "Fatma Aliye: First Ottoman Woman Novelist, Pioneer Feminist." In *Histoire Économique et Sociale de l'Empire Ottoman et de la Turquie (1326–1960): Actes du Sixième Congrès International Tenu à Aix-en-Provence du 1er au 4 Juillet 1992*, ed. by D. Panzac, 783–794. Paris: Peeters, 1995.

——. "La soumise, la subversive: Fatma Aliye, romancière et féministe." *Turcica* 27 (1995): 153–176.

Flather, Amanda J. "Space, Place, and Gender: The Sexual and Spatial Division of Labor in the Early Modern Household." *History and Theory* 52 (October 2013): 344–360.

Fodio, ʿUthmān dan. *Nūr al-albāb*. In *Nigerian Perspectives: A Historical Anthology*, 2nd ed., ed. by Thomas Hodgkin, 254–255. Oxford: Oxford University Press, 1975.

al-Ghazālī, Abū Ḥāmid. *Iḥyāʾ ʿulūm al-dīn*. 5 vols. Beirut: Dār al-Fikr, AH 1414/1994 CE.

——. *Al-Wajīz fī fiqh al-imām al-Shāfiʿī*. 2 vols. Ed. ʿAlī Muʿawwaḍ and ʿĀdil ʿAbd al-Mawjūd. Beirut: Dār al-Arqam ibn Abī al-Arqam, AH 1418/1997 CE.

——. *Al-Wasīṭ fī al-madhhab*. 7 vols. Ed. Muḥammad Muḥammad Tāmir. Cairo: Dār al-Salām, AH 1417/1997 CE.

Giladi, Avner. *Infants, Parent and Wet Nurses: Medieval Islamic Views on Breastfeeding and Their Social Implications*. Leiden: Brill, 1999.
——. *Muslim Midwives: The Craft of Birthing in the Premodern Middle East*. Cambridge: Cambridge University Press, 2015.
Gobillot, Geneviève. "Celibacy." In *Encyclopaedia of Islam*, 3rd ed., ed. by Kate Fleet, Gudrun Krämer, Denis Matringe, John Nawas, and Everett Rowson. Leiden: Brill, 2007.
Goichon, A. M. "Ibn Sīnā." In *Encyclopaedia of Islam*, 2nd ed., ed. by P. Bearman, Th. Bianquis, C. E. Bosworth, E. van Donzel, and W. P. Heinrichs. Leiden: Brill, 1960–2005.
Goldberg, J. P. "Life and Death: The Ages of Man." In *A Social History of England: 1200–1500*, ed. by Rosemary Horrox and W. Mark Ormrod, 413–434. Cambridge: Cambridge University Press, 2006.
Graham, Terry. "Abū Saʿīd Ibn Abī'l-Khayr and the School of Khurāsān." In *The Heritage of Sufism*, vol. 1: *Classical Persian Sufism from Its Origins to Rumi (700–1300)*, ed. Leonard Lewisohn, 83–135. Oxford: Oneworld, 1999.
Green, Nile. *Sufism: A Global History*. Chichester, U.K.: Wiley-Blackwell, 2012.
Grewal, Zareena. *Islam Is a Foreign Country: American Muslims and the Global Crisis of Authority*. New York: New York University Press, 2014.
Gutas, Dimitri. *Greek Thought, Arabic Culture: The Graeco-Arabic Translation Movement in Baghdad and Early ʿAbbāsid Society (2nd–4th/8th–10th Centuries)*. London: Routledge, 1998.
Guthrie, Shirley. *Arab Women in the Middle Ages: Private Lives and Public Roles*. London: Saqi Books, 2001.
Haj, Samira. *Reconfiguring Islamic Tradition: Reform, Rationality, and Modernity*. Stanford, Calif.: Stanford University Press, 2008.
al-Ḥākim al-Naysābūrī, Muḥammad ibn ʿAbd Allāh. *Al-Mustadrak ʿalā al-Ṣaḥīḥayn*. 5 vols. Ed. Muṣṭafā ʿAbd al-Qādir ʿAṭā. Beirut: Dār al-Kutub al-ʿIlmīya, AH 1422/2002 CE.
Halevi, Leor. *Muhammad's Grave: Death Rites and the Making of Islamic Society*. New York: Columbia University Press, 2007.
Halim, Fachrizal A. *Legal Authority in Premodern Islam: Yaḥyā ibn Sharaf al-Nawawī in the Shāfiʿī School of Law*. London: Routledge, 2015.
Hallaq, Wael B. *Authority, Continuity, and Change in Islamic Law*. Cambridge: Cambridge University Press, 2005.
——. *A History of Islamic Legal Theories*. Cambridge: Cambridge University Press, 1997.
——. *The Impossible State: Islam, Politics, and Modernity's Moral Predicament*. New York: Columbia University Press, 2013.
——. *Sharīʿa: Theory, Practice, Transformations*. Cambridge: Cambridge University Press, 2009.
Halley, Janet. "What Is Family Law? A Genealogy, Part I." *Yale Journal of Law & the Humanities* 23, no. 1 (2011): 1–109.
al-Hamadhānī, Abū al-Faḍl Aḥmad ibn al-Ḥusayn. *Maqāmāt Badīʿ al-Zamān al-Hamadhānī*. Ed. Muḥammad ʿAbduh. Beirut: Dār al-Kutub al-ʿIlmīya, AH 1426/2005 CE.
Hassan, Mona. *Longing for the Lost Caliphate: A Transregional History*. Princeton, N.J.: Princeton University Press, 2017.

——. "Modern Interpretations and Misinterpretations of a Medieval Scholar: Apprehending the Political Thought of Ibn Taymiyya." In *Ibn Taymiyya and His Times*, ed. by Yossef Rapoport and Shahab Ahmed, 338–366. Oxford: Oxford University Press, 2010.

Heffening, W., and G. Endress, "Tadbīr al-manzil." In *Encyclopaedia of Islam*, 2nd ed., ed. by P. Bearman, Th. Bianquis, C. E. Bosworth, E. van Donzel, and W. P. Heinrichs. Leiden: Brill, 1960–2005.

Hefner, Robert W. "Shari'a Law and the Quest for a Modern Muslim Ethics." In *Shari'a Law and Modern Muslim Ethics*, ed. by Robert W. Hefner, 1–34. Bloomington: Indiana University Press, 2016.

Hennigan, Peter C. "Al-Khaṣṣāf (D. 261/874)." In *Islamic Legal Thought: A Compendium of Muslim Jurists*, ed. by David Powers, 107–110. Leiden: Brill, 2013.

al-Hibri, Azizah Y. "An Introduction to Muslim Women's Rights." In *Windows of Faith: Muslim Women Scholar-Activists in North* America, ed. by Gisela Webb. Syracuse, N.Y.: Syracuse University Press, 2000. 51–71.

Hidayatullah, Aysha. *Feminist Edges of the Qur'an*. Oxford: Oxford University Press, 2014.

al-Ḥimyarī, ʿAbd Allāh ibn Jaʿfar. *Qurb al-isnād*. Beirut: Muʾassasat Āl al-Bayt li-Iḥyāʾ al-Turāth, AH 1413/1993 CE.

al-Ḥimyarī, Muḥammad ibn Muḥammad ibn ʿAbd al-Munʿim. *Al-Ḥāwī jumalan min al-fatāwī*. Ed. by Muṣṭafā Maḥmūd ʿAlī Shaḥāta. Damascus: Dār al-ʿAṣmāʾ, 1441/2020.

Hinz, W. "Farsakh." In *Encyclopaedia of Islam*, 2nd ed. Ed. by P. Bearman, Th. Bianquis, C. E. Bosworth, E. van Donzel, and W. P. Heinrichs. Leiden: Brill, 1960–2005.

Hoover, John. "Fiṭra." In *Encyclopaedia of Islam*, 3rd ed., ed. by Kate Fleet, Gudrun Krämer, Denis Matringe, John Nawas, and Everett Rowson. Leiden: Brill, 2007.

——. *Ibn Taymiyya*. London: Oneworld Academic, 2019.

al-Ḥubayshī, Abū ʿAbd Allāh Muḥammad ibn ʿAbd al-Raḥmān al-Waṣṣābī. *Al-Baraka fī faḍl al-saʿy wa'l-ḥaraka*. n.p., n.d.

Hurvitz, Nimrod. *The Formation of Hanbalism: Piety into Power*. London: Routledge, 2002.

Ḥusayn, Ṭahā, and Ibrāhīm al-Abyārī. *Sharḥ Luzūm mā lā yalzam*. Vol. 1. Cairo: Dār al-Maʿārif, n.d.

Ibn ʿAbd al-Ḥakam, ʿAbd Allāh. *Al-Mukhtaṣar al-kabīr*. Ed. Aḥmad ibn ʿAbd al-Karīm Najīb. Dublin: Manshūrāt Markaz Najībawayh, AH 1432/2011 CE.

——. *Sīrat ʿUmar ibn ʿAbd al-ʿAzīz*. Ed. Aḥmad ʿUbayd. n.p.: ʿĀlam al-Kutub, AH 1404/1984 CE.

Ibn Abī'l-Dunyā, Abū Bakr ʿAbd Allāh ibn Muḥammad. *Kitāb al-ʿiyāl*. 2 vols. Ed. Najam ʿAbd al-Raḥmān Khalaf. Al-Dammām: Dār Ibn al-Qayyim, AH 1410/1990 CE.

——. *Kitāb Mujābū al-daʿwa*. In *Majmūʿat rasāʾil Ibn Abī al-Dunyā*, vol. 4, ed. by Ziyād Ḥamdān, 1–88. Beirut: Muʾassasat al-Kutub al-Thaqāfīya, AH 1414/1993 CE.

——. *Kitāb al-Qanāʿa wa'l-taʿaffuf*. In *Majmūʿat rasāʾil Ibn Abī al-Dunyā*, vol. 1, ed. by Muṣṭafā ʿAbd al-Qādir ʿAṭā, 1–80. Beirut: Muʾassasat al-Kutub al-Thaqāfīya, AH 1413/1993 CE.

——. *Kitāb al-Tahajjud wa-qiyām al-layl*. Ed. Musʿad ʿAbd al-Ḥamīd al-Saʿdanī. Cairo: Maktabat al-Qurʾān, n.d.

——. *Kitāb al-Zuhd*. Beirut: Dār Ibn Kathīr, AH 1420/1999 CE.

Ibn Abī Shayba. *Muṣannaf Ibn Abī Shayba*. 9 vols. Ed. Saʿīd al-Laḥḥām. Beirut: Dār al-Fikr, AH 1428–1429/2008 CE.

Ibn al-ʿAdīm. *Bughyat al-ṭalab fī taʾrīkh Ḥalab*. 11 vols. Ed. Suhayl Zakkār. Beirut: [Dār al-Fikr], 1988.

Ibn al-ʿAṭṭār, Muḥammad ibn Aḥmad al-Umawī. *Kitāb al-Wathāʾiq wa'l-sijillāt*. Eds. P. Chalmeta and F. Corriente. Madrid: Academia Matritense del Notariado Instituto Hipano-Árabe de Cultura, 1983.

Ibn Baṭṭāl, ʿAlī ibn Khalaf ibn ʿAbd al-Malik. *Sharḥ Ibn Baṭṭāl ʿalā Ṣaḥīḥ al-Bukhārī*. 10 vols. Ed. Muṣṭafā ʿAbd al-Qādir ʿAṭā. Beirut: Dār al-Kutub al-ʿIlmīya, AH 1424/2003 CE.

Ibn Ḥabīb, ʿAbd al-Malik. *Kitāb Adab al-nisāʾ al-marsūm bi-Kitāb al-Ghāya wa'l-nihāya*. Ed. ʿAbd al-Majīd Turkī. Beirut: Dār al-Gharb al-Islāmī, AH 1412/1992 CE.

Ibn Ḥanbal, Aḥmad. *Musnad al-Imām Aḥmad Ibn Ḥanbal*. 52 vols. Ed. Shuʿayb al-Aranaʾūṭ. Beirut: Mu'assasat al-Risāla, AH 1421/2001 CE.

——. *Al-Zuhd*. Ed. Muḥammad ʿAbd al-Salām Shāhīn. Beirut: Dār al-Kutub al-ʿIlmīya, AH 1420/1999 CE.

Ibn Ḥazm, ʿAlī ibn Aḥmad. *Al-Muḥallā bi'l-āthār*. Ed. ʿAbd al-Ghaffār Sulaymān al-Bindārī. Beirut: Dār al-Kutub al-ʿIlmīya, AH 1425/2003 CE.

Ibn Hudhayl, ʿAlī ibn ʿAbd al-Raḥmān.*ʿAyn al-adab wa'l-siyāsa*. Cairo: Al-Maṭbaʿa al-Iʿlāmīya, AH 1302/[1884–1885] CE.

Ibn al-Humām, Muḥammad ibn ʿAbd al-Wāḥid al-Sīwāsī. *Sharḥ Fatḥ al-qadīr*. 10 vols. Ed. ʿAbd al-Razzāq Ghālib al-Mahdī. Beirut: Dār al-Kutub al-ʿIlmīya, AH 1424/2003 CE.

Ibn Jabrīn, Shaykh ʿAbd Allāh. "Wujūb khidmat al-marʾa zawjahā." Saaid. Accessed May 29, 2020. http://www.saaid.net/Doat/ehsan/141.htm.

Ibn al-Jawzī, Abū al-Faraj. *Ṣayd al-khāṭir*. Ed. ʿAbd al-Qādir Aḥmad ʿAṭā. Beirut: Dār al-Kutub al-ʿilmīya, AH 1412/1992 CE.

——. *Ṣifat al-ṣafwa*. Ed. Khālid Ṭarṭūsī. Beirut: Dar al-Kitāb al-ʿArabī, AH 1433/2012 CE.

Ibn al-Jazarī, Muḥammad ibn Ibrāhīm. *Taʾrīkh ḥawādith al-zamān wa-anbāʾihi wa-wafayāt al-akābir wa-l'-aʿyān min abnāʾihi al-maʿrūf bi-Taʾrīkh Ibn al-Jazarī*. Ed. ʿUmar ʿAbd al-Salām Tadmurī. 3 vols. Ṣaydā, Beirut: Al-Maktaba al-ʿAṣrīya, AH 1419/1998 CE.

Ibn Juzayy, Muḥammad ibn Aḥmad. *Al-Qawānīn al-fiqhīya*. Ed. Muḥammad Mawhūb ibn Ḥusayn. ʿAyn Malīla, Algeria: Dār al-Hudā, 2000.

[Ibn Māja, Muḥammad ibn Yazīd]. *Sunan Ibn Māja*. Vaduz, Liecht.: Thesaurus Islamicus Foundation, 2000.

Ibn Manẓūr. *Lisān al-ʿarab*. 15 vols. Beirut: Dār Ṣādir, AH 1410/1990 CE.

Ibn al-Marzubān, Muḥammad ibn Khalaf. *Al-Murūʾa*. Ed. Muḥammad Khayr Ramaḍān Yūsuf. Beirut: Dār Ibn Ḥazm, AH 1420/1999 CE.

Ibn Māza, Maḥmūd ibn Aḥmad. *Al-Muḥīṭ al-burhānī fī al-fiqh al-nuʿmānī*. Ed. ʿAbd al-Karīm Sāmī al-Jundī. Beirut: Dār al-Kutub al-ʿIlmīya, AH 1424/2004 CE.

Ibn al-Mubārak, ʿAbd Allāh. *Kitāb al-Jihād*. Ed. Nazīh Ḥammād. Jedda: Dār al-Maṭbūʿāt al-ḥadītha, n.d.

——. *Kitāb al-Zuhd wa-yalīhi Kitāb al-Raqāʾiq*. Ed. Ḥabīb al-Raḥmān al-Aʿẓamī. Beirut: Dār al-Kutub al-ʿIlmīya, AH 1425/2004 CE.

Ibn Mufliḥ, Muḥammad Shams al-Dīn. *Kitāb al-furūʿ*. 12 vols. Ed. ʿAbd Allāh b. ʿAbd al-Muḥsīn al-Turkī. Beirut: Muʾassasat al-Risāla / Riyadh: Dār al-Muʾayyad, AH 1424/2003 CE.

Ibn Muḥammad, Abū ʿAlī Aḥmad "Miskawayh." *Tahdhīb al-akhlāq wa-taṭhīr al-aʿrāq*. Beirut: Manshūrāt Dār Maktabat al-Ḥayāt, n.d.
Ibn al-Mulaqqin, ʿUmar Ibn ʿAlī. *Mukhtaṣar istidrāk al-ḥāfiẓ al-Dhahabī ʿalā Mustadrak Abī ʿAbd Allāh al-Ḥākim*. 8 vols. Ed. ʿAbd Allāh ibn Ḥamd al-Luḥaydān and Saʿd ibn ʿAbd Allāh Āl Ḥamayyid. Riyadh: Dār al-ʿĀṣima, AH 1411.
Ibn al-Mundhir, Abū Bakr Muḥammad ibn Ibrāhīm. *Al-Iqnāʿ*. 2 vols. Ed. ʿAbd Allāh ibn ʿAbd al-ʿAzīz al-Jabrīn. Riyadh: Maṭābiʿ al-Farazdaq al-Tijārīya, AH 1408.
——. *Al-Ishrāf ʿalā madhāhib al-ʿulamāʾ*. 10 vols. Ed. Abū Ḥammād Ṣaghīr Aḥmad al-Anṣārī. Raʾs al-Khayma: Maktabat Makka al-Thaqāfīya, AH 1426/2005 CE.
Ibn Nujaym, Zayn al-Dīn. *Al-Baḥr al-rāʾiq sharḥ Kanz al-daqāʾiq*. 9 vols. Ed. Zakarīyā ʿUmayrāt. Beirut: Dār al-Kutub al-ʿIlmīya, AH 1418/1997 CE.
Ibn Qayyim al-Jawzīya, Muḥammad ibn Abī Bakr. *Ighāthat al-lahfān fī maṣāyid al-shayṭān*. Ed. Muḥammad ʿUzayr Shams. Dār ʿĀlam al-Fawāʾid, n.d.
——. *Iʿlām al-muwaqqiʿīn ʿan rabb al-ʿālamīn*. 4 vols. Ed. Muḥammad ʿAbd al-Salām Ibrāhīm. Beirut: Dār al-Kutub al-ʿIlmīya, AH 1417/1996 CE.
——. *Rawḍat al-muḥibbīn wa-nuzhat al-mushtāqīn*. Ed. Muḥammad ʿUzayr Shams. Jedda: Majmaʿ al-Fiqh al-Islāmī, n.d.
——. *Zād al-maʿād fī hady khayr al-ʿibād*. 5 vols. in 9. Ed. Muḥammad al-Anwar Aḥmad al-Baltājī. Ṣaydā, Beirut: Al-Maktaba al-ʿAṣrīya, AH 1428/2007 CE.
Ibn Qudāma, Muwaffaq al-Dīn ʿAbd Allāh ibn Aḥmad. *Al-Mughnī*. 15 vols. Beirut: Dār al-Kutub al-ʿIlmīya, 2009.
——. *Al-Muqniʿ*. 32 vols. Ed. ʿAbd Allāh ibn ʿAbd al-Muḥsin al-Turkī. Giza: Hajar, AH 1415/1995 CE.
Ibn Qudāma al-Maqdisī, Shams al-Dīn ʿAbd al-Raḥmān ibn Muḥammad. *Al-Sharḥ al-kabīr*. Published with Muwaffaq al-Dīn ibn Qudāma, *Al-Muqniʿ*. 32 vols. Ed. ʿAbd Allāh ibn ʿAbd al-Muḥsin al-Turkī. Giza: Hajar, AH 1415/1995 CE.
Ibn Rāshid, Maʿmar. *The Expeditions: An Early Biography of Muhammad*. Trans. Sean Anthony. New York: New York University Press, 2015.
Ibn al-Rifʿa, Najm al-Dīn Aḥmad ibn Muḥammad. *Kifāyat al-nabīh sharḥ al-Tanbīh fī fiqh al-imām al-Shāfiʿī*. 21 vols. Ed Majdī Muḥammad Surūr Bāssalūm. Beirut: Dār al-Kutub al-ʿIlmīya, 2009.
Ibn Rushd, Abū'l-Walīd al-Qurṭubī. *Al-Bayān wa'l-taḥṣīl wa'l-sharḥ wa'l-tawjīh wa'l-taʿlīl fī masāʾil al-Mustakhraja*. 20 vols. Ed. Muḥammad Ḥijjī. Beirut: Dār al-Gharb al-Islāmī, AH 1408/1988 CE.
——. *Al-Muqaddamāt al-mumahhadāt*. 3 vols. Ed. Muḥammad Ḥijjī. Beirut: Dār al-Gharb al-Islāmī, AH 1408/1988 CE.
Ibn Saʿd. *Al-Ṭabaqāt al-kubrā*. 8 vols in 4. Beirut: Dār Iḥyāʾ al-Turāth al-ʿArabī, n.d.
Ibn Saḥnūn, Muḥammad ibn ʿAbd al-Salām ibn Saʿīd al-Tanūkhī. *Fatāwā Ibn Saḥnūn*. Ed. Muṣṭafā Maḥmūd al-Azharī. Riyadh: Dār Ibn al-Qayyim li'l-Nashr wa'l-Tawzīʿ/ Cairo: Dār Ibn ʿAffān, AH 1432/2011 CE.
Ibn Sīnā, Abū ʿAlī. *Kitāb al-Siyāsa*. Ed. ʿAlī Muḥammad Isbar. Jableh, Syria: Bidāyāt, 2007.
Ibn al-Sirrī, Hannād. *Kitāb al-Zuhd*. Ed. ʿAbd al-Raḥmān ʿAbd al-Jabbār al-Faryawāʾī. Al-Ṣabāḥīya: Dār al-Khulafāʾ li'l-Kitāb al-Islāmī, AH 1406/1985 CE.
Ibn Taymīya, Majd al-Dīn Abū'l-Barakāt. *Al-Muḥarrar fī al-fiqh ʿalā madhhab al-imām Ahmad ibn Hanbal*. 2 vols. [Cairo]: Maṭbaʿat al-Sunna al-Muḥammadīya, AH 1369/1950 CE.

Ibn Taymīya, Taqī al-Dīn Aḥmad ibn ʿAbd al-Ḥalīm. *Bayān al-dalīl ʿalā buṭlān al-taḥlīl.* Ed. Ḥamdī ʿAbd al-Majīd al-Silafī. Beirut: Al-Maktab al-Islāmī, AH 1418/1998 CE.

——. *Al-Jawāb al-ṣaḥīḥ li-man baddala dīn al-masīḥ.* 7 vols. Ed. ʿAlī ibn Ḥasan ibn Nāṣir, ʿAbd al-ʿAzīz ibn Ibrāhīm al-ʿAskar and Ḥamdān ibn Muḥammad al-Ḥamdān. Riyadh: Dār al-ʿĀṣima, AH 1419/1999 CE.

——. *Majmūʿ al-fatāwā.* 37 vols in 21. Ed. Muṣṭafā ʿAbd al-Qādir ʿAṭā. Beirut: Dār al-Kutub al-ʿIlmīya, AH 1421/2000 CE.

——. *Al-Siyāsa al-sharʿīya fī iṣlāḥ al-rāʿī wa al-raʿīya.* Ed. ʿAlī ibn Muḥammad al-ʿImrān. Mecca: Dār ʿĀlam al-Fawāʾid, AH 1329.

Ibn al-Zayyāt, Yūsuf ibn Yaḥyā al-Tādilī. *Al-Tashawwuf ilā rijāl al-taṣawwuf.* 2nd ed. Ed. Aḥmad al-Tawfīq. Rabat: Kullīyat al-Ādāb, 1997.

al-ʿIrāqī, Zayn al-Dīn ʿAbd al-Raḥīm ibn al-Ḥusayn, and Abū Zurʿa al-ʿIrāqī, *Tarḥ al-tathrīb fī sharḥ al-Taqrīb.* Beirut: Dār Iḥyāʾ al-Turāth al-ʿArabī, n.d.

ʿIyāḍ ibn Mūsā al-Yaḥṣubī, al-Qāḍī. *Ikmāl al-muʿlim bi-fawāʾid Muslim.* 9 vols. Ed. Yaḥyā Ismāʿīl. al-Manṣūra: Dār al-Wafāʾ, AH 1419/1998 CE.

——. *Madhāhib al-ḥukkām fī nawāzil al-aḥkām li'l-qāḍi ʿIyāḍ wa-waladihi Muḥammad.* Ed. Muḥammad ibn Sharīfa. Beirut: Dār al-Gharb al-Islāmī, 1990.

——. *Al-Tanbīhāt al-mustanbaṭa ʿalā'l-kutub al-Mudawwana wa'l-Mukhtaliṭa.* 4 vols. Ed. Muḥammad al-Wathīq. Beirut: Dār Ibn Ḥazm, AH 1432/2011 CE.

——. *Tartīb al-madārik wa-taqrīb al-masālik li-maʿrifat aʿlām madhhab Mālik.* 8 vols. Rabat: Wizārat al-Awqāf wa'l-Shuʾūn al-Islāmīya, AH 1403/1983 CE.

Izutsu, Toshihiko. *Ethico-Religious Concepts in the Qurʾān.* Montreal: McGill-Queen's University Press, 2002.

Jabr, Saʿdī Ḥusayn ʿAlī. *Fiqh al-imām Abī Thawr.* Beirut: Muʾassasat al-Risāla / Amman: Dār al-Furqān, AH 1403/1983 CE.

Jamil, Nadia. *Ethics and Poetry in Sixth Century Arabia.* Cambridge: Gibb Memorial Trust, 2017.

Johansen, Baber. "Die sündige, gesunde Amme: Moral und gesetzliche Bestimmung (*hukm*) im islamischen Recht." In *Contingency in a Sacred Law: Legal and Ethical Norms in the Muslim Fiqh*, 172–188. Leiden: Brill, 1999.

——. "The Muslim *Fiqh* as a Sacred Law: Religion, Law and Ethics in a Normative System." In *Contingency in a Sacred Law: Legal and Ethical Norms in the Muslim Fiqh*, 1–76. Leiden: Brill, 1999.

——. "Secular and Religious Elements in Hanafite Law: Function and Limits of the Absolute Character of Government Authority." In *Contingency in a Sacred Law: Legal and Ethical Norms in the Muslim Fiqh*, 189–218. Leiden: Brill, 1999.

——. "The Valorization of the Human Body in Muslim Sunni Law." *Princeton Papers: Interdisciplinary Journal of Middle Eastern Studies 4* (1996): 71–112.

al-Juwaynī, ʿAbd al-Malik ibn ʿAbd Allāh. *Nihāyat al-maṭlab fī dirāyat al-madhhab.* 20 vols. Ed. ʿAbd al-ʿAẓīm Maḥmūd al-Dīb. Jadda: Dār al-Minhāj, AH 1428/2007 CE.

al-Kalwadhānī, Abū'l-Khaṭṭāb Maḥfūẓ b. Aḥmad. *Al-Hidāya ʿalā madhhab al-imām Abī ʿAbd Allāh Aḥmad ibn Muḥammad Ibn Ḥanbal al-Shaybānī.* Eds. ʿAbd al-Laṭīf Humayyim and Māhir Yāsīn al-Faḥl. Kuwait: Ghirās, AH 1425/2004 CE.

Kamali, Mohammad Hashim. *Principles of Islamic Jurisprudence.* Rev. ed. Cambridge: Islamic Texts Society, 1989.

Kant, Immanuel. *Religion Within the Boundaries of Mere Reason and Other Writings*. Ed. Allen Wood and George di Giovanni. Cambridge: Cambridge University Press, 1998.

Kar, Mehrangiz, and Homa Hoodfar. "Personal Status Law as Defined by the Islamic Republic of Iran: An Appraisal." In *Shifting Boundaries in Marriage and Divorce in Muslim Communities*, ed. by Homa Hoodfar, 7–36. Women Living Under Muslim Laws Special Dossier, 1996.

Karamustafa, Ahmet T. "Islamic *Dīn* as an Alternative to Western Models of 'Religion.'" In *Religion, Theory, Critique: Classic and Contemporary Approaches and Methodologies*, ed. by Richard King, 163–171. New York: Columbia University Press, 2017.

al-Kāsānī, ʿAlāʾ al-Dīn. *Badāʾiʿ al-ṣanāʾiʿ fī tartīb al-sharāʾiʿ*. 10 vols. Ed. ʿAlī Muḥammad Muʿawwaḍ and ʿĀdil Aḥmad ʿAbd al-Mawjūd. Beirut: Dār al-Kutub al-ʿIlmīya, AH 1424/2003 CE.

Katz, Marion Holmes. "Shame (*Ḥayāʾ*) as an Affective Disposition in Islamic Legal Thought." *Journal of Law, Religion and State* 3 (2014): 139–169.

Kaʿwāss, Al-Mīlūd. *Ḥaqq al-zawja fī al-kadd wa'l-siʿāya*. Rabat: Markaz al-Dirāsāt wa'l-Abḥāth wa-Iḥyāʾ al-Turāth, 2008.

Khalīl ibn Isḥāq al-Mālikī. *Mukhtaṣar al-ʿallāma Khalīl*. Ed. Aḥmad Jād. Cairo: Dār al-Ḥadīth, AH 1426/2005 CE.

al-Khalīlī, Luʾayy ʿAbd al-Raʾūf. *La'ālī al-muḥār fī takhrīj maṣādir Ibn ʿĀbidīn fī ḥāshiyatihi Radd al-Muḥtār*. 2 vols. Amman: Dār al-Fatḥ, AH 1431/2010 CE.

Khan, Arsalan. "Pious Masculinity, Ethical Reflexivity, and Moral Order in an Islamic Piety Movement in Pakistan." *Anthropological Quarterly* 91 (2018): 53–77.

al-Khaṣṣāf, Abū Bakr Aḥmad ibn ʿAmr al-Shaybānī. *Kitāb Adab al-qāḍī*, with commentary of Abū Bakr Aḥmad ibn ʿAlī al-Rāzī, known as al-Jaṣṣāṣ. Ed. Farhat Ziadeh. Cairo: American University in Cairo Press, 1978.

——. *Kitāb al-Nafaqāt*, with *Sharḥ* of al-Ṣadr al-Shahīd ʿUmar ibnʿAbd al-ʿAzīz Ibn Māza. Ed. Abū'l-Wafā al-Afghānī. Bombay: Al-Dār al-Salafīya, n.d.

al-Khayrmītī, Maḥmūd ibn Ismāʿīl. *Al-Durra al-gharrāʾ fī naṣīḥat all-salāṭīn wa al-quḍāt wa al-umarāʾ*. Ed. Aḥmad al-Zaʿbī. Beirut: Ibn al-Azraq Center for Political Heritage Studies, AH 1433/2012 CE.

al-Khiraqī, Abu'l-Ḥasan 'Umar ibn al-Ḥusayn. *Mukhtaṣar al-Khiraqī*. Ed. Muhammad Zuhayr Shāwīsh. Damascus: Mu'assasat al-Salām li'l-Ṭabāʿa wa'l-Nashr, 1378/[1958–1959].

Kinberg, Leah. "What Is Meant by *Zuhd*." *Studia Islamica* 61 (1985): 27–44.

Kızıltan, Mübeccel, ed. *Fatma Aliye Hanım: Yaşamı, Sanatı, Yapıtları; ve-Nisvan-ı Islam*. Istanbul: Mutlu Yayıncılık, 1993.

Knysh, Alexander. *Islamic Mysticism: A Short History*. Leiden: Brill, 2000.

Krakowski, Eve. *Coming of Age in Medieval Egypt: Female Adolescence, Jewish Law, and Ordinary Culture*. Princeton, N.J.: Princeton University Press, 2017.

Kraut, Richard. "Aristotle's Ethics." *Stanford Encyclopedia of Philosophy*. Stanford University. June 15, 2018. https://plato.stanford.edu/archives/sum2018/entries/aristotle-ethics.

Krawietz, Birgit. "Body, in Law." In *Encyclopaedia of Islam*, 3rd ed., ed. by Kate Fleet, Gudrun Krämer, Denis Matringe, John Nawas, and Everett Rowson. Leiden: Brill, 2007.

——. "Transgressive Creativity in the Making: Ibn Qayyim al-Ǧawziyyah's Reframing Within Ḥanbalī Legal Methodology." In *A Scholar in the Shadow: Essays in the Legal and Theological Thought of Ibn Qayyim al-Ǧawziyyah*, ed. by Caterina Bori and Livnat Holtzman, 47–66. Rome: Istituto per l'Oriente C. A. Nallino, 2010.

Laḥmar, Ḥamīd Muḥammad. *Fatāwā Ibn Abī Zayd al-Qayrawānī*. Beirut: Dār al-Gharb al-Islāmī, 2004.

——. *Fatāwā Ibn Abī Zayd al-Qayrawānī (Mālik al-Ṣaghīr)*. 2 vols. Cairo: Dār al-Laṭā'if, 2012.

al-Laknawī, ʿAbd al- Ḥayy. *Al-Fawā'id al-bahīya fī tarājim al-ḥanafīya*. Cairo: Maṭbaʿat al-Saʿāda, AH 1324.

Laoust, Henri. "Ibn Ḳayyim al-Djawziyya." In *Encyclopaedia of Islam*, 2nd ed., ed. by P. Bearman, Th. Bianquis, C. E. Bosworth, E. van Donzel, and W. P. Heinrichs. Leiden: Brill, 1960–2005.

——. "Ibn Taymiyya." In *Encyclopaedia of Islam*, 2nd ed., ed. by P. Bearman, Th. Bianquis, C. E. Bosworth, E. van Donzel, and W. P. Heinrichs. Leiden: Brill, 1960–2005.

——. "La pensée et l'action politiques d'al-Māwardī (364–450/974–1058)." *Revue des Études Islamiques* 36, no. 1 (1968): 11–92.

——. *Le Précis de Droit d'Ibn Qudāma*. Beirut: Institut Français de Damas, 1950.

Larsen, David. "Al-Ḥamawī, ʿAlwān." In *Encyclopaedia of Islam*, 3rd ed., ed. by Kate Fleet, Gudrun Krämer, Denis Matringe, John Nawas, and Everett Rowson. Leiden: Brill, 2007.

Last, Murray, "Fūdī, ʿUthmān." In *Encyclopaedia of Islam*, 3rd ed., ed. by Kate Fleet, Gudrun Krämer, Denis Matringe, John Nawas, and Everett Rowson. Leiden: Brill, 2007.

Lewicka, Paulina. *Food and Foodways of Medieval Cairenes: Aspects of Life in an Islamic Metropolis of the Eastern Mediterranean*. Leiden: Brill, 2011.

Lipton, G. A. "Secular Sufism: Neoliberalism, Ethnoracism, and the Reformation of the Muslim Other," *Muslim World* 101, no. 3 (2011): 427–440.

Lutfi, Huda. "Al-Sakhāwī's *Kitāb al-nisā'* as a Source for the Social and Economic History of Muslim Women During the Fifteenth Century A.D." *Muslim World* 71, no. 2 (1981): 104–124.

Malamud, Margaret. "Gender and Spiritual Self-Fashioning: The Master-Disciple Relationship in Classical Sufism." *Journal of the American Academy of Religion* 64, no. 1 (1996): 89–117.

——. "Sufi Organizations and Structures of Authority in Medieval Nishapur." *International Journal of Middle East Studies* 26, no. 3 (1994): 427–442.

Mālik ibn Anas al-Aṣbaḥī. *Al-Mudawwana al-kubrā, riwāyat al-imām Saḥnūn ibn Saʿīd al-Tanūkhī*. 9 vols. Ed. Zakarīyā ʿUmayrāt. Beirut: Dār al-Kutub al-ʿIlmīya, AH 1426/2005 CE.

Malti-Douglas, Fadwa. "*Maqāmāt* and *Adab*: 'Al-Maqāma al-Maḍīriyya' of al-Hamadhānī." In *Power, Marginality, and the Body in Medieval Islam*. Aldershot: Ashgate Variorum, 2001.

al-Mamlaka al-Maghribīya, Wizārat al-ʿAdl. *Al-Muqtaḍayāt al-Jadīda li-Mudawwanat al-Usra*. Rabat: Manshūrāt Jamʿīyat Nashr al-Maʿlūmāt al-Qānūnīya wa 'l-Qaḍā'īya, 2004.

Mangera, Abdur-Rahman. "A Critical Edition of Abū 'l-Layth al-Samarqandī's Nawāzil." Ph.D. thesis, School of Oriental and African Studies, University of London, 2013.

al-Mardāwī, ʿAlī ibn Sulaymān. *Al-Inṣāf fī maʿrifat al-rājiḥ min al-khilāf ʿalā madhhab al-imām al-mubajjal Aḥmad ibn Ḥanbal*. 12 vols. Ed. Muḥammad Ḥāmid al-Fiqī. Cairo: Maṭbaʿat al-Sunna al-Muḥammadīya, AH 1374–1377/1955–1958 CE.

al-Marghīnānī, ʿAlī ibn Abī Bakr. *Mukhtārāt al-nawāzil fī'l-fiqh al-ḥanafī*. 4 vols. Ed. Imtithāl Ṣalāḥ al-Dīn al-Ṣaghīr. Damascus and Beirut: Dār al-Muqatabas, AH 1440/2019 CE.

Marghīnānī, Ẓahīr al-Dīn al-Ḥasan ibn ʿAli. *Al-Fatāwā al-Ẓahīrīya*. ms. Universitätsbiliothek Leipzig. B. or. 006-1. https://www.islamic-manuscripts.net/receive/IslamHSBook_islamhs_00000501.

Marlow, Louise. *Hierarchy and Egalitarianism in Islamic Thought*. Cambridge: Cambridge University Press, 1997.

Masuzawa, Tomoko. *The Invention of World Religions: Or, How European Universalism was Preserved in the Language of Pluralism*. Chicago: University of Chicago Press, 2005.

al-Matroudi, Abdul Hakim I. *The Ḥanbalī School of Law and Ibn Taymiyyah: Conflict or Conciliation*. London: Routledge, 2006.

Mattson, Ingrid. "A Believing Slave Is Better Than an Unbeliever: Status and Community in Early Islamic Society and Law." Ph.D. diss., University of Chicago, 1999.

——. "Status-Based Definitions of Need in Early Islamic *Zakat* and Maintenance Laws." In *Poverty and Charity in Middle Eastern Contexts*, ed. by Michael Bonner, Mine Ener, Amy Singer, 31–51. Albany: State University of New York Press, 2003.

al-Māwardī, Abū al-Ḥasan ʿAlī ibn Muḥammad ibn Ḥabīb. *Adab al-dunyā wa'l-dīn*. 2 vols. Ed. Muḥammad Jāsim al-Ḥadīthī. Baghdad: Manshūrāt al-Majmaʿ al-ʿIlmī, AH 1429/2008 CE.

——. *Al-Ḥāwī al-kabīr fī fiqh madhhab al-imām al-Shāfiʿī*. 19 vols. Ed. ʿAlī Muḥammad Muʿawwaḍ and ʿĀdil Aḥmad ʿAbd al-Mawjūd. Beirut: Dār al-Kutub al-ʿIlmīya, AH 1419/1999 CE.

Al-Mawsūʿa al-fiqhīya. 45 vols. Kuwait: Wizārat al-Awqāf wa'l-Shuʾūn al-Islāmīya, AH 1404–1427/1983–2006 CE.

McGinn, Thomas A. J, ed. *Obligations in Roman Law: Past, Present, and Future*. Ann Arbor: University of Michigan Press, 2012.

McGinnis, Jon, and David C. Reisman. *Classical Arabic Philosophy: An Anthology of Sources*. Indianapolis: Hackett, 2007.

Melchert, Christopher. "Asceticism." In *Encyclopaedia of Islam*, 3rd ed., ed. by Kate Fleet, Gudrun Krämer, Denis Matringe, John Nawas, and Everett Rowson. Leiden: Brill, 2007.

——. "Ibn al-Mubārak's *Kitāb al-Jihād* and Early Renunciant Literature." In *Violence in Islamic Thought from the Qur'an to the Mongols*, ed. by Robert Gleave and István T. Kristó-Nagy, 49–69. Edinburgh: Edinburgh University Press, 2015.

——. "Māwardī, Abū Yaʿlā, and the Sunni Revival." In *Prosperity and Stagnation: Some Cultural and Social Aspects of the Abbasid Period (750–1258)*, ed. by Krzystof Kościelniak, 37–61. Kraców: UNUM, 2010.

——. "Māwardī's Legal Thinking." *Al-ʿUṣūr al-Wusṭā* 23 (2015): 68–86.

——. "The Relation of Ibn Taymiyya and Ibn Qayyim al-Jawziyya to the Ḥanbalī School of Law." In *Islamic Theology, Philosophy and Law: Debating Ibn Taymiyya and Ibn Qayyim al-Jawziyya*, ed. by Birgit Krawietz and Georges Tamer, in collaboration with Alina Kokoschka, 146–161. Berlin: De Gruyter, 2013.

——. "The Transition from Asceticism to Mysticism in the Middle of the Ninth Century C.E." *Studia Islamica* 83 (1996): 51–70.

Merry, Sally Engle. *Getting Justice and Getting Even: Legal Consciousness Among Working-Class Americans.* Chicago: University of Chicago Press, 1990.

Metcalf, Barbara. "Islam and Women: The Case of the Tablighi Jama'at." *Stanford Humanities Review* 5, no. 1 (1995): 51–59.

Mojaddedi, Jawid A. *The Biographical Tradition in Sufism: The Tabaqāt Genre from al-Sulamī to Jāmī.* Richmond, Surrey: Curzon, 2001.

Monavvar, Moḥammad ebn-e. *Asrār al-Tawḥīd fī maqāmat al-shaykh Abī Saʿīd.* 2 vols. Ed. Muḥammad Riẓā Shafīʿī Kadkanī. Tehran: Muʾassaseh-i Intishārāt-i Āgāh, AH 1367/[1989 CE].

——. *The Secrets of God's Mystical Oneness or The Spiritual Stations of Shaikh Abu Sa'id.* Trans. John O'Kane. Costa Mesa, Calif.: Mazda with Bibliotheca Persica, 1992.

Molendijk, Arie L. "Religious Development: C. P. Tiele's Paradigm of Science of Religion." *Numen: International Review for the History of Religions* 51 (2004): 321–351.

Motzki, Harald. *The Origins of Islamic Jurisprudence: Meccan Fiqh Before the Classical Schools.* Trans. Marion Holmes Katz. Leiden: Brill, 2002.

"Mudawwanat al-Usra." Al-Mamlaka al-Maghribīya, Wizārat al-ʿAdl. Accessed September 22, 2021. https://adala.justice.gov.ma/production/legislation/ar/Nouveautes/%D9%85%D8%AF%D9%88%D9%86%D8%A9%20%D8%A7%D9%84%D8%A3%D8%B3%D8%B1%D8%A9.pdf.

Musawah for Equality in the Family. "Who Provides? Who Cares? Changing Dynamics in Muslim Families." Accessed April 15, 2021. https://www.musawah.org/wp-content/uploads/2018/11/WhoProvidesWhoCares_En.pdf.

Muranyi, Miklos. *Beiträge zur Geschichte der Ḥadīṯ- und Rechtsgelehrsamkeit der Mālikiyya in Nordafrika bis zum 5. Jh. D.H.* Wiesbaden: Harrassowitz Verlag, 1997.

——. *Materialien zur mālikitischen Rechtsliteratur.* Wiesbaden: Otto Harrassowitz, 1984.

[Muslim ibn al-Ḥajjāj]. *Ṣaḥīḥ Muslim.* 2 vols. Vaduz, Liecthenstein: Thesaurus Islamicus Foundation, 2000.

Muwasala. "What are some of the etiquettes of service (khidmah)?" Facebook. January 2, 2018, https://www.facebook.com/Muwasala/posts/1938634152832659.

"My Wife and I Married a Long Time Ago . . . ," Sharia Wiz, accessed January 25, 2021, https://halaqa.shariawiz.com/2020/02/03/my-wife-and-i-married-a-long-time-ago-alhamdullilah-we-have-been-blessed-with-beautiful-children-and-abundant-wealth-i-know-that-under-the-sharia-inheritance-rules-my-wife-will-only-recei/.

Najmabadi, Afsaneh. "Crafting an Educated Housewife in Iran." In *Remaking Women: Feminism and Modernity in the Middle East.* Ed. Lila Abu-Lughod, 91–125. Princeton, N.J.: Princeton University Press, 1998.

Nasrallah, Nawal. *Annals of the Caliphs' Kitchens: Ibn Sayyār al-Warrāq's Tenth-Century Baghdadi Cookbook* Leiden: Brill, 2009.

al-Nawawī, Yaḥyā ibn Sharaf. *Minhāj al-ṭālibīn wa-ʿumdat al-muftīn.* Ed. Muḥammad Muḥammad Ṭāhir Shaʿbān. Jedda: Dār al-Minhāj, AH 1426/2005 CE.

——. *Rawḍat al-ṭālibīn.* 8 vols. Ed. ʿĀdil Aḥmad ʿAbd al-Mawjūd and ʿAlī Muḥammad Muʿawwaḍ. Riyadh: Dār ʿĀlam al-Kutub, AH 1423/2003 CE.

——. *Ṣaḥīḥ Muslim bi-sharḥ al-imām Muḥyī al-Dīn al-Nawawī al-musammā al-Minhāj bi-sharḥ Ṣaḥīḥ Muslim ibn al-Ḥajjāj.* 18 vols. Ed. Khalīl Maʾmūn Shīḥā. Beirut: Dār al-Maʿrifa, AH 1414/1994 CE.

Nongbri, Brent. *Before Religion: A History of a Modern Concept.* New Haven, Conn.: Yale University Press, 2013.

Özturan, Hümeyra. "The Practical Philosophy of al-Fārābī and Avicenna: A Comparison." *Nazariyat* 5, no. 1 (May 2019): 1–35.

Paul, Jürgen. "*Khidma* in the Social History of Pre-Mongol Iran." *Journal of the Economic and Social History of the Orient* 57 (2014): 392–422.

Perry, Craig. "The Daily Life of Slaves and the Global Reach of Slavery in Medieval Egypt, 969–1250 CE." Ph.D. diss., Emory University, 2014.

Pouzet, Louis. *Damas au VIIe/XIIIe siècle: Vie et structures religieuses d'une métropole islamique.* Beirut: Dar el-Machreq, 1988.

Qāḍī Khān, al-Ḥasan ibn Manṣūr. *Fatāwā Qāḍī Khān fī madhhab al-imām al-aʿẓam Abī Ḥanīfa al-Nuʿmān.* 3 vols. Beirut: Dār al-Kutub al-ʿIlmīya, 2009.

al-Qaraḍāwī, Yūsuf. "Hal tajib ʿalā al-zawj khidmat zawjatihi?" Islam Online. Accessed September 3, 2008. http://www.islamonline.net/servlet/Satellite?pagename=IslamOnline-Arabic-Ask_Scholar/FatwaA/FatwaA&cid=1122528600720.

al-Qayrawānī, Ibn Abī Zayd. *Kitāb al-Jāmiʿ.* Ed. ʿAbd al-Majīd Turkī. Beirut: Dār al-Gharb al-Islāmī, 1990.

——. *Al-Nawādir wa'l-ziyādāt ʿalā mā fī al-Mudawwana min ghayrihā min al-ummahāt.* 15 vols. Ed. Muḥammad Ḥijjī. Beirut: Dār al-Gharb al-Islāmī, 1999.

Quadri, Junaid. "Moral Habituation in the Law: Rethinking the Ethics of the Sharīʿa." *Islamic Law and Society* 26 (2019): 191–226.

——. *Transformations of Tradition: Islamic Law in Colonial Modernity.* Oxford: Oxford University Press, 2021.

Quraishi, Asifa, and Najeeba Syeed-Miller. "No Altars: A Survey of Islamic Family Law in the United States." In *Women's Rights and Islamic Family Law: Perspectives on Reform*, ed. by Lynn Welchman, 177–229. London: Zed, 2004.

Quraishi-Landes, Asifa. "A Meditation on *Mahr*, Modernity, and Muslim Marriage Contract Law." In *Feminism, Law, and Religion*, ed. by Marie A. Failinger, Elizabeth R. Schiltz, and Susan J. Stabile, 173–195. Farnham, Surrey: Ashgate, 2013.

al-Qurṭubī, Muḥammad ibn Aḥmad. *Al-Jāmiʿ li-aḥkām al-Qurʾān.* 21 vols in 11. Ed. Sālim Muṣṭafā al-Badrī. Beirut: Dār al-Kutub al-ʿIlmīya, AH 1424/2004 CE.

al-Qurṭubī, Muḥammad ibn Faraj. *Aqḍiyat rasūl Allāh ṣallā Allāhu ʿalayhī wa-sallam.* Aleppo: Dār al-Waʿy, AH 1396/[1976] CE.

al-Qudūrī, Aḥmad ibn Muḥammad. *Al-Tajrīd.* 12 vols. Eds. Muḥammad Aḥmad Sarrāj and ʿAlī Jumʿa Muḥammad. Madīnat Naṣr, Egypt: Dār al-Salām, AH 1424/2004 CE.

al-Qushayrī, Abū al-Qāsim. *Al-Risāla al-Qushayrīya fī ʿilm al-taṣawwuf.* Beirut: Dār al-Jīl, n.d.

Rabb, Intisar A. *Doubt in Islamic Law: A History of Legal Maxims, Interpretation and Islamic Criminal Law.* Cambridge: Cambridge University Press, 2015.

al-Rāshidī, ʿAbd al-Raḥmān ibn ʿAbd al-Qādir. *Al-Taʿrīj wa'l-tabrīj fī dhikr aḥkām al-mughārasa wa'l-taṣyīr wa'l-tawlīj.* Ed. Khālid Bushma. Beirut: Dār Ibn Ḥazm, AH 1426/2005 CE.

Rapoport, Yossef. "Ibn Taymiyya's Radical Legal Thought: Rationalism, Pluralism and the Primacy of Intention." In *Ibn Taymiyya and His Times*, ed. by Yossef Rapoport and Shahab Ahmed, 191–226. Oxford: Oxford University Press, 2010.

——. *Marriage, Money and Divorce in Medieval Islamic Society*. Cambridge: Cambridge University Press, 2005.

al-Rāfiʿī, ʿAbd al-Karīm ibn Muḥammad. *Al-ʿAzīz sharḥ al-Wajīz al-maʿrūf bi'l-Sharḥ al-kabīr*. 13 vols. Eds. ʿAlī Muḥammad Muʿawwaḍ and ʿĀdil Aḥmad ʿAbd al-Mawjūd. Beirut: Dār al-Kutub al-ʿIlmīya, AH 1417/1997 CE.

Reinhart, A. Kevin. "Islamic Law as Islamic Ethics." *Journal of Religious Ethics* 11, no. 2 (Fall 1983): 186–203.

——. "Law." In *Key Themes for the Study of* Islam, ed. by Jamal Elias, 220–244. Oxford: Oneworld, 2010.

——. "What We Know About Maʿrūf." *Journal of Islamic Ethics* 1 (2017): 51–82.

Riḍā, Muḥammad Rashīd. *Tafsīr al-qur'ān al-ḥakīm* [*Tafsīr al-manār*], 2nd ed. 12 vols. Cairo: Dār al-Manār, AH 1350/1931–1932 CE.

Ritter, H. "Abū Saʿīd Faḍl Allāh b. Abi 'l-K̲h̲ayr." In *Encyclopaedia of Islam*, 2nd ed., ed. by P. Bearman, Th. Bianquis, C. E. Bosworth, E. van Donzel, and W. P. Heinrichs. Leiden: Brill, 1960–2005.

Rowson, Everett. "Al-ʿĀmirī." In *Encyclopaedia of Islam*, 2nd ed., ed. by P. Bearman, Th. Bianquis, C. E. Bosworth, E. van Donzel, and W. P. Heinrichs. Leiden: Brill, 1960–2005.

Ruffle, Karen G. *Gender, Sainthood, and Everyday Practice in South Asian Shi'ism*. Chapel Hill: University of North Carolina Press, 2011.

Rustow, Marina. "Formal and Informal Patronage Among Jews in the Islamic East: Evidence from the Cairo Geniza." *Al-Qanṭara* 29 (2008): 341–382.

al-Rūyānī, ʿAbd al-Wāḥid ibn Ismāʿīl. *Baḥr al-madhhab fī furūʿ madhhab al-imām al-Shāfiʿī*. 14 vols. Eds. Aḥmad ʿIzz and ʿInāya al-Dimashqī. Beirut: Dār Iḥyā' al-Turāth al-ʿArabī, AH 1423/2002 CE.

Sadeghi, Behnam. *The Logic of Law-Making in Islam: Women and Prayer in the Legal Tradition*. Cambridge: Cambridge University Press, 2013.

al-Ṣadr al-Shahīd (ʿUmar ibn ʿAbd al-ʿAzīz Ibn Māza). *Sharḥ Adab al-qāḍī li'l-Khaṣṣāf*. 4 vols. Ed. Muḥyī Hilāl al-Sarḥān. Baghdad: Al-Dār al-ʿArabīya li'l-Ṭibāʿa, AH 1398/1978 CE.

al-Ṣaffūrī, ʿAbd al-Raḥmān. *Nuzhat al-majālis wa-muntakhab al-nafā'is*. 2 vols. Cairo: Maktabat al-Qāhira, 1991.

Sait, M. Siraj. "Our Marriage, Your Property? Renegotiating Islamic Marital Property Regimes." In *Changing God's Law: The Dynamics of Middle Eastern Family Law*, ed. by Nadjma Yassari, 245–286. London: Routledge, 2016.

al-Sakhāwī, Shams al-Dīn Muḥammad ibn ʿAbd al-Raḥmān. *Al-Ḍaw' al-lāmiʿ li-ahl al-qarn al-tāsiʿ*. 12 vols. Beirut: Dār al-Jīl, [AH 1412/1992 CE].

Ṣāliḥ ibn Junāḥ. "Kitāb al-adab wa'l-murū'a." In *Rasā'il al-bulaghā'*. Ed Muḥammad Kurd ʿAlī, 302–314. Cairo: Muṣṭafā al-Bābī al-Ḥalabī wa-Akhawayhi, AH 1331/1913 CE.

al-Samarqandī, Abū'l-Layth. *Fatāwā al-nawāzil*. Ed. Al-Sayyid Yūsuf Aḥmad. Beirut: Dār al-Kutub al-ʿIlmīya, AH 1425/2004 CE.

——. *Tanbīh al-ghāfilīn*. Ed. al-Sayyid al-ʿArabī. Cairo: Maktabat al-Īmān, 1998.

——. *ʿUyūn al-masāʾil fī furūʿ al-ḥanafīya*. Ed. Sayyid Muḥammad Muhannā. Beirut: Dār al-Kutub al-ʿIlmīya, AH 1419/1998 CE.

al-Samarqandī, Muḥammad ibn Yūsuf al-Ḥusaynī. *Al-Multaqaṭ fī fatāwā al-ḥanafīya*. Eds. Maḥmūd Naṣṣār and al-Sayyid Yūsuf Aḥmad. Beirut: Dār al-Kutub al-ʿIlmīya, AH 1420/2000 CE.

al-Ṣanʿānī, ʿAbd al-Razzāq ibn Hammām. *Al-Musannaf*. 12 vols. Ed. Ḥabīb al-Aʿẓamī. Beirut: Al-Majlis al-ʿIlmī, n.d.

al-Sarakhsī, Shams al-Dīn. *Kitāb al-Mabsūṭ*. 31 vols in 15. Beirut: Dār al-Maʿrifa, AH 1409/1989 CE.

Schacht, Joseph. "Abū 'l-Layth al-Samarḳandī." In *Encyclopaedia of Islam*, 2nd ed., ed. by P. Bearman, Th. Bianquis, C. E. Bosworth, E. van Donzel, and W. P. Heinrichs. Leiden: Brill, 1960–2005.

——. *Introduction to Islamic Law*. London: Oxford University Press, 1964.

——. "Umm al-walad." In *Encyclopaedia of Islam*, 2nd ed., ed. by P. Bearman, Th. Bianquis, C. E. Bosworth, E. van Donzel, and W. P. Heinrichs. Leiden: Brill, 1960–2005.

Schielke, Samuli. "Being Good in Ramadan: Ambivalence, Fragmentation, and the Moral Self in the Lives of Young Egyptians." *Journal of the Royal Anthropological Institute* 15, no. s1 (2009): S24–S40.

Schimmel, Annemarie. *My Soul Is a Woman: The Feminine in Islam*. Trans. Susan H. Ray. New York: Continuum, 1997.

al-Shāfiʿī, Muḥammad ibn Idrīs. *Al-Umm*. 9 vols. in 5. Beirut: Dār al-Maʿrifa, [1973].

al-Shanqīṭī, Muḥammad. "Ḥuqūq al-zawj 1." YouTube. Accessed May 29, 2020. https://www.youtube.com/watch?v=x38Qq-IIb5I.

al-Shaybānī, Muḥammad ibn al-Ḥasan. *Al-Aṣl*. 13 vols. Ed. Muḥammad Boynukalın. Qatar: Wizārat al-Awqāf wa al-Shuʾūn al-Islāmīya, AH 1433/2012 CE.

——. *Al-Jāmiʿ al-ṣaghīr maʿa sharḥ al-Nāfiʿ al-kabīr li'l-ʿallāma al-shahīr Abī al-Ḥasanāt ʿAbd al-Ḥayy al-Laknawī*. Karachi: Idārat al-Qurʾān wa'l-ʿUlūm al-Islāmīya, AH 1411/1990 CE.

al-Shaykh ʿAlwān, ʿAlī ibn ʿAṭīya al-Hītī. *Nasamāt al-asḥār fī manāqib wa-karāmāt al-awliyāʾ al-akhyār*. Ed. Aḥmad Farīd al-Mazīdī. Beirut: Dār al-Kutub al-ʿIlmīya, AH 1421/2001 CE.

al-Shīrāzī, Abū Isḥāq. *Al-Muhadhdhab fī fiqh al-imām al-Shāfiʿī*. 6 vols. Ed. Muḥammad al-Zuḥaylī. Damascus: Dār al-Qalam/Beirut: Al-Dār al-Shāmīya, AH 1412–1417/1992–1996 CE.

Shatzmiller, Maya. *Her Day in Court: Women's Property Rights in Fifteenth-Century Granada*. Cambridge, Mass.: Harvard University Press, 2007.

——. *Labour in the Medieval Islamic World*. Leiden: Brill, 1994.

Sezgin, Fuat. *Geschichte des arabischen Schrifttums*. Leiden: Brill, 1967.

al-Shubrāmallisī, Nūr al-Dīn ʿAlī ibn ʿAlī. *Ḥāshiya*, in margin of Shams al-Dīn Muḥammad ibn Aḥmad al-Ramlī, *Nihāyat al-muḥtāj ilā sharḥ al-Minhāj fī'l-fiqh ʿalā madhhab al-imām al-Shāfiʿī*. 8 vols. Beirut: Dār al-Kutub al-ʿIlmīya, AH 1424/2003 CE.

Sibṭ Ibn al-Jawzī, Yūsuf ibn Qizʾūghlī. *Mirʾāt al-zamān fī tārīkh al-aʿyān*. 23 vols. in 22. Ed Kāmil Salmān al-Jabūrī. Beirut: Dār al-Kutub al-ʿIlmīya, AH 1434/2013 CE.

Siegel, Reva. "Home as Work: The First Women's Rights Claims Concerning Wives' Domestic Labor, 1850–1880." *Yale Law Journal* 103 (1993–1994): 1073–1217.

——. "The Modernization of Marital Status Law." *Georgetown Law Journal* 82 (1993–1994): 2127–2211.

Silbaugh, Katharine. "Turning Labor into Love: Housework and the Law." *Northwestern University Law Review* 91 (1996): 1–86.

Spectorsky, Susan A. *Chapters on Marriage and Divorce: Responses of Ibn Ḥanbal and Ibn Rāhwayh*. Austin: University of Texas Press, 1993.

Stephens, Julia. *Governing Islam: Law, Empire, and Secularism in South Asia*. New York: Cambridge University Press, 2018.

Stroumsa, Guy G. *A New Science: The Discovery of Religion in the Age of Reason*. Cambridge, Mass.: Harvard University Press, 2010.

al-Subkī, Tāj al-Dīn. *Ṭabaqāt al-shāfiʿīya al-kubrā*. 10 vols. Ed. Maḥmūd Muḥammad al-Ṭināḥī and ʿAbd al-Fattāḥ Muḥammad al-Ḥilw. Cairo: Fayṣal ʿĪsā al-Bābī al-Ḥalabī/Dār Iḥyāʾ al-Kutub al-ʿArabīya, AH 1383/1964 CE.

al-Sulamī, Abū ʿAbd al-Raḥmān Muḥammad ibn al-Ḥusayn. *Early Sufi Women: Dhikr an-Niswa al-Mutaʿabbidāt aṣ-Ṣūfiyyāt*, Ed. and Trans. Rkia Elaroui Cornell. Louisville: Fons Vitae, 1999.

—. *Ṭabaqāt al-ṣūfīya wa-yalīhi Dhikr al-niswa al-mutaʿabbidāt al-ṣūfīyāt*. Ed. Muṣṭafā ʿAbd al-Qādir ʿAṭā. Beirut: Dār al-Kutub al-ʿIlmīya, AH 1424/2003 CE.

al-Suyūṭī, ʿAbd al-Raḥmān ibn Abī Bakr. *Al-Ḥāwī li'l-fatāwī*. 2 vols. Ed. ʿAbd al-Laṭīf Ḥasan ʿAbd al-Raḥmān. Beirut: Dār al-Kutub al-ʿIlmīya, AH 1421/2000 CE.

al-Suyūṭī, Jalāl al-Dīn [attributed]. *Nuzhat al-mutaʾammil wa-murshid al-mutaʾahhil*. Ed. Muḥammad al-Tūnajī. Beirut: Dār Amwāj, 1989.

al-Suyūṭī, Jalāl al-Dīn, and Muḥammad Quṭb al-Iznīqī, *Nuzhat al-mutaʾammil wa-nuzhat al-mutaʾahhil*. Ed. Jūrj Kadar. Beirut: Aṭlas li'l-Nashr wa'l-Intāj al-Thaqāfī, 2012.

Swain, Simon. *Economy, Family, and Society from Rome to Islam: A Critical Edition, English Translation, and Study of Bryson's "Management of the Estate."* Cambridge: Cambridge University Press, 2013.

Swidler, Ann. *Talk of Love: How Culture Matters*. Chicago: University of Chicago Press, 2001.

Syed, Mairaj. *Coercion and Responsibility in Islam: A Study in Ethics and Law*. Oxford: Oxford University Press, 2016.

al-Ṭabarānī, Sulaymān ibn Aḥmad. *Al-Muʿjam al-awsaṭ*. Eds. Ṭāriq ibn ʿAwaḍ Allāh ibn Muḥammad and ʿAbd al-Muḥsin ibn Ibrāhīm al-Ḥusaynī. Cairo: Dār al-Ḥaramayn, AH 1415/1995 CE.

—. *Al-Muʿjam al-kabīr*. 25 vols. Ed. Ḥamdī ʿAbd al-Majīd al-Silafī. Cairo: Maktabat Ibn Taymīya, n.d.

al-Ṭabarī, Muḥammad ibn Jarīr. *Jāmiʿ al-bayān ʿan tawīl āy al-Qurʾān*. 30 vols in 15. Beirut: Dār al-Fikr, AH 1408/1988 CE.

al-Ṭaḥāwī, Aḥmad ibn Muḥammad. *Mukhtaṣar Ikhtilāf al-ʿulamāʾ*. Abridged by Aḥmad ibn ʿAlī al-Jaṣṣāṣ. 5 vols. Ed. ʿAbd Allāh Nadhīr Aḥmad. Beirut: Dār al-Bashāʾir, AH 1416/1995 CE.

—. *Mukhtaṣar al-Ṭaḥāwī*. Ed. Abū al-Wafā al-Afghānī. Hayderabad: Lajnat Iḥyāʾ al-Maʿārif al-Nuʿmānīya, n.d.

al-Ṭahṭāwī, Rifāʿa. *Al-Murshid al-amīn li'l-banāt wa'l-banīn*. Ed. Munā Aḥmad Abū Zayd. Cairo: Dār al-Kitāb al-Miṣrī /Beirut: Dār al-Kitāb al-Lubnānī, AH 1433/2012 CE.

Talbi, M. "Saḥnūn." *Encyclopaedia of Islam*, 2nd ed., ed. by P. Bearman, Th. Bianquis, C. E. Bosworth, E. van Donzel, and W. P. Heinrichs. Leiden: Brill, 1960–2005.

Taştan, Osman. "Al-Sarakhsī (D. 483/1090)." In *Islamic Legal Thought: A Compendium of Muslim Jurists*, ed. by David Powers, Susan Spectorsky, and Oussama Arabi, 239–259. Leiden: Brill, 2013.

al-Tāwīl, Muḥammad. *Ishkālīyat al-amwāl al-muktasaba muddat al-zawjīya: ruʾya islāmīya*. Fez, 2006.

Tiele, Cornelis. *Elements of the Science of Religion*. 2 vols. Edinburgh: William Blackwood and Sons, 1897.

——. "Religions." In *Encyclopædia Britannica*, 9th ed. Vol. 20. Edinburgh: Adam and Charles Black, 1886.

Tietze, Andreas. *Muṣṭafā ʿĀlī's Description of Cairo of 1599: Text, Transliteration, Translation, Notes*. Vienna: Verlag der Österreichischen Akademie der Wissenschaften, 1975.

[al-Tirmidhī, Muḥammad ibn ʿĪsā]. *Sunan al-Tirmidhī*. 2 vols. Vaduz, Liecht.: Thesaurus Islamicus Foundation, 2000.

Tottoli, Roberto. "Ahl al-Ṣuffa." In *Encyclopaedia of Islam*, 3rd ed., ed. by Kate Fleet, Gudrun Krämer, Denis Matringe, John Nawas, and Everett Rowson. Leiden: Brill, 2007.

Tsafrir, Nurit. *Collective Liability in Islam: The ʿĀqila and Blood-Money Payments*. Cambridge: Cambridge University Press, 2020.

al-Ṭulayṭilī, Aḥmad ibn Mughīth. *Al-Muqniʿ fī ʿilm al-shurūṭ*. Ed. Francisco Javier Aguirre Sáda. Madrid: al-Majlis al-Aʿlā li al-Abḥāth al-ʿIlmīya, Maʿhad al-Taʿāwun maʿa al-ʿĀlam al-ʿArabī, 1994.

al-Ṭuyūrī, Abū'l-Ḥasan al-Mubārak ibn ʿAbd al-Jabbār. *Al-Ṭuyūrīyāt*, selected by Abū Ṭāhir Aḥmad ibn Muḥammad al-Silafī al-Iṣbahānī. 12 vol. in 4. Eds. Dasmān Yaḥyā Maʿālī and ʿAbbās Ṣakhr al-Ḥasan. Riyadh: Maktabat Aḍwāʾ al-Salaf, AH 1425/2004 CE.

Uddin, Asma T. *When Islam Is Not a Religion: Inside America's Fight for Religious Freedom*. New York: Pegasus, 2019.

al-Ūshī, Sirāj al-Dīn ʿAlī ibn ʿUthmān. *Al-Fatāwā al-Sirājīya*. Ed. Muḥammad ʿUthmān al-Bustawī. Lenasia, Johannesburg, S.A.: Dār al-ʿUlūm Zakarīya, AH 1432/2011 CE.

al-ʿUthaymīn, Muḥammad ibn Ṣāliḥ. *Al-Sharḥ al-mumtiʿ ʿalā Zād al-mustanqiʿ*. 15 vols. Unayza: Dār Ibn al-Jawzī, AH 1422–1428/2002–2007 CE.

Vogel, Lise. "Domestic Labor Revisited." *Science & Society* 64, no. 2 (Summer 2000): 151–170.

Wakīʿ ibn al-Jarrāḥ. *Kitāb al-zuhd*. Ed. ʿAbd al-Raḥmān ʿAbd al-Jabbār al-Faryawāʾī. Medina: Maktabat al-Dār, AH 1404/1984 CE.

Walton, Jeremy. "The Institutions and Discourses of Hizmat, and Their Discontents." In *Hizmet Means Service: Perspectives on an Alternative Path Within Islam*, ed. by Martin E. Marty, 41–56. Berkeley: University of California Press, 2015.

al-Walwālijī, Ẓahīr al-Dīn ʿAbd al-Rashīd ibn Abī al-Ḥanīfa. *Al-Fatāwā al-Walwālijīya*. 5 vols. Ed. Miqdād ibn Mūsā Qaryawī. Beirut: Dār al-Kutub al-ʿIlmīya, AH 1424/2003 CE.

Walzer, R., and H. A. R. Gibb. "Akhlāḳ." In *Encyclopaedia of Islam*, 2nd ed., ed. by P. Bearman, Th. Bianquis, C. E. Bosworth, E. van Donzel, and W. P. Heinrichs. Leiden: Brill, 1960–2005.

al-Wansharīsī, Aḥmad. *Al-Minhaj al-fā'iq wa al-manhal al-rā'iq wa al-maʿnā al-lā'iq bi-ādāb al-muwaththiq wa-aḥkām al-wathā'iq*. 2 vols. Ed. ʿAbd al-Raḥmān ibn Ḥamūd ibn ʿAbd al-Raḥmān al-Aṭram. Dubai: Dār al-Buḥūth li'l-Dirāsāt al-Islāmīya wa-Iḥyā' al-Turāth, AH 1426/2005 CE.

——. *Al-Miʿyār al-muʿrib*. 13 vols. Ed. Muḥammad Ḥijjī. Rabat: Wizārat al-Awqāf wa'l-Shu'ūn al-Islāmīya, AH 1401/1981 CE.

Wario, Halkano Abdi. "Reforming Men, Refining Umma: Tablīghī Jamāʿat and Novel Visions of Islamic Masculinity." *Religion and Gender* 2, no. 2 (2012): 231–253.

Weiss, Bernard. *The Search for God's Law: Islamic Jurisprudence in the Writings of Sayf al-Dīn al-Āmidī*. Salt Lake City: University of Utah Press, 1992.

Weitz, Lev. "Al-Ghazālī, Bar Hebraeus, and the 'Good Wife.'" *Journal of the American Oriental Society* 134, no. 2 (2014): 203–223.

Wollina, Torsten. *Zwanzig Jahre Alltag: Lebens-, Welt- und Selbstbild im Journal des Aḥmad ibn Ṭawq*. Goettingen: V&R unipress, 2014.

al-Zabīdī, Murtaḍā. *Tāj al-ʿarūs min jawāhir al-qāmūs*. 40 vols. in 20. Ed. ʿAbd al-Munʿim Khalīl Ibrāhīm and Karīm Sayyid Muḥammad Maḥmūd. Beirut: Dār al-Kutub al-ʿIlmīya, AH 1428/2007 CE.

al-Zāhidī al-Ghazmīnī, Mukhtār ibn Maḥmūd, *Qunyat al-munya li-tatmīm al-Ghunya*. ms. Jāmiʿat al-Malik Suʿūd, al-raqam al-ʿām 7382, raqam al-ṣinf 217.4 qāf j, folio 52a. https://makhtota.ksu.edu.sa/makhtota/7824/65#.XtpuA0RKiYk.

al-Zamakhsharī, Jār Allāh Maḥmūd ibn ʿUmar. *Ru'ūs al-masā'il*. Ed. ʿAbd Allāh Nadhīr Aḥmad. Beirut: Dār al-Bashā'ir al-Islāmīya, AH 1428/2007 CE.

Zeigler, Sara L. "Wifely Duties: Marriage, Labor, and the Common Law in Nineteenth-Century America." *Social Science History* 20, no. 1 (Spring 1996): 63–96.

Ziadeh, Farhat J. "Equality (*Kafā'ah*) in the Muslim Law of Marriage." *American Journal of Comparative* Law 6 (1957): 504–517.

——. "Al-Khaṣṣāf." In *Encyclopaedia of Islam*, 2nd ed., ed. by P. Bearman, Th. Bianquis, C. E. Bosworth, E. van Donzel, and W. P. Heinrichs. Leiden: Brill, 1960–2005.

Zomeño, Amalia. "Kafā'a in the Mālikī School: A fatwā from Fifteenth-Century Fez." In *Islamic Law: Theory and Practice*, ed. by Robert Gleave and Eugenia Kermeli, 87–106. London: I. B. Tauris, 2010.

Zonta, Mauro. "Bryson." In *Encyclopaedia of Islam*, 3rd ed., ed. by Kate Fleet, Gudrun Krämer, Denis Matringe, John Nawas, and Everett Rowson. Leiden: Brill, 2007.

Zurayk, Constantine K. *The Refinement of Character: A Translation from the Arabic of Aḥmad ibn Muḥammad Miskawayh's "Tahdhīb al-Akhlāq."* Beirut: American University of Beirut, 1968.

Index

Fahmy, Khaled, 26
falsafa (philosophy): al-Ghazālī and, 128–129; Ibn Taymīya and, 194–195; and marriage, 83–88; al-Māwardī and, 108–114, 248n132; al-Sarakhsī and, 150–153; as a source of Islamic ethics, 19. *See also* Aristotle, Bryson
family: contracts of hire within, 53, 141–144, 168; hierarchical relationships within, 122–123, 257n115; as private sphere, 7–8, 26, 32, 187
family law, 209, 213–215
al-Fārābī, 83
al-Fārisī, ʿAbd al-Ghāfir ibn Ismāʿīl, 123
faskh. *See* annulment
Fāṭima (daughter of Prophet): asks for servant, 41, 59–60, 75, 183–185, 212; grinds grain, 63, 70, 236n116; Prophet's admonitions to, 197, 235n101; Prophet assigns housework to, 11, 57, 62–63, 75–76, 79, 141, 149, 161–162, 183, 203, 234n90, 234n92, 263n8
fiqh: definition, 220n26; and Qur'anic exegesis, 178, 191; relationship to ethics, 76–77, 79–80, 107–109, 113–114, 117–118, 150, 159, 163, 167, 179, 184–185, 191–195, 197–199; 208–213, 215–217, 225n102, 254n55
fiṭra (innate nature), 203, 205, 211–212, 273n26
Fodio, ʿUthmān dan, 201
food, 93, 95, 102, 125–126, 170–172, 226n115. *See also* bread, baking, cooking

genitals. See *buḍʿ*
Geniza, Cairo, 28
al-Ghazālī, Abū Ḥāmid, 14, 116, 127–130
grain, grinding of: in home or at mill, 102, 175; by Fāṭima, 41, 63; as onerous task, 29, 50, 58; wife's refusal of, 231n40, 272n14
Greek philosophy. See *falsafa*
grooming products, 95
Gutas, Dimitri, 83
Ḥabīb ibn Maslama, 42
hadith: changing role of, 75–76, 141–142; Ibn Saḥnūn and, 62–63
Hallaq, Wael, 26–27, 208, 223n60, 276n53
Halley, Janet, 213–214
al-Hamadānī, Badīʿ al-Zamān, 28–29, 190
al-Ḥamawī, ʿAlī ibn ʿAṭīya. *See* Shaykh ʿAlwān
Ḥanafī school, 153–158; on *buḍʿ*, 130–131; ethico-religious obligation in, 24–25, 137–139, 157, 210; model of marriage, 148; on *nafaqa*, 132–133; on usufructs of free person, 93; on wages for religious obligations, 134–136, 140. See also *al-Mabsūṭ*, al-Sarakhsī
Ḥanbalī school: on conditions in marriage contracts, 167, 264n30; on contracts between spouses, 165–166; geographic focus, 161; on husbands' sexual obligations, 174; on *nafaqa*, 180. *See also* Ibn Qayyim al-Jawzīya, Ibn Qudāma, Ibn Taymīya
Harb, Mona, 15–16
al-Ḥasan al-Baṣrī, 42
Hassan, Mona, 118–119, 194
al-Ḥāwī al-kabīr (al-Māwardī), 36, 82–83, 90–109, 113–114, 119
Hefner, Robert, 15, 20
hierarchy: gender, 5, 88, 103, 142, 186–187, 191; love and, 187–188; service and, 122–123, 145–146, 164; social, 104–107, 114, 117
al-Hibri, Azizah, 3
al-Hidāya (al-Kalwādhānī), 166
Hidayatullah, Aysha, 187–188
high-status wives. *See* elite wives
Ḥilyat al-awliyāʾ (Abū Nuʿaym), 43
honor. See *murūʾa*
Hoodfar, Homa, 274n39
household management. See *tadbīr al-manzil*
housework. *See* baking, cooking, domestic labor, *khidma*, spinning, sweeping, wages

al-Ḥubayshī, Muḥammad al-Waṣṣābī, 198
human nature. See *fiṭra*
humility, 7, 14, 18, 42–45, 78, 127, 139, 199, 209, 277n70.
Hurgronje, Snouck, 23–24

Ibn Abī'l-Dunyā, 77–78, 80
Ibn Abī Shayba, Abū Bakr, 75–76, 161–162
Ibn Abī Zayd al-Qayrawānī, 67–73, 79–81, 200–201
Ibn al-Jawzī, 194–195
Ibn al-Jazarī, 190
Ibn al-Mājishūn, 56–57, 68, 70–71
Ibn Maslama, 57
Ibn al-Mubārak, ʿAbd Allāh, 43–44
Ibn al-Mundhir, 46
Ibn al-Qāsim, 47–49, 52–54, 68, 71, 78, 80–81, 231n42
Ibn Ḥabīb, Abd al-Malik, 55–61
Ibn Ḥanbal, Aḥmad, 78, 174. *See also* Ḥanbalī school
Ibn Juzayy, 192
Ibn Khuwayz Mandād, 73–74
Ibn Māza, Burhān al-Dīn, 147
Ibn Māza, ʿUmar ibn ʿAbd al-ʿAzīz. *See* al-Ṣadr al-Shahīd
Ibn Nāfiʿ, 57
Ibn Qayyim al-Jawzīya: genre of works, 270n142; Ibn Taymīya and, 183; on marriage, 183–188; rediscovered in modernity, 203–205
Ibn Qudāma, Muwaffaq al-Dīn: and "contract" model of marriage, 214–215; Ibn Taymīya and, 169; on jealousy, 194; life, 161; on marriage, 160–168
Ibn Qudāma, Shams al-Dīn, 169
ibn Saḥnūn, Muḥammad, 62–67
Ibn Saʿd, 43
Ibn Shihāb al-Zuhrī, 41–42
Ibn Sīnā, Abū ʿAlī, 87–88, 242n30
Ibn Ṭawq, 28
Ibn Taymīya, Majd al-Dīn, 168–169, 174
Ibn Taymīya, Taqī al-Dīn: explanations for views, 188–195; genres of writing, 192–194, 270n142; life of, 168–169; on marriage, 37–38, 170–183; rediscovered in modernity, 203–205, 274n31
Ibn ʿAbbās, 169
Ibn ʿUthaymīn, 205–206
Ibrāhīm ibn Adham al-Balkhī, 43
ibtidhāl. *See* degradation
Iḥyāʾ ʿulūm al-Dīn (al-Ghazālī), 127–130
īlāʾ (oath to abstain from intercourse), 72, 174, 176
intimacy, 85, 148, 151
Al-Iqnāʿ (al-Māwardī), 90
al-Isfarāyinī, Abū Ḥāmid, 115
Isḥāq ibn Ḥunayn, 83–84
istimtāʿ (sexual enjoyment): as husband's prerogative, 73, 91–92, 132, 136, 162, 177; as objective of marriage, 95, 107–108; as one of a woman's two usufructs, 52, 93–97, 184; as sexual indulgence, 108, 112–113; of *umm walad*, 50–51; wife entitled to, 176–177, 186, 268n108
ʿiwaḍ (countervalue): dower as, 90, 243n42; maintenance as, 92–93, 180, 243n46; maintenance not, 132–133
ʿIyāḍ, al-Qāḍī, 57, 234n97

Jaʿfar ibn Muḥammad, 59
al-Jāmiʿ (Maʿmar ibn Rāshid), 39–41, 60
jealousy, 85, 151, 194
Jews, 122–123
Johansen, Baber, 22–26, 247n101, 262n180
Judaism, 23
al-Juwaynī, Imām al-Ḥaramayn, 116–118, 120
al-Jūzajānī, Abū Isḥāq, 75, 161–162

kafāʾa (social parity), 105–107, 118, 148
Kahmas ibn al-Ḥasan, 43
al-Kalwādhānī, Abū'l-Khaṭṭāb, 166
Kant, Immanuel, 23, 224n80
Kar, Mehrangiz, 274n39

GPSR Authorized Representative: Easy Access System Europe, Mustamäe tee 50, 10621 Tallinn, Estonia, gpsr.requests@easproject.com

www.ingramcontent.com/pod-product-compliance
Lightning Source LLC
Chambersburg PA
CBHW022139020426
42334CB00015B/963
* 9 7 8 0 2 3 1 2 0 6 8 9 1 *